LIONS AND LAMBS

NOAH BENEZRA STROTE

Lions and Lambs

CONFLICT IN WEIMAR AND THE
CREATION OF POST-NAZI GERMANY

Yale UNIVERSITY PRESS NEW HAVEN AND LONDON

Yale University Press books may be purchased in quantity for educational, business, or
promotional use. For information, please e-mail sales.press@yale.edu (U.S. office) or sales
@yaleup.co.uk (U.K. office).

Set in Scala and Scala Sans type by IDS Infotech Ltd.
Printed in the United States of America.

ISBN 978-0-300-21905-0
Library of Congress Control Number: 2016956973
A catalogue record for this book is available from the British Library.

This paper meets the requirements of ANSI/NISO Z39.48-1992 (Permanence of Paper).

10 9 8 7 6 5 4 3 2 1

"Certainly we have not, overnight, become completely different people because of the war, so that for instance the lions and the lambs among us can wander next to each other peacefully."

—*Friedrich Meinecke, politician and professor of history at the University of Berlin, 1917*

CONTENTS

ACKNOWLEDGMENTS

Many different people contributed to the labor that went into the production of this book, and it gives me special pleasure to acknowledge them here.

First and foremost, the editors with whom I worked at Yale University Press—Erica Hanson, Phillip King, and Chris Rogers—have my unending thanks for their enthusiasm as they prepared the project for publication. The suggestions that they and two anonymous reviewers made after reading the original manuscript sharpened the final product in key ways.

Special thanks are due to colleagues and friends in the place I have called home for the past five years. The faculty of the History Department at North Carolina State University, and in particular Steven Vincent, David Zonderman, and the dearly missed Jonathan Ocko, created the conditions in which a junior scholar could thrive. I can barely imagine now not having met Judy Kertész, whose friendship has been of incalculable importance. Coming here also brought me into the orbit of powerful minds in the Triangle Intellectual History Seminar, a group that in my experience approaches the ideal of a scholarly community. Tony LaVopa, Malachi Hacohen, Emily Levine, and James Chappel took a special interest in my work and generously shared of their time, knowledge, and wisdom. The North Carolina German Studies Seminar, led by Konrad Jarausch and Karen Hagemann in a space called the "Incubator Room" at UNC Chapel Hill, provided a fertile environment for cultivating my arguments about modern German history.

This project would not have been thinkable without the masters of the historical craft under whom I was lucky enough to study. The book's structure, with its dialectical pairs, owes much to the influence of Martin Jay, who directed my dissertation at Berkeley. The late Gerald Feldman taught me respect for the archival document. John Connelly reminded me to build the sustained argument in all its necessary twists and turns. John Efron brought me back to the big story. Peggy Anderson showed me the pedagogical power of vivid narration. Before graduate school, it was Yosef Hayim Yerushalmi's lectures on antisemitism and Simon Schama's seminar on writing narrative history at Columbia University that inspired me to consider this as a profession. Samuel Moyn and Michael Stanislawski provided encouragement while also dutifully warning me about the difficulties of life in academia.

At the end of the day, my friends proved to be my most helpful critics and advisers as I conceived, researched, and wrote this project over almost ten years and in multiple cities. At the top of the list by far is Eliyahu Stern, who read almost every sentence of the manuscript in its various versions and counseled me faithfully on all matters large and small over home-cooked meals and countless phone calls. Elli often intuited what I was trying to do well before I understood it myself, and his edits pushed me toward what I now consider my most important insights. Another dear comrade, Zvi Septimus, helped me realize that much of my dissertation had to be scrapped before it could become the book it is now. In the Bay Area, Amos Bitzan, Grahame Foreman, Shaun Halper, and Will Schachterle were my lifelines. In New York, Louis Abelman and David Moore were there when I first began thinking about postwar Germany as a topic of research and kindly dedicated precious shelf space in their Brooklyn apartment to bulky books on Nazism. I am grateful for the intellectual companionship of Gideon Lewis-Kraus in Berlin, Ben Letzler in Munich, Julia Creet, Samuel Goldman, and Ari Joskowicz in Washington, D.C., and Steve Milder in the Research Triangle. My oldest and most loyal friends, Karthik Pandian and Shiben Banerji, helped me with some tricky problems of language as I put the finishing touches on the manuscript.

Researchers incur many unrepayable debts to librarians and archivists, whose assistance in producing a book too often goes unacknowledged. I would like to thank the staff at the Staatsbibliothek Preussischer Kulturbesitz, the Archiv am Institut für Wirtschaftspolitik, the Historisches Archiv des Erzbistums Köln, the Archiv für Christlich-Demokratische Politik, the Bundesarchiv in Koblenz, the Ludwig-Erhard-Stiftung in Bonn, the Deutsches Exilarchiv, the Institut für Sozialforschung-Archiv, the Archiv des Instituts für Zeitgeschichte, the Deutsches Literaturarchiv Marbach, the Archives of the Wisconsin Historical Society, the Hoover Institution Archives, and the special collections departments of the libraries at the University of Groningen, the University of Chicago, Temple University, Georgetown University, and the University at Albany-SUNY. Special thanks are due to Christian Müller, who helped me with the papers of Wilhelm Röpke in Cologne; to Stephen Roeper, who treated me to coffee at the Frankfurt University Library as we discussed German politics and the legacy of Max Horkheimer; and to Tonnis Musschenga, whose staff patiently scanned hundreds of letters to and from Helmuth Plessner. The interlibrary loan office at D. H. Hill Library at North Carolina State procured obscure books from all over the world, free of charge.

During my research in Germany, I communicated with many people who personally knew the figures I write about in this book, and who patiently answered the often naive questions of a young American. I owe an enormous debt of gratitude to Julius Schoeps, Marianne Leibholz, Erika Bergstraesser, and Balthasar Benz, who granted me access to the literary estates of their fathers. Balthasar Benz deserves further mention for hosting me graciously in Marburg, where we unearthed his father's papers in a musty abandoned garage. I would also like to thank Karl Dietrich Bracher, Jürgen Habermas, Detlev Claussen, Mario Kessler, Alfons Söllner, Yael Geis, Ludwig von Friedeburg, Axel Honneth, and Alfred Schmidt for meeting and corresponding with me in the beginning stages of the project when my ideas were still embarrassingly inchoate.

Numerous people read individual parts of the book in their more awkward stages of construction and pointed me to important source material. Thank you to Carl Caldwell, Dick Buxbaum, Bill Patch, Udi Greenberg, Dirk Moses, Eric Oberle, Erich Geldbach, Daniel Bessner, and David Kettler for their critical feedback. Thank you as well to Spiros Semitis, Bernhard Emunds, Jonas Hagedorn, Carola Dietze, Douglas Morris, Jan-Werner Müller, Michael Brenner, Stefan Müller-Doohm, Detlef Lehnert, Atina Grossmann, Martin Otto, Hans Jörg Hennecke,

Michael Grüttner, Wolfgang Schröder, Matthias Möhring-Hesse, Günter Behrmann, Raphael Gross, Susannah Heschel, Stefan Vogt, Martin Treml, Stephanie Zibell, Anthony Kauders, Tobias Freimüller, Hubertus Buchstein, and Donald Kommers for their help with sources.

Of course, the production of a book also costs money. The Emerging Scholars Program at the Mandel Center for Advanced Holocaust Studies, United States Holocaust Memorial Museum, gave me space and financial support to finish writing the book, as well as funds for indexing. During the research phase, the German Academic Exchange Service (DAAD), the American Historical Association Conference Group for Central European History, the George C. Marshall Foundation, U.C. Berkeley, and North Carolina State University provided travel and living expenses. Finally, I would be remiss if I failed to mention the establishments that provided subsidized office space: Gaylord's Caffe Espresso in Oakland, Atlas Cafe in San Francisco, the now defunct Cafe Pick Me Up in New York, Bateau Ivre and Café Chagall in Berlin, Cup-A-Joe in Raleigh, and Cocoa Cinnamon and Mad Hatter in Durham.

Perhaps most of all, this work is a product of a family whose members like to bicker but also always try to understand the other's point of view. Stephanie was my intellectual sparring partner as well as confidante and consigliere. My parents, strong believers in education, showed me the value of logic, conviction, and empathy, and I hope they recognize their formative influence within the pages of this book.

LIONS AND LAMBS

Introduction

FOR MANY AMERICANS, it was a symbol of their nation's powerful new role in the world: John F. Kennedy, surrounded by a joyful crowd in faraway West Berlin, vowing to protect German liberal democracy against Soviet aggression as if he were a citizen of Germany himself. "As a free man," Americans heard their young president say in a televised speech not far from the newly erected wall dividing the western part of the city from the east, "I take pride in the words 'Ich bin ein Berliner.' " It was the summer of 1963, and the United States was reaching the apogee of its global popularity. As Kennedy's government turned its attention to non-European conflict zones such as the Congo, Vietnam, and even the American South, where an incendiary civil rights movement was mounting, Germany could be claimed as an epochal victory in what Kennedy called the "worldwide struggle" to promote freedom wherever it was endangered. Less than two decades after Adolf Hitler's Third Reich collapsed, a majority of Germans now lived in a strong and prosperous state called the Federal Republic, otherwise known as West Germany. Images of the cheering masses welcoming Kennedy seemed to suggest that America's investment in the western part of Germany since World War II had paid dividends in the form of a stable liberal democratic order and a faithful military ally. Meanwhile, the Soviet-allied German Democratic Republic, or East Germany, was mired in economic stagnation and had lost almost a fifth of its population to western defection.

1

The reporters covering the U.S. president's tour through West Germany presented Americans back home with images of a German society that would have been perceived, in the language of the time, as eminently "modern." The two politicians accompanying Kennedy into Berlin, German chancellor Konrad Adenauer and West Berlin's mayor Willy Brandt, were leaders of parties that together managed a functioning bipartisan legislature, much like Republicans and Democrats in the United States or Conservatives and Labourites in the United Kingdom. A strong judiciary, including a supreme constitutional court founded after the war, protected the civil rights of citizens from alleged government abuses. Newscasters reported that young Germans exhibited little of the nationalism made infamous by previous generations, and that most supported political union between Germany and its erstwhile European enemies. In addition, the people on the German streets looked ethnically diverse, a far cry from the monochromatic columns of Nazi marchers that had once transfixed newsreel viewers around the world. It was easy to draw the conclusion that Western influence, especially American influence, had profoundly reshaped German society.

Indeed, the celebration of Kennedy's triumphal tour was just one example of how Americans imagined a Germany that had moved from darkness into light under Western auspices. The older generation remembered the German interwar era, when Hitler began his rise to power, from news reports of hyperinflation and unemployment or through the Weimar cinema popular in American movie houses. Black-and-white films from the 1920s such as *The Cabinet of Dr. Caligari* or *Nosferatu*, with their jagged sets and ominous shadows, suggested a German world of danger and hostility. By contrast, the Federal Republic that welcomed Kennedy in the summer of 1963 appeared bright and sunny on television. Critics at the American magazine *Architectural Forum* described the new buildings sprouting up in bomb-shattered West Berlin as "cheerful" and "colorful"—words they would never have used to characterize the now destroyed German cityscapes of the past.[1] Meanwhile, American journalists depicted the Soviet-supported German state under construction on the other side of the Iron Curtain as drab and dull. A Time-Life publication comparing the two sides reported to readers in 1968, "Life in East Germany lacks natural colors."[2]

The emergence of a liberal democratic, prosperous, peaceful, and pluralistic nation-state in West Germany so soon after the fall of Nazism seemed staggering to observers who had been following politics in that country since the end of World War I. By the 1960s, the vocabulary of "partnership," "cooperation," and "order" dominated public discourse in the Federal Republic, whereas "struggle," "crisis," and "chaos" had been political keywords for much of the preceding half century. The transformation was so shocking that even hard-boiled commentators used religious language to describe it. West Germany's average growth rate of over eight percent from 1950 to 1960 despite the devastation of the war was termed an "economic miracle," and the country's return to world-power status under the sign of peace and community with its European neighbors was a "political miracle."[3] In 1966, a few years after Kennedy's visit, an American adviser declared the "rebirth" of Germany "one of the historic phenomena of the mid–twentieth century—the full meaning of which is still beyond our comprehension."[4]

Comprehending Germany's rebirth as a liberal democracy remains necessary today not only because it marks the beginning of that country's return as the most powerful force in Europe, but also because Western politicians have held it up as a success story whose putative lessons can be applied to other conflict zones all over the globe. In the 1970s and 1980s, policy makers pointed to the non-communist Federal Republic as a model of economic development and social harmonization as they competed against the Soviet Union for the hearts and minds of leaders in "Third World" nations.[5] Following the collapse of communism in "under-developed" Eastern Europe after 1989, economists looked to the experience of post-Nazi Germany for an example of how to convert a command economy into a market-driven civil society. And after September 11, 2001, American strategists used the German case as historical evidence that military intervention and regime change could help transform an extractive and aggressive dictatorship into a prosperous and peaceful liberal democracy. Noah Feldman, a specialist in constitutional law who served as an expert adviser for the U.S. authorities there, remembered his shock as he made his way on a Baghdad-bound government plane and observed that his colleagues were "without exception reading new books on the American occupation and reconstruction of Germany and Japan."[6]

Most books about the American-led reconstruction, like those that Feldman's colleagues were likely reading, emphasize the importance of security, resources, and the battle for hearts and minds during the early

Cold War as the former Allies divided the defeated country into Western and Eastern parts. They focus on the forced dismantling of the cartels that had once supplied Hitler's war machine, the financial reforms that reopened the German market after years of protectionism and austerity, and the programs that sent billions of dollars in relief and development aid to a war-weary population. They linger on dramatic American policies that ostensibly helped win over Germans to cooperation with the West, such as President Harry Truman's insistence on trying the major Nazi war criminals before a court of law instead of summarily executing them (as per Joseph Stalin's original proposal), and the decision to airlift supplies into the liberal democratic Western sector of Berlin as Soviet authorities attempted to starve it into submission. Books on the American occupation also tend to speculate on the effects of the U.S. government's mission to help Germans "learn democracy" before returning full sovereignty to the defeated nation. The problem with these tales is that they often say more about what Americans want to believe about their postwar humanitarian efforts than about the realities of the reconstruction.[7]

Lions and Lambs presents an alternative explanation of the creation of post-Nazi Germany. Instead of focusing on economic development and American influence, this book turns attention to changes within Germany before American occupation troops arrived and long after they left. It looks closely at the various social, religious, and political groupings of German society and their shifting relations with one another from the turbulent era of the 1920s and 1930s to the more stable postwar years of the 1950s and 1960s. Instead of examining foreign actors and their purported impact on the local population, this book explores the ideas, values, and decisions of the Germans who were themselves responsible for the creation of post-Nazi Germany. It is a history of how former enemies partnered together and how a region with a tradition of internal strife became pacified.

The book provides a counternarrative to stories that have been told in the West to justify interventions in other regions of the world based on the "model" of Germany. Western narrators have often portrayed post-Nazi Germany in ways that suggest universal lessons because of the sheer magnitude of the Federal Republic's success according to factors valued by social scientists as "modern" and politically mature: a stable liberal democratic constitutional order, a strong and flexible market-based economy, and a pluralistic and diverse society whose leaders have confronted the darker parts of their collective past. Those stories about Germany's supposed triumphs of modernization have all too often worked symbiotically with social-scientific models of nation building, development, conflict resolution, and international relations to reinforce policies of intervention around the globe.

MODERNIZATION THEORY AND GERMANY'S TWENTIETH-CENTURY "DEVELOPMENT"

When historians write about post-Nazi Germany, the most common narrative structure is the *Bildungsroman,* or coming-of-age story. Germans move collectively, but fitfully, from adolescence into maturity. They begin to develop into a liberal democracy in the early part of the twentieth century, with a parliamentary revolution midway through the First World War and the establishment of a progressive constitutional order in 1919. This maturation process, however, is uneven and awkward, because the population develops faster in some areas (the cosmopolitan urban centers) than in others (the more custom-bound agricultural parts) and because healthy growth is stunted by vindictive older relatives (the French and British leaders who imposed the Treaty of Versailles). As Germans move along this distorted or "special" path, many lose their minds— seized by a schizophrenic break in early adulthood (Nazism). Because of the size and strength of this young nation, positioned in the middle of the world's most powerful continent, the seizure of power does not remain confined to its own borders but instead affects the entire globe in a massive murder-suicide (World War II). After this catastrophic trauma, the story goes, a majority in Germany begins to learn its lesson and move toward peace and liberal democracy under Western, and especially American, tutelage. A minority breaks away from the body altogether, attempting an experiment on the model of the Soviet Union in a state called the German Democratic Republic, but eventually they, too, learn and reunify in 1990 to form the Germany that exists today.

Germany's particular coming-of-age story was often told in tandem with a general theory of how societies mature, or "modernize." Crafted in the 1950s by political scientists and sociologists in the West, especially the United States, where it became the guiding ideology of foreign policy in the Kennedy era, "modernization theory" defined certain basic preconditions for development into a functioning liberal democracy. In the concise description of one recent historian, modernized society was "cosmopolitan, mobile, controlling of the environment, secular, welcoming of change, and characterized by a complex division of labor," whereas its opposite, traditional society, "was inward looking, inert, passive toward nature, superstitious, fearful of change, and economically simple." According to the theory, there was a direct relationship between economic openness and political maturation: the free circulation of resources led to urbanization, stronger communication networks, and ultimately greater empathy and cooperation between traditionally conflicting groups, a necessity for liberal democratic success.[8] Some societies, such as those encompassing most of Asia and Africa, fell on the extreme traditional side of the spectrum, whereas others, such as Germany in the early twentieth century, contained a volatile mixture of both modern and traditional elements.

The scholars who contributed most to modernization theory were the very same people who told the first historical narratives of German twentieth-century "development." None were more prominent than Karl W. Deutsch, a German-speaking émigré who fled occupied Prague in 1939 and, after studying at Harvard University, became a renowned scholar of international peace and adviser to several American administrations during the Cold War. As he was postulating a paradigm for healthy nation building, he also published the first major study of the Federal Republic's successful stabilization, titled *Germany Rejoins the Powers* (1959). Urging readers to regard Germans as "a close relative recovering from a very grave illness," he explained the rehabilitation of liberal democracy there by pointing mainly to the Western-supervised transition to a free, open, and independent press and the removal of protectionist economic forces such as the large landowners of Prussia and the industrial cartels.[9]

Since those early theories and narratives, Western historians have told and retold stories of Germany's "development" in conversation with the newest social science on modernization. Some have foregrounded economic factors, arguing that the prosperity of the post-Nazi decades finally allowed Germans to mature politically on the course they began in the Weimar Republic, when they had unfortunately been plagued by sanctions, hyperinflation, and worldwide depression. Others have focused on the less measurable effects of the shock of defeat in 1945, or American-led programs to "re-orient" Germans toward liberal democratic values through a vast network of transatlantic bridges and information transfer such as cultural exchange programs for students, teachers, and business-people. Still others have emphasized the emergence of a new generation coming to age in the early 1960s, Germans who grew up after the war looking to the West and were able to liberalize what was still a fairly conservative and culturally closed-off society in the immediate postwar years. At each point, the advocates of different explanations for German postwar success have engaged with social-scientific theories of how liberal democratic modernity proliferated globally in the twentieth century.[10]

A recent example of the symbiotic relationship between modern German history and modernization theory is Konrad Jarausch's book *After Hitler: Recivilizing Germans, 1945–1995* (2006). The most comprehensive narrative of the reconstruction to date, the book takes a nuanced approach to the study of post-Nazi Germany in conversation with current social science. According to Jarausch, the experience of military defeat in the Second World War transformed Germans psychologically, creating what he calls the "willingness to learn" necessary for political maturity. In the Western occupation zones, the book argues, military governments helped Germans build institutions that provided checks and balances in government and promoted the free circulation of goods and ideas, including a powerful independent judiciary, a regulated but market-based economy, networks of European cooperation, and pluralist cultural organizations. In this narrative, the liberal democratic institutions built in the wake of Nazism were the real agents of German postwar success. Although the entire population did not achieve its "breakthrough to a modern civil society" immediately after the war, the institutions allowed for "gradual self-correction," as a new generation that came of age in the 1950s and 1960s began examining its people's past and learning from its earlier misdevelopment.[11]

Recent narratives of political modernization such as Jarausch's represent a significant improvement upon the earlier explanations popular during the Cold War. While not denying the crucial role of the Allied military occupations, historians now typically avoid triumphal representations of the United States as democratizing savior and recognize the agency of Germans themselves and the importance of generational shifts.[12] Also, in light of poststructuralist and postcolonial critiques, historians and social scientists alike have begun to distance themselves from whiggish models that posit a "Western" (British, American, French) developmental path toward liberal democracy as the "normal" standard against which all other national developments must be measured.[13]

But in other ways, the new dominant narratives and social-scientific theories exhibit some of the same problems inherent in the older modernization models. They still assume a direct correlation between liberal democracy, prosperity, and stable peace, simply flipping the older causal explanation on its head. While modernization theorists of the 1950s and 1960s regularly assumed that prosperity and social peace develop as a precursor of liberal democracy, newer theories hold up data suggesting it is the other way around, arguing that the introduction of liberal democratic institutions creates the conditions for prosperity and social peace. Such is the flipped model of the celebrated book *Why Nations Fail: The Origins of Power, Prosperity, and Poverty* (2012) by Daron Acemoğlu and James Robinson, who have suggested that wealthy nations do not necessarily morph into liberal democracies (early-twentieth-century Germany being one of their examples), but those that introduce liberal, inclusive institutions, for whatever contingent historical reasons, tend to develop more measurable "success"—that is, prosperity and peace—as a society over the long term.[14]

Current social science, dominated by theories of neo-institutionalism such as Acemoğlu and Robinson's, tends to look at what institutions do once they are introduced into a society: how they force or coax people to learn and develop in particular ways. One might study how a nation's political culture is affected by the introduction of laws protecting free speech or secular schooling. In doing so, however, scholars often pay insufficient attention to the role of value consensus, or lack thereof, in the long-term sustainability of those institutions. One forgets how much argument and conflict and reconciliation between contested value systems accompany their establishment. Without factoring in the problem of values, social scientists frequently assume a set of categories about what liberal democratic institutions are and then predict that they can produce development wherever they are introduced.

This book does not search for societal "development" in Germany. Instead, it examines changes that took place during the mid–twentieth century to create a German society that was not necessarily more mature, but was certainly new. In particular, it looks at the reconciliation of historical conflict groups in the country. I depart from the work of the sociologist Mario Rainer Lepsius, who pointed out that the German nation-state from its formation in 1871 contained multiple "social-moral milieus": networks of like-minded people who, while by no means homogenous, functioned as discrete groups and organized to fight for their own "social-moral ideals." These milieus—socialist, liberal, Catholic, and Protestant conservative—closely corresponded to the country's largest political parties.[15] They were also often said to promote fundamentally incompatible "worldviews" (*Weltanschauungen*). But by the 1960s, talk of a clash of worldviews was over, and leaders of those older milieus collaborated with each other in the establishment of new liberal democratic institutions, based on new, common animating ideals. Explaining these changes requires a longer view than the typical narrative that begins with German defeat in 1945.

THE GENERATION OF CONFLICT AND PARTNERSHIP

It is impossible to understand the creation of post-Nazi Germany without understanding the changing relationships between the nation's conflict groups before, during, and after Hitler's regime. *Lions and Lambs* begins with the questions that all German elites were posing on the brink of their first liberal democracy in 1918: How could they reach political consensus among such a socially and culturally divided population? How could a collection of parties based around different interests and cultural outlooks take on full legislative responsibilities without collapsing into chaos? This was far from a novel topic of public debate in Germany, a state whose constitution since 1871 had provided for the creation of mass parties and a parliament elected through universal male suffrage. However, the discussions took on a heightened significance near the end of the devastating world war, when elected officials began to perceive their country's defeat as imminent and called the existing monarchical system radically into question. Although Germans had indeed been "practicing democracy" through elections for decades, parliamentary representatives had never acquired the power to choose the ruling government; according to the old Imperial Constitution, a hereditary executive head of state, the kaiser, appointed a chancellor who in turn appointed government ministers only in consultation with parliament. The defenders of that system justified the existence of a strong monarchy by pointing to the need for benevolent, nonpartisan leadership capable of representing national unity in a state riven by social, religious, and cultural conflict.[16]

Nearly three years into a losing military campaign, popular trust in the system had so far eroded that in May 1917, a majority of members of parliament voted to pursue a peace settlement—against the wishes of the regime—and began discussing a transition toward parliamentary sovereignty along the lines of Great Britain and France. Tellingly, one of the transition's supporters, Friedrich Meinecke, who taught German history at the main university of the nation's capital in Berlin, justified "parliamentarization" only by assuring right-wing critics that the war experience had unified the people sufficiently that they were now capable of ethical self-government. "Certainly we have not, overnight, become completely different people because of the war, so that for instance the lions and the lambs among us can wander next to each other peacefully," he wrote in November of that year, emphasizing: "*We again have fierce and deep partisan oppositions among us.*" But he expressed hope that "under the violent lessons of the war, we have found great, common goals that have bound us together, as one binds together a bundle of arrows so that it can no longer be broken."[17]

When the will to continue fighting finally faltered and the kaiser was forced to abdicate, the "partisan oppositions" to which Meinecke referred emerged in full public view during the process of democratic self-determination. The first moment of the revolution, November 9, 1918, was marked by a deep split within the country's largest political party, the Social Democratic Party of Germany, placing the cabinet leaders of the provisional government in the precarious situation of having to decide whether to work with a minority Communist faction, whose spokespeople were demanding social change on the level of what was happening in Soviet Russia, or to use force to suppress them. (They chose the former.) Journalists dubbed the new German political entity the "Weimar Republic" because demobilized soldiers with oppositional visions of their nation's political future had kept their weapons and formed paramilitary groups facing off on the streets of Berlin, rendering the capital city too unsafe for a constitutional convention and displacing representatives to the nearby city of Weimar. Still, after the passage of a liberal democratic constitution in August 1919, the subsequent four years of national political life were defined by assassinations, crumbling coalitions, declarations of emergency, and radical public debate on the future of the country. The coup attempts in 1923, one led by Adolf Hitler and the other by communist groups, were only the most extreme manifestations of a generally volatile political situation.

While the Weimar Republic exposed deep-seated political rifts among the German population, it also generated competing visions for the future. One must not imagine the 1920s as an anteroom of Nazism or a den of cultural despair where disaffected intellectuals fumed over Germany's defeat and simply bemoaned the chaos in their country as they awaited a political messiah. Scholars of German history have recently recognized the Weimar Republic as a place where visions of modernity first shaped in the empire encountered each other in a fateful contest. As Rüdiger Graf and others have recently shown, young Germans, in particular, were full of diverse visions for shaping the future, socially, politically, and culturally.[18] In fact, the discourse around "youth" at this time was often explicitly tied to one's capacity for envisioning such futures. The prominent journalist Hans Zehrer, writing in 1930, included in the category of "youth" Germans born as early as 1890, because, he explained, they had the will and the imagination to fight for a new type of national and global politics.[19]

This book is on one hand a collective biography of that "young" political generation born between 1890 and 1910, and on the other an analysis of how they reconciled their conflicting visions for the future. In the years before Hitler's ascent to power, this cohort of young men—and significantly, they were all men, as males dominated public life—often described their respective visions as mutually incompatible, speaking about political options as if they were, in Graf's words, "two existentially different possibilities."[20] Beginning their careers as lawyers, economists, advisers, and educators in a period of tumult after the First World War, they advanced their ideas with language such as "struggle" and "offensive." And yet, over the course of National Socialist rule, many of those same men who had fought against one another politically during Germany's first republic began to imagine new conciliatory ways forward based not on "struggle" but on "cooperation" and "partnership."

Whereas scholars and readers know this generational cohort born around the turn of the twentieth century as the young men and women who supplied the Nazi Party with storm troopers, recent historians have begun to recognize the non-Nazis among them as the people who built post-fascist Germany and postwar Europe.[21] None of the protagonists in this book were what the American military occupation called "ardent Nazis"—that is, party members before 1937, when Hitler's government required all state workers to join. While the nationalists in the group did accept Hitler's rule at first, they soon regretted their initial support. By 1937 at the latest, all of the figures featured here, from the most left-wing to the most conservative, found their visions for the future of Germany extinguished and their material existence potentially in danger. Some fled the country into exile in the United States, Great Britain, Switzerland, the Netherlands, Turkey, or Sweden. Others remained in Germany in quiet retreat from politics, so-called "inner emigration." And still others were publicly loyal to the Nazi government but privately began imagining life after Hitler. After 1945, they emerged as societal leaders in the postwar zones that became known as West Germany. By the early 1960s, when Kennedy visited the successfully constructed Federal Republic, these men were all nearing retirement, their generation having come to represent the founding fathers of the new liberal democracy.

This book shows the work of consensus building in a divided society: a type of labor that, in Germany at least, involved engagement with the ideas of other social identity groups and the will to find a common denominator of values out of a mix of competing worldviews. After decades of conflict over the shape of the nation's future, leaders of Germany's different social milieus ultimately reached agreement on several core values. They committed themselves to a limited constitutional democracy in which an unelected judiciary checks popular sovereignty. They accepted the legitimacy of church involvement in politics. They pledged loyalty to European unification. They promised to support only defensive wars in the future. Finally, they embraced the value of cultural diversity, at least within limits. Finding agreement on these values, which were viciously contested during the Weimar Republic, required direct communication between previously hostile groups.

Focusing on the subset of Germans known as intellectuals—people who communicated for a living as teachers and writers—allows us to see this process of consensus building in its totality. A recent study by a group of historians led by Axel Schildt and Alexander Gallus found that German intellectuals across all levels of society in the 1950s demonstrated a "readiness to discuss," as compared with the ideologically "fissured and hostile" environment of the 1920s.[22] The shift from a will to power to a will to dialogue was not confined to any one realm of political discussion, either the constitution, the churches, foreign policy, or education. Other studies that concentrate on only one of these aspects, or on one particular medium in which the debates took place, will be able to delve into the finer details of the process described in this book. But they will not be able to show how broad and pervasive it was. Nor can they draw out the ideological themes that emerged over and over again, like a leitmotif, in the creation of what became today's Federal Republic of Germany. The intellectuals chosen for inclusion here spanned nearly the entire range of possible political outlooks and contributed decisively to the creation of the educational ideology of post-Nazi Germany. The only ones excluded are communists, who, for a number of reasons, did not participate with the others.

A further note is in order to justify my emphasis on Christianity, so much so that it is a prophecy from the biblical Isaiah that gives this book its title. Many have noted that post-Nazi German society, and post-fascist Europe west of the Iron Curtain more generally, experienced an astonishing revival of Christian influence in the two decades of reconstruction after the Second World War. The historian Samuel Moyn has called the postwar period "Christianity's last golden age on the continent," characterized by the leadership of political parties and social groupings that identified as Christian as they helped build a legal framework designed to buttress liberal democracy against the kind of collapse experienced in the interwar period.[23] But the reasons behind this remarkable return or restoration of Christianity in ostensibly secular Europe have remained largely unexplained. So, too, has the fact that in the mid-1960s the Christian language of post-Nazi German society seemed to dissipate as quickly as it reemerged. Too often, it is assumed that Christian ideology served simply as an alibi for Germans' past complicity with the Nazi regime and the Holocaust, or as a weapon of psychological warfare against Marxist "materialism" in the Cold War.[24]

While the whitewashing function of Christianity in postwar German politics is indisputable, only when we focus on the efforts of Germans to reconcile conflicts and create partnerships can we understand the overwhelming attraction of Christian ideas. Theodor Heuss, the Federal Republic's first president and a confessed Protestant, argued in a speech about Germany's future after the war that to be a true democrat one must "see in the opponent also the partner."[25] The idea of partnering with opponents resonated with the spirit of the biblical Prophets' yearning for a conflict-free age as well as Roman Catholicism's appeal for social "solidarity" in the face of division. It was no coincidence that the chancellor who oversaw West Germany's reconstruction, Konrad Adenauer, was a devout Catholic, or that President Kennedy, a Catholic himself, received the greeting he did in the Federal Republic. In his inaugural address as president in 1961, Kennedy called for a "beachhead of cooperation" to "push back the jungle of suspicion" among different groups, referring to Isaiah, a figure who, in his own time of great turbulence in ancient Israel, demanded an end to conflict.

Indeed, the "partnership" ideal promoted by the founders of post-Nazi Germany was not unique to them, for leaders across the West held it up during the Cold War as a contrast to the leonine power politics of the Soviet Union and their communist sympathizers. As the British author Max Warren pointed out in *Partnership: The Study of an Idea* (1955), the word derived from the medieval Anglo-French *partecener,* meaning co-heirship of a family estate. It suggested a renunciation of internecine struggles between groups that once laid exclusive claim to the inheritance of the future: to use another biblical reference, a reconciliation of Jacob and Esau. Used in the business world to refer to a plurality of owners, the partnership ideal was a powerful alternative to the imagined ideal of uniformity in so-called "totalitarian" societies. "There can be no question of absorption whereby the identity of the partners is lost," Warren explained in his definition. "The essence of partnership is that it is a relationship entered upon in freedom by free persons who remain free."[26] The founders of the West's anticommunist security alliance, NATO, used the phrase "Atlantic partnership" to describe their cooperation in contrast to the forced alliance of the Moscow-led communist bloc, the Warsaw Pact; the European Union, too, was declared a "partnership" of the sovereign economies of Western Europe rather than the coerced economic integration of Eastern Europe under the boot of the Comecon. Still in 1967, Kennedy's successor President Lyndon B. Johnson mobilized the idea of partnership as a contrast to the values of the West's adversaries, who, he said in his State of the Union address, used "force and terror to settle political questions."[27]

This book is split into two corresponding parts that mirror each other: Part One ("Conflict") and Part Two ("Partnership").

The narrative of Part One, consisting of five chapters, focuses on the most divisive political questions Germans faced in the first fifteen years after the inauguration of a republic in late 1918, as well as the many domestic and international pressures that conspired against the formation of consensual answers. Chapter 1 explores both sides of the country's deep-seated class conflict, which revealed itself in a public debate about constitutional democracy between the highest levels of the judiciary and the leaders of Germany's powerful labor unions. Chapter 2 examines the failure of elites to build consensus on a proper policy response to the onset of worldwide economic depression after the crash of the New York Stock Exchange in October 1929. In the third chapter, I explore the volatile debate about the future of German youth and the ability of the schools to turn them away from nationalism and toward a vision of international understanding. Chapter 4 turns to the no-less-vexed question of cultural identity and cultural minorities, and in particular the state's proper relationship to the values associated with Christianity and Judaism, the two main religions represented among the nation's population. Finally, Part One also considers the Nazi rise and consolidation of power after 1933—and its leaders' novel attempt to unite the nation along racial lines—as just one, if the most devastating, of the many attempts in the years after the Great War to resolve the profound conflicts in German society. Chapter 5 examines the radical efforts of National Socialists and their supporters to create order out of the "chaos" of Weimar-era dissensus, as well as the difficulty they faced because of a fundamental internal conflict within the movement itself.

Part Two of the book, also five chapters, turns to critiques of Nazism and the creation of a post-Nazi Germany along self-consciously "Western" lines.

The narrative of Chapter 6 picks up midway through the Nazi regime, in 1938, when Hitler began preparing for a major offensive in Eastern Europe and Christian conservatives began to show signs of potential opposition within Nazi Germany: it demonstrates how, over the following decade, leaders of the old judiciary and the old labor unions attempted to find resolution to the class conflict that had pitched their forces against each other during the Weimar years, ultimately laying the foundation for the constitutional consensus of a post-Nazi, Western Germany in 1948. Chapter 7 explores how German elites, once the Western occupying forces in the emergent Federal Republic allowed them to organize themselves into national parties to rebuild a liberal democratic state, molded a bare majority to support a "Christian" policy to respond to the dire economic situation still facing the country, under the leadership of the first post-Nazi chancellor, Konrad Adenauer. The following chapter examines the main political opposition in parliament, the Social Democrats, and the compromises on values they felt forced to make—in particular the abandonment of their previous platforms of pacifism and internationalism—in order to resonate with West German voters in the climate of the Cold War. Chapter 9 charts the creation of a post-Nazi state whose leaders celebrated cultural pluralism instead of uniformity, focusing in particular on the remarkable public campaign of the late 1950s to reintegrate Jews, the victims of the largest government-planned genocide in recorded history, into German culture. The final chapter follows the careers of the Federal Republic's left-wing intelligentsia, demonstrating how Germans who had once been outspoken Marxist critics of the Western liberal democratic nation-state came to publicly endorse it, at least in Germany, in light of their experience with both Nazism and Soviet Communism. Importantly, they defended the institutions of post-Nazi Germany, and the partnerships that underpinned them, against the country's left-wing students of the 1960s.

Although the voices of many German actors are represented in this book, ten men appear prominently throughout like threads in the tapestry. My choice to focus on these individuals was both formal and substantive. From a narrative standpoint, following the careers, writings, networks, and movements of specific people helps impose order on what otherwise could become a chaotic jumble of dates and events over a fifty-year period from 1918 to 1968. With regard to content, these men fulfill another important purpose in the larger argument of the book. In order of appearance, Gerhard Leibholz, Ernst Fraenkel, Wilhelm Röpke, Oswald von Nell-Breuning, Arnold Bergsträsser, Helmuth Plessner, Hans-Joachim Schoeps, Ernst Benz, Max Horkheimer, and Theodor W. Adorno all belonged to a generational cohort that was born between 1890 and 1910 and retired between 1960 and 1980: in other words, their adult lives spanned both liberal democracies, the pre-Nazi Weimar Republic and the post-Nazi Federal Republic. Furthermore, they were active and outspoken public figures who came from very different milieus; looking at them alongside one another can show how Germans who were once at odds in the Weimar years came to embrace partnerships in the rebuilding of a post-Nazi Western state. They were not necessarily any more "representative" of their respective social milieus than other figures. In fact, I chose them not because of their typicality but because of their exceptionality, for they were able to survive the war and leave abundant traces of their thinking that historians can use to piece together a narrative in the first place. Last but not least, their presence in the story highlights not only the continuity of male dominance in the German public sphere, but also the rupture of masculinity through the experience of Nazism.

No doubt, I have made many other, perhaps sometimes unconscious, choices and interpretations that reveal my own predilections, interests, and philosophy of the forces driving change over time. But in general I have attempted to faithfully reconstruct the logic intended by the actors themselves, with close contextual reading of their many writings and careful attention to their changing audiences. Luckily for the student of history, Germans in the twentieth century were extremely articulate in public and in private about their intentions, with the aforementioned exception of Germans living under the censorial Third Reich. "More than any other people, the Germans examine and observe themselves," the French author Pierre Viénot once wrote after living in Berlin in the 1920s. "They have a morbid genius for national introspection. Let us follow them on this track."[28]

IN THE LAST DAYS OF A LONG WAR that cost millions of human lives and discredited the leadership of several major empires, news spread to the United States via telegraph that Friedrich Wilhelm Viktor Albrecht, otherwise known as King Wilhelm II of Prussia and Emperor of Germany, had abdicated his throne amid massive street protests in Berlin. As journalists reported further details received through the wire about the German revolution of November 9, 1918, two things became clear. First, the military of the last-standing belligerent on the losing side of the conflict raging in Europe for more than four years had fallen under the authority of new leaders who wanted peace. The Great War was finally ending. Second, in the trail of the kaiser's abdication, the monarchs of all the individual states that made up the German Reich had also stepped down, and the central provisional government in Berlin announced national elections for a convention to constitute a new democratic republic.

American observers who shared the idealistic vision of their president, Woodrow Wilson, expressed hope that the transition from monarchy to republic signaled a maturation process for Germans. Germany was known at the time in the United States as culturally advanced—its universities had produced fourteen of the twenty-four Nobel Prize winners in science and medicine since the turn of the century, and "the nation of thinkers and poets" maintained its reputation for great literature—but also as politically immature. During the war, American propaganda painted Germans as the blindly obedient subjects of reckless rulers who had launched the catastrophic war. "Just as Versailles stands as a monument of royal extravagance," wrote Ralph Lutz, a historian at Stanford University who documented the German republican revolution while serving with the American Military Mission in Berlin, "so the innumerable royal palaces of Germany will remain symbolical of an era of political tutelage."[1]

Yet for more than three years after the establishment of a liberal democratic constitution in August 1919, readers in the Anglophone world continued to receive word of conflict, instability, and chaos in Germany. American newspapers reported the assassinations of two influential government ministers, as well as turmoil between the German government and its neighbors to the east and to the west. Riots and skirmishes were taking place in Silesia at the border with Poland and Czechoslovakia, and late in 1922, the French army occupied the industrial Ruhr Valley of northwest Germany, leading to massive strikes and talk of an impending new war between those two historic enemies. All the while, one read about dangerously rising prices, exacerbated by the annual reparations imposed by the Western Allies in the Treaty of Versailles, and culminating in a hyperinflation of the currency that wiped out the fortunes of many middle-class Germans and helped incite a communist uprising in the north as well as a right-wing coup attempt in the south. The name Adolf Hitler made its first appearance in the pages of the *New York Times:* "New Idol Rises in Bavaria."[2]

American administrations tended to identify economics as the root cause of political disorder in liberal democratic Germany. Looking to avoid further government involvement in European conflicts after losing more than one hundred thousand lives in the recent war, President Calvin Coolidge recruited as his main adviser on German affairs the banker and Republican Party member Charles G. Dawes, who insisted that the chaos in Germany could be ended through private-sector investment in economic development. The promise of what became known as the Dawes Plan, which guaranteed loans to Germany from a consortium of major American lenders, was that prosperity would bring about political peace there and in Europe more generally.

Meanwhile, in Germany itself, talk about peace and stabilization in the new republic was not only about economics but also about the importance of developing common political values and ethical ideals that would unite the nation. Critics of the reckless course of the kaiser during the war spoke of the need to cultivate a new class of political leaders who would combine patriotic responsibility with a shared sense of morality. Friedrich Curtius, a member of the country's intellectual aristocracy and a founder of the Party of Progress in Alsace-Lorraine, noted at the end of the war that "the question of the relationship between ethics and politics" was being debated "more vigorously than ever before."[3] In a celebrated lecture delivered as he helped draft Germany's new constitution, the professor Max Weber urged a rising generation of Germans to imbue their political judgment with both "passion and a sense of proportion" and to "reach for the impossible" without losing sight of the pragmatic.[4]

Many of these elder figures who had been critical of the power politics of the German Empire placed stock in the fact that the younger generation set to take control of the nation in the coming decade had grown up in a cultural atmosphere influenced by a youth movement that stressed the importance of using one's time as a student to form ideals, not simply to obtain the technical skills necessary for making money. Leonard Nelson, an educator in Göttingen and outspoken critic of the old regime, used the metaphor of a ship at sea. "We have sailed in a false direction; it is necessary to chart a new course," he told a group of students in 1921. "That will only succeed, however, when we first find the pole to which we can orient ourselves. . . . Just as one cannot become a seafarer without having acquired the methods of astronomical positioning, so one remains a political charlatan when one believes himself, as a guide of the destiny of peoples, able to dispense with the preliminary philosophical work that first creates clarity on endgoals."[5]

The founders of Germany's first republic also taught that ethical ideals should be not solely national, or interested only in the good of one's own people, but global in scope. This was perhaps in part the legacy of a century-old heritage of German educational idealism, a philosophical tradition in which one's value judgments were understood to be formed in connection with one's broader imagined view of the natural world, a *Weltanschauung*, which transcended local boundaries. Probably even more important was the fact that these generations lived in an age of global consciousness, knowing that people from the remotest parts of the earth could be connected through new technologies such as radio and air travel, but also convulsed collectively in a world war. For the first time, it was possible to gather together representatives from every part of the globe in a new institution called the League of Nations.

But the emerging leaders of democratic Germany also grew up in different milieus, with different teachers who helped them develop different—often radically different—ideals that they brought into the complex negotiations of realistic politics. In times of national emergency, the clashes between these various milieus troubled the older generation. On New Year's Eve, 1923, just after the devastating hyperinflation of the currency, President Friedrich Ebert sent an open letter to the country's umbrella organization of youth groups, to which half of all young people in Germany belonged. He praised their commitment to ideals, rather than simply material self-betterment, while at the same time pleading for peace between the competing camps. "German youth! Preserve and strengthen in yourselves this public spirit and this idealism!" he told them, but also develop "a healthy national feeling, a civic ethic, a consciousness of responsibility for the community, social empathy, and, not least of all, respect for different worldviews and for the honest convictions of national comrades who think differently."[6]

Clashes of worldview and competing visions for the future were less reported in the American media of the time, and they still fade into the background of most popular histories of interwar Germany, which tend to focus more on economic upheavals and the rise of extremism than on philosophical debates among would-be leaders of the nation. But as Part One intends to show, these debates, many of which revolved around dilemmas central to all liberal democracies, reveal the dynamics not only of Weimar's collapse and Hitler's rise, but also of the ultimate reconstruction of Germany after the Nazi Party's downfall.

CHAPTER ONE

The Constitutional Crisis

THE YEAR 1924 WAS SUPPOSED TO BE when Germany finally began coming into its own as a liberal democracy. Or so believed many American experts observing European politics at the time. After five years of chaos following the Great War, during which time the country's resources had been drained, its currency rendered worthless, and its government forced to default on international debts, Germans were set to receive an enormous bailout loan from American banks that would supposedly set them back on the path toward democratic stability. The bailout, called the Dawes Plan after the American banker and politician who negotiated it, Charles G. Dawes, guaranteed hundreds of millions of dollars in foreign investment intended to return prosperity to Germany's middle class and shore up support for the republican forces that in 1918 had deposed the imperial monarchy, signed an armistice with the Western Allies, and constituted the nation's first republic. The U.S. government, which had designs to establish itself as the arbiter of world affairs in the new century, was now literally invested in the success of a foreign state in the heart of Europe. With economic development, American leaders argued, Germans' attraction to anti-democratic ideologies would fade, the popularity of the republic would grow, and the long-standing conflicts between Germany and its European neighbors would disappear. Dawes received the Nobel Peace Prize for his efforts.[1]

As we know, stability did not come to Germany or Europe in the subsequent years. Already by 1930, Adolf Hitler was leading the Nazi Party to its first major victory in national elections, the German president was declaring a state of emergency just to create a viable coalition government, and observers in neighboring nations were worrying what might happen if the constitutional order there broke down. The collapse of liberal democracy in Germany puzzled contemporaries and still poses a question for anyone attempting to understand the course of world history in the twentieth century. Remarkably, the explanations given by the very first American observers of German politics in the interwar period have to this day remained fairly consistent. One popular theory was that the economic recovery fueled by the Dawes Plan after 1924 simply did not last long enough to rebuild the German middle class before the crash of the New York Stock Exchange dried up foreign capital, and that a desperate populace turned to radical anti-liberal solutions. The other argument, made for example by Simeon Strunsky, a respected editor at the *New York Times,* was that most Germans had never been "converted" to a belief in liberal democracy in the first place. Historians who attempt to explain the undoing of the Weimar Republic often combine those two causes, pointing to both material circumstances and the continuation of a "traditional" authoritarian mind-set carried over from pre-republican times.[2]

The problem with relying on those explanations is that they cannot account for the paradox that the liberal democratic order in Germany survived the crises of the immediate postwar period but began to disintegrate precisely when national prosperity and prestige were on the upswing over the subsequent years. In the national elections of 1924, despite a difficult economy, a majority of Germans rallied around the defenders of the republican constitution and rejected anti-liberal movements such as National Socialism and Communism. By 1930, however, many of those same Germans voted for anti-constitutional parties despite the fact that key economic indices for the middle class were demonstrably better than they had been six years earlier. If material conditions cannot explain decreasing support for the Weimar Republic, neither can the theory of anti-democratic traditions. As recent research by such historians as Margaret Lavinia Anderson have shown, Germans had been practicing democracy under universal manhood suffrage since their unification as a nation-state in 1871—longer than any other European country—and had embraced voting and representative government to a much greater extent than previously assumed.[3]

Unlike those previous explanations, this chapter aims to show that the main obstacle faced by defenders of liberal democracy in Germany was not insufficient popular support of republicanism per se, but rather lack of agreement on the values and institutions that would provide legitimacy to the new republican state. Legal theorists often emphasize the importance of reaching consensus on moral principles for the stability of a constitutional system.[4] In Germany, that consensus did not exist. The political representatives whom Germans elected after the Great War to draft a constitution could agree that the new German state should be a republic as opposed to a monarchy. But they could not find common ground regarding as foundational a question as the authority of the three branches of government and their proper relationship to one another. Most important, minds diverged on whether the state should embrace parliamentary supremacy: the idea that the legislative branch, not the judicial or executive, should enjoy final authority in national decision making. The constitutional system of the Weimar Republic faced continual crisis, the scholar Carl Schmitt pointed out, not primarily because of internal anti-republican opponents, but because of conflicts inherent within the ranks of German liberal democracy itself.[5] And if one examines discussions among German political elites at the time, one finds that these conflicts became more divisive, not less, as the economy stabilized.

A public debate on the moral foundations of the Weimar constitution erupted during the first months of 1924, just as the financial situation began to improve. It started with an apparently technical conflict between leaders of the judiciary and top representatives in the legislature. In early January, a group of judges serving on the nation's highest court, led by Chief Justice Walter Simons, published an open letter to the chancellor and his ministers warning them against issuing a set of laws reportedly under consideration to resolve the difficult economic problems left behind by the hyperinflation in 1923. After complaints had poured in from throughout the country that banks were charging exorbitant interest rates and profiting on the backs of suffering compatriots, a majority in parliament had empowered the government to draft emergency decrees to protect German consumers. Simons and his colleagues, however, while recognizing the importance of economic justice, informed the cabinet members that the high court would be monitoring such legislation closely. The court, they said, reserved the right to strike down any measures it found to be unconstitutional or "immoral," for example if the laws protected consumers but violated the banks' right to collect debts.[6]

Beyond the specific questions of profiteering and debt revaluation, the judges' assertion of the right to strike down national laws opened a more profound question about the legitimacy of democratic lawmaking powers. It was a question faced by all liberal democrats: If the will of "the people" was the source of all law and all liberty, as democratic constitutions generally proclaimed, then which institutions could be said to best represent that legislative will? Was it always the group of men and women elected to the legislature? Or could unelected judges also be said to speak in its name? An admirer of the legal system of the United States, one of the few countries at this time where judges were empowered to strike down national laws, argued that American judges could be regarded as a "living voice of the people, because they are in each State the guardians of that Constitution through which the people have spoken and are still speaking till such time as it pleases them to amend the fundamental instrument."[7] But others, particularly the defenders of democracy as it had emerged on the other side of the Atlantic since the French Revolution, regarded the right of judicial supremacy as inherently undemocratic. None of the established liberal democracies there, including Great Britain, France, the Netherlands, and Belgium, allowed their judges to call into question the validity of national laws duly proclaimed by the people through parliament. A German-born professor named Carl J. Friedrich, reporting to American readers about the debates in his home country in the 1920s, thus wrote that a decision to grant judges such power in Germany would have "epochal significance" in Europe.[8]

The framers of the German Reich Constitution in 1919, like all the founders of new republics after the end of the world war, were aware of arguments on both sides of the debate. Rushing to establish a legal foundation for the country in a time of revolution, however, they had not waited for a full resolution. The members of the drafting committee, all eminent jurists, had come to a virtual standoff: they voted against a proposal to establish a court with powers of judicial review by a margin of eleven to ten. For the sake of expediency, the question was tabled at the plenary sessions of the constitutional convention in Weimar and left unaddressed in the final draft of the constitution passed on August 11, 1919. Instead, it was left up to future legislators to decide.⁹ The letter from Chief Justice Simons and his colleagues in early 1924 was so provocative because they claimed a power that legislators had not yet recognized judges to have.

The battle that broke out in Germany in 1924 over the question of judicial review was not like a normal dispute over policy. What made it a constitutional crisis was that it required a decision between two competing claims of legal sovereignty and equality left ambiguous in the text of the constitution itself. The battle pitted two groups supporting conflicting visions for the future of the nation against each other. Leading members of Germany's judiciary, the self-described liberal guardians of private property and individual freedom, coalesced around the value of "equality before the law" to argue for a check against what they considered an over-reaching legislature. On the other side, leaders of Germany's largest party in parliament, the Social Democratic Party, which broadly represented the tradition of democratic socialism, argued that liberal judges were cynically attempting to roll back the legislation for economic equality won by the working class under the new republican regime.¹⁰

The very public battle for legal supremacy in Germany, though rarely reported in the American press, deserves attention because its lack of resolution helped undermine the already precarious popular support for a liberal democracy. In sociological terms, political parties representing the interests of business and international trade on one hand and the interests of the propertyless working class on the other together formed the initial core of support for the republic when it was first declared at the end of the war. A fissure among their leaders on fundamental principles was therefore capable of calling into question the functionality of the new system. Understanding their conflict can help explain why, during the Weimar Republic's so-called golden age under the Dawes Plan after 1924—as the German economy bounced back, foreign currency poured in, and Berlin, the nation's capital, became better known internationally for cabaret and carousal than for street combat—the foundations of German liberal democracy seemed to become less stable, not more.¹¹

THE LIBERAL VISION AND THE CASE FOR JUDICIAL REVIEW
The timing of the high justices' open letter asserting their right of judicial review was not coincidental. At the turn of 1924, for the first time since

the republic's creation five years earlier, no member of the Social Democratic Party of Germany (SPD)—the main source of political opposition to the idea of judicial supremacy—served in the national government. Although Social Democrats remained the country's largest party in parliament, much of the German population as well as Germany's potential lenders abroad blamed Social Democratic leadership for having precipitated the events that led to the hyperinflation in 1923. As a result, at the end of that year, President Friedrich Ebert (a former member of the SPD himself) had advised the sitting chancellor, Wilhelm Marx, to form a cabinet primarily with members of liberal, pro-business parties. For the leaders of the high court, this must have seemed like an auspicious moment to make their case. The chancellor's pick for justice minister, a Bavarian named Erich Emmiger, appeared sympathetic to the judges' claim to review and strike down national laws.[12]

The high judges turned to legal scholars at the University of Berlin to counsel them on the constitutionality of the government's post-inflation ordinances, enlisting Heinrich Triepel, one of the faculty's specialists in public and international law. As a founder of the Association of German Constitutional Law Theorists, a network that connected legal experts from the nation's universities, Triepel was a well-known critic of parliamentary supremacy and a supporter of judicial review. Already in 1920, during the controversy over the people's right to confiscate the personal property of the aristocratic families after the fall of the monarchy, Triepel had argued in the nation's main legal journal that "judicial review is, if not the only, then certainly the most important, protection of liberal freedoms against a power-hungry parliament." Like most liberals, Triepel was proud of Germany's legal tradition of protecting the individual against government overreach, a tradition he associated with the deepest level of Prussian and German culture: the idealist philosophy of Immanuel Kant. Whereas he had been confident in the old emperor's stewardship of that tradition, trusting him to veto unjust laws emerging out of the national legislature, he expressed no such faith in its new parliamentary leaders now that the kaiser was gone.[13]

Triepel used the opportunity afforded to him by the high court to begin making a case for the institution of judicial review. In his first publication on the constitutionality of the recent economic decrees, in the spring of 1924, he homed in on one ordinance in particular: a requirement for the executives of joint-stock corporations to submit to the national government precise records of their past bookkeeping. The intention of that part of the emergency legislation had been to verify that businesses had not profited from the inflation to the detriment of German consumers. But Triepel argued that the ordinance discriminated unreasonably between joint-stock and private companies, in violation of the first article of the Constitution's catalog of "Basic Rights" (Articles 109–165). The first in that catalog, Article 109, read: "All Germans are equal before the law." Because corporations were to be understood as individuals—that is, legal personalities—before the law, the legislation arguably violated Germans' constitutional rights.[14] If it seemed like a minor technicality upon which to build a much larger case, it was. Triepel was meanwhile working with one of his most talented doctoral students, Gerhard Leibholz, on the deeper philosophical and jurisprudential justification for judicial review.

Gerhard Leibholz was a young legal scholar at the University of Berlin who had been afforded all the privileges of an elite education despite the fact that his family belonged to a group once treated as legally inferior in Germany. Barely twenty-three years old, he had been born into tremendous wealth, raised in a villa in the western suburbs of the nation's capital, and sent to one of the elite humanistic schools of the German Empire. Like not a few patriotic German Jews of that era, his mother had converted to the majority religion in the country, Lutheranism, and insisted that Gerhard be baptized and raised that way as well. His father, who was also born Jewish, owned factories in the textile and automotive industries, conducted business throughout continental Europe and Great Britain, and participated actively in local Berlin politics as an unpaid city councilman.[15] Such an upbringing likely convinced Leibholz that even a once despised minority such as the Jews, who had faced legal discrimination in German lands before the unification of the empire in 1871, could thrive as long as their equal rights were protected.

Barely out of high school, Leibholz had been recognized by his professors as an outstanding student, and it was clear that a distinguished legal career awaited him.[16] It was not only his keen mind, but also his commitment to the German liberal tradition that had earned him the praise of his elders. His first published work was an analysis of the writings of Johann Gottlieb Fichte, the German patriot who in the nineteenth century had sought to translate the philosophy of Immanuel Kant into a vision for a future national and international politics. Like Fichte, Leibholz demonstrated a belief that people who belong to the same culture should share the same national borders; at the end of the war in November 1918, when the territory of Germany came under threat, Leibholz volunteered with the Border Guard East's campaign to preserve historically German-speaking lands at risk of being lost to the new Republic of Poland or Soviet Russia. He also adopted Fichte's vision of a league of nations, where self-determined, independent nation-states would come together peacefully to agree on just laws for the world. Leibholz considered this vision to be a secularization of the central idea of Christianity: the harmonization of liberty and equality.[17] It is no surprise that despite his Jewish ancestry, Leibholz endeared himself to the liberal patriots of the German legal establishment, as well as to the patrician parents of his fiancée, Sabine von Bonhöffer, whose twin brother Dietrich was a young student of Protestant theology also at the University of Berlin. Like many well-to-do families in Germany, the Bonhöffers cared more about Leibholz's class background than his Jewish heritage when it came to his suitability for their daughter.[18]

Near the beginning of 1925, Leibholz published the dissertation he had been writing under Triepel, simply titled *Equality Before the Law*.[19] The work consisted of three parts: the first a philosophical reflection on the centrality of equality in a moral legal system; the second a more empirical survey of equality before the law in practice; and finally, a discussion of implications in the spheres of both domestic and international law. As a whole, it presented an argument for why the immanent logic of liberal democracy required the judicial organ of a state to place what Leibholz called a "limit" or "barrier" to the otherwise "omnipotent legislative organ."[20] Because Leibholz's argumentation grew so influential among constitutional lawyers in the years that followed, it deserves close analysis.

Leibholz began from first principles. Liberty and equality, the two basic values underpinning modern politics, he wrote, are not in "natural harmony" with each other but rather exist "in tension." Both values depend on a recognition of the inherent dignity of the human being. However, taking either one of them to its logical end endangers the other. The result of total liberty—both liberation *from* domination by a foreign power and freedom *to* form oneself as an individual or a collectivity—is anarchy and a false morality of might-makes-right. Total equality, on the other hand—the demand for exactly the same rights or resources for all—oversteps natural barriers of difference between members of society; different kinds of people sometimes need different rights and resources in order to be free. Modern politics therefore needed to strike a balance between these two necessary values.[21]

Liberal democracies offered a way to "contract" the values of liberty and equality and stabilize the tension between them, Leibholz argued. First, there must be total equality among adults of a nation in the right to elect legislative representatives. Only then could citizens regard the laws of the land as products of their own "creation." They would be more likely to embrace limitations to their individual liberty if they felt they had played a part in setting those limitations. Universal voting rights thus contained a potential to "unify" or "bind" the nation together—provided that citizens recognize the laws written by their representatives as fair and moral. This, according to Leibholz, was where unelected judges played their crucial role. Only judges could verify whether lawmakers had complied with the imperative developed by Kant in his *Grounding for the Metaphysics of Morals* (1785): that laws were ethical only if they aimed toward maximum generality; if legislators treated, as far as possible, "like as like," and special rules were not accorded arbitrarily to individual members within a reasonably classified category of people. Kant's "categorical imperative," Leibholz wrote, was expressed in the words "equality before the law," a clause the founders of all liberal democratic republics in continental Europe after the Great War had placed near the beginning of their constitutions.[22]

Leibholz attempted to show German readers that they could learn from foreign countries where judges were allowed to apply the equality clause as a check against arbitrary legislation—first and foremost the United States, and to a lesser extent Switzerland—while at the same time retaining the specificity of the German legal system. American and Swiss courts demonstrated that judges were capable of serving as "objective" guardians of the people's will by protecting individuals (including juridical persons such as associations and corporations), religious minorities, immigrants, and other potentially suppressed groups against arbitrary discriminatory legislation based on "unreasonable classification." (Like many liberal Europeans, Leibholz seemed somewhat confused by the decisions of the U.S. Supreme Court to uphold racial segregation laws based on an argument that services would be "separate but equal," but he was willing to assume that they coincided with the "legal consciousness of the American people" regarding the reasonableness of racial classification.)[23] At the same time, Leibholz found the federated legal system of the United States and Switzerland too decentralized for adoption in the new German republic. Instead, he recommended the creation of a central German constitutional court, much like the Austrian Constitutional Court created in 1920, but with the preservation of "equality before the law" as its primary standard for judicial review in a democracy.[24]

Finally, Leibholz's *Equality Before the Law* drew implications for the political system taking shape after the Great War in the League of Nations, whose governing structure included a legislature, an executive, and a judiciary called the Permanent International Court of Justice (otherwise known as the "World Court"). Like the new constitution of Germany, Leibholz noted, the covenant of the League in 1919 recognized equality in voting rights among its constituent members, with one vote each in the legislative organ, the Assembly. However, in practice the dominant organ was the executive League Council, composed of a smaller group of permanent members: Great Britain, France, Italy, and Japan. This "de facto primacy of great powers," he wrote, was "incompatible with the principle of absolute equality of the states," and risked the appearance of unfairness without a check on its actions. Just as the new German republic required a constitutional court to protect equality before the law, Leibholz argued, so, too, did the League of Nations require a World Court capable of protecting equality among its member states if it hoped to achieve the appearance of legitimacy.[25]

By the time Leibholz published his treatise and experts began reading it, the political situation in Germany had again changed in a way that affected both domestic and international dynamics. In February 1925, Friedrich Ebert, the republic's first president and a proponent of parliamentary supremacy, died shockingly in a botched medical operation. By the end of March, Germans had a new president: Paul von Hindenburg, a wizened war hero and large landowner who expressed little faith in parliament and had once suggested that Social Democrats were traitors to the nation.[26] This development perhaps emboldened judges on the high court to issue an unprecedented, confusing, and what one historian called "revolutionary" statement on November 4, 1925. While not actually hearing arguments on or formally reviewing parliament's post-inflation Law on the Revaluation of Mortgages and Other Claims, which classified different revaluation rates for different types of debt, the justices officially asserted their jurisdictional right to do so based on the equality clause. It was unclear which authority had called upon the court to release such a decision.[27]

Over the course of 1926, the argument for the role of the judiciary as a check against the legislative power of the people left the confines of legal argumentation and scholarly journals and became the source of heated public debate in the country's newspapers. Early that year, Social Democratic members of parliament, who still made up the largest delegation even though they were shut out of the governing coalition, made a controversial decision to join the Communist Party in bringing the question of whether to confiscate the property of the old aristocracy to the people for a plebiscitary vote that would have the force of law. Social Democrats argued that the socialization of private property was constitutional because it rested on Article 153 in the basic rights catalog of the constitution: although "Property is guaranteed by the constitution," expropriation could be legislated or decreed for the purpose of public welfare "executed with appropriate compensation, *unless specified otherwise by Reich law.*" When the left-wing parties secured the signatures necessary to bring a plebiscite and scheduled a vote for June, President Hindenburg published a scathing letter in the nation's most important liberal newspaper. The president warned that such a law, which would apply only to the princes and no other property holder, would be arbitrary and a grave violation of "morals." In the weeks leading up to the referendum of June 20, as thousands of polling stations were set up across the country, Germans became well acquainted with the legal conflicts involved.[28]

The referendum ultimately failed (with thirty-six percent in favor), but it only further convinced the legal establishment of the necessity of judicial review. In the fall of 1926, the justices of the high court and a group of legal experts in Triepel's Association of German Constitutional Law Theorists submitted to parliament a proposal for a formal constitutional amendment to ensure that the high court's power of constitutional review be recognized as valid. The proposal called for the State Court of Justice (*Staatsgerichtshof*), the highest civil court of appeals within the Reich Court of Justice (*Reichsgerichtshof*), to obtain jurisdiction of constitutional review over all national legislation, whether passed in parliament, decreed by government ordinance, or directly voted by popular plebiscite. In line with Leibholz's suggestions, unlike the Austrian Constitutional Court, individual parties would be able to bring claims directly to the State Court if they felt their rights to equality before the law in Article 109 had been violated by national legislation—even if the legislation in question technically conformed to the language in the subsequently enumerated basic rights, articles 110–165, as, for example, the confiscation referendum would have.[29]

"Class conflict" and "class struggle" were phrases often heard on the streets and in the cafés of Germany's big cities in late 1926. The leaders of the Social Democratic and Communist delegations to parliament were set on blocking the judges' proposal as soon as it arrived in committee, claiming it was class-motivated. Meanwhile, Walter Simons, chief justice of the State Court, caused an uproar on the anniversary of the republic on November 9 with an inflammatory speech at the University of Munich law school about class and the Social Democratic Party. Accusing Social Democrats of opposing the constitutional amendment so that laws unfairly favoring workers could be passed or ordained with impunity, Simons cast doubt on whether they could be trusted as legislators, civil servants, or judges until they renounced their "worldview of class struggle." To favor one class of Germans over another, he said, was to advocate "conscious unjustness" and to disqualify oneself from responsible leadership.[30] This was, for Social Democrats, essentially an accusation of treason. It recalled a time not too long before, within living memory, when Hindenburg was a young man and the SPD had just been formed, when leaders in the German Empire had empowered the police to ban organizations "in which emerge social democratic, socialist, or communist efforts to subvert the existing state or societal order, in a way that endangers the public peace, in particular the harmony of the population's classes."[31] Class tension was enough of a theme in the popular imagination that the producers at Germany's largest film studio, Universum, decided to give top promotion to a film about the battle between capital and labor, Fritz Lang's *Metropolis,* set to be released in the new year.

THE SOCIAL DEMOCRATIC VISION AND ECONOMIC DEMOCRACY

Meanwhile, in 1926, Social Democratic representatives in parliament were attempting to clarify their party's political positions more effectively as they attempted to regain power in government.[32] Since the hyperinflation, SPD leaders had been struggling to correct misrepresentations of their message not only by liberals such as Chief Justice Simons, but by a vocal minority within their own camp. A majority of those at the recent party convention in Heidelberg had therefore publicly distanced themselves from the call issued by the former director of Germany's largest union (the German Metal Workers' Federation) to break off all negotiation with the liberal parties and wage "unconditional class struggle."[33] Led by party chairman Hermann Müller and former finance minister Rudolf Hilferding, delegates had instead voted overwhelmingly for a platform that described negotiation with non-socialist parties in parliament as "the most favorable ground" for building toward the party's goals, just as negotiation between unions and owners was the path forward in civil society.

The goals articulated in the SPD's Heidelberg Platform of 1925 were generally the same as they had been since the origins of a self-identified Marxist workers' movement before the turn of the century, only now updated in light of the world war that Social Democratic leaders argued had resulted from the competition of capitalist world powers. The party called for the "resistance of the ever-growing working class" against "the capitalist masters of the economy and those controlled by them." However, it wanted to make clear to voters who did not consider themselves part of the proletariat that breaking the grip finance capital held on the basic means of production and transferring control over key industries to the people would benefit not only workers, but "society as a whole." The drive of capitalist owners toward expansion "permanently threatens society with conflicts and the threat of war," the platform explained. Therefore only the overcoming of the capitalist system and the strengthening of workers' rights in both the national and international legal spheres could lift up society from "general strife to self-government in harmonious solidarity."[34]

Another goal of SPD leaders in 1926 was to better communicate to their base and to potential voters the real, if slow, progress the party had been making toward reducing class strife in Germany through legislative means—much of it by building on the crucial final section of the constitution's catalog of basic rights, Article 165, which called for "workers and salaried employees to participate on equal footing in community with employers" in the regulation of wages and working conditions and in the development of the economy in general. This key article, drafted at the constitutional convention with the help of the party's labor law expert Hugo Sinzheimer, was the legal basis for some of the SPD's largest victories in parliament, such as the Works Council Law of 1920, which Sinzheimer considered the "most important piece of legislation since the revolution": a mandate for every business with more than twenty employees to establish a council (*Betriebsrat*) where employees gained a vote in determining their own working conditions.[35] Perhaps most significant, Article 165 provided the constitutional basis—for the first time—by which wage agreements signed between unions and employers must be recognized as binding legal contracts, justiciable in courts of law. SPD leaders could also point to the fact that in late 1926 they were able to gain a majority in parliament to pass a law creating new labor courts especially for contract arbitration and adjudication, staffed in part by lay judges trained in labor issues. Germany's communists often denigrated these plodding advances as the sign of a moribund workers' movement.[36] But Social Democrats presented them as the movement's lifeblood. They used institutions such as the Academy of Labor, founded by Sinzheimer in the commercial hub of Frankfurt, to educate union leaders, workers, and the general public about their legislative progress in the young republic.

Sinzheimer, like most democratic socialists in Germany and beyond, was skeptical about the judicial establishment's efforts to create a constitutional court to check legislation based on the principle of "equality before the law." Although he wholeheartedly embraced the ethical validity of Kant's categorical imperative and in fact based his life's work on it, he worried that the majority of the judiciary considered it arbitrary and unethical to create special laws for workers and would strike down such legislation if they had the chance. He was not alone. The legal scholar Édouard Lambert, who was close to the Socialist Party in France, meticulously traced how the justices of the U.S. Supreme Court had conducted a "war against social legislation" by striking down laws meant to protect workers from exploitation in order to safeguard the freedom of contract;

many believed that if judicial review were instituted in Europe, judges might similarly scuttle what another French scholar called "the socialist vision of law." "Social law" of the sort they wanted to create, Sinzheimer explained, "is unequal law. It favors the weak over the strong. It contradicts the abstract ideal of equality of purely liberal legal thought in order to balance out material inequality."[37]

The rising cohort of young Social Democratic leaders in 1926 was particularly active in this struggle to defend the future of social legislation, none more so than Ernst Fraenkel, a young lawyer whom Sinzheimer had handpicked as his assistant at the University of Frankfurt. Fraenkel was a passionate and quick study of the development of labor law in the new republic. Having lost both parents as a boy, and then returning from the war front injured—he volunteered at age eighteen to fight for his country—this idealistic but now also disillusioned student had thrown himself into socialist politics and its efforts to ensure peace through the empowerment of the weak. Although he had been training to be a judge, through his collaboration with Sinzheimer lecturing at the Academy of Labor during the inflation years Fraenkel had decided instead to join the workers' movement more actively as a private lawyer for labor organizations. By 1926, at just twenty-eight, he was already a chief legal adviser to the German Metal Workers' Federation, the nation's largest and most powerful union, and had begun training labor organizers and members at the Federation's newly opened School for Economics near Leipzig, just kilometers away from the seat of the nation's high court.[38]

Because of his efforts to bring labor politics into the era of mass participatory democracy and because of the respect he enjoyed among workers, some pegged Fraenkel to serve as a future justice minister if the SPD regained control of the German government. At the School for Economics, Fraenkel taught that the mentality of union leadership remained stuck in the first years of the workers' movement, when being a Marxist was still dangerous and organizers sat around in secret speculating on the historical necessity of socialism. Now that new legal pathways had opened up, union leaders needed to learn how to apply Marxist theory and worldview to realms of everyday action. They needed to be able to raise consciousness of worker exploitation through the organization of youth and the use of powerful new technologies of communication such as film, as the deep-pocketed opponents of the workers' movement were already doing. It was necessary to learn legal strategy and take the struggle from the shop floor to the politicians, the courts, and the population at large. Fraenkel's arguments corresponded with the dominant Marxist theory in his party, known as Austro-Marxism, whose proponents held that the goal of socialist revolution was not to upend liberal democracy (as the Soviets in Russia had done), but to integrate workers into it and ultimately seize control over it for the good of the entire society.[39]

In early 1927, Fraenkel published a pamphlet titled *The Sociology of Class Justice,* which in clear terms laid out a Social Democratic position on the question of judicial review and on the future of socialism in a liberal democracy. The text served two related purposes. First, it analyzed the liberal judges' push for judicial supremacy to show how capitalist forces would inevitably react to the empowerment of the working class and how their arguments for morality masked naked class interests. Second, and most crucially, it presented a vision for the future of the workers' movement, which he hoped that all Germans, including the non-proletariat, would adopt as their own instead of embracing the "moral" positions of the high judges.

Fraenkel opened his discussion with an empathetic, almost sympathetic, analysis of the "tragic" position of the judiciary in German society. Before the republic was declared in 1918, he wrote, judges had deeply identified with the rectitude of the old monarchy—not out of any special attachment to monarchism, per se, but because civil servants in those days had been commanded simply to apply the law and never to question it. By psychological necessity they had been compelled to convince themselves that the laws were morally correct; otherwise they would either have become revolutionaries, or gone mad. The monarchy's unreasonable demand to anchor the laws of the state as an absolute, godly ideal, Fraenkel argued, was a holdover from an earlier stage of human development in which people used religion to justify obedience to state laws, an anachronism in a disenchanted world where Christianity was no longer relevant to politics. The jab against the mingling of Christian morality and law was a clear attack on judges such as Chief Justice Walter Simons, who in his work for the World Church Congress and elsewhere rejected any group attempting to disentangle those two categories.[40] Fraenkel's position reflected the official platform of secularism in the SPD, which advocated the separation of church morality from all realms of the state, including the criminal code (where it advocated the decriminalization of abortion), the tax code, and the public school system.[41]

The young socialist Fraenkel expressed something close to pity for the civil servants whose sense of self-purpose had collapsed along with the monarchy at the end of the world war and now needed to be rebuilt. This "crisis of the German judiciary's soul," he wrote, was exacerbated by its class consciousness during the inflation years, which he had personally witnessed unfold as a judge-in-training. Never highly paid, at least relative to the amount of training necessary for the job, and often related by family or marriage to wealthier businesspeople, judges had always felt a certain sense of resentment, but they had never felt their class position threatened until the inflation ruined their savings and they saw that the new regime they served was led by Social Democrats who could further threaten the security of their remaining property. Suddenly, Fraenkel pointed out, the same members of the judiciary who had always disclaimed the right of judicial review under the monarchy now vehemently asserted it. This farce revealed a truth that "any Marxist" would understand, he concluded: "that the judge's concept of morality is determined by his class position, indeed, that their entire approach to law and right are dependent on the class relations in which they find themselves."[42]

Fraenkel then shifted gears to convince readers of the real threat unelected judges would pose to the future of social legislation if allowed to review laws based on the test of the equality clause. He pointed to a decision by the high court from February 1926, where the justices found that the members of a labor union had no standing to bring suit on an alleged violation of their constitutional rights because the basic right they claimed had been violated, Article 165, was really only "programmatic law"—that is, a kind of aspirational resolution, rather than a legally binding part of the constitution. "With the power to designate certain constitutional provisions as programmatic, the Reich Court of Justice has claimed a dangerous right of control over the constitution," Fraenkel wrote. The current proposal for a constitutional court was to be rejected so long as judges claimed the right to hold up one aspect of the constitutional document—the equality clause—over the just-as-constitutive protection of the worker's right to participate on equal footing in the economy. It must be a goal of the Social Democratic Party, he wrote, to awaken a moral outrage among working people that employers and the judges who supported them were keeping them from attaining all the rights to which they were constitutionally entitled.[43]

Although the influence of Fraenkel's *Sociology of Class Justice* is difficult to judge—it was reviewed in most of the major political, legal, and cultural journals and newspapers—there is no doubt that it contributed to the rising consciousness among the ordinary reading public on all sides of the political spectrum that a constitutional crisis was playing out, and that it revolved around the proper role of the judiciary.[44] The media critic Ernst Feder, who surveyed the coverage of political issues in the German press, felt that the crisis might actually be a healthy sign for the new democracy. "As unhappy as the existence of a crisis of the judiciary is in the modern state, and as urgently as a remedy must be demanded," he wrote in 1927, "the very fact that the public is taking such lively and active part" in legal questions was an "important and welcome" new development. By the end of the year, another observer noted that discussion on legal foundations of the republic was going to continue and that the judicial review bill sitting in parliamentary committee was not going to come to a vote any time soon.[45]

Just as Leibholz's argument for the centrality of equality before the law was part of a liberal vision for the equalization of power among sovereign nation-states in the League of Nations, so too was Fraenkel's defense of social law in Germany part of a larger socialist vision of international politics. An educational work titled *Economic Democracy*, jointly written by labor lawyers in the Social Democratic circle around Sinzheimer and published in early 1928 by the nation's largest umbrella group of unions, explained in its conclusion that the continuing globalization of the economy had created multinational concerns and trusts more powerful and more capable of exploiting workers than ever before. The authors pointed hopefully to the institution of a new International Labor Office in Geneva connected to the League of Nations, which would help implement international labor rules. But most important, they wrote, workers around the world needed to integrate themselves completely into the most powerful channels of their own nation's economy, from the universities to the workplaces and to the commissions that advised the government on policy. Only through this arduous and slow process "from stage to stage over the democratization of the economy," it read, could there be an "unfolding of the cultural forces of the entire people" and the "securing of the peaceful cohabitation and communal cultural work among the peoples."[46]

Germany's next parliamentary elections, in June 1928, revealed a significant rise in popularity for the Social Democrats, but shrinking possibilities for cooperation between the parties in parliament. The SPD's share of the vote rose to thirty percent (from twenty-six four years earlier), more than double that of any other party; this result gave its leaders a clear mandate to return to governance for the first time since the hyperinflation. President Hindenburg, known for his hostility to Social Democratic leadership, likely held his nose and invited Hermann Müller, the SPD's chairman, to form a cabinet as chancellor. After piecing together a shaky majority coalition with three smaller parties (the Center Party, the German Democratic Party, and the German People's Party), Müller expressed hope, upon the occasion of the tenth anniversary of the revolution in November 1928, that the new SPD-led government could build on Article 165 and the pro-labor legislative victories achieved just after the war.[47] But as the historian William Patch has shown, Müller's regime ended up being the least productive period in the legislative history of the Weimar Republic, in large part due to what Patch called "the sudden revival of hostile class stereotypes dividing 'bourgeois' [liberal] from 'proletarian' in 1927–1928." One of the most important of the many failed bills in parliament that first year of Müller's government was a second attempt by the liberal parties to pass a constitutional amendment for judicial review, identical to the bill introduced two years earlier.[48]

TWO CONFLICTING VIEWS OF NATIONAL (AND INTERNATIONAL) INTEGRATION

In its book catalog for 1928, the prestigious Berlin-based publisher Duncker & Humblot, whose scholarly wing was directed by the lawyer Ludwig Feuchtwanger, released two important tomes that gave a theoretical language to the constitutional conflict playing out between liberals and Social Democrats without mentioning those two groups by name. The first was a text titled *Constitutional Theory*, by Carl Schmitt, a political theorist and strategist who had just moved to Berlin to seek an advisory position within government circles. Schmitt argued that constitutional systems become unsustainable when internal conflict over their normative "foundations" reaches a certain intensity. At that point, he wrote, the people's perception of the justness and reasonableness of their laws becomes "problematic," and the people might have to re-constitute the nation.[49] The second book, *Constitution and Constitutional Law*, was a more technical but also much-discussed work by the Berlin professor of comparative law Rudolf Smend, who proposed that the success of any constitution should be judged by how well its institutions are able to "integrate" the population into the normative value system that frames it.[50] Both Schmitt and Smend argued for the necessity of a minimum consensus on values for the durability of a constitutional order.

These works resonated because of the current "crisis of trust" in the judiciary and because of the conflicts in liberal and socialist visions exposed by the debates on judicial review. They were also made relevant by several highly publicized legal cases at the end of 1928. In the industrial northwestern part of the country, iron and steel company owners had locked out more than two hundred thousand workers represented by the German Metal Workers' Federation for three months, refusing to recognize as valid law a wage contract mandated by an SPD-led government arbitrator. In another case in December, this one regarding the Reich-owned railway system, Walter Simons dramatically resigned as chief justice of the high court, declaring his disgust for what he regarded as the SPD-led national government's flagrant disregard for the role of judges in the country.[51] Both cases seemed to reveal a serious lack of consensus between judiciary and the most powerful party in the legislature on the issue of labor's relationship to capital.

Gerhard Leibholz, who had finally finished his studies in Berlin—under the very Rudolf Smend whose theory about integration and the legitimacy of a constitutional order had attracted so much attention—suggested a method for "integrating" a German population divided by class and ideology. The way to achieve such a difficult goal without doing away with parliament, Leibholz argued in *The Essence of Representation* (1929), was to create a constitutional court to enforce equality before the law as a control against the legislature.[52] The only other option was dictatorship, a style of government that privileges legislation based on executive decree over freely willed consensus among popular representatives. Leibholz had studied the techniques that Benito Mussolini's Fascist-led government in Italy was using to integrate its own deeply divided nation-state: the ban on opposition parties, the forced reconciliation of labor and capital, the construction of a top-down corporative economic structure. Dictatorship, Leibholz argued, was a "typically Roman product" and could not be imported into Germany, whose dominant cultural tradition made it a nation of laws.[53] In April 1929, Leibholz welcomed the fact that the most celebrated civil lawyer in the country, Max von Rümelin, had published a speech advocating the use of the equality clause as an "inte-grating" factor in the development of a unified nation. Leibholz agreed wholeheartedly with Rümelin that in order to maintain social peace between labor and capital, judges should have the right to refuse to apply certain types of "class-differentiating" national legislation that "clearly" violated the equality clause of Article 109.[54] Judges would thus ensure the unity of the legal system and prevent any popular perception that the law, as created in parliament, was subject to arbitrary power. The same would be true for an international court that could ensure the recognized legiti-macy of legislation issued through the League of Nations.

The labor lawyers around the Social Democratic Party, who at the time were also thinking deeply about the constitutional problems theo-rized by Smend and Schmitt, suggested a very different model of inte-grating the nation. The legal adviser to the SPD executive board, as well as the general counsel of the Federation of General German Unions and the former Social Democratic justice minister Gustav Radbruch, all spoke out against using the equality clause as a method of easing class conflict.[55] In an issue of the SPD's journal *Society*, Ernst Fraenkel presented a policy proposal intended to postpone the standoff between the judiciary and the SPD and develop practical ways to incorporate workers into national life in the meantime. In reality, he wrote, now that the republic had become a bureaucratic welfare state, the actual power behind legislative decisions was less in the hands of party leaders and more in the hands of private organizations such as employers' associations, labor unions, and advo-cates for other specific social groups. Legislators always consulted such organizations before implementing economic policy. If they could be institutionalized into an actual body that brought together workers and owners "on equal footing" in the spirit of Article 165, he argued, then their "collective-democratic" decision making could be what Smend called a "means of political integration," sustaining the state and avoiding a collapse of the system into civil war.[56] Internationally, Social Democrats were working with colleagues abroad, especially in France, to propose a permanent economic council at the League of Nations that would incorporate workers into decision-making processes for the world economy.[57]

At the marking of the Weimar constitution's tenth anniversary on August 11, 1929, it would have been difficult to predict which model of national integration—the liberal model of constitutional review, or Social Democratic economic democracy, if either—the future leaders of the democratic republic would adopt. It is clear that political elites from across the political spectrum identified class conflict as connected to a constitutional crisis and therefore looked for a decisive solution. But aside from the suggested liberal and Social Democratic methods for uniting the nation under the current constitution, few other models seemed available—except, as we will see in the following chapter, a Catholic-inspired economic order and various fringe ideologies such as National Socialism, neither of which took democracy as its source of ethical legitimacy.

A decision on the constitutional crisis over the separation of powers would have to be tabled, however. The crash of the U.S. economy at the end of October 1929, and its almost immediate domino effect in Germany, struck the thorny question of judicial review from the political agenda and shifted the public's attention to a much more pressing arena of conflict. Markets across the Atlantic had lost over thirty billion dollars in just two days, prompting U.S. bank executives to begin recalling loans that had previously allowed the German government to pay off its still massive war debts. German businesses had begun laying off workers at an average rate of forty thousand per month. The SPD-led coalition government, under Chancellor Hermann Müller, could not find a reliable majority in parliament to take legislative action. Members of the largest liberal party in the coalition—the pro-business German People's Party—blamed the Social Democrats for having irresponsibly pushed through expensive welfare programs in the preceding years (in particular unemployment insurance) that had both weakened German businesses and now left the federal government on the hook for bills it could not afford.[58] In March of the following year, after a marathon of failed negotiations with the umbrella groups of employer associations and organized labor to create an acceptable budget, a physically exhausted and politically humiliated Müller resigned his post as chancellor and announced the breakup of the cabinet, leaving in its wake a power vacuum at a time of dire economic crisis and parliamentary fracture.

Looking back on early 1930 several years later, one of the SPD's legal advisers, Franz L. Neumann, wrote that the "final decision of the struggle between judiciary and parliament" was "prevented by the breakdown of Weimar democracy."[59] But viewed from another perspective, it might have been the other way around: the struggle itself, the inability to arrive at common values and consensus on democratic constitutional norms, had also been a cause of the breakdown.

CHAPTER TWO

Sectarian Visions of the Economy

"And had not the Prophet Isaiah, in anticipation of the Lord Jesus
and the birth of the divine child, long before announced peace when
he foretold that swords would be forged into plowshares and that
lions and lambs would live together in peaceful and sincere
harmony? Instead of speaking to men of peace and calm, of mutual
goodwill and beneficence, the Holy Father will speak only to God of
such things; for men do not listen, or do not want to listen."

*Pope Pius XI, in a Christmas address of December 1931, as quoted by a
German Catholic youth leader*

Economic crisis overwhelmed all other public discussion in the early
spring of 1930, when the Social Democratic chancellor Hermann Müller
and his cabinet were forced to resign. By March, the number of registered
unemployed workers in Germany's labor market had doubled since the
previous October. Experts worried about the possibility of further downward spiral and began proposing policies meant to foster job creation as
well as improve class relations. In this potentially dire situation, Paul von
Hindenburg decided to use his constitutional prerogative as president to
declare a national emergency. Instead of announcing national elections
for a new parliament—as a president would normally do after the collapse
of a government coalition—Hindenburg appointed his own choice of
chancellor, whose government would be tasked with solving the social and
economic crisis.[1] It was in this way that the German public first became
acquainted with Heinrich Brüning, a middle-aged policy expert from the
country's Center Party, which had formed in the nineteenth century to
represent the interests of Germany's Catholic population and was still
strongly affiliated, if not as much as before, with the Catholic Church.

The choice of Brüning revealed some of Hindenburg's own aspirations for the future of German politics. First, the old Prussian war hero spoke to his advisers of his desire to exclude the Social Democrats from leadership during the economic crisis. In Hindenburg's eyes, not only had the Müller regime failed to formulate a response to the downturn, but more fundamentally, they had divided the national community, stoking class conflict and alienating the religious communities by advocating a complete separation of church and state.[2] Second, Hindenburg wanted to build a minority cabinet capable of solving the crisis through decree without having to muster a majority coalition in a sometimes dysfunctional parliament. Because that required a sustained presidential invocation of emergency powers based on Article 48 of the constitution—measures that could easily be seen by defenders of the republic as the beginnings of military dictatorship—Hindenburg needed a chancellor who could work as a liaison between the president's office and the legislative body.

Brüning was known, if not for his charisma, then for his experience in budgetary matters and his ability to negotiate in parliament. Significantly, he was also a self-described "*Christian* politician," over and above being a Catholic in a Catholic party. For Hindenburg, that must have been an important attribute for a chancellor at a time when the governments of several republics in continental Europe were using appeals to national religious heritage as a way to overcome class conflict and integrate the nation-state.[3] Like their neighbors in Belgium, France, Austria, and Poland, Germans were overwhelmingly Christian by religious tradition: roughly ninety-eight percent of the population. However, instead of enjoying confessional homogeneity, the demographic was split, with Protestants outnumbering Catholics by a ratio of roughly two to one. Furthermore, Germany's recent past had been plagued by sectarian conflict. In the first years after the country's founding, especially in the kingdom of Prussia that dominated national policy, Protestant-led governments had passed laws to monitor, jail, and even expel Catholic leaders suspected of showing more obedience to the pope in Rome than to the kaiser in Berlin.[4] Though the last of those laws was struck by the end of the Great War, the political and cultural tensions of the *Kulturkampf* remained palpable. As recently as 1921, a team of right-wing former military officers assassinated the most prominent member of Brüning's Center Party, apparently because they perceived the values of the Vatican to conflict with Germany's national interests.[5] Brüning's pedigree as a devout Catholic who envisioned the conversion of the Center Party to an interconfessional "Christian" party would therefore be useful to Hindenburg on a number of different levels.[6]

Encouragingly for the advocates of interconfessional Christian collaboration on social and economic policy, the years during and after the hyperinflation had seen a relative easing of tensions between churchgoing Protestants and Catholics, often due to the common cause they found against the secularist and Marxist ideologies of Germany's left-wing parties, the Social Democrats and the Communists. In 1923, Heinrich Hermelink, a church historian, celebrated what he called the end of mutual attempts by Protestants and Catholics "to find in the other confession only intellectual and cultural backwardness."[7] Protestant and Catholic religious associations came together at various points to lobby against legislation proposed by the left-wing parties, especially against attempts to remove religious instruction from schools and to decriminalize abortion and homosexuality. In 1927, a delegation of German Catholic priests attended a Protestant-led ecumenical conference in Lausanne, where one speaker looked forward to the creation of a unified "Christian International" to fight against the anti-church propaganda of Moscow's Communist International in a "unified front." One young Protestant theologian at a seminary near Frankfurt hoped in 1929 that Catholics could overcome their past grievances and instead join the new "cultural struggle": not Protestantism against Catholicism, but "Christianity against Marxism."[8]

At the same time, those who hoped for a unified Christian politics in Germany faced major obstacles in the years before Brüning took power in 1930. Pope Pius XI responded in 1928 to the participation of German Catholics in international ecumenical conferences by officially prohibiting "pan-Christian activities," lest they "give countenance to a false Christianity," and he gave the Federation of Catholic Academics in Germany special instructions to remind their co-religionists that the "de-secularization of intellectual, economic, and social life" could "only be carried out in, with, and through the Catholic Church." He also tapped several Jesuit scholars in Germany to prepare a set of moral guidelines for economy and society that would explicitly reject "modern" (that is, Protestant) Christian solutions to social problems.[9] Meanwhile, the majority of Protestants in Germany appeared uninterested in making Christian metaphysics the ideological basis for their politics and suspicious of too much church involvement in governmental affairs. Many checked the box for "Protestant" on their tax returns and took advantage of the services the church offered for life-cycle events such as marriage and burial, but also described themselves as "modern" or "liberal" in the sense that they relied on science, reason, and the national interest to form their political opinions. Many also resented the Vatican's interference in German domestic affairs. In 1928, politicians in Brüning's home state, Prussia, faced difficulty forming a coalition because of worries among Catholics that the German People's Party (DVP) and the German Democratic Party (DDP), which were dominated by Protestant voters, might block negotiations for a treaty with the Vatican.[10]

Chancellor Brüning thus had his work cut out for him when, on his first day in office in late March 1930, he was instructed by his advisers and President Hindenburg to infuse his government's economic policies with "Christian" and "conservative" values. Many questions were raised. What would constitute a specifically Christian response to the unemployment crisis? Since there was no such thing as a "Christian church" in Germany, only Protestant and Catholic "confessions"—both associated in the German popular imagination with different social value systems—would one tradition predominate? Would it matter that Brüning himself was a devout Catholic?

A MODERN WORLDVIEW: THE PROTESTANT ETHIC AND THE ENGINE OF CAPITALISM

From its first months in office, Brüning's government confronted not only a social and economic crisis, but also a delicate political situation. Although the chancellor held a legal directive from the president to combat unemployment through emergency legislation if necessary, he also wanted his government's decrees to have the support of the labor and business umbrella organizations as well as the pro-labor and pro-business parties in parliament in order to claim a democratic mandate. When labor and management representatives broke off talks and the pro-business parties rejected the government's proposal in June 1930 to protect unemployment benefits through a special tax on the wealthy, President Hindenburg decided to dissolve the parliament and call for new elections in September, two years ahead of schedule.[11] When it came time to vote, however, with registered unemployment numbers climbing steadily during the summer to fifteen percent of the labor force, and youth unemployment much higher, many Germans supported parties that offered radical anti-establishment solutions. The National Socialist German Workers Party, nicknamed by the press the "Nazis," won a shocking eighteen percent of the vote with its calls to expel foreign workers and repeal the Treaty of Versailles, catapulting Adolf Hitler as the leader of the second-largest party, behind the Social Democrats. The Communist Party also gained ground among urban voters, bringing it to thirteen percent nationwide. These ominous signs motivated Brüning's government to act all the more quickly on the financial situation.

At the end of 1930, Brüning decided to form an independent, nonpartisan group of ten experts—a Commission for the War on Unemployment—to advise the cabinet on ordinances that would be enacted as soon as possible by emergency decree. Many in the press called the commission an "ersatz parliament," because the emergency budget decrees based on its recommendations would be subject to parliamentary confirmation only after they had already been put into effect. Brüning entrusted a colleague from his own Catholic party, the priest and long-time labor minister Heinrich Brauns, with the task of making the group as inclusive as possible while avoiding naming any Marxists. Brauns gathered a diverse group of lawyers, professors, and bureaucrats, including members from the main social and regional milieus: a politician with connections to the large banks, a large landowner from the Prussian territory east of the Elbe River to speak for agricultural interests, the director of the labor office in the western territory of Hesse to represent industrial workers, and a social worker from Bavaria in the south to advocate on behalf of families with many children. Careful to achieve confessional parity, Brauns also included one expert each from the two Christian confessions: Antonie Hopmann, an experienced leader in social policy and member of the Catholic German Women's League; and the Protestant Eduard Heimann, an economist, self-described pro-market "Christian socialist," and member of the Association for Social Policy (*Verein für Socialpolitik*).[12]

The Association for Social Policy, essentially a think tank that promoted scholarship on the economy, had been known since its establishment sixty years earlier as a semi-official advisory board for the national government dominated by Protestants.[13] Founded by Gustav Schmoller in 1873, the association had helped craft Germany's renowned social insurance laws, an employer-based system of health, accident, and disability insurance unrivaled in the industrialized world. Its members vehemently defended the practices of capitalism—private ownership of the means of production—and often supported measures intended to boost national production, such as subsidies for agriculture and tariffs on foreign imports. In fact, their detractors in the left-wing parties called them "state socialists" who were attempting to steal the thunder of the workers' movement by offering the promise of both economic growth and social welfare.[14]

When Heimann, the original Protestant appointee, announced his resignation from Brüning's commission, the chairman took the bold step of appointing a less experienced but brilliant thirty-one-year-old scholar in the Association for Social Policy named Wilhelm Röpke. Röpke was known as a protégé of the association's expert on unemployment (Walter Troeltsch) and one of the most promising young economists in the country. The child of patriotic parents in a family of doctors and pastors, he had grown up under the empire in a prosperous (and what he later remembered as idyllic) village between Hamburg and Hanover, attending a private school run by a charismatic former Protestant theology student who tutored him in math, Latin, Greek, French, and English. After returning from service on the western front during the war, Röpke expressed optimism about his people's new opportunity to shape the nation-state as equal citizens; however, he also found that the postwar inflation had devastated the middle class and tragically driven many of his generation into extremist politics.[15] At the University of Marburg, he studied law and economics with Troeltsch and quickly excelled in the field, earning the prestigious title of full professor already in his twenties. Although he did not belong to any officially "Protestant" organizations and rarely attended church, Röpke can be seen as broadly representative of educated Protestants in Germany in that he considered his "modern" and "liberal" worldview to derive from the secularization of his religious tradition.[16]

The rising reputation of Röpke marked a shift in the orientation of the Association for Social Policy, from an emphasis on welfare spending and protective tariffs to a focus on capital formation and free trade. Many members came to believe that the economic nationalism of the great powers beginning around the turn of the twentieth century had caused the catastrophic world war. The young economist Röpke combined patriotic idealism with free trade ideology. At university during the inflation years, he wrote a rousing call for his generation to serve the nation in the spirit of the old patriots "Fichte, Stein, Hegel, and Lagarde" while at the same time resisting isolationism.[17] Together with several other young economists, he led a movement in the association arguing that government was spending too much on social welfare, overregulating businesses, preventing trade, and thereby contributing to the source of international strife. His mission, Röpke told a friend in 1923, was to remind government leaders of "the cruel exercise of inexorable laws" in the market and to protest against the "irrational" protectionist policies that prevented Europeans from returning to the glorious achievements of the modern industrialized world before the turn against free trade. "Liberals of the world unite to win back this vanished world!," he exclaimed.[18] In his first major scholarly work, *Money and Foreign Trade* (1925), Röpke criticized all efforts to hem in freedom of economic movement, insisting that "national romanticism" must not prevent the free international flow of capital.[19]

Röpke's self-consciously "modern" worldview was shaped by an understanding of the historical relationship between religion and political economy best articulated by one of the most famous (if not the most representative) members of the Association for Social Policy, Max Weber. In *The Protestant Ethic and the "Spirit" of Capitalism* (1904), Weber argued that Protestant theology, through its emphasis on the divinity of asceticism, thrift, industry, and individual communion with God, had encouraged the secular values and behaviors associated with capitalism, democracy, and the "modern" world of rationalism and individualism, while Catholic theology had served sociologically to perpetuate "traditional" and hierarchical forms of politics and economy. Röpke likely took from Weber the metaphor of the modern economic world as a technological machine, which could either lift people up or entrap them in an "iron cage," depending on how people shaped its future.[20]

Also like Weber, Röpke regarded the United States as the epitome of a modern economy shaped by the Protestant ethic. After a six-month tour in

1926 and 1927, which he described to an American acquaintance as "one of the most important steps in my mental development," Röpke returned with several lessons he hoped would help solve the problem of class conflict and international struggle in Germany.[21] His perception of the contrast between North America and its Latin American neighbors to the south confirmed for him the hypothesis that Protestant majorities produced cultures of capitalist entrepreneurship and the rule of law, whereas Catholic majorities produced cultures of collectivism and dictatorship. Though unimpressed with the protectionism of President Calvin Coolidge's administration, he marveled at the standard of living in the United States, which made politics there so "unfavorable to the growth of mass anti-capitalist sentiment" and so favorable to the "inactivation, or at least attenuation, of class consciousness." "What a prospect!" he wrote in 1927, in light of rising class consciousness in Germany. "Does this not mean a solution to the social question through 'prosperity' . . .?")[22] Röpke especially wanted his compatriots to consider attempts by leading (Protestant) American social scientists, such as Edward Ross of Wisconsin, to maintain a basic level of prosperity for all through state-sponsored techniques of population control, including contraceptive access for women, sexual education, immigration restrictions, and eugenic sterilization.[23]

The year before his appointment to the Commission for the War on Unemployment in early 1931, Röpke spoke out against the increasingly popular international tendency toward economic protectionism. In May 1930, he told a group of Dutch law students about the basic law of optimization: the only way to build prosperity and overcome wealth inequality was to free up markets while simultaneously inhibiting population growth. All other methods of state intervention, such as price and wage fixing, property redistribution, and high trade tariffs were "fanatical," he said, because they drew not on science but on "romantic" wishes for national togetherness. Interestingly, Röpke's critiques of Catholic-inspired economic proposals were difficult to distinguish from his propaganda against the economic platforms of the Nazi Party during the election campaign of September 1930.[24] Despite some reported concern in Catholic circles that Röpke was too committed to free markets to serve on Brüning's Commission on Unemployment, the chairman Heinrich Brauns enlisted the young scholar because of his reputation as an expert on capital formation and an enemy of extremism.[25]

Thus, by the time Röpke moved to the German capital in February 1931 and joined the rest of the commission, he had already formulated a clear view of the origins of the economic crisis and the decisive action necessary to solve it. He argued in a seminar at the Berlin College of Commerce that the government's continued "assaults" against "market laws" through overregulation were perpetuating the downward spiral. The situation could be improved, he argued, by reversing the policies that deflated the currency and decreased production, as well as cutting back taxes and the most expensive worker-protection programs (such as unemployment insurance) into which small business owners were required to pay.[26] Some of the other members of the commission, on the other hand—especially the experts from labor offices and welfare organizations with more direct contact with workers and families—offered a different perspective. They shared hundreds of heartbreaking letters they had received from ordinary people affected by the downturn who depended on government to intervene on their behalf. Unfortunately no minutes of the negotiations exist, but retrospective accounts and the final language of the recommendations suggest that Röpke's opinions did not enjoy general acceptance.

When the commission submitted the first two installments of its recommendations on unemployment to Brüning's government in March and April 1931, they seemed to be a self-contradictory mix of regulatory and laissez-faire policies. The first, released against Röpke's wishes, suggested regulations designed to distribute the jobs that already existed in Germany, especially those funded entirely or partly by the state, the nation's largest employer: a prohibition on working overtime, so that others could be hired to work those hours; a prohibition on working two jobs; the discouragement of "double-earning" households, meaning the employment of women whose husbands were employed; and incentives for private businesses and unions to reduce current employee hours and to hire additional workers.[27] The second recommendation, this one penned largely by Röpke, suggested one-time deficit spending by the government to provide an "initial ignition" (*Initialzündung*) for private enterprise, which would then presumably create jobs with no further government regulation. (The metaphor came from the ignition required for an automobile or a locomotive.)[28] The editor of the *Industry and Commerce Newspaper*, who shared many of Röpke's ideas about the dangers of overregulation, noted that the commission bore the "clear stamp of compromise" between interventionists and free-market advocates.[29]

The commission's recommendations thus met with widespread disapproval among both organized business and organized labor.[30] Business leaders saw in the commission's work a continuation of government overregulation to keep prices low. Leaders of the largest union umbrella group, meanwhile, rejected the idea of financial stimulus recommended by Röpke because it seemed geared toward tipping the already skewed balance of class power decisively in favor of employers. As they had seen in the Ruhr Valley metal workers' lockout two years earlier and in several incidents since, the private companies that stood to gain from such an "ignition" were challenging the very legality of collective bargaining and government arbitration of private contracts.[31]

Röpke, sensing that the negative feedback would influence the government's actions, launched a publicity blitz. Throughout the month of May 1931, he published articles in mainstream newspapers and numerous industry and labor-oriented journals, urging business leaders to support short-term credit expansion, despite the fear of inflation, and promising labor leaders that workers would ultimately benefit from long-term economic growth despite lower wages at first.[32] The implementation of ignition combined with deregulation, he argued, would require a faith in the promise of private enterprise that the masses seemed to have lost. But if Brüning's government refused to take decisive action against popular opinion, and instead continued its unsuccessful attempts to "heal" the economy through regulatory decrees, then the radical parties that called for the death of the capitalist system would continue to grow, paralyze parliament, and destroy the German economy.[33]

In the end, free-market advocates such as Röpke would be sorely disappointed by the budget that Brüning's cabinet released at the beginning of June 1931 in its Emergency Decree for the Protection of the Economy and Finances. While it put into effect some of the commission's proposals from its first recommendation on labor regulation, the budget decree completely ignored Röpke's suggestion for an "initial ignition" for private enterprise. Instead, it mandated an increase in taxes and fees, including a new "crisis tax" designed to fund public sector work relief and sustain emergency welfare assistance for the unemployed.[34]

Röpke could not understand why the government failed to recognize basic market laws. In his recap of the commission's work for a journal dedicated to the world economy, he bemoaned that capitalism and the free market were "moving into the museum" like artifacts of a bygone past. He did not share the view of a Catholic participant on the commission, Antonie Hopmann, who congratulated Brüning for having brought together leaders from "the most diverse domains of life" to solve a common problem.[35] Instead, he ridiculed their lack of expertise. "The situation is enormously serious," he wrote in a book titled *The Path to Calamity*, in which he cataloged the crushing pressures driving Germans toward the radical economic nationalism of the Nazi Party. With his proposals for deregulation he had clearly traced "a way out," but for whatever reason, Brüning's cabinet was unable to follow it.[36]

A CATHOLIC WORLDVIEW: REGULATING THE ECONOMIC ORGANISM

We know from private documents that the Prussian, mainly Protestant entourage around Paul von Hindenburg—led by the president's trusted adviser Kurt von Schleicher—was increasingly concerned as 1931 wore on by the influence they felt the leaders of the Catholic Church might be exerting on the Brüning government's economic policies.[37] Such suspicions would have been fed by the tremendous excitement the Vatican had generated in May 1931 with a document entitled *Quadragesimo anno*, or *In the Fortieth Year*, an official statement on Catholic economic morality circulated to all the dioceses of the world on the occasion of the fortieth anniversary of the last great papal pronouncement on social issues, Leo XIII's *Rerum novarum* (1891). By coincidence, Pope Pius XI's message was translated into German and discussed at length in the political press precisely in the midst of government deliberations over the commission's recommendations on unemployment. The specter of "influence" would have also been raised by the fact that Chancellor Brüning himself, as well as the man he had appointed to lead the commission, Heinrich Brauns, and the one he had made his minister of labor, Adam Stegerwald, had always associated themselves with the same theory of moral economy that was said to shape the Vatican's views.

That moral theory, "solidarism" (*Solidarismus*), which its earliest proponents sometimes called "Christian democracy," was a system of thought associated with the entire Catholic social milieu of Germany. It had its own terminology and its own canon, beginning with the foundational works of Heinrich Pesch, S.J. (1854–1926), a scholar who wrote at a time when Catholics were still attempting to convince political authorities of their loyalty to the new German state. One of the laws directed against Catholics in Germany banned members of Pesch's order, the Society of Jesus (or Jesuits), who were considered the intellectual elite of the Catholic Church hierarchy, from teaching on German soil. Pesch became known therefore mainly as an author in exile, his ideas spread through what was at first an openly anti-Protestant as well as anti-Marxist organization called the People's Association for Catholic Germany (*Volksverein für das katholische Deutschland*).[38]

Pesch formulated a theory intended to reintroduce Christian ethics into what Max Weber had correctly called a modern "disenchanted" society based on rationalism and private accumulation. In his influential multi-volume *Textbook of National Economy,* published the year after Weber's *Protestant Ethic,* Pesch analogized the moral national economy not to a machine, but to a self-reproducing organism: an economy in which members of the nation cooperate to sustain a common life. Those who embraced "solidarism," he wrote, imagine an order of "natural law" in which leaders of professional organizations in the various branches of the economy work together to ensure the health of the whole and all of its parts.[39] Near the end of the Great War, when parliament lifted the forty-year ban on the Jesuit order, Pesch and his colleagues in the People's Association began arguing that "Christian," that is, Catholic, morality was the necessary foundation for a peaceful reconstruction of the German nation—indeed, of an entire modern world that had fallen into conflict because of greed and the unbridled competition of interests. The People's Association became one of the staunchest supporters of the new League of Nations, which the Vatican called an originally Catholic idea.[40]

As many scholars have begun to rediscover, the decades after the Great War saw a boom in the popularity of the Catholic Church in Europe—in both church attendance and number of converts, and perhaps more important in the reach of its "ideas," even among those who did not consider themselves Catholic or religious at all. The new and at first glance surprising postwar resonance of Catholicism, especially in the non-Catholic-majority German Reich, begins to make more sense as a phenomenon when it is understood not in isolation but in relation to the lack of faith among a growing part of the majority Protestant population in the ability of their own church leaders to provide material support and principled moral guidance in a social crisis. Siegfried Kracauer, the cultural editor at the prestigious *Frankfurter Zeitung*, put his finger on something when he noted in 1922, "If the [Catholic] Church is again taking hold of many souls precisely in Germany and is experiencing an unexpected rejuvenation, then it is due, beyond all positive religious reasons, to the weighty arguments it can lead into the field against the worldview-position of German Protestantism."[41] None of those arguments were weightier than the solidarism associated with Pesch.

The papal message of May 1931, *Quadragesimo anno,* so closely resembled the canon of solidarism because the Vatican had specifically chosen a group of German Catholics from the People's Association to draft it, led by the forty-year-old scholar Oswald von Nell-Breuning, the flag-bearer of Pesch's legacy after the master's death in 1926. Like Pesch, Nell-Breuning was a member of the Jesuit order. Hailing from the majority-Catholic region of the Rhineland, he had been born into aristocracy. His paternal family owned a large wine-growing estate, and his maternal side included a number of doctors and lawyers, some of whom had been friends with Ludwig van Beethoven; Kaiser Wilhelm II had personally allowed Oswald von Nell to change his name to Nell-Breuning when his maternal uncle Maximilian died in 1909 without children, which would have meant the end of the noble name.[42] But Nell-Breuning renounced his family wealth to become a theologian and teacher. After serving as a volunteer medic during the war, he studied sociology and law with one of the main Catholic framers of Germany's republican constitution, Joseph Mausbach, and began teaching in 1926 at the first Jesuit seminary allowed to open in unified Germany. In the fall of 1930, when Pius XI decided to respond to the world economic depression with a special message, Nell-Breuning was tapped to lead the drafting committee in consultation with a small group of other German Catholic intellectuals.

The decision-making process at the Vatican is not always transparent to outsiders, but Nell-Breuning must have caught the attention of the Vatican because of his leadership in the People's Association for Catholic Germany. After the hyperinflation, Nell-Breuning had led a cadre of young Jesuits traveling on tour through Germany teaching solidarism in the ever more intricately connected network of Catholic associations and political youth groups, in a movement that one Protestant minister of education in the southwest of the country called a "cultural offensive" that "flows today like a powerful stream into the Occidental world."[43] A contemporary historian of German Catholicism boasted that "never before" had a country possessed such a developed and active system of associations. By the early 1930s, the People's Association even maintained an anti-Marxist intelligence-gathering bureau within its organizational structure. The organization circulated copies of the dozens of pamphlets Nell-Breuning wrote on economic topics in the tens of thousands, also to the Catholic youth associations, whose membership numbered roughly 1.5 million in 1931.[44]

Most important for Nell-Breuning's reputation in particular, perhaps, was his book *Basic Principles of Stock Exchange Morality*, published in 1928. In it, Nell-Breuning argued that the modern practice of stock trading was not in itself immoral. Catholic teaching sanctioned the acquisition of private property. However, a government must prevent what he called the "hyena-like" behavior of professional speculators who took advantage of the financial market to pursue unending accumulation and deprived others of their share of the community's finite resources. To combat the potential for immoral uses of property in a capitalist system, Nell-Breuning suggested a government oversight commission for the stock exchange: a financial regulatory institution that did not yet exist anywhere in the world (though the Securities and Exchange Commission would soon be founded in the United States, headed by the Democratic politician and devout Catholic Joseph Kennedy). This, he argued, would help the economy accord better with the "natural law" of a healthy organism.[45]

Nell-Breuning's suggestions to regulate the stock market revealed an approach that distinguished Germany's mainstream Catholic milieu from the dominant voices in the other historic German-speaking center of Catholicism: Austria. In the wake of the hyperinflation of 1923 (which also catastrophically affected the Austrian currency), leading bishops of the Austrian dioceses had attacked capitalism and its political equivalent, liberal democracy, as intrinsically unethical.[46] Their counterparts in Germany, however—where Catholics were decisively a minority among Protestants—had taken a more nuanced stance. In response to the Austrian bishops, German cardinals in 1927 issued a set of guidelines that did not condemn capitalism per se (defined as an economic system based "on the use and increase of private capital") but did call for prevention of the system's abuse. Nell-Breuning defended these guidelines against Austrian claims that German Catholics had accommodated themselves to an immoral conception of life. Catholics, he wrote in 1929, can live in many different types of economy, just as they could live in many different forms of state. What mattered was whether the economic order or state form in question was embodied institutionally in a spirit of individualistic materialism, or in a spirit of communal solidarity.[47]

The lack of understanding between German Catholics and Austrian Catholics on the issue of capitalism pained Nell-Breuning, because he believed that the two sides fundamentally agreed on the common enemy in their "war" against immoral economic behavior: they both wanted to correct a warped view of man's position in society.[48] In a series of pamphlets published by the People's Association before and after the U.S. stock market crash, Nell-Breuning argued that the free-market and Marxist viewpoints on the economy suffered from a false belief that the individual person was entitled inviolably to the fruits of his labor. The Christian view, he explained, saw the community of the state as an organism; it looked to determine not only whether property was legitimately owned, but also whether it was being legitimately *used* toward the purpose of sustaining the whole and all its parts. According to Catholic teaching, the individual could claim rights to property as part of one's dignity as a member of society, but each was always "duty-bound" to the other members. Therefore, the members of the state-organized society should rightfully decide whether property and the labor opportunities created by it were rationally and healthily distributed at any given moment.[49]

Nell-Breuning's approach might have won the Vatican's favor because it allowed for maximum flexibility in the Catholic war against economic immorality. Nell-Breuning insisted that each national body politic had its own internal dynamics and therefore demanded different tactics for self-healing.[50] The constitution of the German republic, he noted in the summer of 1930 as the unemployment rate skyrocketed, offered a legal path toward self-healing. Article 152 prohibited "usury" (an unjustly high interest rate) and allowed annulment of other "immoral" legal transactions; Article 153 entitled the state to expropriate for the common good; Article 155 enjoined the state to supervise the distribution of the country's land, in order to prevent its "misuse," and to secure living quarters for all Germans and economic opportunity for all families, especially those with many children. Although Nell-Breuning bemoaned the constitution's lack of explicitly Christian language, he argued that the republic's founding document was a door through which to usher in the Catholic spirit of economic life: the idea that man "is not free to act in the economy as he pleases," but rather becomes, when he begins working, "a living member" of the community.[51]

While the Commission for the War on Unemployment convened from February through May 1931, Nell-Breuning and his colleagues argued against free-market proposals such as Röpke's and called on the government to use the opportunity of crisis to revivify the national economy from within. Nell-Breuning suggested using public funds to resettle Germans from the overpopulated western and southwestern regions—especially farmers struggling to sustain their large families—to the underpopulated northeastern parts, where large landholders owned large tracts of currently unused land. A redistribution of resources to counteract the "unhealthy one-sidedness" of industrialism in the west with a stronger agricultural body in the east, Nell-Breuning wrote, would put into practice what he called the uniquely Catholic idea of "autarky": the creation of self-sufficiency in the organism. "The national economy should not close itself off against other national economies where mutual complement and advancement is possible," he clarified, but "the economy of a people united in a state should certainly hold within itself the foundations and assurances of an existence worthy of men, and provisions for the sustenance of the entire people in the state."[52]

Gustav Gundlach, a German Jesuit helping Nell-Breuning draft the much anticipated papal encyclical on economic morality, further explained why the Catholic vision of autarky ruled out free markets. In late April 1931, he wrote that Röpke's proposal to use foreign loans to restart the German economy and then immediately deregulate it—as if the economy were a machine that simply needed a "cranking up" (*Ankerbelung*) before it ran by itself again according to so-called "market laws"—would be "disastrous" because the system left to itself resulted in a "completely unhealthy distribution of individual property over the means of production," with no force to supply capital to the sectors of the organism that needed it most. The capitalist order of the economy, while not an evil in itself, Gundlach insisted, offered no immanent means of healing and regulating itself.[53]

The release of Pope Pius XI's encyclical *Quadragesimo anno* on May 15, 1931, was a major media event that dwarfed the coverage of the commission's recommendations. As Chancellor Brüning later remembered, it seemed like a "momentous" statement on the economic depression now affecting the greater part of the globe. The document was parsed in the press all over Germany and Europe and beyond.[54] In no uncertain terms, Catholicism's highest authority called for a Christian solution to the social and economic crisis where the free market had proved "utterly incapable." *Quadragesimo anno* insisted on the inherently *social* character of property; it pronounced that individuals had no natural right to determine the use of surplus property beyond their needs for self-sustenance; it beseeched employers to negotiate just wages and salaries for the good of workers and the good of the whole to which they all belonged; and it condemned as a "grave evil" the class-divided society.

Like the dream of an international free-market economy envisioned by Röpke and other modern liberals, the vision of the Vatican articulated in *Quadragesimo anno* was also a "world" view. The document looked ahead to a system in which the leaders of all nations implemented policies to counteract social instability and promote economic harmony within their own borders. While the creation of trade unions and collective bargaining had been important to ensure dignity for the worker, Pius XI pronounced, the "true healing" of societies could only occur when the opposition between employers and workers was overcome by arranging the "social body" into "orders" (*ordines*): orders into which "men may be inserted not according to the function they may have in the labor market, but according to the various social roles that they perform."[55] The definition of the word "orders" remained necessarily vague to accommodate the particularities of all nations. To accommodate different types of government from parliamentary to authoritarian, the encyclical also allowed for interpretation in how "men may be inserted" into them, by choice or by coercion. (Nell-Breuning translated the Latin *ordines* into German as *Berufsstände*, "vocational estates" or "corporative orders.")

The dramatic events in Europe during the months of May and June 1931 intensified the timeliness of the encyclical's critique of free-market capitalism. Just four days before the official release of *Quadragesimo anno*, the Credit-Anstalt, a bank founded by the Rothschild family in Vienna and Austria's largest loan provider, declared bankruptcy, sending shock waves through European markets and setting the stage for a run on German banks. The press reported that a number of German department stores and other large concerns lost enormous amounts of money on speculation; businesses laid off more workers, and unemployment levels continued to rise. Political youth groups grew increasingly receptive to criticism of global capitalism. As numerous observers noted and historians have now confirmed, the Vatican's powerful critique of the free market and its call to arrange society based on the solidarity of workers and owners within particular economic sectors became modish far beyond Catholic circles. The People's Association for Catholic Germany, which had been in dire financial straits since the depression, appeared at the vanguard of an important social movement and began receiving a flow of monetary contributions to continue spreading the message of solidarism.[56]

The moral grandeur of the papal encyclical lent a kind of gravitas to other proposals, including non-Catholic and Fascist-inspired ones, to overcome class struggle in free-market capitalism through the construction of "orders" that would encourage workers and owners to cooperate for the common good. In particular, the leaders of Hitler's rapidly ascendant Nazi Party, whose grassroots organization had grown from sixty regional party branches in January 1930 to roughly four hundred by the spring of 1931, railed against finance capitalism and spoke often of ordering the economy by vocation, a central part of their original party platform.[57] Indeed, the founders of the Nazi Party borrowed much of their language on economic issues from the theoretical repertoire of the Catholic Church. In an article on *Quadragesimo anno* in June 1931, the political journalist Theodor Heuss, a Protestant liberal who like Röpke belonged to the German Democratic Party, drew parallels between what he considered the "anticapitalism" of both Catholic and Nazi rhetoric.[58]

Catholic political economists in Germany attempted to distance themselves from the proposals of Nazi leaders who used a similar and perhaps Catholic-inspired language of organic "orders" or "estates." In an article published in October 1931, just before the Brüning-led government released another set of major economic ordinances, Nell-Breuning noted that while Catholics should be pleased that their idea of rearranging the social organism was "today on everyone's lips," its popularity put it in danger of hijack and misuse. The pope was *not* calling for a return to a "medieval" system of orders in which individuals would be unequal before the law, he wrote. The Catholic conception was indeed "romantic" in the sense that it was a view of the social body as an organic "structure of members" as opposed to an "enormous mass of grains of sand," Nell-Breuning explained, but "the analogy of the organism may not be stretched too far." If understood responsibly, it would convince people of the necessity to organize voluntarily into units where employers and workers cooperate instead of struggle in the marketplace. He clarified the position of the People's Association by referring to Fascist Italy's recent attempt to dictate cooperation: Mussolini's ban on strikes and lockouts was "without question a thousand times better than the perfect disorganization that liberalistic individualism has brought," Nell-Breuning wrote, but German solidarists would prefer a system in which unions and employer organizations chose to unite freely without coercion from the state.[59]

Although the unemployment rate in Germany did not improve in the second half of the year 1931, Brüning's cabinet took several executive actions praised by solidarists and designed to curb the abuses of capitalism. In September, Brüning announced the creation of a new national government office of bank commissioner to oversee financial transactions. In October, he released another set of emergency budget decrees, cutting wages to correspond to the levels of capital available in the shrunken national coffers, raising unemployment-insurance premiums, and hiking up tariffs to protect domestic industry. The regime began considering the proposal pushed by Nell-Breuning to resettle unemployed workers from the densely populated western regions to the underpopulated agricultural east. Furthermore, Brüning announced an Economic Advisory Council consisting of roughly twenty-five leaders from different sectors of the economy to advise the regime on such questions—to be chaired by none other than President Hindenburg, who was himself an owner of agricultural lands in the east.[60] In December, the cabinet decreed measures to keep prices on consumer goods and interest rates low and created yet another national government office, that of price commissioner.[61]

Prominent Catholic voices in Germany proclaimed that Brüning's cabinet was helping transform the nation into the type of well-ordered national economy envisioned by the Vatican in *Quadragesimo anno*. At the end of 1931, Friedrich Dessauer, a biophysicist, politician, and publisher of a popular Catholic newspaper, attempted to sell the government's accomplishments to Germany's young people, who were suffering from the unemployment crisis more than any other age demographic and who many believed would not endure austerity much longer without revolting. Brüning had a philosophy and a plan, Dessauer assured them. Understanding the nation-state as an organism, the government was counteracting "life-threatening atrophy" by boosting circulation of already existing capital into its underserved sectors.[62] Nell-Breuning noted in Dessauer's newspaper that the government's latest decrees would not cure the depression immediately, but represented a giant step toward overcoming the individualistic free-market spirit that had helped cause it.[63]

ENTRENCHMENT OF THE FRONTS

By early 1932, two years after Brüning's initial appointment, no one could say that liberal Protestants and Catholics had gotten any closer to formulating a recognizably "Christian" social policy that could steer the national economy forward without the help of the "godless" Social Democrats. On the contrary, as unemployment worsened and anti-republican parties gained strength in regional elections, a conflict over fundamental questions of the economy had been laid bare.

To be sure, no bright line can be drawn between "Protestants" who advocated free international trade on one front, and "Catholics" who professed an autarkic healing of the economy on the other. But an ominous feeling of sectarian divide on the morality of political economy was palpable. Several influential individuals in the entourage advising President Hindenburg—many of them Protestant landowners and military men from aristocratic families in the east of the country—voiced concern over Brüning's apparent lack of respect for individual property, which they attributed to his Catholic confession.[64] Even before the drastic deflationary decrees of December 1931, which Hindenburg reluctantly signed, the president's adviser Kurt von Schleicher applied pressure on Brüning to sack his interior minister, Catholic politician Joseph Wirth, who promptly noted that the president's office was losing patience with Catholic influence.[65] These developments were not unconnected to Hindenburg's own self-image as a guardian of liberal, free-market values. Even though he was a large landowner and was often accused by critics of pushing protectionist policies for his Prussian "friends" in agriculture, he was known abroad as something quite different. Harry Louis Nathan, an M.P. in England from the free-trade-oriented Liberal Party, reminded readers of a statement Hindenburg made to the Chamber of Commerce near the end of the war: "Keep open the doors of international commerce for ever for anybody."[66]

Hindenburg still needed Brüning to help him campaign for reelection as president in March 1932 against the rising star of populist politics, Adolf Hitler, whom they both feared. Gerhard Ritter, a Protestant professor of Prussian history and supporter of Hindenburg, urged the Evangelical League for the Protection of German-Protestant Interests (*Evangelischer Bund zur Wahrung der deutsch-protestantischen Interessen*) to suspend its anti-Catholic propaganda against Brüning as he campaigned for Hindenburg's reelection.[67] Hitler was drawing crowds in the tens of thousands, especially young people. But after the aging war hero Hindenburg emerged victorious in a second-round run-off on April 10, 1932, with a vote of fifty-three percent to Hitler's thirty-seven, political journalists predicted that Brüning's tenure would not last much longer.

But the struggle for an appropriate response to the ever worsening social and economic situation was far from over. Around this time, the newly formed Society for Free Market Economy, of which Röpke was an original member, held its first conference dedicated to the refutation of the Catholic-inspired conception of the economy as an ideally "autarkic" organism. The free-trade economist Wilhelm Lautenbach, a longtime civil servant in the ministry of economics, continued to push a plan similar to Röpke's, to reduce wages and expand credit to restart the economy.[68] In the first book that would gain him international attention, entitled *Crisis and Cycles* (1932), Röpke lashed out against all organicist conceptions of the economy, skewering the idea that government could reestablish "equilibrium" within the system by a general lowering of prices and interest rates to correspond to financial constriction. Instead, he argued, it would further upset the system because the difficulties of the transition from one level to the other threw new sand into the economic machine and further decreased much-needed confidence among producers and investors. He also singled out for critique the land settlement proposals pushed by Catholics: they were the result of "unsystematic" and "romantic" thinking "that has no foundation in hard fact."[69]

Meanwhile, the People's Association for a Catholic Germany, fresh from financial infusions because of the popularity of *Quadragesimo anno*, held its first major conference on practical possibilities for the "vocational order" in mid-May 1932. Widely reported in the popular press, the meeting included several leading self-described Catholic economists who called for the creation of a national economic parliament. (Such an institution had existed briefly in the earliest years of the republic before collapsing in strife between employers and workers during the hyperinflation.)[70] This new economic council, they said, would bring together the members of each vocational sector of productive society, this time with decision-making power to cooperate in negotiating uniform wages, working conditions, and so on, delegating only purely non-economic decision making to the regular parliament, the Reichstag. In his report of the conference for an Austrian audience, Nell-Breuning boasted that German Catholics were attempting to become "knights of human freedom in the midst of the breakdown of individualism," while avoiding the mistakes of the "totalitarian state" in Fascist Italy.[71]

Contemporaries noticed the development of these fronts. Observing from across the border, the Austrian economist Josef Dobretsberger wrote in 1932 that there were broadly two main "conceptions" behind the struggle. Both sides seemed to believe the capitalist system could be fixed if only it could be returned to an imaginary ideal state. On one side, there were the mainly Protestant economists associated with the Association for Social Policy, who in general accepted the classical idea associated with Adam Smith that "economic freedom *per se*" was the "source of the wealth of nations." The world economic crisis was pushing them into a defensive position, for until then the economic laws provided by classical theory "exercised the function of anchoring the free-exchange economy as the only thinkable, or at least only economic, form of supplying demand." Citing a recent address Nell-Breuning had given in Vienna, Dobretsberger wrote, "Not so for the critics of the present. To them, the immediate intellectual value of the theory dominated by the principle of competition, is, in the era of 'cartel-and monopoly-capitalism,' at the very least diminished; the 'theory of the new economy' is yet to be created."[72]

Catholic organizations such as the People's Association could claim to have the energy of the public on their side in the war against individualism, but Protestants in Germany still held the levers of national power.

As the cabinet shifted its attention after the presidential election toward blocking the rise of National Socialism, creating public works, subdividing eastern lands into homesteads, and negotiating a final reduction of war reparations and equal rights for Germany in the League of Nations, Hindenburg and his advisers were already searching for Brüning's replacement. The government was also undermined from within the Catholic milieu itself. A prominent nationalist publisher and fringe member of the Center Party with ties to big business, Franz von Papen, was attempting to confirm Protestant fears about the influence of Catholic ideology in the current government. In his newspaper *Germania,* Papen accused the Center Party leadership of placing "worldview"—code for social ideas coming from the Vatican—ahead of pragmatic action for the future of Germany.[73] Under heavy pressure from the president's office, Brüning tendered his resignation on May 30, 1932.

Brüning's departure left behind another void in political leadership—nothing new for Germans in the Weimar Republic, who had seen the rise and fall of more than ten different cabinets in just over ten years. But this one seemed more serious, considering that what was becoming the most popular political group in the country among youth, the Nazis, was actively seeking the destruction of the existing constitution. One thing was certain: government policy moving forward would not be rooted in a Christian consensus between self-described Protestants and Catholics.

CHAPTER THREE

The Battle over National Education

"Truly, the proponents of mutually opposing standpoints and
programs are not killing each other, but rather graze together like the
lions and lambs of the prophesied time of paradise."

Siegfried Kracauer in the Frankfurter Zeitung *after visiting a "labor
camp" for students in summer 1932*

Battles over national education can be a window to the soul of a liberal
democracy in crisis. In the republic declared after the overthrow of the
French king in 1792, competing proposals for a unified system of public
instruction revealed the social conflicts that would play out during the
Reign of Terror. In the years running up to the American Civil War,
the fundamental divisions that would pit northerners against southerners
in 1861 were apparent in the debate over a common curriculum for the
country's youth.[1] The history of education is such a useful indicator of
conflict because of the special task assigned to schoolteachers and university instructors in the national unification of a divided society. As one
French revolutionary wrote in 1793, "the constitution will give to the
nation a political and social existence; public instruction will give it a
moral and intellectual existence."[2] There are thus few better places to look
for the character of conflict in the Weimar Republic than in debates about
German schools.

After the resignation of Heinrich Brüning in May 1932, a battle over
the future of national education exposed a dangerous ideological fault
line running through Germany. Although conflicts over constitutive
issues such as the separation of legal powers and political economy had
been fierce in the preceding years, German journalists began writing
about the actual possibility of "civil war" only in the summer of 1932. It

was the precise point at which a new national government, led by Brüning's replacement as chancellor, Franz von Papen, began laying plans for a radical centralization of educational policy. It was the first time since Germany's political unification sixty years earlier that the national regime in Berlin took administration of schools and curriculum away from the individual states and began centralizing decision making in the capital.

The advisers around President Hindenburg, led by his army comrade and most trusted confidant Kurt von Schleicher, had drawn up plans to replace Brüning's failed cabinet. The political situation appeared volatile. Almost a third of the population was sapping the national budget through unemployment insurance claims; the voices of communist rioters who called for revolution were rising; and the populist firebrand Adolf Hitler, who spoke openly of burning up the peace treaty signed with Germany's former enemies, was demanding government leadership. Hindenburg's entourage decided in May 1932 that calling for new elections and allowing the parliamentary process of government formation to play out would be too dangerous, given the splintering of the parties and the very real possibility that the Nazis could win sufficient votes to rule alone. Instead, the president appointed his friend, the inexperienced politician Franz von Papen, to serve as titular head of what the government press secretary called a "Christian-conservative" cabinet of "national concentration," chosen directly by the president's office.[3] Schleicher, who negotiated Papen's appointment and positioned himself as minister of defense, persuaded Hitler to tolerate the new government (that is, not call for a parliamentary vote of no confidence) for at least two months, until the next national elections at the end of July.[4]

The ministers of the new cabinet immediately announced their intention to protect Germany against potentially subversive forces by suspending constitutional liberties and uprooting the causes of national disunity through emergency educational reform. On June 11, the new interior minister, a conservative Protestant lawyer named Wilhelm Baron von Gayl, told members of the upper house of the legislature (the Reichsrat) that the government was considering an administrative take-over of Germany's largest state, Prussia, as part of a larger plan to centralize and coordinate national control of unstable regions. Gayl also announced his authorization of censors to "weed out all un-German influences in artistic and intellectual realms," including especially schools. He notified the country's radio commissioner Hans Bredow that the government would require at least half an hour daily on all regional stations between 6:30 and 7:30 P.M., to promulgate new emergency legislation. (Normally laws would have to be published in the government's *Gazette,* not simply announced via radio, before attaining force.)[5]

Meanwhile, Chancellor Papen announced that the main foreign policy goal of his cabinet was to persuade France and England to revise the conditions of the postwar peace agreement, the Treaty of Versailles, which required Germans to pay massive reparations for the expenses of the war and limited their military defenses to a size that German generals such as defense minister Schleicher said was insufficient even for the maintenance of order within their own country. Schleicher had recommended Papen as chancellor in no small part for the purpose of representing German interests at the upcoming conference with France and England, set to begin on June 16 in Lausanne, Switzerland. A wealthy aristocrat, Papen spoke fluent French and English and enjoyed many connections in those countries through both business and marriage. In Lausanne, Papen and his foreign minister, Konstantin Baron von Neurath, would try to talk their former enemies into signing a new peace treaty ending reparations once and for all. In nearby Geneva, at the ongoing Conference on the Reduction and Limitation of Arms, government delegates would attempt to achieve equality for Germans so that they could grow their armed forces at least to the level of other members of the League of Nations.

National education and foreign policy were linked because German educators did not agree on the question of whether the League of Nations, and the ideal of international law it represented, should be taught to German youth as an unequivocal good. Many German professors were dedicated to the League's vision of fair and legal international conflict resolution. But it was also true that a significant portion of Germany's younger teachers and university students rejected the legitimacy of the League and its ideals. This was particularly true of those young people who had affiliated themselves with the Nazi movement, which a reporter from the *New York Times* estimated in early 1932 was "by all odds the dominant political force among the students."[6] These young nationalists saw no moral imperative to recognize the strictures of international law when the national interest was at stake.

The debates between the two groups revealed a deep schism among Germans who had otherwise supported the republic since the war: between idealists, who envisioned a world of international understanding based on international law, and hard-nosed realists, who argued for the irreducibility of national sovereignty and the inevitability of armed conflict. The position of educators on fundamental questions of value mattered for the future of liberal democracy in Germany. What was the essence of good citizenship, they asked, and how should young people be taught to conceive of the relationship between their nation and the rest of the world? Was the ultimate goal of instruction in one's national history to overcome young people's sense of national exceptionalism and to promote self-criticism and global citizenship? Or, on the contrary, was it to foster inner communion with their fellow nationals and to celebrate and defend a common heritage? The professor and adviser on educational policy Friedrich von der Leyen put the choice bluntly: educators would have to choose between two competing worldviews, "the international" and "the national."[7]

THE VALUE OF INTERNATIONAL UNDERSTANDING AND INTERNATIONAL LAW

Under the mounting pressure exerted by Hitler's Nazi movement, Chancellor Papen's negotiations with French and British leaders at the end of June 1932 seemed like the "last chance for great and lasting solutions" within the international order of the League of Nations, at least according to the later recollections of the ousted chancellor Brüning.[8] German supporters of the League, despite their general disdain for the repressive police-state tactics of Papen's new undemocratic government, had to admit that the chancellor, unlike Hitler, seemed at least dedicated to maintaining relations with the rest of the world and committed to a *legal* revision of the Treaty of Versailles. Nazi leaders, meanwhile, demanded unilateral annulment of international agreements and savagely criticized the government for bargaining on Germany's future.[9] In that sense, Papen still represented the values inscribed in the Weimar constitution calling for a generation of youth dedicated to both "German national culture" *and* "reconciliation among the nations" (Article 148).

One sometimes forgets that Germans were at the forefront of the movement for "reconciliation among the nations" in the years after the

Great War. Dispelling their country's reputation for militarism abroad was a major aim of the republic's founders, which included a number of university professors who had dedicated their scholarship even before the war to the resolution of international conflicts.[10] The German government hosted the Twenty-third International World Peace Congress in the Reichstag itself in 1924. The most famous public intellectual of the postwar decade, the philosopher Max Scheler, developed a philosophy intended to foster understanding between people from different social milieus. Scheler was raised by a Protestant father and a Jewish mother before converting to Catholicism and then leaving behind religion altogether; he represented a hope among many German educators that differences, including those between Germans and other peoples, could be respected but overcome through the recognition of larger commonalities. Scheler's ideas were intimately associated with the university where he taught, Cologne, an internationally oriented city led by a mayor, Konrad Adenauer, who championed international styles and hosted Germany's first major League of Nations event, the International Press Exhibition of 1928.[11]

When Scheler died unexpectedly, his ideas were carried on by his younger colleague in Cologne, the thirty-five-year-old Helmuth Plessner. The visions of these two men were so similar that Scheler once accused Plessner, unjustly, of plagiarism. Plessner had arrived at the University of Cologne after the war with the reputation of a talented and ambitious, if not terribly innovative, young academic. His exact contemporary Walter Benjamin noted in 1920 with tepid approval that of all the newly minted young professors in Cologne, Plessner appeared poised to have the most promising professional future.[12] Raised in privileged circumstances among a family of doctors and musicians, Plessner studied at the most prestigious university in the country, Heidelberg, with professors who were patriots but had founded an Association for International Understanding in opposition to the tensions leading up to the Great War. One of them, the famed biologist and League of Nations supporter Hans Driesch, lavished praise on Plessner for what he called the young scholar's attempt to establish foundations for intercultural communication. A private foundation that awarded one of Germany's most prestigious academic prizes chose Plessner for encouraging international understanding through the sciences.[13]

The older internationalists who promoted Plessner's work must have seen in it a contribution to their efforts to foster a generation of responsible political elites who would be attentive to national interests while avoiding another world conflict at all costs. Educators such as the sociologist Max Weber, who included Plessner in his exclusive Sunday seminars in Heidelberg, and Paul Rühlmann, who founded the new German Academy for Politics (*Deutsche Hochschule für Politik*) in Berlin the same year as the foundation of the republic, blamed Germany's entrance into the Great War on the empire's inability to produce such leadership.[14] From his first days in Cologne, Plessner announced his intention to help in this educational project to cultivate what he called a new "race" of young Germans committed to "statecraft for humanity's sake." He lauded the German Academy for Politics and other new educational institutions designed to train Germans to cooperate on specific goals "before all partisan fissure in worldview" and to pursue a "politics of understanding."[15]

Plessner worried about the emergence of a German governing elite committed instead to a politics of force and power, what Machiavelli called the politics of the lion. When the leaders of several large German youth groups during the hyperinflation called for a revolutionary break with liberal democracy and the immediate creation of a more communitarian system, Plessner published a widely read pamphlet titled *The Limits of Community*, a kind of guidebook for responsible governance, similar in that way to Machiavelli's *The Prince* but written for an age in which leaders derived their authority from democratic election instead of noble heritage. The "social radicalism" of so many young Germans, he wrote in 1924, stemmed from "impatience," characteristic of a developmental phase of youth when people have "faith in the redemptive force of the extreme" and pursue "the method of making a front against all traditional values and compromises," without having yet learned the valuable "logic of diplomacy."[16] *The Limits of Community* inaugurated what would become Plessner's lifelong practice of analogizing the psychological development of young human beings with the political development of the young German nation. The editors of one of Germany's most respected newspapers, the *Frankfurter Zeitung*, were so impressed by Plessner's analysis of Germany's condition that they offered him a position as education critic and asked him to pen a more extended defense of the republic.[17]

In the "stabilization" years after 1924, Plessner attempted to show that the harmonious balance between community and individual freedom he had argued for in *The Limits of Community* was not only a positive political goal, but also a "natural" function in the science of human behavior. In an article titled "The Interpretation of Mimic Expression," researched and written collaboratively with a biologist from the Netherlands, Plessner argued that extreme communitarianism was biologically unnatural. The authors found that from the earliest phases of development—as an infant mimics the behavior of its parents before pushing away to form its own sense of self—humans seek both "emphatic fraternity" with others as well as "distance" from them.[18] Later, in his prize-winning book *The Stages of the Organic and Man* (1928), Plessner developed that same idea into an entire theory of "philosophical anthropology," the study of humanity's essential characteristics. Humans were different from other animals in that they are both closed off from and open to the world at the same time, capable of recognizing the limited "horizons" of their embodied selves and their contingent, time-bound existence. It was thus uniquely human to envision what he called an "absolute" beyond one's horizon and the possibility of human "unity." That drive to look beyond one's place, the "utopian standpoint," Plessner argued, led ineluctably and teleologically to the "idea of the one world."[19]

What was true for the human body should also be true for the larger body politic, Plessner suggested. His ideas fit well into the educational policy of the German national government under the leadership of Gustav Stresemann, who as foreign minister from 1923 to 1929 pursued a "politics of understanding" with Germany's former enemies, negotiating a major agreement on borders with the French (the Treaty of Locarno) in 1925, overseeing the country's admission into the League of Nations in 1926, and signing the General Treaty for Renunciation of War as an Instrument of National Policy (otherwise known as the Kellogg-Briand Pact) in 1928. Although the Weimar constitution placed curriculum development under the authority of the regional state governments, the national ministry of the interior released nonbinding guidelines to encourage teachers throughout the country to develop lessons for students that would balance the inculcation of national pride on one hand with the fostering of respect for international law on the other.[20]

The first author of the interior ministry's guidelines, the curriculum theorist Theodor Litt, used Scheler's and Plessner's idea of organic development in his recommendations on teaching history, civics, and social studies.[21] In his *History and Life* handbook for teachers, which entered its second edition in 1928, Litt argued that it was imperative to integrate young children into community life by inculcating love of their nation; but as they grew older, instruction in history should reveal the provincial limitations of their communal horizons. One of Litt's sample lessons imagined a scenario in which a teacher asks students what they associate with the concept "the Russian people." After collecting answers, the teacher could then demonstrate the "paltriness" of the students' knowledge and the "randomness" with which they had obtained it, asking them: "What would the same concept mean for someone who had traveled in Russia for several years?" Litt called this style of learning "education for historical self-critique," in which the teacher facilitated the transcendence of received wisdom through "the light of critical thinking . . ., as a view would be opened for someone who was shortsighted." The goal was to help dispel "misunderstanding that divides peoples, parties, and groups in questions of foreign and domestic politics, of social and economic life, of culture and worldview," and to explicitly reveal the value of the new League of Nations.[22] The Prussian ministry of culture, which organized the institute responsible for the guidelines, also called for the rewriting of nationalistic textbooks in order to dispel harmful stereotypes about historical enemies and to examine more critically Germany's own history of malfeasance.

Foreign observers who hoped for the success of the German government's efforts to turn German youth away from aggressive nationalism reported mixed results. The editor of *L'Europe Nouvelle*, a French periodical dedicated to understanding after the war, wrote glowingly in 1926 that the delegation of German university students in the new International University Federation stood at the "*avant-garde* of the League of Nations."[23] German students also made up a significant contingent of a program, financed by the League, that brought together top French and German scholars and students for an annual three-week summer colloquium in Davos, Switzerland, to discuss the conditions for "supra-national understanding." At the same time, an American scholar who studied education in Europe reported that a generation of Germans who had grown up under what many perceived as anti-German actions sponsored by the League—not only the Treaty of Versailles, but also the French occupation of the Ruhr and the continuing stationing of French troops in the Rhineland—were actually becoming more nationalistic than their fore-bears, not less.[24] That impression was corroborated by the anecdotes of German high school teachers who discussed their students' rejection of the curriculum pushed by the national government. One teacher at an elite school noted in 1926 how his students bridled, sometimes violently, at lessons designed to demonstrate the deficiencies of past German leaders.[25]

The negative reactions of nationalist students seemed to intensify as the reputation of the League of Nations in Germany continued to decline over the issue of Germany's unsettled eastern borders with Czechoslovakia and Poland in the late 1920s. While the Treaty of Locarno marked agreement on the western borders with France (Alsace-Lorraine and the Saar), the fate of the territory known in German as the Sudetenland, the Polish Corridor, and Danzig still required resolution under the auspices of the League. When France, which was allied militarily to both Czechoslovakia and Poland, appeared to be blocking German claims to those territories, German students expressed growing suspicion that the ideal of international law represented by the League was merely a front for the national interests of its core members. At the summer colloquium in Davos sponsored by the League in 1929, many teachers were taken aback when the German university students in attendance publicly flouted the philosophy of myth-busting, self-critique, and international law advocated by the philosopher Ernst Cassirer in favor of the ideas of Martin Heidegger, who called for a decisive, all-or-nothing commitment to a particular cultural tradition.[26] At the end of 1930, the national interior ministry judged students' nonreceptivity to be enough of a problem to convene a four-day lecture and discussion series on it in the eastern city of Breslau, with nearly four hundred teachers in attendance.[27]

The nature of the problem came into clearest focus, perhaps, in 1931 at a conference of educators hosted in Cologne, where Plessner taught. The meeting was organized in June by the national interior ministry, in conjunction with the national office of foreign affairs, to discuss the depiction of the League of Nations in German school curricula. Attendees were to discuss a proposal, drawn up by a high school teacher and adviser to the regional Rhineland school system named Hugo Lötschert, to convene a nationwide commission for the revision of textbooks. Lötschert expressed horror that most teachers gave their lessons based on prewar-era material from the German Empire that fostered what he considered exaggerated enthusiasm for the fatherland. Updated textbooks, he suggested, should "awaken the feeling of the new international soli-darity," and in their depiction of the past emphasize not Prussian military might, but instead traditions of "supra-national authority" from the medi-eval Catholic Church to the League of Nations. Furthermore, they should not avoid aspects of the German past that "might arouse national shame."[28] The reaction to the proposal among many teachers and admin-istrators was so negative that the conference convener closed the gath-ering with the words: "We have been jolted, we have become uneasy, and we will pursue the ideas further."[29] Wilhelm Mommsen, who edited the country's trade journal for social studies teachers and was present at the gathering in Cologne, explained that whether or not teachers themselves found historical self-critique a desirable pedagogical goal, the *students* they taught were rejecting it. They wanted to feel empowered by, not ashamed of, their people's past, he noted.[30]

In the summer of 1931, now facing an economic depression that had driven German youth even further toward radical nationalist movements than the hyperinflation had in 1923, Plessner frantically wrote a text commissioned for use by social studies educators.[31] In this short book, titled *Power and Human Nature,* Plessner recognized the students' need for a strong and proud national cultural identity: the cover featured a full-page-size image of the imposing German imperial eagle. But inside the pages, Plessner warned against the temptation of "self-enclosure" and the rejection of international law. He criticized the argument gaining so much traction among German youth, made by the philosopher Heidegger, that the goal of authentic education was to "ground" one's self in "commu-nion" with one's cultural tradition. On the contrary, Plessner wrote, humans' biological distinctiveness lay precisely in their *inability* to ground themselves: a human individual does not achieve selfhood by communing with others, but rather through struggle against others. The process of self-formation, he argued, begins with a child's recognition of his own bodily interests and the separation from his parents' authority. But while struggle was necessary for self-assertion, the goal of education was to "civilize" struggle by curbing the pursuit of unending self-interest and learning the authority of agreement with others. Translated into the terms of the body politic, one might well say: all nations have the right to self-determination within their borders, but "civilized" nations should respect and abide the strictures of international law.[32]

At the end of *Power and Human Nature,* Plessner outlined the beginnings of a universal theory of global understanding in education. One's belonging to a "people" or "nation" (*Volk*), he admitted, could lay claim to a certain type of "absoluteness," for it was only within one's "blood and tradition" that one could "expect to be understood." Communication outside one's own group was "dissonant" and "non-transparent," an inevitable obstacle arising out of the biological fact of being confined to a culture and having a restricted "field of view." However, if a teacher could cultivate in students a "consciousness of the randomness of the character of one's own people"—an imagining of universal "humanity" from the perspective of God—then the difficult process of intercultural understanding could begin. Echoing one of his old mentors, Hans Driesch, Plessner argued in philosophical terms that if peoples of different nations shared the consciousness of living within one large global organism, then the struggle between them would be "directed not toward the maximum, but rather the optimum, for one's own situation of being." He urged German teachers to resist the temptation to submit to the nationalist "politics of the hour" embraced by much of the country's youth.[33]

Calls for international understanding and cooperation as stipulated in the Weimar constitution resonated less and less as geopolitical events unfolded over the last months of Heinrich Brüning's chancellorship. In February 1932, Plessner delivered a soaring speech about international cooperation at the Bauhaus College in Dessau, where young architects and artists of all cultures and ideologies from around the world, including Soviet Russia, gathered to envision the elements of a new universal and functional design. That same month, students and young professors at several German universities organized demonstrations in the hope that the delegations from Europe's powers gathering in Geneva to discuss world disarmament would agree to rectify the inequality of arms imposed on Germany in the Treaty of Versailles.[34] As the conference failed to produce a resolution, students continued to flock to the Nazi Party, swayed by Hitler's realist message that the French and British governments would never agree to Brüning's demands to reduce the size of their militaries to that of the Germans. To students, idealistic educators such as Plessner increasingly appeared as Professor Rat in Josef von Sternberg's 1930 hit film, *The Blue Angel*: the stuffy bourgeois who can neither inspire nor control the middle-class students who grew up in a world blighted by the injustice of Versailles.

The modest diplomatic success of Brüning's successor, Franz von Papen, did not improve the popularity of international negotiation among nationalist youth. On the contrary, young Germans already predisposed against the authority of the "international community" were further jaded by news from the Lausanne Conference, which lasted from mid-June to early July 1932. Citing the unemployment rate of German youth, which topped forty percent, Papen persuaded the French and British to let the Germans discontinue regular reparations, pending American approval. But the German government remained on the hook for a final payment of three billion marks, and there was no discussion of equality of arms. When Papen's delegation returned to Berlin, nationalist students pelted his entourage with rotten eggs.[35] Giselher Wirsing, a twenty-five-year-old student of political economy in Heidelberg who considered himself a spokesperson for the country's youth, condemned Papen's cabinet during the campaign for parliamentary elections at the end of July. By slashing unemployment benefits and waiting passively for the international community to save them, he wrote, the government had placed a quarter of the population "on the brink of hunger" and literally threatened "the existence of the nation."[36]

THE LIMITS OF INTERNATIONAL UNDERSTANDING AND INTERNATIONAL LAW

In the lead-up to the elections of July 1932, Papen and his cabinet began centralizing national control over the education system, beginning with a controversial and constitutionally questionable takeover of Germany's largest and most important regional government. On July 20, the chancellor announced a presidentially approved decree to dismiss the state cabinet of Prussia and replace it with an emergency national governor. From a domestic perspective, this authoritarian action represented a radical departure from Germany's tradition of self-administration in the individual states that made up the territory of the Reich. But the "Prussian coup," as it came to be known in the press, worried foreign policy experts in the countries west of Germany for a different reason. For them, the upheaval, and the constitutional uncertainty it created, signaled chaos in the very heartland of the country.

Prussia was not only Germany's economic engine, but also its bedrock of stability. Historically, foreigners knew Prussians not only as the inhabitants of Germany's largest state—which encompassed essentially the entire northern half of the country, from the border with France, the Netherlands, and Belgium in the west to the disputed borders with Poland and Czechoslovakia in the east—but also as the area responsible for the very existence of Germany. It had been the government of Prussia, headed by Otto von Bismarck, that had persuaded the leaders of other German-speaking states, such as Bavaria and Baden, to join with their northern neighbors in what began as a military alliance and ended in political unification in 1871. In the decades since, the Prussian government had attempted to unify the country culturally through the model of its educational system. As a result, what subsequently came to be known internationally as German values—the love of order, discipline, duty, and obedience to lawful rules—were virtues that had been stressed by Prussian schoolteachers since the days of Immanuel Kant, himself a subject of the Kingdom of Prussia.

Prussians were known to prize gradual change and hate revolution. Indeed, even the workers' movement in Prussia, which is where the Social Democratic Party of Germany first emerged, was dominated by politicians who favored constitutional reform rather than violent upheaval, despite being associated with a Marxist platform that called for revolutionary social change.[37] It was in large part thanks to that political culture that the Prussian government had become, in the years after the republican constitution was ratified in 1919, what one historian called a "rock" of loyalty to the Weimar constitution compared with other parts of the country.[38] Unlike other states, Prussia had been governed by the same set of pro-constitutional coalition partners—the SPD and the Center Party—and the same prime minister, Otto Braun (SPD), continuously since 1920.

But by 1932, the SPD-led Prussian state government faced political crisis in the state assembly and political violence in the streets. Hitler's National Socialists, which had collected less than two percent of the vote in the state elections of 1928, suddenly received a shocking plurality of more than thirty-six percent in the elections of April 24, 1932. The long-standing coalition of the SPD and the Center Party, which barely mustered that many votes combined, could no longer build a majority. Prime minister Braun publicly refused to take part in any negotiation with the Nazis, claiming they would destroy the rights of workers. Meanwhile, Nazi grassroots organizers in small localities all over Prussia led unruly marches, attracting tens of thousands of young supporters into their paramilitary force and violently clashing with members of communist groups. It was in this context that Chancellor Papen, citing the Prussian government's inability to keep order and Braun's unwillingness to work with the state's most popular party, announced the national takeover on July 20.[39]

Foreign observers who worried about the instability of Germany watched as the presidentially backed national government used its takeover of Prussia to assert unprecedented power over regional policy and initiate new educational institutions in the lead-up to the national parliamentary elections. On July 26, 1932, defense minister Schleicher announced that the government would begin training young people for participation in a national guard, given that the Western powers in the League of Nations would not allow Germany to raise an actual army large enough to protect its people.[40] Two days later, interior minister Gayl used the threat of further regional takeovers to warn the ministries of instruction in the sixteen states outside Prussia that any school or university instructor who subverted national unity "no longer has a place in the instructional system." These strict measures, Gayl told the regional heads, were necessary in this time of ideological schism to ensure that German young people were trained to value "service, responsibility, and self-sacrifice to the whole."[41] The day before the election, Papen delivered a radio address in English to assure foreign politicians and international investors that his government did not intend to establish a permanent dictatorship in Prussia, and that all the measures taken there and elsewhere were designed as only temporary actions to establish order in the face of a potential civil war between rival political factions. The communists were particularly dangerous; the Nazis, he said, despite their extreme tactics, were at least dedicated to "national regeneration" and the alleviation of the desperate economic situation of German youth.[42]

The results of the national election at the end of July 1932 and the events that followed it convinced many foreign journalists that liberal democracy in Germany was dead or dying. The electoral results were unmistakably a protest against the current government: the Nazis received a plurality of thirty-seven percent, the SPD twenty-two, and the Communists fourteen, all parties whose leaders called for the resignation of the Papen-led cabinet. And yet, with no possibility of a viable majority coalition, Hindenburg and his adviser Schleicher decided to make no changes to the sitting cabinet. The Nazi M.P. Hermann Göring, as leader of the largest party delegation in the Reichstag and thus the inside candidate for speaker, called for a vote of no confidence against the government, but Hindenburg simply signed an order to dissolve parliament and set new elections for later in the year.[43] George Soloveytchik, a political commentator who wrote for British and American magazines, wrote at the end of the summer that Germans faced the option of either "chaos" or "dictatorship" if Papen could not garner more popular support.[44]

Thus, in September 1932, the Papen-Schleicher-Gayl government unfurled a major publicity campaign specifically targeting the country's nationalist youth. Outlined in a pamphlet titled *The New State,* the platform consisted of three main policy goals. First, in foreign affairs, the cabinet would no longer negotiate for, but would instead demand, legal equality in armaments. Second, the cabinet would spend more money for public works and require that all capable unemployed Germans participate. Third, and perhaps most significant, the nation's youth groups would be organized into a mandatory national service program. The cabinet decreed the creation of a new office in the ministry of the interior called the National Board for the Strengthening of Youth (*Reichskuratorium für Jugendertüchtigung*), an institution that defense minister Schleicher had been planning for more than a year. The stated goal was to heal the "disastrous" splintering of the country's youth groups into ideologically warring parties by bringing them together in common labor.[45]

Perhaps no one in the country was more qualified to help lead this bold new endeavor than one of Schleicher's new advisers, a thirty-six-year-old educator widely beloved by the nationalist youth groups named Arnold Bergsträsser. Bergsträsser had been involved with patriotic youth groups for the better part of two decades, beginning in Stuttgart with his own membership in the Wandervögel, a large organization akin to the

Boy Scouts.[46] His experience fighting in the Great War on the western front, where he suffered a severe head injury and witnessed the death of close friends, deepened his commitment to the youth movement. Upon his return to civilian life, Bergsträsser presided over an umbrella organization of student representatives from universities across the country, as well as from German-speaking regions in the new republics of Austria and Czechoslovakia and the free city of Danzig, who campaigned for a self-determined German republic. He had continued involvement with political youth organizations as a young professor at the University of Heidelberg. In late summer 1932, just as the Papen government announced its new platforms, Bergsträsser emerged as a countrywide hero among nationalist students when he helped strip the teaching credentials of a Heidelberg colleague accused of insulting the honor of Germany's veterans.[47]

Before emerging as a nationalist hero, Bergsträsser was known as one of the promising young responsible German political leaders that the older generation of educators had hoped for at the dawn of the republic. He was a star graduate student at the Institute for Social and State Sciences (*Institut für Sozial- und Staatswissenschaften*), an institution founded after the war in Heidelberg and partly funded by the Rockefeller Foundation to train a generation of liberal democratic leaders in Germany. As president of the German Federation of Students, Bergsträsser fought against xenophobia and racism, and he sharply criticized those young people who called for a "messianic" leader-savior instead of engaging in the messy task of self-government.[48] Above all, he made his name as an organizer of the nation's first academic exchange program, a student-run, government-funded institution headquartered at the Heidelberg Institute committed to the notion that middle-class youth hit hard by inflation would be less susceptible to radicalization if they experienced foreign cultures.[49]

Bergsträsser subscribed to a romantic, patriotic theory of education popular in Germany's youth movement since the turn of the century. In those circles, the teacher's role was not merely to transmit knowledge and foster critical thinking, but to inspire and lead. Martin Spahn, the director of a new college for political leadership in Berlin whose board included future interior minister Gayl and several representatives of German big business, argued that the future of the nation's youth depended on whether teachers were "able to bring electricity before the youth in our telling of the history of the fatherland" and inculcate love for a common tradition. The educator Elisabeth Blochmann, Heidegger's student and one of the few women active in university youth leadership with Bergsträsser, reminded readers of the old Prussian practice of using history-telling to unify a religiously divided population.[50] In 1927, the youth expert Bergsträsser told a gathering of professors who may have been skeptical of taking on such a leadership role that the post-Versailles generation then entering university was yearning for more than just technical expertise. They rejected the "coldness and intellectuality of our modern life" and looked to their teachers for something to believe in. Most important, he said, the older generation could not expect these students to become political leaders in the new liberal democratic republic if instructors failed to serve as role models.[51]

These romantic ideas stemming from the youth movement about teaching and the nation helped inspire an experimental type of educational institution near the end of the 1920s: the "labor service camp," or simply "labor camp" (*Arbeitslager*). Conceived by a student and youth leader named Helmuth James Graf von Moltke (the great-grandnephew of the military hero of German unification, Helmuth von Moltke) and supported financially by the national government (thanks to the lobby of politicians including Brüning and military leaders such as Schleicher), the labor camp was intended to resolve conflicts between historic enemies in Germany—or, as one skeptic at the *Frankfurter Zeitung* put it, allow "proponents of mutually opposing standpoints and programs" to "graze together like the lions and lambs of the prophesied time of paradise." Indeed, Moltke's university adviser compared the project to the "Bible's great vision of peace, that lion and lamb should lie down peacefully together."[52] Its supporters hoped that divisions among Germans based on class, religion, party, ideology, race, and region could be overcome by bringing diverse groups of university students together with workers and farmers in underserved areas of the country over the course of a summer, united through national service. Moltke solicited support to found the first camp in the impoverished eastern agricultural region of the country, Silesia. He traveled to Heidelberg to meet Bergsträsser, who agreed to advise the organizers on the economic and political situation of the Silesian region.[53]

The broad coalition of romantic educators, students, politicians, and military leaders who supported the labor camps celebrated the project as a model of national unification, but many also saw them as potential garrisons in the heavily disputed eastern borderlands. The conflicts over territorial demarcations and minority rights there had been intense after the war. In 1921, the Council of the League of Nations had administered a plebiscite in the upper part of Silesia, a mixed region of ethnic Germans and Poles, to determine whether it should belong to Germany or Poland, but the contested results in favor of Germany had been followed by an armed uprising of Polish nationalists and the mobilization of German paramilitary groups; the Inter-Allied Military Control Commission led by France had intervened and awarded parts of the territory back to Poland.[54] Ever since, German nationalist groups consistently lodged complaints that German speakers on the other side of the border were being mistreated, especially after Józef Piłsudski, a general close to the Silesian fighters who had a reputation as an aggressive nationalist, took over the Polish government in a military coup in 1926. The town where the first labor camp opened in 1928, Löwenburg, was known by Poles as Lwówek Śląski and claimed by some as rightfully theirs. During the second summer of the labor camp, in 1929, Moltke and his co-organizers encountered difficulty reining in student participants who engaged in skirmishes with Poles at the border, prompting the national government to defund the project for budget year 1930.[55]

For leaders of the German nationalist youth groups, the withdrawal of support for the labor camp in Silesia would have appeared as more evidence that their government was too beholden to international law and too cowardly to fight for their people who lived on the other side of current state borders. Whenever confronted with Polish offenses against ethnic Germans in the eastern regions, instead of responding like a lion, with a demonstration of power, German government officials instead deferred, lamb-like, to the legal authority of arbitration commissions in the Council of the League of Nations. Considering that the French-dominated League consistently discriminated against Germans, such meekness was not only humiliating, but also treasonous. In late 1930, after months of press reports about the disenfranchisement of the German-speaking minority in Poland, nationalist German students held a series of mass meetings calling on their government to act. Yet the most the foreign minister, Julius Curtius, was willing to do was to call the situation to the attention of the League.[56]

In 1930, Bergsträsser began to publicly support the nationalist youth groups in their criticism of the League. To be sure, Bergsträsser had been involved with efforts to forge economic and intellectual ties with Germany's former enemies, France and England: he was a founding member, along with Franz von Papen and several other German elites, of the German-French Study Committee (*Deutsch-französisches Studienkomittee*), as well as the political editor of the journal published by the pro-entente European Federation of Culture (*Europäische Kulturbund*).[57] But Bergsträsser also emphasized the "limits" of understanding between nations: there came a point, he suggested, at which national leaders must pursue the interest of their people regardless of whether that meant sacrificing the ties that bound them together with other nations. When the Nazi Party became the second-largest party in parliament in the elections of September 1930, running largely on a platform to revise the Treaty of Versailles, Bergsträsser explained to his French interlocutors in the Study Committee that students were flocking to the Nazis out of justifiable rage at the former Western Allies for contributing to their economic immiseration.[58]

The French supporters of the League of Nations in the German-French Study Committee worried about what they called Bergsträsser's aggressive "turn" as representative of a larger process of German self-abandonment to the emotional forces of nationalism. The pacifists Pierre and Andrée Viénot, who worked closely with Bergsträsser on economic and cultural exchange for several years, blamed it on their friend's head injuries from the western front, speaking of it as a synecdoche for the entire postwar German body politic. "His profound disequilibrium, his lack of judgment, of stability, of steadiness, is getting worse and worse," Andrée Viénot wrote about his "dangerous" and "deplorable" turn toward "*quasi* national socialism" at the turn of 1931. "He increasingly abandons himself to political passions whose source he does not critique." Although Bergsträsser had "made a serious effort toward comprehension and rapprochement," she continued in another letter, "in the present hour he is certainly passing through a crisis of nationalism, sustained by the milieu of the students of Heidelberg, in whose eyes he always has too much desire to appear as the great man."[59]

The Viénots were mistaken: Bergsträsser's support of the German nationalist youth groups was not the manifestation of a mental disorder, but rather the logical conclusion of a realist worldview in which the value of the national interest always takes precedence over the value of international law. In a series of books written for German university students in 1930, Bergsträsser ridiculed "utopian" German politicians for their belief that international law could tame the anarchic nature of international relations and criticized the Council of the League of Nations for its "imperialistic" suppression of member states. The League, he wrote, was bankrupting Germans by preventing the expansion of their domestic market to include Austria and the Polish Corridor. The League was hypocritical, because even as it celebrated national "self-determination," it blocked or reversed plebiscites in regions where a significant portion of the population appeared to support German annexation, much as it kept Arab nations under its colonial dominion. German society, Bergsträsser explained, unlike French and British society, remained racked with class and religious divisions and under threat of a communist uprising that could exploit its instability. National leaders could not rely on international law to solve those problems. His view aligned with one of the political theorists whose articles he edited, Carl Schmitt, who made similar realist critiques of the League in his arguments to educators and students.[60] While Bergsträsser never denied that intercultural exchange was important, he made his position clear: as one of his colleagues in the German-French Study Committee put it succinctly, Bergsträsser simply placed "reason of state above everything."[61]

Nor was Bergsträsser alone, for his worldview was shared by many German political elites who after the war had appeared to support international cooperation but in the early 1930s sided with the nationalist youth of Germany against the League. The political journalist Hans Zehrer, who until the end of the 1920s had edited the free-trade-oriented *Vossische Zeitung*, began advising the Heidelberg-based nationalist student journal *Die Tat*, supporting its calls for an exclusive economic pact with the Danube valley states Austria, Czechoslovakia, Yugoslavia, Hungary, and Romania.[62] As the historian Adam Tooze has shown, even someone such as Ernst Wagemann, a leading official in the German economics ministry whom foreign leaders had known as a fierce advocate of free trade, turned toward the economic nationalism of the Nazis, inspired by the energy of German youth.[63] And raison d'état was certainly the worldview expressed by the leadership of the German government in mid-1932, when

Chancellor Papen, defense minister Schleicher, and interior minister Gayl announced their vision for "the new state."

Bergsträsser, who by that point had become a full professor of "state sciences" at the University of Heidelberg and an adviser to Schleicher, defended his country's new government against critics in the League of Nations who feared that Germany was descending into dictatorship. In August 1932, after Papen took control over Prussia and instituted drastic measures to make Germany's economic and education policy more nationalist in orientation, Bergsträsser visited the chancellory and sent a communication to the French members of the German-French Study Committee explaining that the emergency action was a necessary response to the "strong growth of the communist danger" in Prussia. The SPD-led Prussian government, he wrote, had been persecuting the Nazi Party when everyone in Germany knew that the *only* way back to a demo-cratic coalition there depended on the inclusion of Hitler's party. Attempting to assuage French fears about Schleicher's call for a youth-led national guard, Bergsträsser referred to the "justified necessity of adequate military security, above all in the east."[64]

Bergsträsser's values at this time, like those of many of the students he was mentoring in Heidelberg at the time (including one, Franz Alfred Six, who joined the Nazi Party in 1932), can be described as fascist. As defined by various historians of the interwar period, "fascism" was different from "conservatism" and included the following basic principles of political leadership: exaltation of youth above other stages of life; appeal to the importance of "authenticity" rather than "traditionalism"; emphasis on the emotional, mystical, and aesthetic aspects of national belonging; desire to "integrate" the national economy through government action to prevent disunity; celebration of military and traditionally masculine virtues in education; willingness to expand national territory through the use of violence; conception of the nation as a living "organism"; and most important, precedence of national "culture" and national law over universal "civilization" and international law.[65]

Elements of these fascist conceptions of political leadership were evident in Bergsträsser's speech of September 1932, as he justified the German government's more assertive stance toward the League of Nations to a group of university students preparing to study abroad. The idea of nationalism, he reminded them, was born in the late eighteenth century in resistance to the universalism of English and French Enlightenment thinking, which flattened out cultural difference and created laws ostensibly applicable to all nations, such as the civil code that Napoleon once sought to impose on German lands during the imperialistic Napoleonic Wars. The League of Nations, he suggested, was the current-day Napoleon. "In all the people who consciously and actively take up life here" in Germany, Bergsträsser declared in Heideggerian terms of authenticity, "resistance against Napoleon is justified by the certainty that in Germany one leads a spiritual existence, with its own law, newly formed out of its original relationship to the world, which is also capable of defending its external existence and is legitimized through its eternal maintenance." It was Germany's historical task, he told the students, to teach the other nations of the world that they, too, must preserve their right of national resistance against the imperialism of the League's international law.[66]

Despite his fascism and his call for the inclusion of Hitler's party in government, Bergsträsser was no Nazi himself. He could support parts of their protectionist economic program, but could not abide their proposed racial policy. After all, the first issue of the Nazis' academic journal contained an article condemning Bergsträsser as a "descendant of a foreign people" because of his partial Jewish ancestry. (His maternal grandfather was Jewish from a Czech-speaking region of the Austro-Hungarian Empire.)[67] Nor could Bergsträsser approve of Hitler's loyalty to a political party over loyalty to the German state as such. In a speech on political education at a leadership seminar for student groups in late 1932, as the Nazis campaigned for the next parliamentary election in November, Bergsträsser criticized the instrumentalization of young people as "storm troopers of party promotion." The elevation of one party over all others was "diametrically opposed," he said, to the type of national education promoted in the new state led by Papen's government, which aimed to bring all elements of the people together under common service to the nation.[68]

THE DIVERGENCE OF MINDS ON EDUCATIONAL IDEALS

German educators in the fall of 1932 faced two competing ideals of national education. The decision was sometimes described in the press in terms of geographical orientation. Would they teach students national history with an emphasis on Germany's common heritage with countries to the west, its contribution to the creation of an international legal order represented by the League of Nations? Or would they stress Germany's similarity with the "young" peoples of the east, who were not yet done growing after having been stunted by imperial powers for so long? "Minds divide in the inclination toward the east and toward the west," wrote the young journalist Hans Friedrich in September 1932. If so disposed, he wrote, teachers could easily look into the past for a long list of German contributions to the development of international law. But there was also a history, almost as long, of Germans rejecting universal norms and claiming legal particularity and territorial self-determination. The problem for educators, he noted, was that middle-class German students were beginning to demand textbooks that stressed an "eternal political opposition" between the two positions.[69]

Nobly promoting a synthesis between these two apparently conflicting worldviews, Helmuth Plessner did what he had done for a decade when faced with "radicalization": he gave a lecture. In mid-October 1932, several weeks before the next parliamentary elections, he delivered a sobered keynote address in Berlin to the German *Werkbund,* a prestigious group of designers working on boundary-crossing international forms. The collective was suffering at the time from a reputation of being hopelessly out of touch with popular German taste.[70] Meanwhile, the university semester was beginning at the University of Heidelberg, and energy was high in the packed lecture hall of Arnold Bergsträsser, who was leading a class on the historical formation of German national consciousness. In one lecture on the contribution of humanist educators to the birth of German nationalism, he emphasized the importance of physical forms of instruction such as horseback riding, fencing, dancing, and chivalry, activities that discipline and unify an otherwise disordered group. "By hemming in the unruly of temperament and passion, it gives the whole a higher title and sophistication," he jotted in his notes. This ideal was especially important, he wrote, for the humanists who lived in the Silesian realms in the eastern regions of the former Holy Roman Empire, for they knew that the "Turks could invade" if the "Reich was disunited."[71]

During the month leading up to the parliamentary elections of November 6, 1932, the contrast between these two educational frameworks was stark and ominous. Papen and his cabinet's call for a national education had summoned a cacophony of voices. "National education!" mourned the educator Carl Baustaedt in October 1932, reporting on a government-funded seminar on civic instruction held at the German Academy for Politics in Berlin. "That means, if I am correct, that the path to the national education of our youth goes over the cultural history of our people," he wrote. But "many history teachers have gone there in the last years, and still we have not reached the goal of a civic education. Despite increased cultural studies instruction in history, German, and geography, we cannot get around the sad result that the young people who have gone through this instruction widely reject the current state, without being agreed on a future one."[72]

Three days after a massive strike sponsored independently by both the Communist Party and the Nazi Party paralyzed the transportation system of the capital, the elections of November 6 suggested yet another clear referendum against the national government. Hitler's party won thirty-three percent of parliamentary seats: down significantly from the thirty-seven percent it received in July, but still a large plurality. The Communist Party gained votes, reaching nearly seventeen percent. Yet again, fully half of German voters rejected the existing societal order. These factors were enough to convince Schleicher and Hindenburg that it was best for Papen's cabinet finally to resign, after failing in its mandate to create policies acceptable to the nation. Papen announced the resignation of his government on November 17, 1932.

The foreign press speculated over what would come next. Hindenburg invited leaders of the Nazi Party, the Protestant-led German National People's Party, and the Catholic-led Center Party to meet with him, but most expected that a majority parliamentary coalition would still be impossible and that another presidentially appointed cabinet would be necessary. Hindenburg dramatically rebuffed Hitler's request for the chancellorship. "The President thanks you, my dear Herr Hitler, for your willingness to assume the leadership of a presidential cabinet," read a missive from Hindenburg's office on November 24. But "the President must fear that a presidential cabinet led by you would inevitably develop into a party dictatorship, with all the consequences of a drastic intensification of the antagonisms within the German nation that that would involve."[73] Thus, the reappointment of Papen with a new collection of cabinet ministers appeared as the likely outcome, or, alternatively, the

appointment of a new chancellor who would then retain the old ministers. Papen, like most of the press outlets, assumed it would be the former.

In the end, however, Schleicher had apparently lost patience with
Papen, the political novice he had helped install six months earlier. He
was particularly concerned that Papen had lost the support of German
labor organizations, whose large membership increasingly flocked to
the radical parties. On November 25, Schleicher invited President
Hindenburg to the ministry of defense, where strategists presented the
findings of a war game intended to demonstrate that Germany's forces as
they currently existed under Papen would not be able to prevent a coup
attempt in the hypothetical event of a nationwide strike called simultaneously by Nazis and communists. The meeting had its intended effect: it
turned the president and Papen's former ministers against the prospect
of reappointing the man who had served as chancellor for the past half
year. Hindenburg is reported to have told an adviser, "Our only hope is to
let Schleicher try his luck."[74]

CHAPTER FOUR

The Problem of Culture

WHEN PLANNERS AT THE LEAGUE OF NATIONS began designing an international legal order after the Great War to ensure the protection of minorities against discrimination in the new nation-states formed out of the collapsed European empires, they were primarily concerned with cultural minorities: groups that considered themselves to belong to a culture that was different from the majority culture in which they lived. As a precondition of entry into the League, therefore, the governments of new states in central and eastern Europe with a regional history of ethnic strife—such as Czechoslovakia, Hungary, and Yugoslavia—were required to negotiate treaties guaranteeing specific rights for people who did not identify as the national majority and thus faced a danger of discrimination. The new German republic was included in that list of new states. Led by the British and French delegations, the League Council pressured the German government to implement special legal protections for the large Polish-speaking population in Germany, such as provisions for the availability of Polish-language schools.[1]

The council's commission on minorities had not, however, required the German government to sign any special protection treaty regarding a small group of people who in 1932 appeared increasingly threatened with the prospect of legal discrimination as nationalist sentiment in Germany intensified: the Jews. Leaders of the central Jewish organizations in

Germany had never sought a legal minority status. On the contrary, they claimed to be an integral part of the German cultural community, a religious faith group just like Protestants or Catholics whose members were inseparable from and contributed actively to German culture *as Jews*. "There is as little a thing as a German who is not somehow defined additionally as Jew or Protestant or Catholic or Northern German or Southern German or craftsperson or farmer or worker, as there is a tree in the abstract, which is neither beech nor oak but simply tree *per se*," said Hugo Preuss, the primary drafter of Germany's constitution as well as a proud Jew.[2] Unlike their co-religionists living farther east in Poland, Hungary, Romania, or Palestine, most Jews in Germany did not speak a Jewish-specific language such as Yiddish or Hebrew. As people whose families had resided in the German-speaking regions of Europe for centuries, they often claimed to be simply one of the many branches (*Stämme*) that together composed German culture. Indeed, German Jews had not faced legalized discrimination or segregation in Germany for several generations.

Observers from abroad were at something of a loss, then, when the rollback of Jewish civil rights became a real possibility in 1932 with the rise of Hitler's antisemitic Nazi Party and the increasing possibility of its potential coalition with nationalist Christian conservatives to form a majority government. Even today historians have difficulty explaining why so many Germans seemed willing to acquiesce in the prospect of the marginalization and segregation of a part of the population that long before had acquired legal equality. Some have sought answers in class dynamics, pointing to resentment among middle- and lower-class Germans who jealously took out their frustration with the economic downturn on the relatively wealthy Jewish population. Others have taken a more psychological approach to the conundrum of complicity, noting elements of anti-Jewish sentiment transmitted through German religious education and secular education for generations.[3] While there are elements of truth in both explanations, one context has largely eluded the grasp of scholars. Too often, historians have seen Germans' non-resistance to Nazi anti-Jewish policies as evidence of active hatred of this minority, when in reality, it was also partially the result of dynamics that related only indirectly to the Jews. For reasons that should become clear in this chapter, nationalist Christian conservatives (both Protestant and

Catholic) were apt to sacrifice the Jewish population in the lead-up to the Nazi takeover of power in a larger struggle they were waging against *secularists,* Social Democrats and Communists especially, over the role of Christianity in state institutions.

The question of the Christian churches' role in the republican state had occupied Germans' attention since the passage of the constitution in 1919, especially during the volatile debates on the development of a "national school law" (*Reichsschulgesetz*). Publicly supported elementary school education in Germany had always been extremely decentralized: depending on the region and community, some parents sent their children to all-Protestant schools, others to all-Catholic schools, still others to mixed "inter-confessional" schools. More recently, the large cities had seen the founding of schools that did not teach Christian religion in their curriculum at all: so-called "secular" schools, as well as a growing number of all-Jewish schools.[4] Some delegates to the Weimar constitutional convention expressed concern that such splintering would undermine the stability of a new liberal democracy and called on parliament to develop a national school law, one that would create an integrated system in which Protestants, Catholics, Jews, and nonbelievers were educated together.

The creation of such a national school law proved extremely difficult, however. Carl Heinrich Becker, the head of the Prussian cultural ministry, spearheaded a national campaign to craft proposals that would be acceptable to both the religious communities and the secularists, but in the process he alienated several key conservative blocs, including the influential Evangelical Parents' League. Friedrich Winckler, one of the highest Protestant church leaders in Prussia and an active member of the Protestant conservative German National People's Party, accused Becker in an open letter of allying himself with the Marxist enemies of religion. By 1927, Becker declared the probability that a school bill would pass through parliament to be almost nil.[5] "The tremendous difficulties of the school problem," wrote one law student who studied the debates, lay in the fact that "it is, after all, about the 'religious question.' Worldview stands against worldview." Detlev Peukert, the great historian of the Weimar Republic, noted that the attempt to create common schools as a basis for a common national culture "led to bitter and unappeasable controversy."[6] In the academic year 1931–1932, of all the elementary schools where German children were educated in their first nine years (*Volksschulen*), fifty-five percent were still confessionally Protestant and thirty percent confessionally Catholic.[7]

But in 1932, with the rising talk of civil war, the national takeover of Germany's largest regional government, and finally, President Hindenburg's appointment of a powerful military man, Kurt von Schleicher, to secure order as chancellor and emergency governor of Prussia, the prospect of forced cultural integration through non-Christian institutions was suddenly back on the agenda. This time, Christian groups did not have to fear secularist Social Democrats in the national parliament (a body that had been effectively disabled from forming legislation since before 1930), but rather faced a potential military dictatorship. Schleicher was not known as a friend of the churches. One of his first acts in his new post as chancellor was to approach Carl Heinrich Becker, the same Prussian official who had been so dedicated to the prospect of a common school system, with an offer to join his cabinet as a "minister without portfolio," in which capacity he would both oversee the administration of the Prussian cultural ministry and coordinate it with national cultural policy through the interior ministry and the foreign office.[8]

The idea to appoint Becker was part of Chancellor Schleicher's larger plan to piece together a national-unity cabinet and stabilize Germany through military-led government: a maneuver that presented a high level of difficulty given the intense divisions in German society (as we have seen in the previous three chapters), but one that Schleicher, of all statesmen at the time, was perhaps best prepared to complete successfully. Schleicher's influence has been underestimated in the historical literature on Hitler's rise to power. This general, having begun his career working for the high army command during the Great War, had become the chief liaison between the military and the civilian government during the chaotic early years of the republic, President Hindenburg's most trusted *consigliere,* and, with the rise of presidentially appointed cabinets, politically the most powerful man in Germany. After 1930, he held a de facto veto over almost all government decisions. By the end of 1932, he was not only second-in-command of the military (after Hindenburg), but he also wielded tremendous influence in all the major state ministries of finance, justice, the interior, and the foreign office. Hardly a democrat and never a member of a political party, Schleicher had been the tactician behind both the national takeover of the Prussian regional government and the interior ministry's attempt to draft a new constitution in which the cabinet would no longer have parliamentary oversight.[9] Despite his encroachment on liberal democratic institutions, few individuals could boast the broad-based respect among the civil service that Schleicher had built over his many years defending the German state against both foreign and domestic enemies.

Now having stepped into the limelight of the world stage as chancellor of a country whose economic and political instability was the subject of international attention, Schleicher set himself a mission that would have represented the greatest strategic victory of his career. When the recently elected members of parliament met for the first time in Berlin on December 6, 1932, Nazi representatives stormed in, outraged that Hindenburg had appointed a general instead of Hitler, the leader of the country's most popular party. Schleicher told the press that he was committed to building a cabinet that could bring together all layers of society, something that Hitler—who alienated and indeed inspired hatred in several key groups of the German population, especially workers in the labor unions—could not do. In response to the uproar in parliament, Schleicher, with Hindenburg's support, temporarily banned Reichstag members from convening and commenced largely secretive negotiations with the leaders of the unions and the powerful employer associations to start building cross-class support for new economic policies. Even more ambitiously, the new chancellor entertained hopes of pulling away rebel factions of the two largest parliamentary delegations, the Nazis and the Social Democrats, to work together for Germany's stability despite their deep mutual mistrust.[10]

Schleicher outlined his vision for national unity in an address broadcast on all radio stations on December 15, his first communication to Germans as chancellor. After condemning Nazi attacks on Hindenburg as unpatriotic, Schleicher introduced himself as a "soldier" for the people. He was, he said, not a career politician, but a neutral, nonpartisan "social general" who was willing to do "whatever is reasonable at any given moment" to unite the various strata of the population in this "hopefully short" time of economic and political emergency. That seemed to include the willingness to suspend constitutional and other established rights if necessary. The platform of his government would consist, he said, of "one sole point: 'Create jobs!' " In terms of policies aimed at cultivating feelings of national solidarity, Schleicher suggested that he would be apportioning less of the government's precious fund of money to "church, school, and scholarship," and more to the "labor service, the associations for the strengthening of the youth, the professional cooperatives, and similar cells that strive for community . . . from below."[11]

Schleicher's speech left much room for anxious guesswork among groups that relied on the state to support "church, school, and scholarship." Church communities depended on state-collected funds to provide salaries for their pastors, priests, and religious instructors, and many parents depended on those people in turn to transmit Christian values to their children. Furthermore, there was little indication, in the speech or elsewhere in his record, that Schleicher—a military man who unlike the outspokenly Protestant Hindenburg was not known to be religious at all—would be dedicated to preserving a role for the churches if he were successful in forming a government and consolidating the public institutions of Germany. Indeed, there was talk that if the chancellor proved unsuccessful in working with the Nazis, he would dissolve parliament and center his efforts on including the secularist Social Democrats in a dictatorial regime.[12] The nonpartisan Becker, who would be supervising cultural policy as minister without portfolio, was known to have worked closely with Social Democrats over the years and was on record recently for having advocated the removal of church-led instruction from public schools.[13]

The new military-backed authoritarian state led by Schleicher thus reactivated a volatile dynamic in German politics. Unlike Hitler, Schleicher voiced his commitment to equality before the law and to the protection of minorities, such as the Jews, as long as they demonstrated loyalty to the nation. Indeed, Hindenburg's appointment of Schleicher in early December 1932 quelled many of the fears of Jewish groups, both within Germany and abroad.[14] At the same time, Schleicher's rise as chancellor exacerbated longstanding concerns among Christian groups about the potential obsolescence of the churches' role in the state. Understanding this dynamic helps explain Schleicher's failure to create a viable government and prevent Hitler's rise to power in late January 1933. It also provides insight into why so few Germans spoke out publicly when the new Nazi-led government began issuing its first laws discriminating against the Jewish minority in the spring of that year.

THE "JEWISH" VIEW OF THE STATE AND THE IDEAL OF NEUTRALITY TOWARD RELIGION

Leaders speaking for Germany's small Jewish communities, which together constituted only about one percent of the country's total population, took the opportunity of Hindenburg's rebuff of Hitler to reaffirm their loyalty to the fatherland. The rise of the Nazis, with their propaganda campaign that presented Jews as foreign and subversive and their promises to "de-Judaize" German society when in power, had understandably troubled Jewish citizens over the previous two years. Some had even made plans for emigration if Hitler became chancellor. On November 25, 1932, in the auditorium of a government building in Berlin reportedly "filled to the last seat" with top-ranking state officials, the National League of Jewish Frontline Soldiers (*Reichsbund der jüdischen Frontsoldaten*) led a ceremony to commemorate the twelve thousand German Jews who gave their lives for the nation during the Great War. "Perhaps this sacrifice of 12,000," the group's director Leo Löwenstein hoped in his opening comments, will mean "that we German Jews will not experience the least affront from our non-Jewish co-citizens, neither in civic nor in economic relations, nor in any other relations that can arise in the intercourse between the individual citizens of the country." After a series of pomp-filled presentations, the assembled men sang the first verse of the German national anthem: *Germany above everything . . . always, when it clings together fraternally for protection and defense.* Defense minister (and soon-to-be chancellor) Schleicher, who could not personally attend the event, sent his highest subordinate to acknowledge that he and other military leaders honored the memory "of these loyal and true sons of our German people."[15]

The view of the German state expressed at this patriotic gathering—as a community in which belonging depends not on membership in any particular faith tradition, but rather on one's willingness to make sacrifices for the sake of the nation—was nowhere better articulated than by the twenty-three-year-old Hans-Joachim Schoeps, a self-described "loyal and true son" of the German people and leader of a small youth group committed to the defense of the German state against communist revolution. Although too young to have fought in the Great War himself, Schoeps was proud to trace his family tree back through a long line of German Jewish military veterans, including a great-grandfather who fought in the War of the Sixth Coalition against Napoleon, a grandfather who served as one of the few non-Christian officers in the Prussian army during the wars of German unification in the 1860s and 1870s, and a father who ran a military hospital in Berlin during the most recent war from 1914 to 1918. While still a student, by 1932 Schoeps had already made a name for himself in political circles through his controversial public debates with racist youth movement leaders who argued that German Jews did not deserve full belonging in the German national community.

Older Jewish communal leaders, such as Berlin's chief rabbi Leo Baeck, typically supported the young Schoeps even when they did not agree with his more extreme stances, which tended toward a fascist brand of nationalism. After all, the youth leader had committed himself completely and totally to the defense of the Jewish minority's rightful place in the German nation. Schoeps later remembered that he had first felt called to defend his co-religionists in secondary school, around 1926, after an "intellectual wrestling match" with a slightly older youth group friend who was studying Christian theology at the University of Berlin. Schoeps disagreed adamantly with an argument his friend related from one of Berlin's theology professors: that all of Germany's political ethics were rooted ultimately in Christianity and the doctrine of the Holy Trinity. From then on, Schoeps submerged himself "with ardent zeal" in all the literature on Jewish and Christian history he could find and learned the ancient languages of Hebrew and Aramaic, in order to refute those who would claim that Christianity was the only religious tradition in the nation capable of fostering ethical political behavior.[16]

During the years he spent in secondary school after the hyperinfla-tion, Schoeps followed the heated debates in parliament over various proposals for a national school law. One proposal, sponsored by the (Catholic) Center Party, called for the codification of the status quo, main-taining segregated confessional schools and leaving all further decisions on school policy to the individual states and localities. Another, submitted by the Social Democratic Party, called for the creation of a unified system with complete separation of religious instruction from public education (similar to public schools in the United States). And yet another, submitted by the German Democratic Party (DDP), imagined a nation-wide system of interconfessional schools, where children of various religious heritages would be educated together and then separated out several times a week for religious instruction according to their religious identity (they could also opt out, if the student preferred).[17] German Jews tended to favor the DDP's interconfessional plan, as part of what Schoeps called a "liberal" view of the state that "envelops all national comrades with their diverse confessions of faith" and "desires to confer to the confessions every freedom within the common school for all children of the people."[18] Indeed, since its formation after the war, the DDP was the party of choice for most German Jews, including Schoeps, while a smaller number supported the Social Democrats or the Center. The other main parties, such as the German National People's Party and the German People's Party, ran candidates who often expressed explicitly antisemitic messages in their campaigns and were thus less attractive options.[19]

In his first year at university in the city of Heidelberg, Schoeps came into contact not only with student groups and fraternities whose members excluded Jews on racial grounds but, more alarmingly for him, with ostensibly progressive professors close to the DDP who questioned the compatibility of Judaism with an education for ethical German citizenship. Schoeps took one seminar taught by Willy Hellpach, a neurologist, educator, and DDP politician who, during his candidacy against Hindenburg in 1925 for president of Germany, had advocated an interconfessional school plan (like the rest of his party) but limited it to the two Christian confessions, excluding Jewish religion. Although he came out in opposition against the racial discrimination advocated by the Nazis, Hellpach argued in his book *Political Prognosis for Germany* that Jewish parents and teachers of Judaism focused too much on the material, worldly aspects of life—as opposed to Christianity's emphasis on the spiritual—and tended to raise children who were clever, but also coddled, effeminate, anxious, cerebral, critical, analytical, individualistic, and atheistic: values that undermine, he said, the cohesiveness of the German people. Hellpach contended that his fellow neurologist Sigmund Freud, who at the time was imagining a future where humans would dispense with the "illusion" of religion, was the quintessential product of Jewish education.[20]

Schoeps spent his university years in the late 1920s and early 1930s attempting to show, pointing to contemporary trends in German Jewish religion and education, that the self-described "godless Jew" Freud did not represent their values and that Jewish teachings were more than compatible with German values. Martin Rade, the Protestant theologian and DDP politician who had helped draft the articles on state neutrality toward religion in the Weimar constitution, hired Schoeps in 1929 to introduce progressive readers of his newspaper, *The Christian World,* to the educational theories of new institutions such as the Free Jewish Lehrhaus in Frankfurt run by Franz Rosenzweig, and to the ideas of recent Jewish authors such as Martin Buber and the new German translation of the Talmud. Schoeps told his Christian audience that he wanted to contest "the prevailing appraisal from the Christian side" that Judaism failed to foster that "knowledge of human limitation, the need for redemption, and divine grace" that instruction in Christianity provided. For his university dissertation, which he finished at the University of Leipzig, Schoeps researched the history of German Jewish religious thought in the preceding centuries to reveal how Jewish educators themselves might have contributed to the "prevailing appraisal" of Judaism among their Christian co-nationals.[21]

It was above all toward a young audience that Schoeps directed his apologetic defense of the Jewish minority. As he knew from personal experience, many nationalist youth leaders were avid readers of the charismatic antisemite Hans Blüher, a neurologist and brilliant wordsmith who since the war had lobbied German politicians to remove Jewish "influence" from the German public sphere. The chancellors Brüning and Papen counted among his occasional listeners.[22] Blüher contended that Germany suffered from severe cultural division, and that the only way to overcome it was to reinstate a German state, or Reich, that was specifically Christian—not neutral toward the various religions. (In a powerful twist, Blüher actually called on Germans to emulate Zionists, those Jews who were rejecting the bankrupt liberal ideal and heroically reclaiming a specifically Jewish state.)[23] In a widely discussed book published at Christmas 1931, Blüher broadened his "conservative-revolutionary" vision further to encompass Germany's foreign relations. It was only when leaders in the currently secularist French republic reclaimed their people's Christian heritage that they could repair the injustice done to Germany in the Treaty of Versailles. "Christianity and its conception of earthly and divine justice," he wrote, was the only "basis and ground for understanding between the peoples."[24]

Like the recently deceased Jewish writer Franz Kafka (whose unpublished essays he was helping edit at the time), Schoeps was both attracted to and outraged by Blüher's powerful message to German youth.[25] On one hand, Schoeps shared Blüher's hostility toward French-style attempts to remove religious ethics entirely from the public sphere. He agreed with Blüher that the materialist writings of Karl Marx and Sigmund Freud had contributed to the unfortunate decline in both religious faith and social solidarity in the modern world. On the other hand, Schoeps expressed "disgust" with Blüher's argument that materialism was a natural outgrowth of Jewish teachings. In an open letter to Blüher in Germany's largest Jewish newspaper in early 1932, he argued that Marx and Freud were "evil" not because they were of Jewish descent, but because they, also like many Christians, had lost touch with their religious heritage.[26] Whereas Blüher praised Zionists for their efforts to leave Germany to found a Jewish state in Palestine and urged Germans to create a Christian state in their own land, Schoeps condemned both efforts as inherently racist, a claim that angered not a few of his fellow Jews.[27]

Shortly after his public dispute with Blüher, Schoeps developed a more extensive defense of Judaism, titled *Jewish Faith in This Time*, a pamphlet whose publication in 1932 was funded in part by the Jewish community of Berlin. Schoeps argued, provocatively, that German Jews themselves had been partially responsible for the negative perception of their religion. In an attempt to win equal civil rights from state authorities and dispel the notion that Judaism was a religion of superstition, the fathers of modern Judaism in Germany since the eighteenth century (best represented by the famous author Moses Mendelssohn) conflated "enlightenment philosophy and religious tradition" and reduced Judaism to a religion of pure reason. In doing so, Schoeps lamented, they stripped the necessity of "faith" and the "fear of God" from Jewish education. That, in turn, weakened the power of Judaism's religious message and made it difficult for "broad circles of Western European Jews . . . to see why the role and task of religion could not be undertaken from out of the [secular] ethic of justice and the ideal of humanity in the progressive initiatives, or the ideals of the socialist parties."[28] Indeed, a significant number of German-speaking Jews over the previous century had left Judaism behind to pursue largely non-religious lifestyles—a trend that many in the younger generation of Jewish leaders were attempting to reverse by downplaying rationalism and emphasizing the more spiritual aspects of their tradition.[29]

Emulating the attempt of the Christian theologian Karl Barth to convince German students to "turn back" (*umkehren*) to the core truths of the Christian Bible for their political ethics, Schoeps attempted to do the same for German Jewish youth and the notion of "return" or "repentance" (*teshuva*) in the Hebrew Bible. In *Jewish Faith in This Time,* he reminded his readers of the ideas of Ludwig Salomon Steinheim, a Jewish doctor and theologian who lived in Hamburg in the mid–nineteenth century. Like the philosopher Immanuel Kant, Steinheim envisioned a peaceful world order composed of self-determined republics in a league of nations. But like Kant's critic G. W. F. Hegel, Steinheim also argued that a free and peaceful order could be achieved only if state leaders shared the right conception of God. At the most basic level, Steinheim taught, this conception must include belief in the biblical revelation that an all-powerful God created humans to be free.[30]

Schoeps and other young Jewish leaders would have had reason to believe in 1932 that at least some of the majority youth groups in Germany were open to positive depictions of Judaism. One observer who tracked trends among young people carefully noted that racist elements encompassed "only a part" of the country's youth organizations.[31] The famed author Ernst Robert Curtius, whose books were read widely in nationalist youth circles, wrote in 1932 that Germans should be fighting not Judaism or the Jewish race, but rather the *negation of Christianity's truth* with which Jewishness was perhaps falsely associated. Because Germans had so little knowledge of the actual content of Judaism, Curtius wrote, and took their associations mainly from the notoriety of prominent figures such as Marx and Freud, the Jewish population of Germany had "a wide possibility in the intellectual and political sphere to decide for itself on its situation and its appraisal."[32] Indeed, the Jewish communities were waging a publicity campaign in 1932 to show that Judaism promoted patriotic, ethical behavior that would never subvert national unity. The directors of the Central Association of German Citizens of Jewish Faith, Germany's largest Jewish organization, emphasized in a pamphlet it distributed to politicians that year that biblical revelation was the "true source" of all Jewish education and the basis for their loyalty to the nation.[33]

German Jews were also temporarily relieved to see that the group that most threatened their existence in the nation, the Nazis, seemed to have been neutralized by the strength of the military-backed German state by the end of 1932. Hindenburg had apparently preserved order by rebuffing Hitler's demand for government leadership and appointing Schleicher, an army general who publicly recognized patriotic Jews as "loyal and true sons of our German people." In one of his first acts as chancellor in December, Schleicher issued an emergency "civil peace" decree criminalizing all invective speech against legally recognized religious communities through the beginning of January 1933. The order was intended to squelch Nazi publications that blamed the tiny Jewish minority for all the country's ills—clearly a short-term, stop-gap measure—but German Jewish leaders hoped Schleicher would take more decisive action when he formed his new government. Ludwig Höllander, the director of Germany's largest Jewish organization, argued that the violence and threats of boycott perpetrated by Nazis against German Jews would not cease until deeper problems in German society were resolved. "True civil peace cannot reign where there exists unclarity in important questions in the life of the state," he wrote in December.[34]

Nonetheless, there were several indications that Hitler's antisemitic movement had peaked and was now on the decline. The press was reporting that the Nazi Party leaders had borrowed too much money to fund the multiple election cycles of 1932 and that their financial contributors were abandoning them. Local elections in the state of Thuringia, the party's stronghold, showed a decline in votes.[35] These reports allowed Schoeps—who expressed admiration for Hitler's ability to mobilize voters on behalf of the nation but supported Schleicher's measures to sideline his dangerous racist messages—to celebrate what he called the "victory" of "Prussian order" over Nazi chaos. "The youthful élan of the movement is now lost," he wrote in early January 1933, and "the nimbus that encircled Adolf Hitler destroyed."[36]

GERMANY'S CHRISTIAN CHURCHES AND THE FEAR OF OBSOLESCENCE
Just before the ban on anti-Jewish publications expired on January 6, 1933, shocking word spread in the press that Franz von Papen, the recently resigned chancellor, was conducting secret negotiations with Hitler to refill the Nazi Party's campaign coffers and undermine Schleicher's

efforts to form a national unity government. Media outlets reported that Papen and Hitler had even begun putting together their own list for a cabinet, composed of both National Socialist and Christian conservative leaders, to present to President Hindenburg. A wealthy businessman from Germany's conservative Prussian Protestant aristocracy, Kurt Baron von Schröder, part owner of the banking house J. H. Stein, had arranged the meeting and provided key funds—one million Reichsmarks—to revitalize Hitler's movement.[37] The media attention thrust both Papen and Hitler back into the center of the national limelight. One eminent historian of the Weimar Republic has called it, in retrospect, the "Third Reich's actual hour of birth."[38]

Scholars who have speculated on Papen's reasons for allying with Hitler and betraying his former patron have tended to focus on economic or psychological motivations: either the wealthy Papen was making a deal with the Nazis to gain protections for capitalist interests, or he was striking back at Schleicher for forcing his recent resignation. But Papen's own explanation for his betrayal—his divergence from Schleicher on issues of cultural policy and the churches—has received far less attention.[39] In his role as chancellor and emergency governor of Prussia from June to November 1932, Papen—a self-declared Catholic conservative who had long worked with Protestant conservatives to conceptualize a "renewal" of the old Christian *Reich* idea (as described by the young conservative-revolutionary Hans Blüher, among others)—instructed his appointees to begin reestablishing the specifically Christian character of all state institutions.[40] Schleicher clashed with Papen on that issue: he expressed concern that the forced Christianization of state institutions would create further discord in the nation by alienating civil servants and labor leaders committed to state neutrality toward religion. Wilhelm Kähler, the Protestant conservative lawyer whom Papen appointed Prussian minister of culture in November 1932, remembered that Schleicher was deeply disgruntled when the ministry strong-armed the state teachers' union into accepting church oversight of religious curriculum and instructed his staff to prepare a series of decrees aimed at converting the entire Prussian school system, including the secular schools of Berlin, to accord with a "Christian and national popular education."[41]

While Papen and Schleicher clashed at the highest level of cultural policy, influential conservative church educators in Prussia were conceptualizing the details of what a specifically "Christian," rather than exclusively Protestant or Catholic, German Reich might look like in the future. For almost a decade, Erich Seeberg—a conservative-revolutionary theologian who was widely considered the country's greatest scholar of Christianity and oversaw the training of pastors and religious instructors as dean of the University of Berlin's Protestant theological faculty—had been imagining a new type of nonsectarian Christian instruction for public schools. Instead of teaching the dogma of any particular confession, he suggested, religious instruction could consist of the study of church history. Instead of simply telling German students to value Christianity—a tactic that was clearly failing, given the falling rates of church attendance—instructors could show the centrality of their historical religion in the formation and maintenance of the nation. In 1932, Seeberg argued in front of a group of constitutional lawyers that the German state had a vested interest in the perpetuation of Christianity: the religion served as a "dam" against radical and unethical political movements and as a useful aid to unite the nation by promoting individual responsibility, work ethic, and patriotic loyalty.[42]

Ernst Benz, a young theologian rapidly gaining prominence in academic circles, was a strong supporter of Seeberg's plan to re-Christianize German state education through instruction in church history. Benz would go on to be involved in some of the most dramatic changes in the relationship between church and state in twentieth-century Germany, but the important story of his life and work has never been told, in part, perhaps, because his personal papers were only recently discovered. Raised Lutheran in the mixed confessional region of southwest Germany, the cerebral son of a civil servant who worked for the national railway, Benz graduated from an elite high school in Stuttgart, the same one attended by Hegel. He excelled in foreign languages, and after continuing his study of theology in Italy, he moved to the state of Prussia to pursue a career in teaching. A group of older conservative scholars in the Prussian Academy of Sciences hired him to join the prestigious Church Fathers Commission (*Kirchenväter-Kommission*), a monumental project begun at the turn of the century (and sustained by rapidly diminishing state funding) to make the documents of early Christianity available as a resource for instructors of religion.[43]

These older theologians took an interest in Benz not only because of his philological skills, but also because of his impressive ability to articulate what they considered Christianity's persisting value in the rationalized "modern state." Like his mentor Seeberg, Benz focused on the Christian history that might unite Germans of competing confessions rather than the dogma that divided them. During his stay in Fascist Italy, he took private lessons with a charismatic professor named Ernesto Buonaiuti, who introduced him and a handful of other students to the Christian mystical tradition that ran from the writings of Paul the Apostle into the modern era. Benito Mussolini had personally ordered the removal of Buonaiuti, an outspoken critic of the regime, from his professorship at the University of Rome.[44] Benz returned to Germany with a clear idea of the authentic mission of the church vis-à-vis the state as well as a firsthand knowledge of the fate of Christian civil servants when they got on the wrong side of an authoritarian modern government.

In 1932, Benz laid out some of these ideas in a book he published with the misleadingly esoteric title *Marius Victorinus and the Development of the Western Metaphysics of Will*. The importance of this text "is still far from being fully appreciated," the Italian philosopher and astute critic of Christianity Giorgio Agamben recently pointed out. On the face of it, the book was a narrative of ancient history about a man named Marius Victorinus, who lived in the Roman Empire under the reign of Constantine the Great and taught rhetoric at the Academy, Rome's training ground for political leaders. But as one reviewer noted about another of Benz's books, it was not " 'only' about history."[45] For Marius Victorinus was also a convert to Christianity from paganism and one of the first authors in history to make a sustained logical argument for the adoption of Christianity as the official religion of the Roman Empire. Historians knew him for his decisive influence on the illustrious church father Saint Augustine of Hippo. To transmit the opinions of this ancient author to a modern German audience was a way for Benz to express a vision for a future Christian Reich.[46]

Before describing his arguments, Benz positioned Marius Victorinus in the context of the Roman Empire of the fourth century A.D., as various conceptions of Christianity competed with each other for primacy. In 325, Emperor Constantine, intrigued by the prospect of adopting this new religion but wary of its adherents' lack of internal unity, invited a council of

Christian theologians from throughout the imperial realm to convene in the city of Nicaea (in today's Turkey) to come to agreement over the proper conception of God. Although the theologians present at that meeting, later known as the First Ecumenical Council, did successfully produce a single document known as the Nicene Creed, many dissidents remained in the various churches of the Roman Empire, and in 358 Constantine's successor Constantius II requested two further councils (convening in the cities of Rimini and Seleucia) that ended in utter discord and conflict and cast a long shadow of doubt among Roman leaders regarding the long-term viability of Christianity as state religion. Into this fray stepped Marius Victorinus, the rhetorician of the Academy, who for most of his life had practiced the official pagan religious rituals of Rome but at what he called a "ripe age" (in his sixties) converted to Christian faith and began writing treatises defending the original Nicene Creed against its detractors.

Benz first reconstructed Marius Victorinus's defense of Christianity in general against claims by pagan detractors that Christianity was too close to its progenitor, Judaism, a religion that Roman leaders had suspected as subversive ever since the first Jewish revolts against Roman authority several centuries earlier. In particular, Benz highlighted the cooperative relationship Victorinus envisioned between the Christian church and the Roman state, in contrast to the Jewish synagogue's allegedly competitive relationship with the Roman state. Whereas the Hebrew Bible commanded worshipers to practice a set of religious laws that always placed the empire's Jewish minority in potential conflict with state law, Victorinus explained, Christianity preached a spiritual, metaphysical faith. In the distinction between law and faith Benz saw the importance of "will." Christianity's message—belief in the divinity of the son Jesus—was valuable to the state because it developed a young person's will to be good. In emulating Jesus, the young person was taught to envision a messianic age in which humans would freely do good and coercive laws would be unnecessary. In Benz's Lutheran telling, there was "absolute opposition" between Victorinus's conception of the (old) Jewish testament and the (new) Christian testament.[47]

Benz then went on to describe Victorinus's defense of the Nicene Creed in particular against its internal Christian detractors. Arius of Alexandria, a priest who inspired many of those detractors, argued that the creed's concept of a "holy trinity" of the father, the son, and the spirit defied logic: if God the father was holy, then Jesus the son could not be equally holy because something cannot will a creation identical to itself. Jesus could only have been a very special, or near-perfect, creation. Marius Victorinus responded in an extended treatise that the conception of God peddled by Arius was lifted from the pagan notions of Plato and Aristotle, who conceived of gods as architects designing demigods that were similar, but not identical, to themselves. In terms of training the future leaders of the empire, Arius's Christianity would thus add nothing to the existing curriculum of the Roman Academy, beyond the reduction of many gods to one. The conception of God expressed in the Nicene Creed, by contrast, offered something new and useful to the state. To conceive of God and his fleshly son as identical and connected through "holy spirit" was to extend beyond the realm of logic traditionally taught in the Academy into the realm of the mystical. Young leaders would be taught to emulate a divine Jesus who, because he was identical with God, always willed exactly what God willed: to do good. According to Victorinus, it was the pedagogical goal of Christianity to teach that a "spark" of that spirit was inside all humans and that one could develop one's will or desire for that same good.[48]

Benz's narrative also illuminated some of the contemporary anxieties of Christian church leaders and religious instructors in Prussia as the dictatorial powers of the German government grew during the depression years. As civil servants employed by the state, many expressed concern that shrinking budgets would mean the loss of their jobs; the Protestant church communities, which depended on subsidies from the state as membership declined, might be left on the vine to die. Some of their fears were realized in 1931, when the Social Democratic–led Prussian government ordered thousands of teacher positions to be cut. Fully half of the region's state-funded Pedagogical Academies (*Pädagogische Akademien*), crucial institutions for the training of teachers in all-Protestant and all-Catholic primary schools, were closed as young pre-service and untenured teachers staged protests in Berlin and other Prussian cities.[49] In response, Protestant church leaders in Prussia signed a legal deal with the state government, guaranteeing the continuation of public subsidies and the maintenance of theology departments at public universities in exchange for government supervision over the "political acceptability" of all faculty appointments.[50]

Anxiety over the obsolescence of the church in the modern and now economically depressed state led many Christian civil servants in Prussia to steer clear of any possible conflict with the government, claiming that their role in the state was purely spiritual and patriotic, not "political." When nationalist students at the University of Halle intensified a campaign in 1931 and 1932 against a newly hired professor of Christian theology accused of being insufficiently patriotic, the majority of his colleagues, including Benz, who was finishing his doctorate in theology there, maintained a safe distance from the issue. Karl Barth, who taught theology in Bonn, represented an exception when he publicly criticized the Prussian government for failing to protect the professor.[51] Benz judged Barth harshly for creating a perception of the Christian church as watchdog of public policy, and mourned the loss of what he called "true Protestantism" in Germany. In a letter to his mentor Erich Seeberg, Benz wrote that a Christian theologian's intervention in the political sphere overstepped his role as a servant of the state. It also prevented Barth from "saving his own ass" if the government ever decided to come after *him*.[52] (Sure enough, a Nazi-led government soon forced Barth out of his post at the University of Bonn and back to his native Switzerland.)

Like most young church leaders, Benz had little interest in joining the Nazi Party but seems to have been willing to collaborate with it if necessary to achieve conservative goals. Privately, he ridiculed Hitler's racial ideas and expressed surprise at their resonance in historically Protestant northern Germany. When the Nazis won thirty-six percent of the vote in the Prussian state elections of April 1932, Benz told Seeberg that, "as a southern German," he simply could not understand how so many north-erners could celebrate "a Catholic, non-smoking, non-meat-eating, anti-alcoholic, unmarried, piano-playing Austrian"—that is, Hitler—"as a messiah."[53] He found the Nazis' theory of fixed genetic identity entirely opposed to the Christian message of free will. "One belongs to the race one chooses," Benz wrote to Seeberg in late November 1932. He had several friends in Halle who were converts to Christianity from Judaism. At the same time, Benz's primary concern seems to have been the conservation of Christian education in public institutions. He would have opposed the Social Democratic Party, let alone the Communist Party, because of its program to separate church and state.[54] Politically homeless, Benz would likely have voted in elections for the German National People's Party

(DNVP), which at least supported policies aimed at the re-Christianization of state institutions as well as the protection of Protestant German-speakers from persecution in Catholic Poland. The DNVP was the party of Franz von Papen, who allied with Hitler in January 1933 against Schleicher.

Many young conservatives ended up allying with National Socialism not because they wanted racial laws in Germany, but because Hitler promised to help them in their effort to re-Christianize the German state. Unlike Schleicher, who with Hindenburg represented the idea of "the national state" as a liberal sovereign that treated all loyal religious communities neutrally, Hitler promised Christian leaders (both Protestant and Catholic) a privileged and financially protected position under his future government. Nazi campaigners emphasized the Christian nature of their commitment to the reestablishment of a truly German Reich during the election campaigns of 1932. The Organization of National Socialist Women (*Nationalsozialistische Frauenschaft*) released a manifesto in which it emphasized: "We stand for the preservation of Christian belief," and the leaders of the Sturmabteilung, the Nazis' paramilitary group, advertised photographs of its men attending church services. One did not have to be convinced of the Nazis' sincerity to choose cooperation with them over Schleicher's alternative, which appeared likely to sideline and defund the churches.[55]

THE SACRIFICE OF THE JEWISH MINORITY

In the first weeks of January 1933, Chancellor Schleicher's efforts to create a national-unity government failed. His attempt to gain loyalty from the pro-labor "left wing" bloc of the Nazi Party, a maneuver that depended on the successful recruitment of Nazi politician Gregor Strasser, was thwarted by Hitler, who used funds provided by his new conservative benefactors to campaign against cooperation with Schleicher. Additionally, Schleicher's bid to win the toleration of the largest workers' party, the Social Democrats, foundered on his refusal to reinstate the old SPD-led Prussian cabinet, his proposal to restrict the independence of the country's independent unions by folding them into a national state-managed "labor front," and his unwillingness to distance himself entirely from the Nazi Party, whom socialist politicians had condemned in the strongest possible terms. Schleicher officially informed President Hindenburg of his failure thus far to forge a cabinet and requested another emergency dissolution of the parliament in order to avoid a vote of no confidence.[56]

But Hindenburg, still worried about a possible communist coup in the case of a general strike or election boycott (a scenario that Schleicher himself had warned him was plausible), refused to sign an emergency decree, humiliating Schleicher and opening the door to Papen's idea of a Hitler chancellorship. Papen, as well as several influential elites from the military and the conservative DNVP, apparently assuaged Hindenburg's fears that Hitler would create a one-party dictatorship if handed the reins of government. Hindenburg's good friend Elard von Oldenburg-Januschau, a DNVP politician who was almost as old as the president (eighty-five) and shared his Prussian aristocratic commitment to the German state, is said to have told Hindenburg that Hitler's designs, whatever they were, could be checked by the army and the "Christian-conservative ideas among the people."[57] Papen told him that a replacement cabinet consisting of only two Nazi Party members (Wilhelm Frick and Hermann Göring) and eight conservatives (with Papen himself as vice chancellor) had already been assembled and awaited his approval. On January 30, 1933, the head of state, for the first time in modern Germany's history, sanctioned a government whose chancellor advocated a rollback of civil rights for an entire segment of citizens. Hindenburg refused Hitler's request for emergency legislative powers, but he did call for new parliamentary elections in early March.

Hitler took little time to frame the platform of his government in terms meant to court Christian conservatives in the lead-up to the elections, while downplaying the anti-Jewish thrust of his party. In his first official communication to the German people, a nationally broadcast radio address on February 1, 1933, the new chancellor used stirring Christian language to describe his goal of national "renewal" and "rebirth." He ensured his listeners that any government led by his party would take "Christianity as the basis of our entire morality," ending with the reverent words, "May the Almighty God take our work into his grace, bless our insight, and bestow us with the trust of our people." The editors of one Nazi newspaper even titled their report on the speech "Hitler's Confession to the Christian State."[58]

The government's first official appointments also seemed to confirm Hitler's promised commitment to a Christian Reich. One of Hitler's first personnel decisions was the installation of a new cultural minister in Prussia, the Nazi educator Bernhard Rust, who immediately ordered a reduction in the number of secular schools and the introduction of religious instruction in vocational schools that previously had none—an apparent continuation of the work of Rust's predecessor, Papen's Christian conservative appointee Wilhelm Kähler.[59] On February 10, at Hitler's first public appearance as chancellor at a huge indoor arena in Berlin under a banner that read "Free Germany from Marxism," his party leaders made many references to the dangers of liberal democracy and the importance of Christian values, but few to anti-Jewish policy, aside from propaganda chief Joseph Goebbels's cryptic remark that they might "lose patience" with criticism of the new government and "plug the lying mouths" of the Jewish journalists responsible for it.[60]

Those who spoke for the Jewish minority in Germany had little choice but to continue to profess their loyalty to the state and its government, unless they wanted to join the Zionists and advocate mass emigration. A new Jewish Museum had just opened its doors in Berlin on January 24 with a ceremony emphasizing the rootedness of Jews in Germany. Hans-Joachim Schoeps, in an article edited for accuracy by Leo Baeck, the chief rabbi of Berlin, assured readers of the anti-Nazi publication *The Christian World* that the rabbinical tradition in Judaism taught loyalty to state authority even in spite of objective injustice.[61] The editor of the newspaper for the Jewish communities' largest umbrella religious organization, the Union for Liberal Judaism (*Vereinigung für das liberale Judentum*), mourned the fact that Hitler's new government apparently did not appreciate the "blood toll" that Jews had paid for the nation as patriots and soldiers. He insisted that Jews would remain loyal to the "real Germany," which would outlast the current power holders.[62]

Meanwhile, Christians concerned about the future of the churches during this moment of transition and uncertainty attempted to secure their privileged role in state institutions as well as their freedom from potential future governmental intervention. On February 26, Erich Seeberg and the other deans of the major faculties at the University of Berlin (including Rudolf Smend from the law school, Eduard Spranger from the humanities, and Heinrich von Ficker from the natural sciences) paid a personal visit to Vice Chancellor Papen, who had just given a speech to young conservatives at the university promising "never to hand over his name and service to support a political movement that could threaten our holiest assets." According to records, Seeberg and his colleagues expressed anxiety that the independence of German higher learning could be threatened under Hitler. In what could not have been a promising sign, Papen is reported to have hurriedly broken off the meeting without giving any specific details about governmental plans once the next legislative period began.[63]

What happened next—the fateful event that ultimately gave Chancellor Hitler and his regime an opportunity to establish a legal path to obtaining emergency legislative powers—is well known and can therefore be outlined briefly. On February 27, 1933, just a week before the national election, the Reichstag—the parliament building constructed after German unification to symbolize the promise of national unity— was attacked by an arsonist, apparently a young man who had worked with underground communist groups. Hitler claimed that the fire was proof of a foreign-backed communist plot against the state, and he was able to persuade President Hindenburg to grant him temporary emergency authority to suspend civil liberties in light of the threat. The government authorized police forces to arrest leaders of the Communist Party (KPD) without a warrant and banned them from campaigning in the crucial days before the parliamentary election of March 5. On election day the KPD still received almost six million votes (twelve percent)— compared with seventeen million for the Nazis (forty-four percent)—but when Hindenburg authorized the formal dissolution of the KPD several days later, their 120 seats in parliament were eliminated. That gave Nazi leaders a fifty-percent majority, and a sixty-percent majority when combined with the delegates from Papen's conservative bloc (*Kampffront Schwarz-Weiss-Rot*, consisting of representatives of the DNVP and other nationalist groups). Nazi members of parliament began whipping up support among their colleagues to approve a law that would enable the regime to decree legislation for the elimination of the communist threat, formally titled the Law to Remove the Emergency of the People and the Reich (*Gesetz zur Behebung der Not von Volk und Reich*), or simply the Enabling Act, requiring two-thirds of parliament.

Since the support of Social Democratic delegates was out of the question, the swing vote for the Enabling Act fell to the delegates from the Catholic political parties, the Center Party and the Bavarian People's Party, who together composed fifteen percent of the Reichstag and throughout the electoral campaigns of the previous year had presented themselves to voters in their propaganda as the "last bastion of freedom and order" against the Nazis and the Communists. The church hierarchy had previously banned Catholics from membership in either party. But from the Prussian university town of Halle, Ernst Benz wrote to Seeberg on election day, March 5, to report on the radical shift among Catholic leaders since the Reichstag fire. Before the arson attack, he observed, sisters at the local Catholic schools had been putting all the pro-Nazi students into a corner and calling them "little devils." Now, they were praying that "nothing happens to Mr. Hitler."[64] Hitler reciprocated. In his declaration of the regime's platform the day before the vote on the Enabling Act, he told Reichstag delegates, "The national regime sees in both Christian confessions the most important factors in the maintenance of our popular culture."[65] The promise was believable because ever since Hitler had refounded the Nazi Party in Bavaria in 1925, he had been careful not to attack traditional Catholic rights. Hitler assured the Catholic delegations in parliament that his regime would immediately negotiate a new, nationwide agreement, or concordat, with the Vatican to protect Catholic education in all of Germany. Their unanimous vote on March 24 made the Social Democratic Party the only major faction to vote against the legislation. Several days later, Germany's bishops lifted the ban on Nazi membership among their flock.[66]

With support for the Enabling Act secured, Hitler and his new government prepared the regime's first legislative acts, which parliamentarians knew would most likely include a special provision for Jews in the effort to neutralize potential subversives within the state. Jewish leaders' pronouncements of patriotic loyalty did not impede the inclusion of such a paragraph. Rabbi Leo Baeck issued a public statement on April 6, the day before the legislation was set to be announced, declaring that German Jews were well disposed toward the two main goals of the "national German revolution through which we are living: the struggle to overcome Bolshevism and the renewal of Germany."[67] But on April 7, the regime released a law that mandated the immediate release of Jewish civil servants, defined as people "of non-Aryan descent." The fact that the regime, at the urging of President Hindenburg, granted an exception for those Jews who had fought at the front in the world war was cold comfort for a group of people who had not encountered legally sanctioned discrimination in Germany for more than two generations.

State employees who worked as instructors in Christian religion feared the precedent set by this act, the Civil Service Law, but they dared not object out of fear for their own positions. On April 18, Erich Seeberg told his colleague from the law school Rudolf Smend that *someone* needed to express a "clear protest," either directly to Hitler himself or in the press, regarding government incursions into public university life. But "in the Jewish question," he wrote, "I think, selfishly enough, that persecution of Jews is better for us than persecution of Christians."[68] Several days later, Seeberg appealed privately to a retired colleague who he thought might speak out regarding several upstanding Christian theologians who were being persecuted. But Seeberg himself did not want to risk reprisal against his faculty, which for the time being looked forward to increased funding under a new government that at least gave lip service to the reinstatement of Christianity as the official state religion of Germany.[69]

CHAPTER FIVE

Two Competing Ideals for a Third Reich

"Today will be the day we close the book of German history on the recent years of hardship and treason and start a new chapter, and freedom and honor will rest on this chapter as the foundation of the emerging nation."

Nazi minister without portfolio Hermann Göring, January 30, 1933, quoted in The National Socialist Revolution

"That [an] orientation toward conservative revolution is not yet apparent in the consciousness of the broad masses today remains as understandable as it is grave. Understandable, because nationalism is standing in the foreground and temporarily covering conservatism. Grave, because the creative formation of the future rests on the force of the conservative-revolutionary idea."

Edgar Jung, Interpretation of the German Revolution, *c. May 1933*

There are few subjects to which scholars and readers have dedicated more attention than National Socialism—for perhaps obvious reasons. In 1938, five years after assuming dictatorial powers as chancellor, Hitler and his government launched a program of aggressive foreign policy in eastern Europe that eventually provoked an armed response from the powers of England, France, the Soviet Union, and the United States, resulting in the bloodiest and most brutal conflict ever recorded. Mobilizing unprecedented forces, the Nazi-controlled German military invaded, in short order, the territories of Austria, Czechoslovakia, Poland, Norway, Lithuania, Latvia, Estonia, Ukraine, Russia, Yugoslavia, Hungary, Romania, Bulgaria, and Greece. At one point during the Second World War, Hitler ruled over an empire of occupation encompassing nearly half of all Europeans: roughly 250 million people.[1] By the time the Germans were defeated and Hitler committed suicide, more than 60 million people had been killed around the globe, most of them civilians, and many of them in circumstances that defy belief. Entire civilizations had been changed forever, and, in the case of eastern European Jewish civilization, nearly destroyed. The global impact of Nazism was so vast, so profound, and so shocking that authors and scholars to this day devote their careers to understanding it.

Because of the trauma of the Second World War, authors have often found it difficult to write about the first four years of the Nazi regime, 1933 to 1937, without projecting onto their historical representations an anachronistic sense of impending doom. The literary scholar Michael André Bernstein called this often unconscious style "backshadowing." In backshadowed narratives, Bernstein observed, Nazi leaders often misleadingly appear as agents of evil unfurling a secret plan, not as human beings responding to complex political pressures. Conversely, the victims of the regime—Jews, communists, Social Democrats, and ultimately the Christian conservative opposition—come across, tragic-ironically, as having realized too late the magnitude of a supposedly always existing threat.[2]

The shadow cast backward upon those years can easily obscure the truth about the relationship between Nazi Party leaders and that last group, Christian conservatives, who helped the Hitler-led regime to power in 1933 and provided it with key moral legitimacy in its first four years but later wanted to distance themselves from it. Indeed, conservatives may have invented the backshadowing technique as a way to white-wash their own reputations. In 1938, Hermann Rauschning, a Christian conservative politician who had joined and then resigned from the Nazi Party, began publishing a series of best-selling (and, we now know, falsi-fied) memoirs of his conversations with Hitler, in which he attempted to warn readers in Europe and the United States by presenting Germany's leader as an antichrist who seduced and misled peace-loving Christians before revealing his true, demonic nature. Published in Switzerland and immediately translated into English and nearly all other European languages besides Russian, Rauschning's exposé allowed non-German readers to feel vindicated for their initial admiration of Hitler's regime. Before the Munich Conference and the anti-Jewish pogroms of 1938, many foreign observers regarded Hitler as a leader who was forging unity in a divided Germany in line with the Christian tradition and defending Europe against communism. Rauschning reassured these observers that they, too, had been misled as to Hitler's "real aim": to abolish the prophetic Christian vision of lions and lambs and to raise instead a "violent, domineering, fearless, and ferocious upcoming generation" of Germans trained to fight wars.[3]

The problem with Rauschning's narratives, and others that explicitly or implicitly present conservatives as having been manipulated by evil Nazi Party leaders, is not only that they create a caricature of Hitler and his relationship to Christianity, but also that they distract from the history of conservative collaboration in the creation of a violent, anti-Jewish racial state and an imperialistic military machine in the years between 1933 and 1937.[4] Rauschning himself, who joined the Nazi Party in 1932, personally oversaw the passage of laws forbidding non-Aryans from public office in 1933 and advocated the German annexation of the so-called Polish corridor in his role as president of the Senate in the free city of Danzig—facts he neglected to mention in his best-selling memoirs. Franz von Papen, the most infamous conservative politician to help the Nazi Party to power only to regret it later, also vigorously defended the regime's removal of Jewish influence from German public life in 1933 and its aggressive foreign policy in the east, including its withdrawal from the League of Nations, as compatible with the Christian value of love. (That, too, was left out of Papen's postwar memoirs.)[5] Given the pitfalls of backshadowing and the faultiness of memory, this chapter examines the relationship between Nazi Party leaders and their conservative supporters using only sources from this four-year period itself.

Christian conservatives who advocated for an alliance with Hitler in early 1933 knew about the Nazis' call for dictatorship, and many worried about the political gamble they were wagering. But enough of Hitler's program overlapped with conservative causes to make collaboration seem more attractive than the alternatives. First, Hitler's political biography reflected an authentic commitment to the German national interest. A man who could claim having given up his Austrian citizenship in protest against the punitive postwar peace settlement, Hitler railed against the decision of the victorious Western powers to veto the Austrian constitutional convention's declaration of political union with Germany and then to thwart a joint German-Austrian declaration of a customs union that many said would have helped lift those countries (as well as Czechoslovakia, a potential future member) out of their economic depression.[6] Hitler also called for the establishment of a "third German Reich," or empire, a popular ideal among younger conservatives. The phrase referred to a vision of a German state that would be officially Christian again but this time avoid the sectarian divisions that had plagued the (first) Holy Roman Empire and the (second) German Empire. It would be neither Catholic nor Protestant but rather a synthesis of the two, capable of uniting co-nationals harmoniously.[7] Finally, many Christian conservatives found common ground with the Nazis' platform of antisemitism, a program to eradicate "Jewish influence" from German public life and to regenerate a healthy race of political leaders. The founders of the DNVP, the primary political home for Christian conservatives and in 1933 an ally of the Nazis, had made that part of their own platform for at least a decade.[8]

Ill defined as it was, antisemitism was *the* moral foundation of the joint nation-building project launched in 1933 by Nazi Party leaders and their Christian conservative allies. As shown below, there would be many debates within that alliance about what precisely the eradication of Jewish influence should mean. But all involved agreed that the goal would be not simply to remove from public life those individuals defined biologically as Jews, but perhaps even more important to eliminate so-called "Jewish" methods of structuring politics and institutions in order to lay new foundations for the unification of the fractured nation. Their joint target was allegedly Jewish styles of thinking and being in the world, styles that the non-Jewish majority had itself allegedly adopted in the era of the liberal commingling of the races.[9] In his book *Race and State,* published just as Hitler rose to power, the Austrian political observer Erich Vögelin insightfully noted that the movement to cleanse "Aryan" Germany of Jewish influence was fulfilling the same function as the segregation of people of color in the United States during the period of American nation-building. The fact that many self-described "Aryans" were calling Jewish traits "un-German," just as many "Whites" called African, Indian, or Mediterranean traits "un-American," was evidence not of Aryan solidarity but rather its opposite, he argued.[10]

The analogy was apt because both Nazis and their conservative allies were fascinated by the colonial past of the United States and its founders' ability to forge consensus on a way of life amid the political chaos of the New World. In one of his books, Hitler wrote that he wanted Germans "to lead a life analogous to the American people." He meant that Americans had achieved things that Germans had not, such as the colonization of sufficient living space for their people and the institution of racial laws protecting the majority culture from disintegration.[11] Conservatives who allied with Hitler also tended to speak admiringly of American consensus in contrast with German conflict. Edgar Jung, the popular author Vice Chancellor Franz von Papen retained as adviser to help him appeal to a younger generation of conservatives, mourned the fact that Germans tended to envision the world and its future in radically different ways. "An American asked about his 'political worldview' in the German sense," he wrote, "would understandably laugh."[12]

Amid an outpouring of nationalism after the Reichstag fire, the new chancellor and his eleven ministers obtained a mandate from a two-thirds majority in parliament to forge order and unity in Germany. The day before the Enabling Act vote in March 1933, Hitler assured parliamentarians tired of partisan bickering that the measures his government planned to take would be designed not only to put Germans back to work, but also to create the ground of a common way of life upon which Germans could build consensus on controversial issues. "The splitting up of the nation into groups with irreconcilable worldviews means the destruction of the basis of a possible communal life," he said in his address to the Reichstag. "Individuals' fully conflicting attitudes regarding the concepts of the state, society, religion, morality, family, [and] economy, tear open differences that lead to a war of all against all."[13] The text of the Enabling Act, which was initiated by conservative politicians in the DNVP, called for the transfer of legislative power to the cabinet until April 1, 1937.

As we shall see, however, the project to create a common German way of life out of what cultural critics called the "worldview chaos" of Weimar was hampered by the persistence of competing visions of Germany's future among the younger generation of Nazis and conservatives. In particular, minds divided on the question of the Christianization of the state, one of the primary stipulations of conservative support for the Nazi-led project. The tension between German leaders who wanted to separate church from state as a precondition of political unity—such as Nazi Party ideologue Alfred Rosenberg—and those who wanted to "rejuvenate" a Christian body politic was evident from the earliest months of the Third Reich. Papen's adviser Jung, at thirty years old perhaps the most prominent spokesperson for young conservatives in Germany, registered his concern about this tension already in the early summer of 1933. Although he did not object to racial laws, he noted that conservatives were interested in something beyond the physical segregation of the Jews. In order to restore Germany's mission as "protector of the cross" against the anti-Christian forces threatening Europe, Jung wrote, the new government needed to unify the divided views of the Protestant majority and the Catholic minority into one "image of the world."[14]

The internal struggle over the future of the Third Reich played out over the first four years of Hitler's regime, though few foreign observers noticed at first. The big story coming out of Germany was the economic recovery: Hitler was outdoing President Franklin D. Roosevelt in job creation, implementing inventive combinations of economic policy proposals developed during the Weimar years, from deficit spending to labor service camps. Through the economic successes of the new regime, the Nazi Party was able to grow its base and win over more adherents among the general population to the idea of an antisemitic racial state (of which many in Germany were initially skeptical).[15] But the clash of visions became more apparent when the nation's economic situation revealed itself as less sustainable than previously thought. At that point, it became clear that the leaders of the Nazi regime, despite running a dictatorship, were not necessarily better equipped to bridge the deep divisions among Germans than the founders of the liberal democracy in Weimar had been.

THE NAZI VISION OF STABILITY UNDER THE SYMBOL OF THE SWASTIKA

Nazi Party leaders sought to change fundamental aspects of German life with their first antisemitic actions and laws of 1933. It would be mistaken to argue that these actions and laws were directed at non-Aryans alone. The party-organized boycott of Jewish-owned businesses on April 1, for example, was intended to punish Jews, naturally, but also to pressure non-Jewish German consumers to buy German-made products instead of the foreign-made things they often preferred. Those seen buying at Jewish-owned department stores, where imported items were sold, could be tarred as indifferent to the struggles of German workers and subversive to the government's plan for economic nationalism.[16] Likewise, the Law for the Restoration of the Professional Civil Service (*Gesetz zur Wiederherstellung des Berufsbeamtentums*) of April 7, which required the ministries of all regional states to retire tenured public employees "of non-Aryan descent," was designed for a broader purpose than simply removing Jews, who themselves composed only a very small fraction of such positions. According to the law, *any* civil servant could be fired with no legal right of rebuttal if his or her superior found evidence of past political activity (such as membership in the Social Democratic Party, or attendance at a pacifist rally) that suggested unwillingness "to advocate at any time for the nation-state without reserve."

Nothing symbolized the centrality of antisemitism in the Nazi Party's larger program of societal transformation more than the book burning organized by university students in Berlin, the nation's capital, on May 10, 1933. At 11 P.M., students dressed in Nazi paramilitary uniforms listened to an incendiary speech by propaganda minister Joseph Goebbels and then threw an estimated twenty thousand books on to an enormous bonfire. The action represented the culmination of several frenetic months of nationwide purges that journalists called collectively the "National Socialist revolution." A flyer distributed by a Nazi student group laid out the rationale for the book burnings. Under the motto "Against the Un-German Spirit," the students drew a connection between the eradication of Jewish influence and the transformation of German education that they longed to see. By removing the "Jewish spirit" from their cultural life, they said, Germans could transform the university—the training ground for rising leaders—from a factory that produced rootless intellectuals and citizens of the world into a "nursery of German national culture" that cultivated leaders dedicated without reserve to the nation. They demanded that professors and students at the university be selected based not only on intellectual merit but also on proven commitment to cultural unity.[17]

The logic behind the association of Jewish influence on one hand and German national disunity on the other is easier to comprehend when one looks at the background of Alfred Baeumler, the University of Berlin professor Nazi students chose to deliver a lecture directly preceding the book burning.[18] In May 1933, Baeumler, forty-five, had just been appointed by the Nazi cultural minister of Prussia, Bernhard Rust, as dean of the humanities faculty and head of the division responsible for the training of teachers. Like Hitler, who belonged to the same generation, Baeumler came from a disputed German-speaking region outside the political borders of the Reich. (He hailed from Bohemia, which for much of history was considered part of German Europe but at the Paris Peace Conference fell under the territory of the new Czechoslovakia.) After fighting in the war on Germany's side, the academically inclined Baeumler studied philosophy and quickly earned the attention of some of the most respected educators both in Germany and abroad. Since 1931, he had been an active member in an antisemitic organization of scholars who "battled for German culture" as well as co-editor of an international journal he founded with Paul Monroe, the eminent professor of education and close colleague of John Dewey at Columbia University's Teachers College in New York City. Baeumler and Monroe were both interested in the power of public education to forge political consensus in divided societies, especially those at risk of—as Americans put it—"going communist."[19]

Baeumler received recognition during the inflation years with sweeping arguments about the inability of the existing education system to foster consensus and the failure of professors to bridge the generational gap between older and younger Germans.[20] His first acclaimed book was a radical critique of Immanuel Kant, the philosopher whose ideas had most shaped the form of Germany's renowned educational institutions since the nineteenth century. Kant, Baeumler noted, was foundational for German educators mainly because his approach, known as transcendental idealism, offered the promise that human beings, when properly educated, would overcome self-interest and reach consensus on collective ideals. Kant, in one of his mature works, described the future of humanity as a system in which people constructed collective "symbols of morality" in a quasi-divine, "sublime" synthesis of individual opinions, likening it to a beautiful organism whose parts would work together harmoniously in common purpose.[21] The problem with this noble dream, Baeumler argued, was twofold. First, it was inherently elitist: it depended on the existence of privileged intellectuals who had the means and time to arrive at agreement through time-intensive study and logical reflection. Second, it was messianic: Kant anticipated consensus only for a more enlightened time supposedly to come, never for the present. Baeumler traced both pitfalls to what he claimed were the covert Christian assumptions of Kant's secularized philosophy: idealists hoped people would agree on a common secular "idea," just as the Christian church fathers hoped they would come together around the idea of Jesus as messiah.[22]

Although Baeumler was far from alone among German educators in his critique of idealism and its allegedly Christian roots, few made it a weapon of attack against the German political establishment. The attempt to overcome idealist elitism was most associated at the time with Rudolf Steiner, whose new Waldorf school in Stuttgart served children of all classes, minimized the importance of Christian religious instruction, and emphasized physical play for community building.[23] But Baeumler, who was a theorist and not a practitioner, went further, connecting the genealogy of idealist education to other indications of societal breakdown he saw in Weimar Germany: the rise of the unattached, liberated woman in the age of universal suffrage; postwar pacifism and the apparent unwillingness of many Europeans to fight for the preservation of their nations against a communist threat; and more generally, the chaos of an urbanizing society where immigrants threatened to overtake locals. In his introduction to the work of the nineteenth-century philosopher Johann Jakob Bachofen, Baeumler connected German idealism with Christianity's mythical origins in Judaism and what Bachofen called "the law of the mother," a feminine principle that celebrated love, religion, harmony, and equality, often symbolized by the lamb. While beautiful, Bachofen argued, the law of the mother should never be raised above the higher masculine principle best expressed in ancient Greek myth: the creation of order from chaos, often symbolized by the lion.[24] Alfred Rosenberg, the Nazi Party's chief theorist, seized upon Baeumler's ideas in 1930 to argue that liberal democrats, by extending equal rights to all races and sexes, feminized and ultimately Judaized their nations, allowing them to fall into chaos.[25]

During the electoral rise of the Nazi Party, Baeumler used the writings of Friedrich Nietzsche, who famously prophesied in *Thus Spoke Zarathustra* the appearance of a lion (a "blond beast") that would destroy the morality of Christianity to make way for a new type of human, to articulate his political vision for the eradication of Jewish influence and the birth of a unified Germany. Baeumler gained exclusive access to Nietzsche's unpublished literary estate from the philosopher's antisemitic sister, and edited a new set of his collected works as well as a lengthy introduction and companion volume of interpretation. Baeumler painted the Prussian Nietzsche as a political philosopher who as a young man was horrified by the state of Germany he saw founded in 1871.

According to Baeumler, Nietzsche believed that the German state was destined for disunity because its political leaders were too Jewish. This did not mean they had Jewish bodies: it meant they viewed the world in a "Jewish type" of way that Nietzsche called "priestly." Famously, the Jewish priests of antiquity banned anthropomorphic depictions of God, rejected the mythical idols common to the ancient world, and rendered the divine an abstract, imageless idea. They celebrated as moral a lamb-like, ascetic meekness. In so doing, Jews denied what Nietzsche called in 1873 the natural human drive to anthropomorphize the divine, as the Greeks did in their myths, metaphorical images of the good that bound a people together. As students of Nietzsche's *Genealogy of Morals* knew, that originally Jewish "priestly type" was then adopted by Christians and much later by German idealists. The educators who were helping to build German national identity after 1871 embraced a Kantian vision that valued, like the Jewish priests, ideas over images and meekness over heroism. They taught students in their universities to bust myths through critical historical thinking instead of building myths. They hoped for future cultural unity without being willing to fight for it. "We are getting a German Empire at precisely that time when we are on the verge of ceasing to be Germans," Nietzsche wrote in 1873. "I no longer have the courage to claim one simple characteristic as especially German."[26]

Baeumler argued in his lecture to Nazi students in May 1933 that an idealist (that is, "Jewish") type of education could never unite a divided Germany and that only a mythical, "Greek" type was capable. The Nazi movement, with its lively metaphors for the nation and its image of the characteristically German, would bind the people together. By burning un-German books, he told the students, they destroyed a legacy of "imageless idealism," a notion of truth that had dominated the university and prevented national unity for a century. Mere ideas such as equality, Christianity, the nation, or the state could not hold a people together. Backdropped by a giant flag with the Nazi Party swastika, Baeumler asked them to turn idealism on its head: instead of striving *toward* future consensus through endless talk about ideas, commit *now* to a Nazi movement that already provided an image of what German unity could look like.[27]

Baeumler's lecture inaugurated Hitler's efforts in the spring and summer of 1933 to synchronize (*gleichschalten*) Germany's universities, like nodes in a communication grid, by pressuring professors and students to join the Nazi revolution. Most professors had not voted for Hitler, let alone joined the Nazi Party. Most were conservatives who had tolerated the purges of non-Aryans and Marxists from their ranks but still expected to retain the traditional rights accorded their institution since the nineteenth century, such as self-administration of research, teaching, budget, and personnel.[28] At the end of June, the philosopher and new Nazi Party member Martin Heidegger, who was collaborating with Baeumler on synchronization, publicly scolded the assembled professors of Heidelberg, Germany's oldest university, in front of their students. "In Germany there is revolution, and we must ask ourselves: is there also revolution at the university? No," he said through a loudspeaker in the overflowing auditorium. Instead of embracing a communally shared outlook and cultivating leaders committed to the nation, professors were conducting research and teaching as they had for decades, transmitting "only the point of view of the [individual] teacher."[29] It quickly dawned on these university conservatives that the new Nazi-led government might cut their resources if they did not join the party and willingly subordinate their traditional administrative powers.

Chancellor Hitler and the Nazi ministers in his cabinet applied pressure on conservatives not only in the universities but in all realms of public life, beginning with conservative politicians in parliament. In June 1933, after plundering the offices of the labor unions and forcing the leaders of the Social Democratic Party into exile, the Nazi-led interior ministry persuaded the leaders of the main conservative Protestant and Catholic parties (the German National Front and the Center Party, respectively) to dissolve their organizations and embrace one-party Nazi rule.[30] Longtime Nazi member Joseph Goebbels, head of a newly established national ministry for propaganda, suggested that the Center Party "would do well to close up shop" because organizations representing the interests of any particular social group were superfluous now that one Nazi movement represented the people as a whole. By July, when Germany's Catholic bishops pledged loyalty to the government as long as Catholic values were respected, the self-synchronization of the conservative parties to the national revolution was complete.[31] Hitler asked

President Hindenburg to call elections for September 1933: the Nazi Party would be the only party on the ballot.

If these events were not dramatic enough, perhaps the most revolutionary of Nazi-led efforts to remove "Jewish" influence and synchronize the nation was the attempt to undo the federalist structure of Germany and lay the foundation for a common national primary school system. Although the propaganda ministry honored the memory of Germany's first chancellor, Otto von Bismarck, and depicted Hitler as his spiritual successor, it also held Bismarck's constitution of the Reich in 1871—a collection of essentially sovereign states with their own constitutions, governments, and education ministries—responsible for the continuing "chaos" of Germany's cultural disunity. (Ironically, this had been the argument made by Social Democrats and other prominent politicians at the time of the Weimar constitutional convention in 1919, but the conservative advocates of states' rights had blocked their efforts.) On the anniversary of Hitler's appointment, January 30, 1934, with far more than the two-thirds majority required to change the constitution, Nazi members of parliament passed a law that eliminated regional state parliaments, placed their governments under the direct oversight of the national government, and allowed the national interior minister to promulgate decrees for the regional states. Two weeks later, the National Socialist parliament passed another law to dissolve the upper house of the national legislature (*Reichsrat*), a pillar in Germany's federal structure.[32]

As Nazi Party leaders laid the ground for a national school law, legislation that had proved impossible to pass in the Weimar years, many conservatives became concerned that educators who advocated the separation of Christianity from the state (such as Alfred Baeumler) would take an overpowering hand in drafting it.[33] In February 1934, Hitler's government announced the creation of a national education ministry, the first institution of its kind in Germany. Bernhard Rust, whom Hitler personally appointed to head the new ministry, began soliciting proposals even before his office opened in May. One of the first proposals to arrive, from the chapter of the League of National Socialist Teachers in Saxony, foresaw the creation of common schools that replaced the teaching of traditional Christianity with instruction in a paganlike "German faith."[34]

The creation of Germany's first national education ministry revealed a rift among supporters of the Third Reich over the role of Christianity.

This became apparent at the highest echelons of the government. In the spring of 1934, Vice Chancellor Papen's adviser Edgar Jung publicly challenged Hitler to prove that he was, as promised, committed to building the Christian state as a defense against communism. When Papen himself delivered a speech to that same effect on June 17, 1934, at a meeting of young conservatives at the University of Marburg, Hitler's response was violent.[35] During the Night of the Long Knives, a wave of assassinations at the end of June, the Nazi secret police killed Jung and ransacked Papen's office. Papen was briefly placed under house arrest and then dismissed from his cabinet post at the beginning of July, demoted to the office of ambassador to Austria.

Hitler's actions against Jung and Papen in the summer of 1934 did not reveal a hostility to Christianity per se. They did, however, communicate Hitler's view that the moral legitimacy of government derived not from a "responsibility toward God" (as the Catholic Church maintained, and as Jung wrote before his death), but from a responsibility to protect the tribe. In his speech addressed to the nation on July 13, 1934, Hitler took personal responsibility for the extrajudicial executions and referred to himself as a "supreme judge" whose responsibilities included emergency decisions of life or death to avoid "chaos."[36] In using the words "supreme judge," a phrase Christian conservatives reserved for God, Hitler was not rejecting the moral principles of Christianity and the church: he was denying their sovereignty over political affairs. Perhaps to demonstrate this new hierarchy, Hitler proscribed theology students, pastors, and priests in 1934 from becoming officers in the Schutzstaffel (SS), the elite security organization of the Nazi Party.

That crucial distinction—between Christian religion in general and Christian claims to sovereignty in particular—was explained by a leading member of the Nazi Party's legal counsel who defended the legitimacy of Hitler's actions in the summer of 1934. Carl Schmitt, a jurist who had been appointed to help remove Jewish influence from the university law faculties and provide a legal rationale for the new government, argued that those who called a leader into question when the nation was endangered exhibited a typically "Jewish" style of thinking in German jurisprudence. Schmitt traced the genealogy of the Jewish style to the mid–nineteenth century, when Christian conservative lawyers persuaded the king of Prussia to implement what they called a Christian state: a

"state of justice" (*Rechtsstaat*), in which independent judges held government leaders accountable to the law. That kind of thinking, he suggested,
was analogous to orthodox Jewish communities in which adherence to
God's law trumps the integrity of the community.[37]

The fortuitously timed death of conservative President Hindenburg
in August 1934, soon after the Night of the Long Knives, allowed the Nazi
Party leadership to merge the offices of chancellor and president into one,
thereby moving further toward what Hitler and Schmitt called a "total
state," where government and judiciary shared "one worldview."[38] The
new combined officeholder was to be called simply the Führer, a post to
which Hitler was elected by near unanimous popular acclaim on August
19, 1934. In his new role as head of state as well as head of government,
the Führer was now also commander-in-chief of the German armed
forces, the only state institution that leaders of the Nazi Party had not yet
attempted to synchronize. The deal Hitler struck before the purge with
his defense minister Werner von Blomberg included the guarantee that
the generals would retain autonomy over self-administration provided
they willingly incorporated a National Socialist worldview into the political training of their officer corps. Together, the party and the military
would form what Hitler called the "two pillars" of the German state.[39]

Hitler declared the National Socialist revolution complete by September
1934. But the true task of national construction, he said, was just beginning.
"A revolution can, in itself, never realize a platform," read Hitler's opening
statement at the annual party rally in Nuremberg, famously documented
in Leni Riefenstahl's *Triumph of the Will.* "Revolutions only eliminate
the current conditions of power! Evolution alone changes the current conditions of things!" In just one and a half years of dictatorial rule, the new
regime had broken the self-administration of the civil service, decon-
structed the federal structure of the Reich, and made inroads into a largely
unsupervised and aristocratic military—all things, incidentally, that prominent democratic politicians had wanted to do but failed to accomplish by
parliamentary means for fourteen years. Now, with the old "conditions of
power" gone, party leaders called for the construction of a state that would
be strong and sustainable: a common school system, a unified state bureaucracy, and a true people's army.

For that, Hitler said, the coming generation of Germans needed a
common creed, sacred, mythical values that the people held deeply and

expected government to protect. These values could not be invented out of whole cloth. "There is nothing great on this earth that lasts thousands of years and has come about in decades," Hitler wrote. "The tallest tree has also had the longest period of growth."[40] Many believed that the American "way of life" had evolved out of the Calvinist culture of the country's British settlers three hundred years earlier. It remained to be seen what traits, if any, a German way of life would derive from the traditional moral values of its Christian churches, whose histories reached back far longer than that.[41]

THE CONSERVATIVE VISION OF A THIRD REICH UNDER
THE SYMBOL OF THE CROSS PATTÉE

The role of Christianity in the formation of a common German worldview was a heavily disputed matter within the Nazi Party. It is important to note that the composition of this party, which Hitler expected to be the vanguard of national unity, had fundamentally changed between the Enabling Act of March 1933 and the Nuremberg Rally of September 1934. With the dissolution of rival political organizations, many conservatives who earlier belonged to or voted for the German National People's Party or the Center Party were now card-carrying Nazis. Over that period, the Nazi Party more than tripled in size (to nearly three million members), and its social makeup expanded from a largely lower- and lower-middle-class base to encompass bourgeois and upper-middle-class types.[42] Significantly, many of these new joiners included conservatives from the professional civil service who sought to conserve and renew the Christian identity of the state. Their Christian vision for the Third Reich proved to be a source of competition for the pro-separation elements in the party.

The conservatives who joined or supported the Nazi Party after the Enabling Act envisioned a Third Reich in which Germans, united by a Christian view of the world, led Europe in a modern crusade against Bolshevism. Over the first year and a half of Nazi rule, they formed a number of institutions and projects to ensure what Erich Seeberg, dean of the theological faculty in Berlin, called a "symmetry" between the Christian spirit and the new secular power.[43] In July 1933, the members of the country's Protestant churches voted overwhelmingly to form a unified German Evangelical Church (*Deutsche Evangelische Kirche*, DEK), an organization that would place all individual regional churches, including in theory Catholic dioceses willing to break with papal authority, into a single structure capable of collecting tax funds for welfare, standardizing religious instruction in public schools, coordinating military chaplaincy, and presenting a single voice in negotiations with the government. In the fall of 1934, after the Soviet Union was admitted into the League of Nations, prominent Catholic and Protestant conservatives worked together to found a German chapter of the Pro-Deo Commission for the International Struggle Against Godlessness in Berlin, where they hoped to work against communism in concert with the Nazi ministry of propaganda.[44]

Ministers in the Nazi-led regime, including Hitler himself, regarded Christian efforts to unify the confessions as useful and promoted them when possible. Education minister Bernhard Rust saw the creation of a set of supradenominational Christian ethics, free of the dogma that had divided Germans since the Reformation, as a way to solve the difficult school issue.[45] Defense minister Werner von Blomberg looked forward to the introduction of one Christian chaplaincy and one Christian prayer book as an aid to troop camaraderie, and he supported the election of his friend Ludwig Müller, the military chaplain for the East Prussian army, to lead the new DEK.[46] After all, European generals had used the church concept of "militans pro deo," war in the name of God, as a morale-builder from late antiquity through the Crusades and into the modern period.

But conservatives who shared a vision of a unified, fighting Christian ethic faced serious obstacles, due primarily to the intransigence of a significant number of church leaders who refused to abandon their particular confession and conform to a single, uniform Christian culture. The Protestant communities of the DEK, to which the majority of Germans paid church taxes, split into three camps: one supported by the Nazi Party calling itself German Christians (*Deutsche Christen*), whose leaders advocated the self-synchronization of all member churches and the racial exclusion of Jews from pastoral work; another calling itself the Confessing Church (*Bekennende Kirche*), which declared in May 1934 its commitment to the continued self-administration of the DEK's various confessional churches (Lutheran, Reformed, United) and rejected the importation of Nazi racial ideology into church affairs.[47] A third, larger group remained neutral and conciliatory. Meanwhile, the Catholic Church hierarchy, to which roughly thirty percent of Germans paid their dues, flatly denied the possibility of joining what Müller hoped could be a "single church, free of Rome." One archbishop in Bavaria conceded that a national church structure would represent a "profound unification of German people"; but it also stood "in absolutely glaring contradiction to the nature of the Catholic Church," whose rock would always be in the Vatican, he said.[48] By the time of the Nuremberg Rally in September, the project of building a single German Christian faith was effectively stalled when two major constituent Protestant churches in Prussia and Bavaria insisted on autonomy within the DEK.[49]

Some conservatives remained hopeful and urged the national government to continue funding the DEK's efforts in connection with proposals for a common school system. In the fall of 1934, Erich Seeberg and a number of younger conservative theologians in his circle, including Ernst Benz, sent a joint letter to education minister Rust stating clearly: "We German Protestant theology professors request that the Führer and Reich Chancellor protect the connection of the German Evangelical Church with the state." The request included an explicit warning about the potential for chaos, disunity, and security breaches if consensus in the churches could not be achieved. "The Evangelical Church can, furthermore, only in close connection with the Führer provide him with the forces he needs in the battle against the powers antagonistic to the Third Reich," it read, referring primarily to the battle against Bolshevism. "If the Evangelical Church falls into sects and communities separated by the state, it could easily succumb to the danger of becoming a staging area for attitudes harmful to the Third Reich, and alienate the religious from the political order."[50]

The Nazi-led education ministry seems to have recognized the legitimacy of those conservative arguments. At the end of 1934, Rust appointed Ernst Benz to a prestigious post at the University of Marburg. At twenty-seven years old, he became the youngest professor of theology in the country. Benz was not yet a member of the Nazi Party, but he did belong to the academic department of the Nazi paramilitary organization, the Sturmabteilung (SA), despite his initial skepticism about Hitler. In 1933 he taught for several months in a Lutheran academy in the Baltics, where he collected material on Soviet anti-Christian activities and gave a series of lectures for the SA in the disputed city of Danzig. Rust brought Benz to Marburg in 1934 to replace a theologian who had recently been sacked for public opposition to the Nazi regime. It is telling that the education ministry accepted Seeberg's assurance that the young Benz had "slowly but surely grown into the National Socialist body of thought," despite the fact that Benz's superior in the academic department of the SA labeled him "politically unreliable (salon National Socialist)."[51]

Benz argued for the usefulness of Christianity in his book *Ecclesia Spiritualis* (The Spiritual Church). Published in 1934, it told the story of the Italian medieval visionary Joachim of Fiore, whose prediction of a coming "third age" was popularized by the German conservative revolutionary Arthur Moeller van den Bruck in his famous work *The Third Reich*. According to official papal doctrine in the twelfth century, the "first age" of God's plan for the world's development was Jewish (or Mosaic) law, which was then superseded by a "second age" of Christian canon law upheld and sanctioned by the pope in Rome. Disgusted by abuses within the Roman church, especially the indulgences scandal, Joachim introduced the possibility of a "*third* age," a messianic time when the current church would disintegrate and Christians would instead preach a purely "spiritual," as opposed to legal, message of togetherness.[52] King Richard I the Lionheart of England was said to have visited Joachim in his monastery in Messina on his way to Jerusalem, leading a diverse army of Europeans; the monk reportedly inspired the soldiers by predicting a final apocalyptic battle against the Muslim persecutors of Christians. The analogy between medieval Islam and modern Bolshevism would not have been lost on his Nazi audience.[53]

Even more strikingly, Benz appeared to suggest that Hitler's popularity would be weakened if he cut ties between church and state. The second part of *Ecclesia Spiritualis* narrated the life of Cola di Rienzi (or Rienzo), the fourteenth-century populist leader who purported to be the messianic figure Joachim of Fiore prophesied would reunite the fallen Roman Empire. Rienzi was the protagonist in Hitler's favorite tragic opera composed by Richard Wagner; Hitler claimed that Rienzi's life inspired him to enter politics as a young man, and he insisted that the opera's overture be played at the party's annual conventions. The moral of the story the way Benz told it, however, was that Rienzi's effort to unite the Roman Empire was bound to fail because he tragically depended on his charismatic leadership alone and failed to enlist the forces of Christianity in his efforts. "The political foundation of Rienzi's power is too thin and the confidence in the force of his person is too slight to place himself, with bold audacity, in the middle of the cosmos as lord of the world and bringer of the final Reich," Benz wrote. (He used the typical present tense of historical narratives designed for contemporary relevance.) Such "messianic self-conception" in the hands of politicians, Benz concluded, is a "dangerous game."[54]

There is evidence that Hitler himself worried about the breadth of his popular base without the unified support of identifying Christians in Germany. If not, it is difficult to explain why the Nazi regime expended so much time and so many resources on the success of the DEK. In early March 1935, Hitler was reportedly considering appointing education minister Rust to lead the creation of yet another new government ministry, this one devoted exclusively to conflict resolution, or "pacification," within the Protestant churches.[55] The head of the new national ministry of church affairs in July 1935 ended up being a lawyer named Hanns Kerrl, a loyal member of Hitler's inner circle who for the previous two years had been involved in the reordering of communal administration around the country, facilitating the transition from democratic town councils to executive models of mayoral rule.[56] The fact that Rust had been the man originally slated for the job, however, demonstrated the connection of the church struggle to the holdup in the development of a national school law, on which no progress had been made for a year.

The appointment of Kerrl backfired. The lawyer's coercive means of conciliation as minister of church affairs exacerbated the conflicts between the various sects in the DEK and helped bring them to the attention of influential Christian groups abroad. When Kerrl mandated the nationwide creation of "church committees," on which members of both German Christian and Confessing Church groups would be forced to sit down together to reach consensus, leaders in the latter group simply refused and took the matter to the international press. Karl Barth, the leading theologian of the Confessing Church, left Germany for his native Switzerland, where he could more freely condemn the German Christians. A popular young Lutheran pastor and leader in the Confessing Church, Dietrich Bonhöffer, who remained in Germany, published a dramatically worded article in August 1935 arguing that any true Christian must reject the racial ideology of the German Christians "under the onslaught of new nationalism," calling on Christians in the world ecumenical movement to take notice of developments in Germany.[57] The timing was significant because Nazi leaders in the late summer of 1935 were set to announce major new racial legislation, including citizenship and anti-miscegenation laws, at the annual Nuremberg Party Rally that Kerrl was organizing in September.[58] Protestant groups abroad responded immediately to Bonhöffer's call. The Anglican bishop George Bell, a leader in the center of the world ecumenical movement in England (whom we will meet again later), arranged to meet with Hitler's deputy, Rudolf Hess, days after the rally to register the deep concern of the international Christian community.[59]

Hitler reacted negatively to the increased pressure from the renegade conservative Confessing Church camp and their decision to involve international actors in what he considered a purely German national issue. Less than two weeks after the party rally in September 1935, Hitler's minister of justice, Franz Gürtner, enabled Kerrl with administrative powers to legislate ordinances binding for all Protestant churches (overriding traditional synodal authority) and to convene mandatory church committees for all Protestant communities. In November, Kerrl decreed the dissolution of all organizations that refused participation in the committees. The *New York Times* reported that Kerrl was threatening to recommend the discontinuation of church tax collection, a key service the German government had provided since its foundation in 1871 to ensure the upkeep of Christian communities.[60] Rumors spread that the church tax might even be replaced with a general "cultural tax," a measure advocated by vocal proponents of church-state separation within the Nazi Party. In December 1935, some more explicitly anti-Christian members of the party's elite SS were already organizing the replacement of state-funded Christmas celebrations with natural-religious (or "pagan") celebrations of the winter solstice.

Conservative church leaders who were willing to support Kerrl's committees pushed back against the radical anti-Christian elements in the Nazi Party. The antisemite Adolf Schlatter, a retired theologian and respected public intellectual, found resonance among German readers when he warned the party against replicating the work of Jews by removing Christian symbols from the public sphere.[61] The advocates of Christian uniformity also used the fact that the German government would soon fall under increased international scrutiny—when it hosted the Olympic Games for summer 1936—as leverage to advance its vision of the Third Reich. In early January 1936, Ernst Benz and several of his colleagues in Marburg signed a letter to *The Times* of London criticizing what they claimed was the "one-sided" coverage of Germany's church affairs in the foreign press.[62] At the same time, he and a group of prestigious German theologians published a proposal calling for government support of "confession-less" theological faculties ("evangelical," as opposed to separate Protestant and Catholic faculties) that would prepare a new generation of German religious instructors and chaplains free of dogmatic attachment to sectarian teachings. While rejecting all "Catholic" and "Calvinist" mixing of Christianity and politics, they also demanded from the government that church communities as such be protected from charges of heresy against National Socialism and instead recognized as caretakers of "the most fruitful element in German spiritual life."[63]

These Christian conservative supporters of the Third Reich understood Hitler's growing impatience with cultural division in Germany as the Führer began in 1936 to prepare the nation for hardships to come. Many Germans had been put back to work over the previous three years, largely in the arms industry, but the deficit spending that spurred job creation had also led to unsustainable government debt and decapitalized the production of consumer goods, creating shortages in food and other resources.[64] The government protected consumers by keeping costs of basic commodities low through price controls and quality reduction, but in April 1936 journalists in the foreign press speculated that Germany would be able to pay off its massive rearmament debt only through significant tax increases on its population.[65] State finances were further stretched with Hitler's announcement in July to commit the German air force to the fight against communism on the side of nationalists in Spain's civil war.

As is well known, Hitler decided in the late summer of 1936 to solve Germany's financial problems not by implementing traditional economic measures such as tax increases, which carried the risk of losing popular support for the government, but rather—fatefully—by preparing for a large-scale, imperial incursion into eastern Europe. The resources gained in lands conquered by the German military in Czechoslovakia and Poland and perhaps beyond would pay for Germany's current debt.[66] As theologians who had contacts in the regime knew, Hitler's decision had important bearing on the church issue. The new "Four-Year Plan" for war preparation, Hitler wrote in an internal memo to his ministers and generals, would depend first and foremost on the formation of "ideological solidarity" among the current generation of German youth, who would be expected to fight with hard commitment. Such unbreakability, he explained in the memo's very first paragraph, was not possible for peoples riven by conflicts over religion or worldview.[67]

Given the situation, Christian conservatives in or close to the Nazi Party made the case that a government committed to a uniform Christian faith was stronger and harder than one that severed the connection between church and state. Otto Koellreutter, a judge who had joined the party in 1933 and served as dean of Munich's law school, argued that the state's attachment to Christianity was what distinguished Germans and other Europeans from Bolsheviks, connecting them to their past and inspiring them to fight for the preservation of their lifestyle. The crucifix that adorned most courtrooms in Germany symbolized that connectedness. In his popular handbooks on constitutional and administrative law, used by many German law students in 1936, Koellreutter taught that the government was justified in purging the civil service of elements subversive to national solidarity. But he added that the bureaucracy, including the theological faculties and the judiciary, must retain a level of self-administration if Germany was to remain true to its Christian culture and avoid becoming like the communists. Reminding readers of Hitler's declaration on the eve of the Enabling Act, that the churches were the "most important factors in the maintenance of our national culture," Koellreutter campaigned against lawyers in the party who called for the total separation of church and state and the total control of the secular executive over the Christian conservative judiciary.[68]

Pushback was also apparent among Christian conservatives in Germany's state financial institutions, whose sphere of decision making was shrinking due to increasing government intervention in the economic realm. While they had never publicly criticized the government when their offices were purged of Jews during Hitler's "economic miracle" from 1933 to 1936, they did speak up when they perceived that Hitler's insistence on further deficit spending and increasing isolation from Western- and Atlantic-based trade might spell economic disaster for the country. Walter Eucken and Franz Böhm, two national economists at the universities of Freiburg and Jena, respectively, began developing a manifesto for the conservation of what they argued was an economic order of free trade based on Christian principles of freedom and European values of universal truth.[69] Their sentiment was shared by prominent German business leaders, many of whom wished to access consumer markets in the Western hemisphere, and by key figures in the state financial bureaucracy, including the president of the national bank Hjalmar Schacht and price commissioner Carl Gördeler.[70]

Christian conservatives in the military hierarchy also fought to preserve the institution of Christian chaplaincy in soldiers' units as they prepared the country for war. Both defense minister Werner von Blomberg, whom Hitler had promoted in 1936 to supreme commander of all armed forces, and Werner von Fritsch, supreme commander of the army, felt strongly that the military's Christian banner of the cross pattée must wave alongside, not be replaced by, the flag of the swastika: in other words, that officers and soldiers receive both training in National Socialist ideology and a sense of Christian mission. In his new role, Blomberg appointed two field bishops to supervise the chaplaincy, Franz Dohrmann (Protestant) and Franz Rarkowski (Catholic), both strong nationalists who were open to the idea of uniform, supraconfessional Christian services for soldiers.[71] When Nazi Party leader and air force commander Hermann Göring led volunteer units to fight in the Spanish Civil War but failed to organize an accompanying legion of chaplains, officials in the rest of the military spoke out, citing soldiers' wishes for spiritual comfort and inspiration in a fight to the death against Bolshevism.[72]

In sum, Christian conservatives who participated in all sectors of the Third Reich often pushed back against, and sometimes successfully thwarted, those in the Nazi Party who attempted to separate church and state. When a Nazi cultural minister in northern Germany issued a decree in early November 1936 to remove church or other religious symbols from all state buildings, mass protests, in which several high-ranking national party leaders joined, forced the regional politicians to revoke their order.[73] At the same time, Christian conservatives adopted ever more radical tactics when they sensed that Hitler was losing patience with the churches' failure to find a uniform voice. In December, Erich Seeberg— who had been told by Alfred Rosenberg that only war could bring Germans together—wrote a memorandum for Hitler's chief deputy reminding him of the value of Christian ethics to propaganda, security, and morale. The majority of church leaders in Germany could be counted on to eliminate Jewish influence from their ranks, he wrote, and they would be crucial for winning over allies in the German-speaking populations in Poland, the Baltics, and the Soviet Union in the event of war. But if the regime drove traditional religion "into a corner," he warned, the churches could become "reservoirs of opposition," leading to a "fissuring" of the people. "A Christianity that proclaims the moral teaching of Jesus and reveres the authentic image in Christ," Seeberg insisted, "may not be torn away from German being and German culture if one does not wish to provoke a religious crisis of incalculable consequences."[74]

THE FAILURE TO BUILD A UNIFORM STRUCTURE

With the turn of the new year, 1937, Goebbels's propaganda ministry had much to include in its museum exhibit in Berlin celebrating the achievements of the regime since Hitler asked the German people in January 1933 for "four years' time" to build national unity. The exhibit's catalog highlighted, of course, the truly remarkable fact that unemployment had dropped from over six million in 1933 to under two million in 1937, thanks to an aggressive, publicly funded economic modernization program. It emphasized the accomplishments of the engineers and workers who had connected towns and cities with more than a thousand kilometers of the world's first high-speed roads—with another fifteen hundred kilometers under construction—and built the world's first high-speed train line. It highlighted the fact that for the first time, a government had made it possible for millions of working Germans to afford vacations with their families, with the publicly funded "Strength Through Joy" initiative. It praised the spirit of generosity that had emerged among the population, with government welfare agencies having collected fourteen million tons in donations of goods for the needy.[75]

It was highly questionable, however, whether the country's political elites had achieved what Hitler announced at the Nuremberg Rally of 1934 was the primary goal for the younger generation: "that we are able to give to the German people a new idea, and to unify this people in this idea, and lead it to a new form of life." By the turn of 1937, the regime had made enrollment of all school-age children in party-run extracurricular youth programs mandatory, but less than ten percent of the total adult population could be counted on Nazi Party membership rolls. The achievement of consensus on the fundamental vision for Germany's future is difficult to ascertain, as in any society, but one key index suggested that Hitler had fallen short in his four years as chancellor and Reich leader. To the astonishment of many foreign visitors, the regime— despite being a dictatorship that decreed legislation in many other realms of policy—failed to develop a national school law that would bring together students of all backgrounds in a common type of educational institution.[76] The fact that most children still attended primary schools separated by Protestant and Catholic confession was so striking because Hitler had long described cultural unity as a priority and had established a national ministry of education expressly for that purpose.

There is evidence to suggest that this last failure considerably troubled Hitler, and that sometime before the turn of 1937 he decided that the leadership of the existing confessional churches would not be capable of building a state structure in uniformity with the party over the long term. In late November 1936, if the diary of Alfred Rosenberg can be trusted, Hitler told a group of top party officers that Christianity was "incapable of fighting Bolshevism; another worldview must do that." According to the diary of Joseph Goebbels, the Führer also hosted a "debate" on religion among his most trusted advisers on January 5, 1937. Goebbels paraphrased Hitler as saying that Christianity was "ripe for decline. It could take a while still, but it is coming."[77]

Hitler did not move immediately to sever all ties between church and state, but he did begin favoring the anti-Christian elements within the Nazi Party over the Christian conservative elements. In the presence of other government ministers, Hitler ridiculed the minister of church affairs, Hanns Kerrl, when Kerrl suggested that the party had been more popular in 1933 than it was in 1937 and that it was crucial to conserve Christianity in the state structure in order to rebuild mass support.[78] Hitler delegated increasing power to men such as SS leader Heinrich Himmler, who advocated the privatization of Christianity; chief of labor policy under the Four-Year Plan Fritz Sauckel, who dismissed the idea of a uniform German church as a pipe dream; and chief secretary in the office of the deputy führer Martin Bormann, whose anticlerical tracts were suppressed by the regime in years past.[79] Bishop George Bell of England, who by this point was well acquainted with the German church crisis, recorded in his notes in mid-January 1937 that "two currents" existed simultaneously within the National Socialist state: "(1) Those who wished for a compromise between National Socialism and Christianity, (2) Those who wished to *ecraser* [sic] *l'infame*." In 1935, Bell wrote, "the first of these currents was still strong. Now there was no doubt that the second was much stronger."[80]

The shift in power dynamics within the Nazi-led state allowed anti-Christian educators in the party, such as Alfred Baeumler, to assert themselves in policy matters after the renewal of the Enabling Act in January 1937. Some regional governors began shutting down confessionally segregated primary schools, especially in Catholic regions, in favor of "community schools" that would dispense with religious education altogether.[81] The national education ministry sent German teachers to learn from American schools, where Christianity was legally separated from public instruction. On February 10, 1937, Baeumler delivered an address in the Reichstag on behalf of the League of National Socialist Teachers, published under the title "The German School in the Age of Total Mobilization," in which he cited the Four-Year Plan as the impetus for finally passing a national school law. He and Hitler's deputy Rudolf Hess pushed for the adoption of a Waldorf School model, which would include instruction in "spirituality" without actual Christianity.[82]

On January 30, 1937, Hitler required all appointments to the civil service in the future to be based on party membership and approved ultimately by the office led by Bormann. There were some Christian conservatives, including one government minister, who as a result of this development publicly criticized the direction of the regime and lost their jobs because of it.[83] But most did not and continued to advance their vision, within the changed circumstances, of a Third Reich that preserved its connection to Christianity. Ernst Benz, for example, was allowed to join the party in May 1937, despite Bormann's ban on theologians from future membership, after writing an essay presenting Friedrich Nietzsche not as anti-Christian but as a destroyer of existing confessional church structures and prophet of an "evangelical order": a new Christian faith that could inspire young people to defend themselves against threats instead of martyring themselves in "Jesuanic" yearning for a world where lion lies down with lamb.[84] Also in May, the senior chaplain of the German army successfully proposed guidelines for a new type of supraconfessional, uniform Christian service for soldiers. Confessional division was a "grave liability and impairment" for the military units, he wrote.[85]

It is extremely difficult, given the nature of the Nazi dictatorship and the lack of reliable documentary sources, to measure the dynamics between revolutionary and conservative forces within the broader German population. However, as we have seen in this chapter, inside the Nazi Party itself the year 1937 was decisive in Hitler's decision to move toward the separation of Christianity from the German state. That decision was not a foregone conclusion or a revelation of Hitler's "true aim," as some Christian conservative authors would later claim as they sought to distance themselves from the regime and appeal to the international community. Rather, it was the product of a failed attempt, waged by many in good faith, to develop a German way of life that could incorporate the cultural traditions of both Protestantism and Christianity. The government's inability to align a majority of Christian church leaders to a race-centric worldview with a temporal leader as "supreme judge" was only one outward manifestation of a more general problem. In the coming years, as Hitler took supreme command of the armed forces and launched a war ahead of the timeline suggested by his top generals, conservatives would have to weigh their loyalty and duty to political authority against their own visions for the German future. They would have to decide whether to risk their own safety and join forces with other groups that they had tacitly or actively allowed to be persecuted, such as Social Democrats, internationalists, and Jews.

PART TWO OF THIS BOOK, which attempts to chart the creation of post-Nazi Germany, focuses on the forging of partnerships rather than on the effects of conflict. It proceeds from two arguments. The first is that the Germans who built the Federal Republic out of the ashes of Nazism did so not only with economic capital, provided by the United States and their own hard work, but also with cultural capital, derived from their common commitment to the value of reconciliation, forgiveness, and partnership. The second argument is that this political culture of partnership did not emerge spontaneously in 1945, but rather formed piecemeal in the years after 1937 among German leaders who came to oppose the Nazi government either in exile abroad or within the borders of the Reich. Whereas Part One traced successive failed attempts to unify a divided nation, Part Two examines the beginnings of successful partnerships between conflicting interest groups. These emergent "blocs" or "common fronts," as they were often called, were more responsible for the construction of a stable liberal-democratic republic in Germany than any foreign country could ever be.

The story of Germany's transformation from a site of conflict and war into one of partnership and peace is not dramatic in the same way as the tragedy of the Weimar Republic's collapse and the rise of Hitler. A seasoned scholar once remarked to me that modern German history loses

its appeal once the element of "evil" disappears with the Allies' neutraliza-
tion of the Nazis in 1945. This book speaks against that view. It is true that
postwar Germany, at least the non-communist "West Germany" that
formed the basis of today's Federal Republic, lost the sense of danger and
volatility it once had—a welcome transition for the majority of the country's inhabitants, if not the stuff of Hollywood. Konrad Adenauer, the
chancellor of the Federal Republic for its first full fourteen years of existence, was no Brüning, Papen, Schleicher, or Hitler. But postwar Germany
did not become a nation like any other. On the contrary, it became both
the economic engine of Europe and the very emblem of post-conflict
reconstruction, held up by the Western powers as a model for all divided
nations to emulate. To understand Germany's dramatic transformation is
thus to gain insight not only into the beginnings of this one country, but
also into the difficult work of nation building in general.

Because the planning of post-Nazi Germany began years before the
Nazi period was over, two remarks about Nazi-era source materials are
necessary. First, largely because of censorship and fear, the first records in
Germany of common fronts against Nazism, such as those between
socialists and liberals or between Protestants and Catholics, do not necessarily reflect the actual timing of the beginnings of their cooperation. If
one looked only at published material from inside the borders of Germany
itself, one might conclude that postwar partnerships between proponents
of mutually opposing standpoints formed spontaneously only after
Hitler's downfall. For that reason, it is necessary also to look at sources
published by German authors in emigration between 1937 and 1945.
These émigrés often maintained contacts in Nazi Germany but could
write openly in exile, whereas their compatriots who stayed could not.

Second, the partnerships responsible for the creation of post-Nazi
Germany did not form all at once. That is because the National Socialist
regime did not threaten all of Germany's interest groups at once—a fact
memorialized in the serial structure of Martin Niemöller's oft-quoted,
and oft-falsified, statement about the Nazis: "first" they came for the
communists, "then" the trade unionists, "then" the Social Democrats,
"then" the Jews, "then" (in some versions) the Catholics, until finally
"there was no one left" to protest when they came for him, a Protestant
conservative.[1] Partnerships formed between those groups not because
they shared common values, but because they felt their existence

threatened. As the anthropologist Gregory Bateson wrote in the 1930s, "the lion will lie down with the lamb if only it rain hard enough."[2] Indeed, it was only after a majority of Germans came to perceive their material interests as more endangered by the Nazi regime than protected by it—not until midway through the Second World War, at the earliest—that the people featured in this book could imagine the formation of a general consensus for the shape of a future Germany.

No decisive influence can be attributed to these particular men in the creation of post-Nazi Germany. Although they ended up holding positions of power in the Federal Republic—one became a judge on the country's highest court, another held the ear of the chancellor, and another oversaw the creation of several major think tanks—they were not "founding fathers" in the sense that George Washington and Alexander Hamilton were in America. Their lives were more humble. But they did perform important work in reconceptualizing the way Germans should relate to one another in the post-Nazi world. They spent time providing rationales, elaborating tortured proofs, and theorizing the natural legitimacy of partnerships between groups that had often been sworn enemies in the very recent past. While they were not political leaders themselves, their work allows us to see the difficult labor of building consensus in a divided nation.[3]

It is sometimes claimed that the Federal Republic's "democratic miracle" after 1945 was in large part the result of lessons that German elites learned from the United States or other Western countries, either directly from the teachings of the postwar occupiers or indirectly from transatlantic mediators, Germans who traveled abroad and returned with new ideas about how to structure a stable liberal democracy.[4] The five chapters of Part Two include stories of Germans who spent time during and after the war outside Germany, in the United States, the United Kingdom, Switzerland, the Netherlands, and Sweden. Although these stories show that Germans established many contacts and networks with elites in those host countries, they do not reveal the transfer of concepts or practices necessary for a democratic reconstruction. What was decisive in the postwar period was not the importation of foreign ideals, but rather the reconciliation of German ideals that had long been regarded as mutually opposing.

Embracing reconciliation between previously warring groups, Germans forged consensus on the basic constitutional, economic, educational, and cultural questions that had been so divisive in their first liberal democracy. As Sebastian Ullrich has shown, it was also a constitutive part of West Germany's political culture to worry about the reemergence of the "partisan bickering" (*Parteiengezäck*) characteristic of the Weimar Republic.[5] However, the overcoming of old conflicts in Germany did not signal what the Western advocates of modernization theory called "development" or "political maturation," marked by a disappearance of dogmatic and uncompromising belief systems often known as "ideologies." It was instead the beginning of a new dominant ideology, equally dogmatic and uncompromising as the socialisms and liberalisms of nineteenth-century Europe: the ideology of partnership.

What made partnership at first unrecognizable as ideology was that its adherents could claim to have renounced ideologies. After 1945, the evils of Nazism cast a pall over all "isms." By militantly promoting the values of reconciliation, cooperation, and compromise, the founders of post-Nazi Germany could reject as "ideological" any and all people who were unwilling to reconcile, cooperate, and compromise with them. They could dismiss as unserious and politically immature those groups whose leaders sought to achieve their vision through conflict and power politics. Western people, they claimed already in the 1950s, had exhausted that type of juvenile energy and grown past what several sociologists were calling the "age of ideology."[6] This claim often sounded avuncular and moralistic, and it would eventually face pushback from the German student generation of the 1960s. For even as it sought heroically to achieve political stability in Germany through partnership, the founding generation of the Federal Republic also laid itself open to the critique that it had signed away key ideals of the old struggles.

CHAPTER SIX

The Creation of Constitutional Consensus

"The re-education of a defeated nation seems to me to have a chance
of changing the minds and spirits of a people only if it is carried out
by the vanquished themselves."

Gerhard Leibholz, written from England, 1944

Several years after returning to Germany in the wake of the Second World
War, Ernst Fraenkel and Gerhard Leibholz exchanged a series of letters on
the fate of their homeland and the unlikely trajectories of their careers.
The lawyer Fraenkel, a lifelong advocate for workers' rights, had become
one of post-Nazi Germany's preeminent political scholars and Social
Democratic theorists. He taught at a new university founded in the
western sector of the country's old capital, Berlin, which, like the
European continent as a whole, had been occupied by foreign militaries
and divided into two sides—one forming part of "West Germany," the
other "East Germany"—since he last lived there in 1938. Leibholz, once a
wunderkind in the German judiciary, was now serving as the leading
voice on West Germany's new supreme judicial body, the Federal
Constitutional Court.[1] Anyone familiar with the ferocious battles that
used to be waged between the Social Democratic Party and the judges of
the Weimar Republic would have been struck by the fact that these erstwhile adversaries now called themselves partners. They once stood on
opposing sides of an acrimonious conflict that threw the legitimacy of the
old liberal democracy into question. Now they wrote to each other
amicably about their "common work" in its reconstruction.[2]

The two men must have realized that their trajectory from conflict to
partnership was representative of a much larger transformation in the

liberal democracies of Europe. Political leaders across the western part of the continent, with Germans in the lead, were reconsidering their old conceptions of democracy. Whereas most self-described democrats in the first half of the twentieth century imagined "rule by the people" to mean the legislative supremacy of popularly elected representatives in parliament, more and more embraced the idea that the power of unelected judges to overrule the legislature was a fundamental aspect of true democracy. It had been socialists such as Fraenkel, leaders in Germany's largest political party before the meteoric rise of the Nazis, who had led the fight against judicial review in the 1920s, arguing that judges would use the power to protect their class interest and strike down laws detrimental to business. After the war, Fraenkel and many other leading socialists suddenly supported it.[3] Their consensus with the German judiciary enabled a majority of delegates at the Federal Republic's constitutional convention of 1948 to create the first constitutional court in modern German history. The historian Jan-Werner Müller, writing about the "settlement" of one of European democracy's most contested conflicts, called the innovation of the constitutional court "one of the most important in twentieth-century Europe as a whole."[4]

Because the United States was one of the world powers that occupied the country after the German military's surrender in 1945, and the only one that arrived with a tradition of a Supreme Court, political scientists have often misconstrued the constitutional consensus of post-Nazi Germany as a product of American influence.[5] German sources reveal a different story. As we saw in Chapter 1, Germans were acquainted with the idea of judicial supremacy already in the 1920s: they knew it as a debate that divided society along class lines and caused a constitutional crisis in the Weimar Republic. Evidence suggests that German socialists, forced underground by the Nazi government, forged consensus with the country's liberal judiciary on this issue before the Western occupation as part of an effort to heal rifts and create common cause between workers and the property-owning class.

This is not to say that the role of the Western world powers that eventually occupied Germany were unimportant in this story. In the United States and the United Kingdom, especially, Germans who fled the Nazi racial state in temporary exile found well-funded institutions and networks of concerned people willing to help them in their efforts to bridge the divide between socialism and liberalism. These helpful hosts, men such as Reinhold Niebuhr and James Luther Adams in the U.S. and William Temple and George Bell in the U.K., were trying to build the same bridge in their own societies, which they perceived were riven by class warfare just as in Germany and thus also in danger of a home-grown fascist movement. After the Western Allies helped the Soviet Union to defeat Hitler's military and occupied the western side of the Reich in 1945, German socialists and liberals in American and British emigration leveraged the networks they had established since 1937 to support a new vision for the constitution of a liberal democracy in Germany.

The following pages also shed light on how the constitutional consensus enabled partnership between the two largest political parties in Western-occupied Germany: the rebranded Social Democratic Party of Germany (SPD) and the new Christian Democratic Union (CDU), which together received the vast majority of votes in the elections for a constitutional convention in Bonn. Despite their bitter differences on questions of economic and cultural policy, the leaders of these two parties were in near unanimous agreement that the will of the people as represented in a democratic parliament should not be sovereign, and that an unelected, elite judiciary should be able to review and strike down legislation whenever found to be unconstitutional. The agreement distinguished them decisively from their counterparts in the Soviet-occupied zone, who were holding a rival constitutional convention for the future German state in 1948. The leaders of the Socialist Unity Party there were arguing steadfastly against a constitutional court with judicial review, claiming continuity with a Weimar-era Marxist tradition they claimed Western socialists had traitorously abandoned.

A TURNING POINT FOR SOCIAL DEMOCRATS

The contrast between the earlier and later work of the socialist thinker Ernst Fraenkel has accurately been described by historians of the left as emblematic of the transformation of socialism in Western Europe from a revolutionary class-based workers' movement into a left-of-center political orientation.[6] Indeed, socialists like him from Germany—the birthplace of the movement, its international headquarters, and the place Karl Marx himself had believed the revolution would begin—ended up forming the avant-garde of the left's midcentury march toward centrism.[7]

They renounced positions associated with the movement's original Marxist ideology and instead embraced what the historian Erich Matthias described as "liberal" tactics of national statecraft.[8] Scholars have often noted this transition, but they rarely offer explanations for how and why it took place beyond the pressures of the Cold War.

Hitler's government isolated Germany's socialists, driving them underground or into emigration and forcing them to make difficult decisions about the future of the workers' movement. In the first months after the Enabling Act in 1933, Nazi Party security forces raided labor union offices, tarred SPD leaders as Marxist traitors to the nation, banned all their affiliated organizations, and confiscated their property. And yet several years into the new regime, the SPD leadership in exile had no coherent strategy for the future as they smuggled anti-Nazi propaganda back into Germany from neighboring Czechoslovakia and France. The only decision it had made by the mid-1930s was a negative one: the members of the SPD executive committee, convening in Prague, rejected efforts by the Comintern in Moscow to facilitate a "united front of workers' parties" against fascism. In fact, the executive committee went so far as to expel from the party any groups that pressed for cooperation with Communists. The decision frustrated the also-exiled leaders of the Communist Party of Germany (KPD), such as Walter Ulbricht, who had hoped that the two groups could put aside their historic differences in the face of the Nazi threat.[9]

Fraenkel, who remained in Berlin to serve as legal defense counsel for political opponents of the Nazi-led government but wrote under a pseudonym for the Social Democratic press in exile, approached the question of strategy from his perspective within Germany and inside the courtrooms.[10] While he supported the Marxist interpretation that property owners in Germany had allied with fascists to protect a capitalist system in crisis, he also observed in 1936 that Hitler's regime was beginning to work against and repress elite civil servants in the German judiciary and the state financial offices. Around the time that the government was cracking down on Christian civil servants who refused to participate in the pacification of the churches, Fraenkel wrote an article for a German-language socialist journal that was published in France but smuggled into Germany. He made the case to his fellow socialists that the goal of underground work should not be to stage a coup, which was unrealistic at the moment given their meager resources, but rather to get arrested, appear in court, and "demonstrate" the unjustness of the current administration.[11] Convincing the judiciary of the need to partner with them against Hitler, Fraenkel suggested, was the best hope Social Democrats had.

In early 1937, as the tensions between the Nazi Party elites and the high civil service became especially apparent, Fraenkel wrote another series of articles for a socialist audience explaining the inner workings of Nazi Germany, which he labeled a "dual state." He documented how the Nazi Party's security organization, the SS, led by Heinrich Himmler, often sent detained defendants to concentration camps even though they had been officially exonerated by judges. He explained how Nazi-led government agencies were arbitrarily dispossessing legally recognized claims. In general, he argued, Hitler maintained a nominally independent judiciary even as he overrode judicial decisions whenever he pleased. Such a "dual" system, Fraenkel believed, served an economic function for Germany's large business interests: it lubricated the flow of capital through the mostly predictable enforcement of laws, while at the same time creating fictive enemies—the so-called "Jewish threat"—that allowed the administration to intervene at any point to suppress class conflict.[12] Fraenkel made clear in his reports that many of Germany's judges, the longtime defenders of liberal freedoms, were slowly becoming embittered with the regime.

An important aspect of Fraenkel's career in the resistance that has largely escaped the attention of his many interpreters is the collaborative relationship he developed with a slightly younger lawyer named Martin Gauger, who was defending Christian civil servants accused of political crimes in the same court building where Fraenkel defended socialists and communists. Gauger, age thirty, grew up in a strict Lutheran conservative and antisemitic milieu in a small city in the Rhineland—very different from Fraenkel's secular Jewish upbringing around the labor movement in nearby cosmopolitan Cologne. As a student at the University of Breslau in the late Weimar years, Gauger was inspired by the labor camp ideal that promised to bring together young Germans of different classes and political orientations to work in national service.[13] When Hitler declared himself Führer and demanded an oath from civil servants recognizing him as "supreme judge," Gauger resigned his job as public prosecutor and began work in Berlin as a private lawyer to defend the Confessing

Church in its struggle against the German Christians, and then in 1936 to provide legal counsel to the Lutheran wing of the Confessing Church (the so-called Luther Council). The fact that Fraenkel later remembered having long private conversations on theological and legal themes with his new colleague in 1936 and 1937 demands explanation, since Fraenkel's writings up to that point evinced no thoughts on Christianity except for negative reactions to the Protestantism of the German judiciary.[14]

The two men no doubt discussed the divisions among Germany's Protestant churches, the topic of a small book by Gauger that had been published and promptly banned by the national government in 1936. In that book, Gauger criticized the government's attempts to coerce Germany's Christian communities into forming one uniform German Evangelical Church (DEK). The ministry for church affairs and its advisers (such as Ernst Benz) used proof texts from Martin Luther to argue that the Christian churches of Germany should be purely "spiritual" as opposed to "confessing": that members should renounce all confessions to the dogmas that had separated the different denominations of Christianity for hundreds of years. That argument was a distortion of Luther's message, Gauger wrote, because every church needed a creed according to which congregants could legitimately replace "unnatural" legal authority in the church—for example, in order to dismiss a racist pastor if they believed that racial discrimination violated their confession. He did note, however, that the traditions of the Reformed and Calvinist churches (such as the Geneva Confession or the Heidelberg Catechism), let alone the Catholic Church (which had canon law), were clearer than the Augsburg Confession of the Lutheran churches in defining the natural boundaries of authority.[15]

The long manuscript on Nazi Germany that Fraenkel wrote surreptitiously over the course of 1937 and early 1938 in the hopes of having it published abroad and smuggled back into Germany, titled *The Dual State*, bore a strong imprint of his conversations with Gauger. Most notably, the text, which was intended at least primarily for a socialist audience, included a long excursus on Western Christianity as well as a fairly shocking call for a commitment to "natural law" as the basis of anti-Nazi resistance. As an alternative to the Comintern's "united front of workers' parties," Fraenkel suggested instead a "united front of natural law advocates." This unusual and surprising formulation begged for interpretation. In the history of modern socialism, from its founders Karl Marx and Friedrich Engels to its most recent leadership, the concept of natural law had been anathema: an idea of the liberal bourgeoisie. As Fraenkel himself noted, natural law theories were historically associated with justifications for private property from Thomas Aquinas to John Locke.[16] Most recently, liberal jurists such as Gerhard Leibholz had used a natural law argument to justify their assertion of the judicial review of legislation, an institution against which Social Democrats, including Fraenkel, had strenuously fought.

Fraenkel's extended engagement with Christian history and the tradition of natural law thinking can only be explained as an attempt to provide rationale for a partnership between socialists and the liberal judiciary in Germany by pointing to their shared heritage. Belief in natural law, he attempted to demonstrate, was a central characteristic of the European lineage: it emerged in antiquity with a group of Greek philosophers known as the Stoics, who developed a concept of absolute values of moral justice based on natural reason, to which all humans had access. The early Christians adopted that tradition, claiming that God had willed certain natural, absolute values that were valid on earth for all people and could not be legitimately violated. Those early Christian teachings, Fraenkel noted, still survived in Germany among Catholics, Jehovah's Witnesses, and other Christian groups whose traditions taught them to resist state authority when they viewed divine laws as having been violated. Likely drawing from his conversations with Gauger, and certainly from the arguments of the theologian Ernst Troeltsch, Fraenkel mourned the fact that Lutheran church leaders in Germany had fatefully departed from the Stoic and natural law traditions, arguing that the state alone was empowered by God to legislate and demand obedience from its constituents.[17]

In *The Dual State,* Fraenkel also described a second strain of natural law thinking, one that he claimed appeared during the European Enlightenment and formed the worldview of the emerging European bourgeoisie. This "secularized" concept of natural law, elaborated by liberal legal philosophers such as Hugo Grotius, Johannes Thomasius, and John Locke, was separate but "genetically" related to the Christian version. Its supporters posited universal values of natural law, independent of Christian faith, which must not be violated by any state if that state was to be considered legitimate. A careful reader of Max Weber, Fraenkel noted the tendency of judges in modern liberal societies such as the United States and Great Britain to reduce natural law to a single-minded protection of private property at the expense of the common welfare. Nevertheless, he wrote, the modern liberal tradition of natural law was an ethical concept rooted, alongside Christianity, in the European heritage of absolute values.[18]

The most striking part of Fraenkel's narrative for our purposes was his argument that socialism, too, belonged to the European heritage of natural law thinking. Again citing Troeltsch, Fraenkel described socialism as the "heir" to those ancient Christian sects that promoted radical social equality based on Jesus's Sermon on the Mount. He even argued that Karl Marx and Friedrich Engels, who famously rejected natural law as a theoretical basis for the workers' movement, shared a hope for a redemptive age when a universal natural law of justice would reign, a hope he traced back to an ethics related to Christianity. What Marx and Engels found intolerable, Fraenkel tried to explain with tortured logic, was the attempt to implement an order based on natural law prematurely, before the proper economic relations obtained. "If this interpretation of Marx's thought is correct," he concluded, "there is nothing prohibiting the integration of Marxists into the united front of natural law advocates."[19] Fraenkel's manuscript suggested that an alliance of socialists and liberals against the Nazis, who explicitly sought to destroy the universalistic natural law tradition of Europe and replace it with a kind of tribal German law, was more than just politically expedient; it was also historically and philosophically justified.

Fraenkel's *The Dual State,* as one fellow German socialist noted in a review after the book was published, was also an elaborate argument to justify the institution of constitutional judicial review.[20] The use of natural law theory to call for the judicial review of state laws was a recognizable genre—for example, *The Eternal Return of Natural Law* (1936), written in emigration by the German lawyer Heinrich Rommen from a Catholic perspective—but not for a socialist.[21] Fraenkel argued that the practical goal of natural law advocates was to "subordinate the state" to a system of absolute values, which necessarily implied a body empowered with the capability of enforcing it. Fraenkel even praised the ideas of the famously conservative Anglo-Irish philosopher Edmund Burke, who claimed the existence of a higher moral order beyond the will of both kings and even legislators. Such arguments marked a steep departure from a socialist theory that claimed nothing higher than the legitimate will of the people. If Marxists refused to subordinate the state to such a higher order, Fraenkel warned readers in conclusion, they would necessarily follow the path of fascism, which he defined as "rule by will."[22]

Fraenkel had embraced both a "united front" with liberals and the idea of judicial supremacy before having been forced out of Germany. It is therefore not surprising that when he and his wife Hannah Pickel reluctantly fled their homeland by ship in autumn 1938 after hearing that the Nazi Party leadership in Berlin had sanctioned the disbarring and arrest of private doctors and lawyers defined as Jewish, which he was, he was eager to get to the United States and begin studying its judicial system.[23] The couple arrived in New York that November, virtually penniless after the German government drained their bank accounts.

The arrival of Fraenkel and his wife in the United States coincided with a transitional time in the history of the relationship between the American federal legislature and the highest judicial organ, the Supreme Court. At the time, the popularity of social legislation introduced by the most popular president in American history, Franklin D. Roosevelt, was overwhelming a class-entrenched judiciary that had long struck down laws geared to protect working-class interests. But in 1937, after Roosevelt won the U.S. presidential election in a landslide and threatened to use his mandate to curb the independent authority of the court, the Supreme Court justices switched course, suddenly upholding the constitutionality of the social legislation pushed by the White House. American progressives who previously accused the court of using the Constitution's Fourteenth Amendment ("equal protection under the law") to protect oligarchy—and even called for a reduction of the court's powers— changed accordingly. Max Lerner, editor of the left-wing magazine *The Nation,* praised what he called the justices' "restraint" against their class-based tendency to block laws designed for the common welfare.[24]

Given that the anti-labor history of the American courts was a key piece of evidence German socialists used against the institution of judicial review in the Weimar Republic, Fraenkel could cite the new developments he observed in America to argue to his socialist comrades who remained in Germany that the empowerment of judges to subordinate the state did not necessarily result in the suppression of social legislation.[25] At the age of forty, Fraenkel signed up for courses at the University of Chicago Law School in the fall of 1939 with every intention of bringing knowledge of the American constitutional system back home after the fall of the Nazis, whenever that would be. Neither he nor anyone else knew that war in Europe would break out already in September, just before the beginning of his first semester. Fraenkel's final contribution to the German-language socialist press published in Paris, before war engulfed Europe, was a rave review of a book by Lerner, *It Is Later than You Think: The Need for a Militant Democracy* (1939), a defense of what Lerner later called the "uneasy partnership of capitalism and democracy" against a foe, fascism, "that would destroy the world of both."[26]

A TURNING POINT FOR THE GERMAN JUDICIARY

Judges in the U.S. courts were not the only ones reconsidering their practices. Back in Germany in the years directly after 1937, the complicity of jurists with Nazi laws concealed the fact that some of them had taken up a quietly oppositional—or at least what a leading historian of German law has called a "detached"—stance toward Hitler's regime, as Fraenkel predicted.[27] The leading lights of the German judiciary maintained an ambivalent relationship with the Nazi Party. Many admired its decisive action against communists and its apparent ability to "integrate" a divided population in ways that governments adhering to Weimar's liberal democratic constitution had seemed unable to do. At the same time, the liberal judiciary was also the group in Germany most invested in the conservation of individual freedoms such as property rights and religious liberty. Many, such as chief justice of the high court Erwin Bumke, were alarmed by the Nazi regime's flouting of equality before the law and due process.[28]

Germany's rising star of the judiciary in the Weimar years, Gerhard Leibholz, exemplified that ambivalence between attraction to and repulsion from fascism. Leibholz's Jewish ancestry had cost him his prestigious teaching job at the University of Göttingen, despite his devout Lutheran faith. But he continued to be fascinated by Benito Mussolini's non-racial version of fascism in Italy. The law school dean in Göttingen arranged for Leibholz to go on paid retirement, with a comfortable research stipend of ten thousand Reichsmarks a year, enough to keep his servants, take vacations with his wife Sabine and two daughters, and conduct research and publish on the Fascist Italian legal system.[29] He admired Mussolini's attempt to create a homogeneous "community of values." Like his interlocutors in the German legal establishment before 1933, Carl Schmitt and Rudolf Smend, Leibholz argued that only a population that agreed on fundamental values could succeed in sustaining a democracy. At the same time, Leibholz criticized what he called the Fascists' "totalitarian" claim to the sovereignty of the Party as opposed to God and the law, and their tendency to overrule the independent legal decisions of state judges.[30]

Leibholz used his free time in forced early retirement (he was in his mid-thirties) to reconceptualize the proper relationship between Christianity, politics, and the law. In early 1938, just months before Mussolini declared the adoption of antisemitic racial laws similar to those in Germany, Leibholz published an article in an Italian legal journal proposing a way to harness the integrating function of Fascism without sacrificing individual liberal freedoms. He argued that Fascist theorists had recognized a basic truth: that to achieve political solidarity in an age of mass democracy, people needed a common faith (or myth) that a rational commitment to "liberalism" in the abstract could simply not provide. But instead of building a myth of national political unity, Leibholz suggested, one would achieve a higher unifying effect by politicizing religion and formulating a common Christian political faith. The religious scriptures of Christianity, he pointed out, celebrated both commitment to the community and the freedom of the individual person. It was also a tradition to which nearly all Europeans claimed heritage, even if a great many had abandoned it or paid only lip service to it.[31]

Apparently appealing to socialists, Leibholz expressed regret over the loss of the judiciary's prestige in the eyes of the working-class masses and blamed it on judges' abandonment of the Christian social message. In the article, subsequently translated into English and other European languages, he blamed his judicial colleagues for creating a perception that the courts were handmaidens of an oligarchy. In fact, Leibholz wrote, the bourgeoisie as a whole, "the social stratum that carries the liberal idea," spoke too much of individual rights and not enough of social legislation based on the spirit of the Sermon on the Mount. As a result, populist leaders found resonance when they promised to curb the independence of a class-entrenched justice system. A perfect example, Leibholz claimed, was the fact that the justices of the U.S. Supreme Court gained a terrible reputation among the American working class in 1935 and 1936 for striking down the greater part of Franklin D. Roosevelt's social legislation (which Roosevelt sometimes described as Christian-inspired).[32]

With his argument for a politicized Christianity, Leibholz took sides on a question that divided the leaders of Germany's majority Lutheran churches. Was it the proper role of the Christian, *qua* Christian, to engage in political affairs, to speak against secular authorities, or to lobby for social policy? Many non-Lutheran Protestants outside Germany, especially those involved in the new World Council of Churches founded on the model of the League of Nations, were replying with a resounding yes. The Anglican bishop William Temple, one of the founders of the World Council, authored a pamphlet in 1937 titled *Christian Democracy,* in which he described the revelation of a "natural order" contained in Christian scripture as the basis for involvement in political affairs. The leading members of the Church of England in general were arguing that they must become more involved in state and international affairs if they were to remain relevant in an increasingly secular and bureaucratizing world.[33] But many Lutheran leaders in Germany argued that Christians should stay above politics. In the summer of 1937, Ernst Benz recommended to the German national ministry of church affairs to avoid sending a delegation to the world ecumenical conference in Oxford, as conference leaders planned to make a political statement condemning the Nazi government for its treatment of the Jews.[34]

Leibholz, whose parents were born Jewish, was married to the twin sister of Dietrich Bonhöffer, a young Lutheran pastor who was in close correspondence with leaders in the London-based world ecumenical movement. As a result, when the Leibholzes made the difficult decision to flee Germany in September 1938, they chose to reside in England, where they could remain close to the European continent and to their brother, who insisted on staying in Berlin.[35] Bishop George Bell, who had taken a special interest in Germany's church affairs and was now also a member of the House of Lords in Britain, arranged for Leibholz to receive an appointment at Christ Church College at Oxford University, where he would teach in 1939 on the Lutheran approach to law and politics. From there, after a brief period of internment as an enemy alien when war broke out that year, Leibholz wrote texts to be smuggled back into Germany, arguing that the politicization of Christianity was not a "Jewish" influence as supporters of the Third Reich claimed, but rather the essence of the New Testament.[36] For many Lutherans, that was a difficult argument to accept. Even his brother-in-law Bonhöffer, who was considering whether to join the anti-Nazi resistance, searchingly asked Leibholz in a letter in early 1940, "Do there exist principles of law in the creation which could be viewed as absolutely valid? Or is law bound to actual power?"[37]

Leibholz dedicated his work over the next two years, during and after the Battle of Britain, to answering Bonhöffer's question about Christian natural law. In the frequent articles he wrote for the *Christian News-Letter*, whose editorial board included T. S. Eliot, Leibholz praised the pledge of clergymen at a conference at Malvern College in January 1941 to take leadership in "ordering the new society" after the war, both inside and outside England, with talk of cooperation between Protestants and Catholics on the European continent and outlines for what a Christian "natural law" might look like when translated into economic policy. Some proposals at Malvern even included the communal ownership of the means of production, leading *Time* magazine to call the Church of England's new support of traditionally socialist platforms "little short of revolutionary."[38]

The momentous development of the early part of the war was not the particular policy platforms that came out of various meetings and conferences, however, but the general gathering of support among an entire range of church leaders and previously "secular" politicians and intellectuals for the prospect of a Christian postwar policy.[39] In January 1942, weeks after the United States joined the United Kingdom and the Soviet Union in the military alliance against Nazi Germany, Leibholz gave a series of lectures at Oxford titled "Christianity, Politics, and Power," meant also to be published and smuggled back into Germany. Leibholz argued that the Christian must transcend Luther's call to resist secular law only when it encroaches on freedom of conscience, and instead take an active guardianship over the modern political order in general, as Calvinists had long done and Catholics had attempted to do since the late nineteenth century.[40]

Thanks to his connection with Bonhöffer, who was now embedded as a spy in the German military intelligence agency and leaking information to English sources, Leibholz found out earlier than others about a change in the Nazi regime that increased the potential for resistance in Germany.[41] In early December 1941, a pastor in the Confessing Church got hold of an internal memorandum written back in June as Party members planned Operation Barbarossa, the devastating invasion of the Soviet Union. It was written by Martin Bormann, Hitler's new deputy, in response to a regional Party leader who wanted to revisit the idea of a unified German church in light of the difficult task ahead in the east and the need for morale. Bormann's strongly negative reply, circulated to all regional offices, included the definitive statements: "National Socialist and Christian conceptions are incompatible," the national church dream was "conclusively nullified," and "never again may room be made for the influence of the churches on the leadership of the people." By order of the Führer he also gave instructions to prohibit future financial assistance to all churches, including the most pro-Nazi Protestant groups.[42] The local Gestapo inspector who arrested the pastor in possession of the circulating document notified central security in Berlin of the likelihood that hostile foreign countries and Catholic sources had probably already obtained copies. He was correct. The memorandum represented vital intelligence because it suggested that the German conservative elites who had supported Hitler and legitimated his rule would be more amenable to resistance if they saw that their leader had definitely rejected their value system.[43]

A committed anticommunist since his youth, Leibholz worried that Germans, exhausted and demoralized, would fall into civil war once they began turning against Hitler, a situation ripe for Bolshevik exploitation if the British and Americans failed to actively manage a transition to stability. "A defeated Nazi-Germany can no longer stand between the East and the West," he wrote in October 1942, referring to what he considered conflicting Western and communist systems of principles and values. "A non-communist and anti-Nazi régime in a post-war Germany could only be established if such a government could get from the beginning the help of the Anglo-Saxon countries in the same way as a communist Germany would get the help of the Soviet Union."[44] Through George Bell, who took an active role in debating the future of British policy on postwar Germany in Parliament, Leibholz urged the body to recognize and materially support the Christian conservative resistance in the military and the high civil service. It would be disastrous for the prospect of "Western principles" in post-Nazi Germany, he told Bell, if Germans began believing that a majority of the British people agreed with Robert

Vansittart, the politician in the House of Lords who argued draconianly that German territory would have to be occupied and its people "re-educated" for at least a generation to cleanse them of their beastly and militaristic character.[45]

For Leibholz, it was crucial that the British and Americans helped build consensus among anti-Nazi, non-communist groups around the political idea of "Western Christianity," which entailed certain key constitutional principles everyone must accept. In an article published at the turn of 1943 in both Protestant ecumenical and Catholic journals, Leibholz argued that the idea consisted in a balance between the dual foundations of "justice" and "law." Justice, defended by the judiciary, must have the power to invalidate unjust or ungodly acts, such as the kind the Nazi Party had decreed over the past decade. Law, enacted by the legislature, must have the autonomy to represent the will of the people as long as it did not act against nature. In other words, judges would pledge to restrain themselves from striking down all but the most abominable of laws if legislators would grant them the right to judicial review, thus striking a "Christian" symmetry between community and individual liberty.[46] He referred to a comment made by Sir Frederick Pollock, the great jurist from England's tradition of parliamentary supremacy, to Oliver Wendell Holmes, the American Supreme Court theorist of restraint: that judges should have the right to "disregard" laws only when they were "clearly contrary to natural justice." In other words, a high court should have the right to invalidate laws, but only when there was unanimity among the judges on the morality involved.[47]

Germans on the home front had plenty of time to consider such propositions before the end of the war. After the defeat of the German Sixth Army in Stalingrad in February 1943, more than two years elapsed before the Allied militaries occupied German territory. That gave civilians ample opportunity to judge the lack of functionality in their current government, especially in its most basic duty to secure the life of its people. The reports published on the home front in early 1943—that tens of thousands of German young people had been captured by the Soviet military—were evidence that the government had led the country's most precious property, its young, into grave danger. As German civilians themselves came under attack through Western Allied blanket bombing after February 1944, evidence for the chaotic and dysfunctional nature of the government mounted: hence, the new tactic of British and American intelligence at this time, in coordination with subversives in the German military command, to broadcast the (probably untrue) rumor that Hitler, the head and soul of the government, was insane.[48] Whether or not civilians believed that propaganda, it is safe to say that the long period of physical endangerment would have inspired an increasing number among them to consider, if not actively pursue, a realignment of solidarities.

Observed from abroad, there were certain external indications of non-communist German groups coalescing in a common front against the Nazi regime. In a letter to George Bell in May 1944, Leibholz noted the shift in the way the German Social Democratic press in exile wrote about cooperation with Christians. He pointed out with pleasure that the Council for a Democratic Germany—a new organization based in New York whose leaders claimed to bring together the nation's exiled democratic forces "from the Catholic 'Center' to the most extreme left" to prepare for the cleansing of the Nazi spirit from German cultural institutions—was led by the Lutheran theologian Paul Tillich.[49] Leibholz likely did not know that at this very time, Ernst Fraenkel was helping translate Tillich's works into English in addition to working for the U.S. government in Washington to advise on the imminent military occupation.

From inside Germany itself, the most spectacular news was a failed attempt on July 20, 1944, code-named Operation Valkyrie, to overthrow Hitler's government. The coup had apparently been plotted for more than a year by a large network of Germans who together spanned nearly the entire political spectrum of the old Weimar Republic. Had the top-ranking military generals who led the coup attempt been successful, the men who would have taken over the reins of government would have been the former price commissioner and Christian conservative Carl Gördeler as chancellor, and the former union leader and socialist politician Wilhelm Leuschner as vice chancellor. In the event, Hitler ordered the execution of all the conspirators, including Leibholz's brother-in-law Dietrich von Bonhöffer, and the war dragged on for another year despite the inevitability of German defeat. Significantly, however, Operation Valkyrie appeared to prove that the leaders of former conflict groups were prepared to work together to found a new Germany. In October 1944, Leibholz told an English audience that a unified opposition movement in Germany now included "all the Western-minded people remaining in Germany, comprising Conservatives, Liberals, Socialists, Catholics, and adherents of the Confessional Church"—that is, all the major social milieus in Germany besides communists.[50]

WESTERN ALLIED OCCUPATION AND THE DRAFTING OF A NEW CONSTITUTION FOR GERMANY

In May 1945, the military leadership of the United States, the United Kingdom, liberated France, and the Soviet Union accepted the surrender of Alfred Jodl on behalf of the German armed forces and the German government. Hitler and Goebbels had committed suicide, leaving in command the navy general Karl Dönitz, who ordered the surrender. The parties signed the final act in the city of Reims, in a schoolhouse building the Western Allies had commandeered as headquarters, not far from the storied cathedral once used for the coronation of French kings. According to the instrument of surrender, Germans relinquished "unconditionally" to both the Western Allies and the Soviet Union "all forces on land, sea, and in the air who are at this date under German control." This meant that the German Reich ceased to be a sovereign state and was from that point forward occupied territory. Germans would regain sovereignty only when the occupying forces agreed on the terms of their freedom.

Having declared in the summer of 1945 no interest in annexing Germany or occupying it indefinitely, the four government powers, or Allied Control Council, decided to purge German territory of all Nazi elements and return a "denazified" people to self-administration as soon as possible. That required the authorities in the various American, British, French, and Soviet territorial zones to assemble lists of German elites who had not been "compromised" by too close an association with Nazism and could be considered trustworthy founders of a post-Nazi state. The occupation authorities quickly found, however, that there were insufficient numbers of completely uncompromised Germans capable of constituting and running an administrative structure for a population of more than sixty million. They therefore relied heavily on German jurists active in the Weimar Republic who had fled the Third Reich and returned after the war. Many of these returnees, people like Gerhard Leibholz and Ernst Fraenkel, took up high-ranking positions on the courts and in legal faculties, and some served on the drafting committees of the first German state constitutions.[51] But while authorities could ban from participation the allegedly most tainted legal minds of the Nazi era, such as Carl Schmitt and Otto Koellreutter, they could not do without old Weimar-era elites who had served the Hitler government in one way or another.[52]

Many in Germany feared that the restoration of older elites, now mostly in their fifties or sixties, would lead to the same constitutional conflicts that had divided them in the Weimar years. Diverging visions for a future reunified democratic state were already apparent as authorities in the different occupation zones began allowing the formation of political parties and elections for regional constitutional conventions. Theodor Heuss, who was sixty-two and taught the history of those conflicts in a university reopened in the American zone, gave a speech to communists in the Soviet-occupied zone in March 1946 insisting that it was impera-tive for the future of German democracy that one "see in the opponent also the partner."[53] But in the territories composing the "Western zones," at least, it became clear over the course of the following year that basic constitutional consensus existed among the politicians who emerged to found and lead the largest parties.

Socialist leaders in the Western zones demonstrated a major shift in their orientation and platform compared with the Weimar years on two key points. At the first interzonal convention of the re-formed SPD in June 1947, which took place in the American zone in the city of Nuremberg, the chairman of the party's committee for political and constitutional guidelines supported both partnership with Christian politicians and the implementation of a constitutional court, two causes of conflict in the 1920s. "Few great world-historical events have been able to raise the unifying factors [among Germans] over the dividing ones," declared Walter Menzel, the socialist lawyer who, like Ernst Fraenkel, had repre-sented Germans accused of political crimes during the Nazi years. Just as Fraenkel did in *The Dual State*, Menzel compared the Nazis to a non-Euro-pean ("Asiatic") force that had worked as an "adhesive agent" among Germans, convincing them of their common intellectual lineage as a people. Even though socialists in the SPD and self-declared political Christians in Germany still held conflicting views about the correct rela-tionship between church and state, he told the gathering, the "common denominator" that linked them genetically was the idea of "natural law" and commitment to universal "truth and justice." Menzel announced that the party would support a constitution in which power was given to

unelected judges to review national laws, as long as parliament maintained the power to appoint and recall them.[54]

The SPD's announcement was in large part a response to reported
developments in what had emerged as occupied Germany's other largest
party, the new Christian Democratic Union (CDU). In the small southwestern city of Ellwangen, also in the American zone, a group of
Protestant and Catholic lawyers and politicians had been convening since
March 1947 to draft constitutional guidelines for a future state from the
perspective of Germany's first ecumenical "Christian" political party.[55]
The most prominent jurist in the group, the Lutheran Protestant Walter
Strauss, explained the party's commitment to a powerful constitutional
court, an institution he along with most of the liberal judiciary had
supported since the Weimar years.[56] But in a major shift from the Weimar
years, Strauss and other Lutherans, like Leibholz before them, advocated
a mixing of church teachings and politics on the basis of "natural law."
They accepted the vision of the Ellwangen conference's chairman, the
Catholic lawyer Josef Beyerle, who insisted that every member of the new
CDU must "check, down to the details of every important decision, in
particular in the realm of legislation, what Christian doctrine says about it
and whether the planned rule is good or at least justifiable."[57]

The historic nature of the constitutional consensus was not lost
on participants in these events. The newly elected Catholic head of the
Bavarian government under American authority, Hans Ehard, remarked
after witnessing the SPD's shift in the summer of 1947: "What is playing
out here within Western socialism is one of the most remarkable
processes in the intellectual history of our time." He regarded it as a turn
away from a Marxist conception of the state. He even allowed himself to
hope, perhaps somewhat prematurely, that the new commitment of
Lutheran liberals in his party to Christian scripture as the basis of their
political positions could lead to legislative cooperation with the CDU and
the SPD on economic policy.[58]

In the Soviet zone of occupation, meanwhile, the socialist jurists who
were drafting their own constitutional proposals condemned the SPD's
shift as a betrayal to the promise of Marxist social democracy. Karl Polak,
a lawyer who returned from exile in the Soviet Union and became
the leading constitutional theorist of the Socialist Unity Party (SED)—the
product of a united front of workers' parties and the largest party in the

Soviet occupation zone—criticized socialist advocates of natural law such as Walter Menzel as having disastrously misunderstood the nature of Weimar's constitutional crisis. The problem with the Weimar constitution, he claimed in 1947, was not that parliamentarism allowed unchecked legislative power and the emergence of evil or "unnatural" laws. Instead, it was that the founders of Weimar created legal confusion when they enshrined both the sovereignty of the parliament and the unchecked independence of an ostensibly objective liberal judiciary. Repeating the arguments that Ernst Fraenkel and other socialists made in the 1920s, judges would block the progress toward economic democracy if allowed power to strike down social legislation.[59] Indeed, the leaders of the SED declared that their constitutional proposal for a future unified German democratic state was the heir to the original promise of Weimar's founders. In December 1947, the son of Weimar Germany's first president, Friedrich Ebert, Jr., announced at the opening of the SED's People's Congress for Unity and a Just Peace in East Berlin that the party would embrace the traditional German republican colors of red, yellow, and black.[60]

Along with disputes over federalism, the question of judicial review of parliamentary laws and judicial independence proved to be the constitutional issue that most divided German politicians in the Soviet zone from those in the western zones in early 1948, when the Four Powers expected Germans to elect representatives to constitute a sovereign state. For reasons that will become clearer in the following chapter, negotiations between the American and Soviet authorities over the future of Germany had broken down, and to the dismay of both occupation authorities and the majority of Germans, it appeared likely that two separate and opposing republics would emerge on the territory of the old Reich. That summer, the French government agreed to join the Americans and the British in endorsing a temporary German state composed of the three Western zones. The regional governments of the Western zones agreed that the members of the constitutional convention for a Federal Republic of Germany, officially to be called a Parliamentary Council (*Parlamenatrischer Rat*), would not be directly elected but rather appointed by the regional assemblies. When the convention opened in September, in the city of Bonn in the British zone, the overwhelming majority of the appointees came from the SPD and the CDU, with twenty-seven delegates apiece out of sixty-five voting members.[61]

The meetings of the Parliamentary Council, much like the separate meetings of the SPD and the CDU the year before, revealed a striking degree of consensus between the two parties on the questions that had so divided German political elites twenty years earlier. The consensus was particularly evident in the council's Committee for Questions of Basic Principle, a group responsible for drafting the preamble, the section on basic rights, and the section on the individual states' relationship to the federation. It was by far the most powerful committee at the council, convening for the first time at the beginning of September 1948, and then thirty-five further times before their work was done at the end of November.

The personal story of the chairman chosen for the Committee for Questions of Basic Principle reveals, in itself, the complicated makings of the postwar consensus. Hermann von Mangoldt, an expert on U.S. constitutional law and close colleague of Gerhard Leibholz, represented the changed orientation of the liberal judiciary over the course of the Nazi years.[62] In the 1930s, he was a member of Nazi Germany's main legal organization and endorsed the Nuremberg Laws, legislation that segregated Aryans and Jews. He regarded the laws as "unequal" but justified them as beneficial to society, just as he interpreted the Jim Crow laws of the American South. At the same time, after 1937, he used his scholarship on judicial review in the U.S. legal system to push back against Hitler's attack on judicial independence.[63] Untainted by official membership in the Nazi Party, Mangoldt became the leading constitutional theorist of the CDU. Ironically, his argument from the Nazi years against a dogmatic interpretation of equality before the law and his new embrace of natural law theory placed him in a perfect position to forge consensus with socialists.

The question debated at most length by the committee members, led by Mangoldt, was not whether a commitment to basic rights and social law derived from principles of natural law. There was near unanimity on that issue among SPD and CDU representatives. Mangoldt noted that the first plenary meetings of the Parliamentary Council at the beginning of September 1948 could be interpreted as a general call to go "back to natural law!" By that, he said, the council declared that "there are legal postulates prior to written law that, without being written, have a generally binding character."[64]

The debate revolved instead around whether natural law principles should be characterized in the Federal Republic's constitutional document as divine or secular. Would it invoke the idea of God? The CDU members on the committee made their case by referring to what they considered the timeless truth of Christianity, while SPD members made theirs by pointing to Germans' shared commitment to universal truth.[65] On November 9, the committee's nineteenth meeting, Mangoldt told his colleagues that they were under heavy pressure from both the CDU faction of the council and much of the West German public to include a phrase in the preamble declaring "trust in God," as some but not all of the post-Nazi regional state constitutions did.[66] The ranking SPD representative rebutted that his faction harbored concerns about such language and proposed instead, " 'In the consciousness that every state must be carried by moral forces,' or something similar." One committee member suggested combining the two into "Out of trust in God and the moral forces of the German people." At that point, future German president Theodor Heuss, who represented neither party, jested that people would assume the first part of the clause was the contribution from the CDU and the second from the SPD.[67]

Heuss was only half joking, because the decision was serious: it could mean the difference between a document born of compromise—the reputation of the Weimar constitution—and one born of consensus. On November 15, Leibholz, who had returned from England to the British-occupied zone of Germany, made a passionate plea to the Parliamentary Council in favor of the CDU-supported *invocatio Dei*. The men and women in Bonn, he wrote, must be made aware of what he called the ideological "either/or" choice before them: to invoke the Christian God was not only to supplant the traditional democratic idea of popular sovereignty with one limited by a pre-state authority; it was also to provide the common element, or "enzyme," for reconciliation between the legislature and the judiciary. "It is precisely the historical service of the socialist (not Communist) democratic workers' movement to have undertaken the attempt to secure a political existence for people in which freedom and equality are bound together in a way where liberty finds its limits in equality, and equality does not exclude political liberty in the political and economic realm," he wrote. "The big question is only whether this attempt at a synthesis of freedom and equality is possible at all on a purely secular basis." To declare the synthesis divine in a constitutional document would be a way to ensure that courts weighed social legislation coming out of parliament not only against negative liberties, but also against the definition of individuals as divine creatures deserving of social welfare.[68]

We will never know if it was Leibholz's argument that made the difference, but the following day, November 16, after Mangoldt begged them to "bring the formulation to an end," the members of the Committee for Questions of Basic Principles voted to take up the invocation of God in the preamble. Socialist representatives actually outnumbered their Christian counterparts on the committee that day.[69] Aside from a few minor alterations, the language developed from their proposal would be the final language ratified the following year by the constituent states of the Federal Republic:

PREAMBLE
Conscious of its responsibility before God and man, . . . the
German people, in the exercise of their constituent power, has
adopted this Basic Law. [. . .]

BASIC RIGHTS
Article 1
(1) Human dignity shall be inviolable. To respect and protect it
is the holy duty of all state authority.
(2) The German people therefore confess themselves to
inviolable and inalienable human rights as the foundation of
every human community, of peace, and of justice in the world.
(3) The following basic rights bind the legislature, executive,
and judiciary as directly applicable law.[70]

After a list of eighteen individual liberties included under "basic rights," a commitment to social legislation in the abstract followed:

THE FEDERATION AND THE STATES
Art. 20 (1) The Federal Republic of Germany is a democratic
and social federal state.

The most influential committee of Germans at the Parliamentary Council thus reached consensus on basic principles before the three Western military governments issued a memorandum on November 22 with their requirements for a constitution. The German representatives had actually gone well beyond what the occupation authorities required, which consisted mainly in a federal structure and an independent judiciary capable of reviewing administrative acts and conflicts between the federation and states. The memorandum did not include a requirement for judicial review of legislation or a constitutional court.

Furthermore, the system of judicial review that the members of the Parliamentary Council decided to put in place was not modeled after the United States. In the new Federal Republic, only a single Constitutional Court, not lower federal courts, would be able to review federal legislation. Only a chancellor, the federal cabinet, a state cabinet, or one-third of federal parliament members could request the Constitutional Court to review it.[71] Rudolf Katz, a socialist who returned to Western-occupied Germany from American emigration in the summer of 1946 and would soon be appointed as a judge on the new Constitutional Court along with Leibholz, noted that the founders of the Federal Republic did indeed adopt a "principle"—natural law—that emerged as an institution first in the United States. But the system as instituted in Germany was "entirely 'un-American,' " he wrote.[72]

Some have claimed that this institution designed by the Parliamentary Council in 1948, the Constitutional Court, was the difference between the stability of Germany's second liberal democracy and the instability of its first. Donald Kommers, an American scholar of postwar German jurisprudence, has called it "the guardian of democracy" in post-Nazi Germany, and indeed has spoken of the benefit of instituting constitutional judicial review in other fragile, conflict-ridden democracies.[73] One might also consider the possibility, however, that it was not the institution of judicial review itself, but rather the ideological consensus that enabled its emergence, that provided the foundation for a stable liberal democratic structure in Germany.

CHAPTER SEVEN

Christian Economics?

WHILE THE LEGAL EXPERTS WERE BUSY IN Bonn designing a constitutional document for the new Federal Republic, Germans living in the Western occupation zones remained more concerned with the economic situation. A case can be made that the German population as a whole was suffering more in 1948 than in even the worst years of depression before the rise of Hitler. Mass unemployment was not as extreme as it had once been—hovering around ten percent as opposed to almost thirty percent in 1933—but the majority of Germans could be described as working poor. Two economists writing for an American academic journal reported that, even among those who were employed, people living in cities often found it necessary to travel to nearby farm areas to gather beechnuts in the forests and scavenge for stray leftover crops in already harvested fields, cutting tobacco with razor blades and stuffing their own makeshift cigarettes for barter. In a survey overseen by U.S. authorities in their zone of occupation, fifty-nine percent of respondents reported having "no means of livelihood."[1]

The spike in insecurity in 1948 was a shock wave of the controversial economic reforms implemented in June of that year under the auspices of the Economic Council of the Unified Economic Territory (*Wirtschaftsrat des Vereinigten Wirtschaftsgebietes*), a legislative body that American and British military authorities had created the previous year to begin returning autonomy to Germans over public policy. As part of efforts to rebuild industry and reintegrate it into the world network of trade, the council oversaw the introduction of a new currency, the Deutsche Mark, and abruptly banned price ceilings on almost all consumer goods, ending a system where the government kept prices for basic necessities low. The results of the reforms were predictable. First, the announcement of the reforms infuriated the Soviet zone's regional governments, which were not involved in the deal and stood to be adversely affected if they did not cut off interzonal trade. Second, within the Western zones, rapid deregulation caused the cost of consumer goods to skyrocket, leading to heavy profits for business owners, who then reinvested and increased production, but not to corresponding increases in the wages of ordinary workers.[2]

Popular outrage over economic inequality grew, as did the unpopularity of the Economic Council. For months, Germans in the American and British zones protested against the council's administrative wing, which had been responsible for designing and implementing the reforms. They directed their anger in particular at Ludwig Erhard, the rotund, cigar-smoking professor of free-market economics who orchestrated the slashing of price controls and was, according to one critic, "a fighter for such an extreme form of economic liberalism that it would be considered outdated by the economic experts of the American Republican Party."[3] In October 1948, local German police officials were so concerned about the level of discontent at an anti-Erhard rally in the central market square of Stuttgart that they called in tanks from the American military forces to disperse the tens of thousands of protesters with tear gas. Leaders of the umbrella organization of unions called for a general strike, and socialists in the Economic Council began pushing for a vote of no confidence against Erhard.[4] But by the end of 1949, at which point foreign trade had doubled, resentment began to dissipate as worker wages steadily rose and the West German economy entered a period of unprecedented growth that would come to be known simply as "the economic miracle."

These events have provided much grist for interpretation over the years. Some advocates of free-market institutions have seen in postwar Germany an ideal case study of how a controlled economy can be converted overnight into a market-based one. The neoliberal economist Jeffrey Sachs used the example of Erhard's reforms, which he compared to a "shock" to the economic system, to argue that people who have lived in a controlled economy often need to slide down a "valley of tears" before they can summit the heights of prosperity that the free market brings. Others, such as the free-market critic Naomi Klein, have argued that the various social safety nets that West Germans embedded into their economy, such as subsidized housing and government pensions, make the Federal Republic an inappropriate historical example of the neoliberal economy at work.[5] Erhard himself called his reforms part of a vision for a "social market economy" (*soziale Marktwirschaft*). Because of its remarkable success in the 1950s, economists and historians have dissected this West German economy in scores of books and articles in the hopes of deriving economic laws and lessons.

While scholars often attempt to understand the effects of economic policies in West Germany, they less commonly ask how the policies were constructed, what groups were behind them, and what collective values they represented. The first advocates of the "social market economy" argued that the policies underpinning it reflected what Erhard later called "our Christian way of thinking": principles ultimately rooted in Christian scripture.[6] Their party affiliation was either the Christian Democratic Union (*Christlich Demokratische Union*, CDU) or its sister party in Bavaria, the Christian Social Union (*Christlich-Soziale Union*, CSU), whose leaderships ran their campaigns in conjunction with each other and together formed a bloc (CDU/CSU) in national legislative bodies. The last time German politicians had attempted to forge an interconfessional "Christian" economic policy, during the unemployment years under chancellor Heinrich Brüning, Protestant liberals and Catholics had infamously failed in their charge. Twenty years later, however, the attempts met with more success. This chapter seeks to understand the change.

The CDU/CSU was the largest party bloc in the Economic Council and staked its entire reputation on Erhard's deregulatory reforms of 1948. In June, just after the Deutsche Mark was introduced, its representatives used their slim plurality—out of 104 total council members, forty-four were CDU/CSU, four more than the rival delegation from the socialist SPD—to pass a law enabling Erhard's administrative agency with near dictatorial power to eliminate price controls. Several months later, they thwarted the no-confidence vote against Erhard called by socialists after the popular protests.[7] By late October, as working-class outrage grew and calls for Erhard's resignation persisted, the CDU/CSU risked losing credibility as a bloc that promised to translate a Christian social message into ethical economic policy. Even more troubling, the party's delicate coalition of Protestants and Catholics demonstrated signs of splintering into factions. Catholic church leaders expressed deep concern with the free-market policy of Erhard, who was a Protestant. On the same late October day as the violence in Stuttgart, high-ranking members of the Catholic-dominated CSU momentarily joined socialists in calling for Erhard's resignation.[8]

It was in this context that two prominent economic theorists close to the CDU/CSU bloc, one Protestant and the other Catholic, began discussing the possibility of creating future policy on which all Christians in Germany could agree. At the end of October 1948, the Protestant Wilhelm Röpke, perhaps the most famous economist living in Western Europe at this time and a leading booster of Erhard's reforms, invited Oswald von Nell-Breuning, the most respected social theorist of the Catholic Church in Germany and a prominent critic of Erhard, to his home in Geneva, Switzerland, to break bread and talk economics. The two men described their meeting as a tentative success. Writing a follow-up note on his way back from Switzerland to Frankfurt, Nell-Breuning seemed pleased to find agreement between them on some fundamental principles. "I see with full clarity the great step forward which you and your circle of academic friends have taken beyond the liberalism of old, and I value it as progress, to be most greatly welcomed," Nell-Breuning wrote to Röpke on October 31. But he also regretted their inability to overcome all the barriers that had so often separated Protestants from Catholics in the first half of the century. There still existed between them, he noted, an "invisible and wafer-thin, yet nonetheless impermeable, wall through which we are not yet able to break." The two men would correspond fitfully over the next years, with long periods of silence and tension followed by long letters reaffirming their common commitments.[9]

The on-again, off-again relationship between Röpke and Nell-Breuning opens a window on the creation of post-Nazi Germany's most successful political movement—political Christianity—represented by the CDU/CSU and its most successful slogan, the "social market economy." The phrase, with its promise of a humane capitalism, suggested a merger of Protestantism and Catholicism. As this chapter shows, however, the cooperation of Protestants and Catholics in a common political bloc was more akin to a strategic partnership than to a merger. As in a strategic partnership, the Protestant and Catholic wings of the party bloc retained their prior brands, business philosophies, and separate accounting, and retained their right to end the deal. They found the most success when they were able to pool their resources to thwart a common rival, which in the post-Nazi era was always socialism. And like any partnership, the power dynamics between the contracting parties were unequal. In the first several years of the new Federal Republic, the leaders of the bloc's self-identifying Protestant wing—whose members had mostly belonged to the "liberal" parties of the Weimar Republic— depended on the Catholic Church's moral legitimization for their rise to power. The movement's Catholic leaders often leveraged that dependency, threatening to withdraw their support for the project if their demands were not met.

THE PROTESTANT DEMAND FOR CATHOLIC SUPPORT

One of the most significant effects of Allied occupation on political Christianity in the territory that became the Federal Republic was the demographic equalization of the Protestant and Catholic populations. The western region of Germany surrounding the Rhine River, occupied by the French and British, was historically home to a far larger Catholic population than in the mostly Protestant eastern parts of the country occupied by the Soviet Union. The southern region of Bavaria, which fell under American authority, was also heavily Catholic. With the merging of the French, British, and American zones into one country and the exclusion of the Soviet zone, the ratio of Protestants to Catholics was set to become 5:4, compared with a ratio of 2:1 in the former unified Germany. (By contrast, in the Soviet zone that eventually formed the German Democratic Republic, the ratio of Protestants to Catholics was roughly 8:1.)[10] Among other things, this demographic shift forced those Protestants who hoped to rebuild the politics of the shattered nation on Christian foundations to depend far more heavily on the Catholic vote than they would have had Germany not been divided.

During the years of political organization under the occupation, German Protestant politicians—who, as Maria Mitchell has shown, were indispensable in the leadership of the CDU—turned to the ideas of strategists who were theorizing a collaboration between Protestants and

Catholics.[11] Chief among them was Wilhelm Röpke, a German-born economist who since the early years of the Nazi era had lived abroad in neighboring Switzerland but kept close tabs on developments in his native country and had ambitions to advise on German policy. During the war, Röpke had waged a strong publicity campaign for an alliance of Protestant "liberals" and Catholic "conservatives" against what he considered catastrophic socialist proposals for a post-Nazi economy. In 1948, Röpke became a household name in western Germany when his economic principles became associated with Erhard's deregulatory policies. One reporter noted in November of that year that Röpke's ideas had become "almost a fetish," more discussed than any "other recipe for social policy."[12]

Röpke's emergence as something of a celebrity (as economists go) was in part a result of his own self-marketing for over a decade. After voluntarily leaving his native country in protest against the Nazi regime and spending several years teaching in Turkey, Röpke returned west in 1937 to be closer to the German-speaking world, taking up a position at the prestigious Graduate Institute of International Studies in Geneva, Switzerland. He turned down numerous offers to relocate to the United States, including a chair at the New School for Social Research in New York, and stayed in Geneva during the war—despite the threat of German occupation—in order to position himself as the Western Allies' local *consigliere* after what he foresaw would be the inevitable fall of Nazism. "It is becoming ever more likely," he wrote in 1941 to the former minister of economics in Belgium, "that the role of world-arbiter will fall to the United States, and it is thoroughly possible that the rest of this century will be determined by a *Pax Americana*, as the nineteenth was by the *Pax Britannica*. Everything will depend on whether the United States is spiritually and morally ready to take over this historic role, and, when the time comes, whether the men who make decisions know what they want to do and what they should do."[13] Röpke promoted himself as the world's top authority on the "German question," gathering every piece of literature on its details and devoting all his considerable brainpower to its solution.

Given his presence at the dissolution of the Weimar Republic and his involvement in the Brüning regime's failure to create a "Christian" economic policy during the unemployment crisis, Röpke was well positioned to appreciate the power of the Catholic Church and the necessity of coopting its support if his free-market ideas were to gain ascendancy in Germany. In self-imposed exile, he saw the ability of Nazi and other fascist leaders to harness ideas long associated with the cultural conservatism of Catholicism, such as the understanding of the national economy as an "organism" and its separation into "orders." Once German Catholic church leaders began to distance themselves from the Nazi-led government after 1934, however, Röpke hoped they would begin to realize that the "real program" of Christian economy did not lie in fascism's "economic planning, organization and regimentation," but rather in the "spontaneity" of the free market. He began pleading with his fellow advocates of a free-market economy not to alienate Catholic conservatives, who would be crucial for the success of their program.[14]

Indeed, the popularity Röpke achieved as a spokesperson for what became known as "neoliberalism" was a result not of any innovation in the field of economics but of his ability to advertise a free-market vision for the future to a culturally conservative audience. In his book *The Social Crisis of Our Time*, published in 1942 to so much acclaim that it went through four editions in that year alone, Röpke promoted a "broad overall program" for market freedom that was not very different from his liberal policy proposals from the depression years: decentralization, supervision of the market to ensure fair competition, and limitation of state interventions to measures that conform to the "rules of the market."[15] What *was* new was his adoption of the rhetoric and social policy catchwords of traditional Catholic social thought. Röpke began to use the Catholic analogy of the economy as organism (instead of as machine, his preferred metaphor) and wrote of treating businesses as "communities." Most revealingly, Röpke appropriated the term most associated with the Vatican's economic philosophy: a call for a "third way," or "middle way," between laissez-faire capitalism and state-planned socialism. By adopting the Vatican's language, Röpke likely hoped to contribute to what he called the "increasing blurring of earlier oppositions, a *rearrangement of old fronts* and a *growing consolidation into a new, broad front* in which all those of good will and clear-sightedness stand together and subordinate differences that have become insignificant."[16]

Röpke reached out so far to Catholics in *The Social Crisis of Our Time* that his Austrian-born friend Friedrich Hayek, a free-market theorist and a nonpracticing Catholic himself, accused him of being disingenuous in describing his proposals as a "middle way" between laissez-faire and planned economy when in fact they were far closer to the former. "[The book] is a great achievement, and as you will expect I am in almost complete agreement not only as regards the main argument but also with respect of the detail," Hayek wrote him. "[But] I am convinced that we must have the courage openly to confess to the basic ideals of old liberalism and individualism, however much we may criticize the crudity of the way in which people in the 19th century tried to put them into practice."[17] Röpke insisted on the Catholic language, and his marketing strategy paid high dividends. As his recent biographer has noted, in few social milieus did his book receive more attention than in Catholic circles. The editors of the *Solothurn Gazette,* which covered news for the majority-Catholic German-speaking region of Switzerland just south of Germany, editorialized that "Röpke's lines of thought strongly remind the friends of Christian social reform of the teachings of the social Popes Leo XIII and Pius XI."[18] Hayek's competitor text, the anti-socialist treatise *The Road to Serfdom,* which Röpke's wife translated into German and for which Röpke himself wrote an introduction when it was published in Switzerland in 1945, enjoyed no comparable reception among Catholics.

Röpke energetically recruited influential German Catholics to lend credence to his argument that interventionist economic policies—from Bismarck's mandatory health insurance in Germany to Roosevelt's job creation programs in the U.S. to William Beveridge's welfare plan for the United Kingdom—violated the principles of Catholic social teaching.[19] He reacted with almost giddy excitement when Karl Thieme, a Catholic with close contacts in the church hierarchy who had been working for Protestant-Catholic cooperation since the Weimar years, told him that he, too, was trying "to help create the preconditions for an alliance of Catholics and liberals" after seeing "with horror how widely the delusion of planned economy has intruded into so-called 'liberal' and also Catholic circles." Thieme remarked that Röpke was practically begging him to write something endorsing the claim that Catholic tradition promoted a free market. "You, as a Catholic, would second me," Röpke wrote Thieme hopefully, noting that he was reading *Quadragesimo anno* in the original Latin. He also complained about German-speaking Jesuit authors in Switzerland who he felt were sabotaging his "attempts to come to a kind of common front with Catholicism."[20]

By the end of the war, Röpke believed he had positioned himself as the Allies' local expert on the German question. He met with the director of American intelligence in Switzerland, Allen Dulles, and claimed to have secured support for a group he formed with Thieme called the Committee of the Christian Confessions of Germany for Collaboration on Reconstruction. The committee's proposal seems to have been directed against those in the U.S. government, including President Roosevelt's chief adviser Sumner Welles, who believed that Germany's postwar map should be redrawn around Protestant and Catholic regions, given the apparently irreconcilable hostilities between the two groups. The committee argued that Germans of both Christian confessions could remain together as one nation as long as the country was federated and shifted away from government intervention to a free-market system.[21]

One of the educational materials the Committee of the Christian Confessions hoped to circulate among German youth after the war was Röpke's book *Civitas Humana,* which later became one of his most popular pieces of writing. In it, Röpke called for a "shock" (*Anstoss*) to Germany's struggling economic system: the immediate deregulation of price controls, the breakup of the big cartels to promote competition, and a simultaneous lowering of tax obstacles, both national and international. The shock would promote circulation and unclog Germany's economic arteries, he claimed.[22] The policy recommendation was very similar to the one he had made to Brüning's government in 1931, but the metaphor was different: what he had once called "ignition" of the economy he now called "shock." In the text he published, simply titled *The German Question,* in 1945, Röpke described the German economy as a national organism, a body plagued by a romantic addiction to socialist ideals and curable only through "psycho-therapeutical treatment on the vastest scale the world has ever known."[23]

The first few years of the military occupation of Germany were full of frustration for Röpke and other advocates of the free market. It was bad enough that the Allied authorities insisted, based on the Potsdam Agreement between the Four Powers, on retaining price controls until new economic legislation could be drafted by an autonomous, unified German parliament. What was worse, the first economic platform released by the Catholic-dominated regional chapter of the CDU for North Rhine–Westphalia in 1947 called for national policies very close to the socialist addictions Röpke diagnosed as the root of the German disease.[24] The editor of the *Rhenish Mercury,* founded after the war by a close friend of Röpke's to foster neoliberal economic ideas among a Catholic audience, complained bitterly of traditional Catholics who appeared to have learned nothing from the Weimar experience and seemed more willing to support the planned economy proposed by the SPD than the free-market economy of the more pro-Christian neoliberals.[25]

Fortunes for Röpke's ideas changed only when Allied negotiations over the future of Germany began to break down. At the end of 1947, when the Four Powers failed to achieve a common vision for reintegrating Germany into the world economy, American and British officials decided unilaterally to give Germans in their zones more autonomy to draft legislation and administer changes in their own economic policy. They doubled the number of members in the Economic Council of the Unified Economic Territory and created an executive branch with a director general. Röpke jumped at the opportunity to advise the council on policy. In an article titled "The Cure for the German Economy," published in February 1948 in the *Rhenish Mercury* and republished in the information service of the CDU/CSU, he presented an either-or decision to the council. In light of continuing poverty and the opportunity it created for communist agitators, only two paths were available: either separate the western zones from the Soviet zones by instituting radical deregulation reforms, or risk the prospect of having to recruit the American military to prevent a communist revolution. Although the division of Germany would be unfortunate, he wrote, the "building blocks of construction" for a future unified nation could be laid only in the west in partnership with Western Europe and the United States.[26] Röpke recommended proposed legislation in the Economic Council meant to enable its administrative wing, led by the free-market economist Ludwig Erhard, with wide-reaching executive powers to deregulate prices.

In the debates of spring 1948 over this new enabling act—the Law on Guiding Principles of Economic Policy After the Currency Reform, or Law on Guiding Principles for short—Catholic leaders held the swing vote to give Erhard emergency powers of decree. The SPD faction of the council vowed to vote against it, claiming that free-market advocates were using anticommunist scare tactics to manufacture a crisis. The neoliberal wing of the CDU/CSU thus needed to muster the support of all the bloc's members, including those Catholic leaders who expressed skepticism of both the free market and the partitioning of Germany. The Vatican had even criticized the very creation of an economic council in the Bizone. For the second time in fifteen years—the first being March 1933, when they were asked to enable Hitler's government with dictatorial executive powers—Catholics acquired a kingmaker role.[27]

Evidence suggests that Catholic members of the CDU/CSU bloc in the Economic Council made their decision for the Law on Guiding Principles (and against SPD objections) based not primarily on their commitment to the free market, as Röpke had hoped, but because of foreign policy concerns. The leading Catholic on the Economic Council's administrative advisory committee, Oswald von Nell-Breuning, told the group in early 1948 that "in consideration of the psychology abroad, and namely of the Americans, it may be advisable that we blaze the path as far as possible toward bringing the market economy into operation."[28] Not doing so risked losing fragile popular support in America for the U.S. government's dramatic plan, devised in 1947 by secretary of state George C. Marshall, to prevent the spread of communism by investing billions of dollars in the reconstruction of Germany and other European states. Enabling Erhard to deregulate the economy in the American and British zones would be a show of support for Marshall's efforts, which the Vatican wholeheartedly supported, indeed claimed to have initiated.[29]

Whatever their reason for supporting the enabling act of 1948, the critical support of Catholics in the council was won. When the law finally came to a vote at almost four in the morning on June 18, after vigorous debate, a unanimous vote from the CDU/CSU bloc guaranteed its passage, 50 to 37. Hermann Pünder, the Catholic chief executive of the council, later called the vote "the most important parliamentary decision of German postwar history." Several historians have noted that the decision would never have been made had several key Catholic representatives close to workers' interests not been convinced shortly before the roll call.[30]

The critical Catholic support enabled Erhard to put into effect policies largely in line with Röpke's recommendations.[31] Just days after the passage of the enabling act, without notifying American or British authorities beforehand, Erhard decreed the elimination of ninety percent of price controls in the Western zones. Almost simultaneously, the agency proposed steep reductions in income, property, inheritance, and corporate taxes. The draft laws Erhard submitted to the occupation authorities included reductions of fifty percent in income tax, sixty percent in property tax, and forty percent in inheritance tax. French authorities were concerned about emptying public coffers for social spending, but American and British officials persuaded them to approve most of the deductions for the sake of returning autonomy over fiscal policy to Germans. (In the Soviet zone, Germans introduced their own new currency at around the same time but retained price controls and prior tax rates.)[32]

From the first to the second half of the fiscal year 1948, industrial output in the western zones increased by more than twenty percent. Röpke seemed as thrilled in his private correspondence as he had ever been. After an entire career complaining about the irrationality of German economic policy, Röpke could finally express pleasure with the new direction in his home country. He wrote to an Austrian-American friend in September 1948, even as popular protests against Erhard in West Germany mounted, to say that a "fresh wind" was blowing there.[33]

THE (CONDITIONAL) SUPPLY OF CATHOLIC CHURCH SUPPORT

True to the laws of the market, the Catholic supply of support for Erhard's policies came with a price. Following the market reforms of 1948, the German church hierarchy sought to leverage its new power—with over fifty percent of the Catholic population reporting regular church attendance, this was a substantial influence—to pressure the CDU/CSU leadership to ensure passage of legislation in accordance with Catholic principles.[34] Already in August 1948, on the occasion of remembering the patron saint of Germany, Saint Boniface, Germany's bishops publicly criticized the Economic Council's lack of social policies to counteract the spike in poverty caused by the deregulations. "We want to think and hope that in the economic reform, the calculation of the bureaucrat does not wipe the slate clean, and instead that suffering people, too, will be accounted for," read the pastoral letter they circulated to the dioceses.[35] Calls for Erhard's resignation in the CDU/CSU's Catholic wings showed that these warnings were serious—serious enough to persuade Röpke to appeal to Nell-Breuning for continued support for Erhard and the neoliberals.

Nell-Breuning was Catholicism's most respected thinker in West Germany. Not only had the Vatican long recognized him as an authority on social and economic issues, having appointed him to draft *Quadragesimo anno* during the crisis of the interwar depression, but Protestants also appreciated his ability to express the voice of the church in a way that was accessible to non-Catholics. The Protestant co-founder of the CDU/CSU, Walter Strauss, insisted that Nell-Breuning be appointed among the first members of the Economic Council's administrative advisory board, a committee of roughly twenty economists who convened since January 1948 to advise the agency Erhard led.[36] Nell-Breuning did not change out of his clerical clothes when he made the two-mile trek over the Main River from the seminary, where he lived and trained clergy, to the Stock Exchange building where the advisory board convened. He cut a striking image in these bureaucratic circles, with his lanky frame, shaved head, and Jesuit's frock. In his late fifties, Nell-Breuning began a second career in government advising, which would soon garner him a reputation as the country's Catholic "Nestor," after the old counselor to Greek kings in Homer's *Odyssey*. Dolf Sternberger, a scholar in Heidelberg informing the U.S. State Department on trends in German social science, reported in 1950 that Nell-Breuning's work provided the common intellectual foundation for the platforms of Catholic politicians not only in Germany, but in all European states governed by Christian political parties west of the Iron Curtain.[37]

The immense prestige accorded to Nell-Breuning was, in several ways, a reflection of the rising stock of the church as a whole, ever since its hierarchy, for the first time in history, began to express an openness to partnership with Protestants under an interconfessional Christian political banner. The hierarchy's rejection of dialogue during most of the first half of the century had always stifled attempts to form a Christian party in Germany. When it came to economics, the church had been far more willing to endorse fascist policies than free-market ones.[38] However, the church could also claim that it criticized the Nazi government on its eugenic laws as early as 1933 and expressed "burning concern" in 1937 about its suppression of religious freedom. When the war shifted decisively against the Axis Powers in 1942, the Catholic hierarchy opened the door to the possibility of exclusive "partnership" with the liberal-capitalist world. A recent study on wartime diplomacy has shown that Pope Pius XII pivoted in that year toward an alliance with the Western Allies, and especially the United States, in the expectation of leadership in the reconstruction of a post-fascist Christian Europe.[39]

Nell-Breuning's work in West Germany reveals some of the logic of the church's shift toward openness to exclusive partnership with liberals. When Germans began to organize into political parties under the occupation after 1945, Nell-Breuning flatly denied the existence of a social ethics common to both Protestants and Catholics. He did, however, in a text titled *On the Objectives of Political Parties,* grant the church's blessing to the creation of interconfessional "Christian" parties to serve as strategic bulwarks against other parties openly hostile to Christianity.[40] Such a partnership of the two confessions would depend, he wrote, on Protestants' renunciation of laissez-faire economics and their openness to Catholic social principles. "Today we are seeing an extremely formidable neoliberalism, which is striving to take lessons from the experiences of the past hundred years and to strip off the mistakes of classical liberalism," Nell-Breuning explained to a Catholic audience in 1948. In his correspondence with Röpke from late 1948 to early 1949, Nell-Breuning lauded the neoliberals' promise to support social safety net laws, but he made clear his expectation that they would come closer to Catholics' more communitarian positions if they wanted continued support.[41]

Even though the church placed conditions on its endorsement, the Protestant neoliberals in the CDU/CSU needed that support to offset popular frustration with the economic reforms and retain supporters in anticipation of the Federal Republic's first parliamentary elections in August 1949. The Western Allies officially ended their military occupation of Germany in May, but continued to station troops and civilian officials there, still wary of political unrest and perhaps even revolution. Within the first months of independence, seven million workers organized by the umbrella organization of unions close to the SPD in the Western zones struck in protest of Erhard's deregulations. Furthermore, polls showed that much (if not the majority) of the population favored returning to price controls even if it meant fewer goods would be on the market. It was increasingly difficult to dispute the argument of the SPD's economic spokesperson, Erik Nölting, who told Erhard in a public debate that the so-called "social market economy" he and his supporters in political Christianity had promised so far looked "damn similar to a liberal market economy." Nölting singled out Wilhelm Röpke as the blithe theorist behind Erhard's policies. For Röpke, he said sarcastically, "one needs only to allow the economy to flourish and run, and social harmony will form from out of itself in the autonomic course of the exchange of goods."[42]

It was therefore crucial that the Catholic church, whose hierarchy built its social principles around the plight of the dispossessed, continued to defend the price deregulation and promise voters that the CDU/CSU would make progress on social policy. Nell-Breuning spent the months leading up to the elections in the summer of 1949 arguing that the SPD and the union leadership, despite their legitimate concerns about the economy, were still too dominated by an anti-religious worldview for Catholics to support. The German bishops, too, strongly suggested in a pastoral letter released before election day that the CDU and CSU were the only appropriate parties to vote for.[43] The CDU/CSU ticket, running on a platform stressing "social justice for all" in an election that was essentially a referendum on the preceding year's economic liberalization, could point to a robust endorsement from the church in its advertisements.

Catholic support turned out to be the decisive factor in the election on August 14, 1949. It was estimated that nearly all Catholics who cast a ballot in West Germany voted for the CDU/CSU bloc, whereas the Protestant vote was split among Christian and secular parties.[44] The CDU/CSU received thirty-one percent of returns—just barely enough for a slim victory, less than two percentage points, over the SPD. Thanks to the Catholic vote, the bloc gained a plurality and the upper hand in nego-tiating a coalition government with two smaller parties that supported Erhard's reforms, the Free Democratic Party and the German Party. In September, the CDU/CSU faction nominated a Catholic supporter of Erhard and former mayor of Cologne, Konrad Adenauer, to be the Federal Republic's first chancellor. After barely gaining approval in parliament over the protests of the SPD (who claimed that the votes of socialist repre-sentatives of West Berlin were unjustly excluded), Adenauer brought Erhard into his cabinet to transform the administrative wing of the Economic Council into a new ministry of economics.

Meanwhile, leaders of the church prepared to capitalize on their indispensable position within the Christian party by lobbying for legislation derived from specifically Catholic ethics. The principles they endorsed in 1949 were not, in their essence, different from those they had proposed under the Weimar Republic. The conception of the national economy as community and living organism remained, as did their condemnation of selfish materialism. In the official handbook of Catholic economic ethics that Nell-Breuning published after the election, *On the Ordering of the Economy* (1950), several entries were reprinted verbatim from a similar text of twenty years earlier. The entries on topics such as property redistribution, housing subsidies, stock market regulation, the rights of employees to profit sharing and co-management, just wages, and progressive taxation were only updated versions of the same "solidaristic" proposals the church had advocated since the release of *Quadragesimo anno* in 1931.[45] At the first Catholic Day from August 31 to September 4, 1949, a convention of German Catholics during which roughly half a million supporters joined clergy members in the working-class city of Bochum in a massive show of electoral strength, the bishops endorsed economic policies almost identical to those they had endorsed in the Weimar years when the Catholic Center Party had governed in coalition with the SPD, such as employee participation in business management ("co-determination") and public works programs. As the historian Maria Mitchell has noted, the major shift in the German Catholic Church was related not to principle or policy, but to rhetoric: America, the new partner, was no longer described as the epitome of materialist evil.[46]

Nell-Breuning noted that the support of the bishops caused a "tremendous sensation" among "all circles of the working class" in the Federal Republic, and later remembered that Catholic economic teaching "enjoyed *high* respect" in some circles of the SPD at this time. Indeed, despite the church's firm stance against the SPD in the 1949 elections, many of its economic policy proposals showed more affinity with elements in the socialist opposition than with neoliberals in the CDU/CSU.[47] Catholics could thus taunt neoliberals with a threat that if the socialist leadership were to come closer to the Catholic position on such cultural issues as public support for religious schools, then the church might no longer consider the SPD unsafe for Catholic voters. In 1946, Nell-Breuning had written that too many socialists still felt "negative, if not totally hostile, toward the world of Christian values or at least what they take them to be."[48] But in early 1950, he told a Jesuit colleague living abroad that some German socialist leaders were modulating their views. He cited the politician Gerhard Weisser, who, unlike the "orthodox"

Marxist chairman of the SPD, Kurt Schumacher, did not advocate central-ized economic planning or strict non-partnership with the churches on policy issues. "If the SPD were to embrace [Weisser's] program," Nell-Breuning wrote, "they will have stopped being 'socialism' in the sense of *Quadragesimo anno* and we would no longer need a party that does busi-ness under the name of Christianity." He admitted he was growing tired of preaching in vain to Erhard about the necessity of "real economic policy" beyond laissez-faire.[49]

In 1950, in light of its perception of growing inequality and continued poverty throughout Western Europe's increasingly market-based society, the church hierarchy increased its pressure on Christian political parties to better "order" their national economies through social policy. Pope Pius XII, whose support had helped elect interconfessional Christian parties not only in West Germany but all across the western part of continental Europe, from Italy to Belgium to Holland and France, told an interna-tional conference of Catholic social scientists in June that progress on the unemployment problem still plaguing Europeans could not be sought simply in negative measures of deregulation.[50] This did not require breaking partnerships with the free-market-oriented neoliberals. Glossing Pius several days later, Nell-Breuning wrote, "Without being a controlled or planned economy, a clever and skilled policy of national economy can accomplish an extraordinary amount with integrating measures that are 'in line with the market.'"[51]

Now was the time, Nell-Breuning wrote in the market-oriented news-paper where Röpke often published, to make the market economy "social" by introducing "corporative" policies. Other Catholic-led governments in Western Europe had already begun experimenting with corporative poli-cies. The Belgians, for example, under the regime of a coalition of Christian and socialist parties, had created a Central Economic Council that brought together business and union leaders to issue joint recom-mendations on policy. The Dutch government, a coalition of Catholics, Protestants, socialists, and liberals, had passed a Corporative Organization Act allowing for employers and employees in the same economic sectors to cooperate in issuing binding regulations for all businesses in their respective industries. One of the international solutions that both the Vatican and Nell-Breuning strongly supported was the plan introduced in May 1950 by the French government to create a regulatory high authority for the new European Coal and Steel Community composed of West Germany, France, Italy, and the Benelux states—the basis of a future European economic community—with the goal of increasing employment and coordinating working conditions.[52] Neoliberals in the ministry would soon be further frustrated when the U.S. State Department pressured it to roll back many of its economic deregulations in solidarity with the Korean War effort. In October 1950, the State Department forced austerity measures (restrictions on the production of luxury goods) and other controls on the economy.

Neoliberals in Erhard's economics ministry reacted to these recommendations with concern—largely because the ideas were popular among the West German public. Erhard recruited Röpke, whose ideas he endorsed with "complete agreement," to draft an opinion for the government that would refute the church's corporative proposals.[53] Röpke responded quickly. His report, submitted in August 1950 and later published with a foreword written by Chancellor Adenauer himself, suggested that West Germany, after heading in the right direction with the reforms of 1948, was now in danger of becoming a "mixed system of economic policy": neither the fish of the free market nor the fowl of planned socialism. (Röpke no longer wrote of a "third way.") In his pamphlet *Is German Economic Policy Correct?* put out by a Protestant press, Röpke warned that if the government embraced further policies infringing on national and global market forces—such as joint employee administration, profit-sharing requirements, or too many labor protections in the emerging European economic zone—then an "impenetrable underbrush of regulations" would be created, leading to uncertainty and risk aversion among investors and a general flaccidity of the "propulsive powers" of the market.[54] Röpke had cut off his correspondence with Nell-Breuning by this point for more than a year. When, in September, Nell-Breuning introduced his own popular policy proposal on fostering profit-sharing to the economics ministry, Erhard refused to circulate it publicly, forcing Nell-Breuning to publish it in various periodicals himself.[55]

Neoliberals close to the CDU/CSU such as Erhard (he was not yet an official member of the bloc) needed Catholic support to launch them into the driver's seat of West Germany's horse-powered economy. But now the church was asking them to tighten the reins just as the engine was starting to rev. Just as the metaphors they used to imagine the economy were mixed, the tension between the extreme free-market and solidaristic wings of the party threw into question the compatibility of the exclusive partnership.

A PRECARIOUS PARTNERSHIP

By the autumn of 1950, the tension within the CDU/CSU was palpable. When the leading Protestant in the cabinet, Röpke's good friend Gustav Heinemann, was asked to resign as interior minister for opposing the chancellor's stated goal of remilitarizing the country and joining a military alliance with other Western European countries, Adenauer received an angry message from a prominent Protestant member of his caucus suggesting that the Catholic Church was exerting a disproportionate influence in the party. For Adenauer, the short-term solution to the problem, a practice that had become standard in his government, was to replace him with another Protestant, Robert Lehr, to ensure the semblance of religious parity.[56] But he and other leaders of the CDU/CSU knew that this was not sustainable. At the party conference in late October, one politician whose specialty was the recruitment of youth noted, to tremendous applause, that the CDU in Germany would only stop being simply an anticommunist party and actually be able to integrate the country based on Christian principles "when one [member] of the CDU can speak for the other," including "the Catholic for the Protestant, and vice versa."[57]

The "invisible and wafer-thin, yet nonetheless impermeable, wall" that Nell-Breuning had detected between the Catholic and neoliberal standpoints back at his first meeting with Röpke two years earlier had in the meantime become manifest. It was now clear that although they agreed on certain fundamental goals for the future—in particular the importance of private property and its distribution among the greatest number of citizens possible—they had very different ideas about how to achieve them in practice. By 1950, these differences had become especially apparent now that there was more property in West Germany to distribute. The economy had begun to boom again even while unemployment remained over ten percent. Röpke's and Nell-Breuning's conflicting views about specific economic policies, specifically regarding the regulation of both the West German national market and a potential common European market, were reminiscent of the conflicts between liberal and Catholic social thought in the years of the Weimar Republic. But the circumstances had changed: no populist movement such as the Nazis existed to offer the church a more attractive partner than the neoliberals.

And yet, at least at the midcentury marker, neoliberals and the Catholic hierarchy still saw strategic benefits in their continued partnership. As the public debate over worker involvement in corporate governance (*Mitbestimmung,* or "co-determination") reached a boiling point at the turn of 1951 and the leaders of the umbrella organization of unions threatened (with SPD support) to call a general strike if wage workers were not guaranteed the right to equal representation in the administration of their companies, Nell-Breuning and the Catholic hierarchy once again used their more or less collective voice to urge a common interconfessional front in the CDU/CSU against them.[58] Röpke, who complained of the "diabolical pincer strategy of the unions" and warned of "the destruction of the corporate enterprise structure" if workers were allowed to co-direct business operations, was reminded of the indispensability of the church voice. "I cannot indeed convert to Catholicism, but I do not know what would become of the world if it did not exist," he wrote to the wife of one of his colleagues, an active member in the Free Economy Alliance. For neoliberals, it must have been a relief when the CDU/CSU-led parliament passed a law in April 1951 limiting the co-determination rights demanded by unions to large corporations in the coal and steel industries.[59]

In 1952, as the CDU/CSU representatives in parliament entered the second half of their tenure, the tensions in their caucus over the role of government policy in dividing the wealth of the new boom settled into a structural pattern. The partners themselves described the nature of those tensions—their conflicting understandings of what the "social" in the Federal Republic's "social market economy" should be—in the following way.

Alfred Müller-Armack, one of the leading Protestants on the advisory board of the economics ministry and a friend of Röpke's, briefly summarized the neoliberal position in a presentation he gave at a conference of Austrian economists. He took account of the strikingly positive results of the West German economy since Erhard's deregulations of three years before. Industrial production had more than doubled due to lower taxes and the ability of business owners to reinvest. Despite the "heavy strain" on a large portion of the population, millions of new jobs had been created. The lesson to be drawn from the data, he argued, was that government must guard against all impurities hindering free competition in the economy. Only through the free circulation of goods could a robust productive order be created that could then "also serve social progress." The focus of neoliberal policy, he said, must be on breaking up trusts and monopolies: it was precisely the new government commitment to ensuring fair market competition, which allowed people to receive what they worked for, that separated the new liberalism from the old and made it "social." He neglected to say so, but all of Müller-Armack's arguments drew on what he had been saying since the war years: that the spiritual genealogy of the free-market idea was Protestant.[60]

Nell-Breuning, on the other hand, described the dispute between neoliberalism and Catholic social theory in terms of their divergent conceptions of "power." During a debate in the economic ministry's advisory board at the beginning of 1952 meant to garner agreement on core principles for their recommendations to the CDU/CSU-led government, Nell-Breuning criticized Müller-Armack's notion that there was any such thing as a "power-free, pure economy of competition" or power-free market conditions that conduct business transactions like distilled water conducts electricity. He argued that there would always be an imbalance of power among partners in the economy, weak and strong, and that it was the constant job of social policy to help correct those imbalances with the least amount of coercion possible.[61] Although some top Catholics criticized Nell-Breuning's willingness to cooperate with socialist members of the board on social policy, most agreed with his criticism of neoliberalism as it regarded the nature of power.

The conflict between Müller-Armack and Nell-Breuning, as one scholar has recently pointed out, expressed the "deep religious grammar" of conflicts in the CDU/CSU about the "social market economy."[62] Christian bloc politicians were easily able to agree on matters of cultural and foreign policy dear to Chancellor Adenauer, such as the maintenance of Christian confessional public schools and a committed cooperation with the United States. But conflicts over the economy made it difficult for the bloc and its coalition partners to pass social policy without the support of the socialist opposition. In 1952, Protestant politicians in the CDU/CSU founded a separate Evangelical Working Group to articulate particularly Protestant principles, challenge what they perceived as increasing Catholic hegemony in the bloc, and keep fellow Protestants from leaving the party.[63]

As the next parliamentary election cycle approached in 1953, the developments in political Christianity showed that Protestants and Catholics recognized the problems in their partnership but also did not dare to separate. Arkadij Gurland, a socialist political scientist in West Berlin who conducted the first scholarly analysis of the CDU/CSU, noted that the tensions between the Protestant and Catholic wings of the party necessitated a new, aggressive effort in 1953 to show German voters what was specifically "Christian" about their politics and why it was necessary to elect them to hold the country together.[64] Perhaps for that reason, the elections of 1953 would be the most vicious in the history of the young Federal Republic, as the leaders of the Christian bloc struggled to convince voters and themselves of their enduring ties by imagining how much worse things would be if they allowed the socialists into power.

CHAPTER EIGHT

The Education of Western Europeans

POLITICAL ANALYSTS IN THE UNITED STATES, WHICH along with the United Kingdom and France maintained legal supervision over West Germany's foreign policy even though the occupation had officially ended, expressed satisfaction with the results of the parliamentary elections held in the fall of 1953. If they saw the election as a test of the country's political matura-tion and its ability to cultivate responsible leadership among the youth, then West Germans passed with flying colors. With a high turnout from the younger generation, voters demonstrated hardly any support for can-didates on the extreme right and left wings of the political spectrum, and the number of splinter parties represented in parliament shrank by half. Most promising for those looking for signs of stabilization in Germany, perhaps, was the fact that even after a brutally contested campaign in which Adenauer's governing Christian coalition won a resounding vic-tory over the main socialist opposition (forty-five to twenty-nine percent), leaders of the losing party signaled their willingness to work together with the new regime on the policy questions that had most divided them over the first four years of the country's independence.[1] "If the many signs are not misleading," wrote one émigré who covered the politics of his former homeland for an American audience, then "Germany may not figure too large in future headlines, yet achievements are likely to be built on a firmer foundation, and the goals which the Germans set themselves may be more universally acceptable than they were during the turbulent decades behind us."[2]

American social scientists, using an empirical method that sought to explain and predict behavior primarily through the lens of material interests, tended to look at indicators of economic development to explain such signs of political stabilization in foreign countries. Many, such as a panel of Germany experts at the Academy of Political Science in New York in 1954, argued that the growth of extremism in the Weimar Republic had resulted from the hollowing out of the middle class; therefore, political stabilization in the Federal Republic depended on a return to prosperity and social mobility.[3] Indicators of this sort all predicted good news, for West Germany was in the midst of unprecedented growth often referred to as an "economic miracle."

What these analyses often overlooked, however, was that economic success cannot paper over destabilizing disagreements among a population over fundamental questions of national orientation and education. For evidence of that kind of stabilization, spreadsheets on gross domestic product or wealth distribution were unhelpful. In the years after 1953, as the Western Allies turned over sovereign decision-making power over foreign relations to the Federal Republic's government, Germans did indeed show signs of coming to agreement on precisely the issue of values and "ideals" for the German youth that had caused such crisis during Hitler's rise to power in 1933. The common ideal that bound them together, as Chancellor Adenauer noted in the speech he made to parliament in late 1953 announcing his government's goals, was twofold: the value of "Europe" and the foreign policy of "binding to the West" (Westbindung).[4]

In the years leading up to 1953, Germans from across the Federal Republic's political spectrum participated in the creation of educational institutions designed to shape a generation of young people capable of overcoming centuries of conflict in a common "European" identity. In Luxembourg, the administrative center of the new European Coal and Steel Community—an organization that Chancellor Adenauer and his counterpart in France intended as a first step toward linking old enemies in a common market and ultimately a political federation—children of the West German, French, Dutch, Belgian, and Italian bureaucrats who convened there began attending the first European School. Also that year, the professor Bruno Snell founded the Europa-Kolleg in Hamburg, modeled after the College of Europe in Bruges, Belgium, four years earlier, designed for university students from around the continent to attain graduate degrees for jobs in the quickly expanding field of European integration. Young Germans had already founded the first public forum for the promotion of European cooperation, the Europe House, in Bad Marienburg in 1951, and in 1949 the first European youth organization, the League of European Youth, with its headquarters in the Federal Republic's capital of Bonn.

Also in 1953, German educators attended the European Forum, a two-week colloquium held annually in an alpine town just south of Germany in Austria and open to university students from around Europe west of the Iron Curtain. Members of the anti-Nazi resistance founded it directly after the war, with financial support from the United States, to bring together leading thinkers to discuss pressing issues in a "pan-European spirit."[5] The forum of 1953, which was attended by more than four hundred people, most of them students, took place in late August just before elections in the Federal Republic. According to newspaper reports, participants stayed in small guesthouses and ate schnitzel and typical Austrian sweets in between lectures from the leading European thinkers in the fields of philosophy, art, and the natural sciences.[6] Much like the short-lived European University Conference in Davos, Switzerland, a quarter century earlier, which had been sponsored by the League of Nations and intended to encourage international under-standing, the forum in Alpbach took as its topic the question "What is man?" But unlike the Davos debacle, where the two German philosophers Ernst Cassirer and Martin Heidegger clashed spectacularly in front of a rowdy group of German students, the German professors who presented in Alpbach found themselves in genial agreement on fundamental questions and seemed to diverge only on the details.

Those familiar with Germany's older debates would have been inter-ested to see that two German professors who had stood on the opposing sides of Cassirer and Heidegger in the Weimar years now partnered on youth questions at the European Forum. Helmuth Plessner, the rising young philosopher who had been forced into Dutch emigration by nation-alist youth groups in 1933, sat together on a panel on metaphysics with Arnold Bergsträsser, the charismatic educator who had been celebrated by those nationalist youth groups before they turned on him after 1935. (By 1953, he actually used the Western, Latinized spelling Bergstraesser instead of the Germanic Bergsträsser.) Plessner delivered a presentation on philosophical anthropology about man as the sole life form capable of self-representation. Bergsträsser spoke about the way humans had represented themselves specifically in Europe, using the example of Johann Wolfgang von Goethe's "Christian-oriented" self-understanding. After their meeting in Alpbach, Bergsträsser wrote to Plessner that he looked forward to working with him on "the long line of fundamental scholarly and educational questions" facing the leaders of the new liberal democracy in Germany.[7]

The never-before-told story of Plessner and Bergsträsser's arrival on common ground deserves a chapter in the history of the reconstruction for two reasons. First, their scholarly work reveals the rationale (as opposed to simply the opportunism) that Germans used when they supported Adenauer's policy of "binding to the West," meaning joining in partnership with both Western European nations and the United States after so recently being at war with them. Until just several years before, many if not a majority of Germans considered themselves to belong not to the West but rather to Central Europe. Second, their cooperation shows how German educators used the ideal of a "Western" European identity in an attempt to heal a society whose members had turned on one another in a kind of civil war before the emergence of the strongman Hitler. Working together on a common goal to cultivate a generation of German youth committed to a Western European identity and a peaceful future could provide distraction from the painful personal memories of a conflict-ridden past.

THE IDEA OF EUROPE AND THE PROBLEM WITH COOPERATING WITH COMMUNISTS

In the autopsy of their disappointing finish in the elections of 1953, the socialist leaders of Germany's main parliamentary opposition, the SPD, found that they had fatally misread the electorate for the past several years. Erich Ollenhauer, a Weimar-era socialist youth leader who had survived the Nazi years in British emigration and now served as the party's new chairman, noted in his first speech after the election that the SPD had underestimated the existential angst about potential war with the Soviet Union. By overwhelmingly supporting Adenauer's foreign policy message, Ollenhauer said, the majority of Germans showed themselves to feel that it was "better to live in the custody of the West, even when it is in the status of tutelage," than to remain "nonaligned" in the Cold War between the world powers. The SPD's campaign to resist all exclusive partnerships with the West, both in economic and military policy, had been based on the reasoning that alignment would alienate their communist brethren in East Germany and prevent reunification of the nation. But the message failed to resonate.[8]

On the contrary, the SPD's campaign had backfired terribly. In light of the proxy war being fought between the United States and the Soviet Union in Korea, many feared a similar outbreak in divided Germany. Not long before the election, in June 1953, Russian tanks rolled into East Berlin to suppress peaceful demonstrations against low wages, which meant that Soviet troops were just across the border. Chancellor Adenauer and his incumbent CDU/CSU-led government were able to paint the SPD and its refusal to ally with the West as overly idealistic and a threat to national security. The slogan printed on CDU placards around the country read, simply, "Protect us!" Furthermore, in decisively advancing a vision of partnership with Germany's western neighbors under the sign of European and Christian unity, Adenauer exploited the socialist party's Marxist roots. Although the party leadership had abandoned its identity as a workers' party and broadened its tent, there were still enough self-declared Marxists in the SPD to link it genealogically with anti-Christianism and the Soviets. Another CDU slogan that year was "All Paths of Marxism Lead to Moscow!"[9] Ollenhauer expressed concern over evidence that the CDU/CSU bloc received massive support not only from the Catholic population, which was to be expected, but also from more secularized Protestant circles. The good news, on the other hand, was that socialists still controlled five of the ten West German regional governments (counting West Berlin) and, at least in those places, could begin to reformulate the party's message.[10]

Not coincidentally, the education ministries of the regional governments controlled by the SPD were competing in the fall of 1953 to recruit the sixty-one-year-old professor Helmuth Plessner, who had decided several years earlier to return permanently to Germany from teaching in the Netherlands. Remarkably, three of the four socialist-led regions that ran major universities, Lower Saxony, Hamburg, and West Berlin, were vying to hire Plessner to teach philosophy and sociology.[11] Plessner's prestige among socialist circles was clearly not due to partisan loyalty, for he had never joined a political party and didn't intend to in the future. Nor was it due to his reputation as the most prominent philosopher in the country after having been elected president of the German Congress for Philosophy. More likely, it was because of the ideals for Europe and the West that he had been advocating since his emigration.

Plessner himself had a painful past behind him in Germany. In April 1933, after Hitler's announcement of Germany's first antisemitic laws, Plessner's seventy-two-year-old father, who was Jewish, was found dead in his practice. Plessner believed it was suicide. That same month, his seminar in Cologne was canceled.[12] Declared unfit to teach German youth because of his liberal internationalism as well as the Jewish ancestry on his father's side, Plessner was luckily able to use networks he had already established with academics in the Netherlands to obtain a post at the University of Groningen, not far across the border with Germany. The rise of a violent form of nationalism took his father and his job and prevented him from staying with his grieving and sick non-Jewish mother, though he ended up being able to visit her fairly regularly in his hometown of Wiesbaden, before she died midway through the war and Plessner had to flee into hiding from the Gestapo.

While in Groningen, Plessner sought to explain the underlying psychological causes of the growth of Nazism in Germany. In a series of lectures he turned into a book titled *The Destiny of the German Spirit at the End of Its Bourgeois Era* (1935), he argued that the German turn away from Western Europe's "political humanism"—liberal democracy, equal rights, international law, and other values associated with the European Enlightenment and the League of Nations—was more than the result of economic frustration and racial prejudice. It was a "destined" response to a cultural process that had been taking place progressively throughout Europe in the modern era. When Europeans began diverging from the rest of the world in material wealth and gained a sense of superiority from their technological advances, Plessner argued, they began to reject the necessity of their value system, Christianity, for the maintenance of that global dominance. This decoupling of Christianity from their secular identity as Europeans enabled them to export their culture abroad, but it also made many "suspicious" of any closed value system or "ideology" that claimed universal validity beyond the reality of naked material interest. (He knew because he, too, had contributed to that suspicion in the Weimar years.) Germans attempted to build a unified nation in the years after 1871 in this intellectual environment of "suspicion of ideology," he said. To many of them, the biology of race appeared as the only realistic foundation of a people. Their protest as a young people against the political humanism of the older nations of the West was a protest against ideology in general.[13]

Although Plessner diagnosed secularization as the root cause of German protest against the West, he did not, as Christian democrats would, prescribe a return to Christian ideology as the path to German pacification. Instead, he imagined the emergence of a "new humanism" for Europe as a whole, one that would be more open and less "suspect" than the older version against which German nationalists had protested. Specifically, Plessner sought to transcend the dogma of secularism—hostility to all Christian involvement in public life—that had made Western humanism appear to many Germans just as ideological as the Western Christianity it aimed to replace. That secularism was particularly apparent in the ideology of German socialists from the nineteenth century into the twentieth.[14]

As the Nazi regime clashed with both secular socialists and conservative Christians across the Dutch border after 1936, in the Netherlands Plessner laid the groundwork for an academy where he hoped to recruit other exiled German scholars dedicated to the possibility of partnership between science and Christianity in a future unified European federation. The list of invitees demonstrated the reach of the German intellectual emigration throughout Europe: it included the philosopher Ernst Cassirer in Sweden, the political economist Julius Moritz Bonn in England, the biologist Julius Schaxel in the Soviet Union, and the philosopher Karl Löwith in Italy. The plan fell through for imaginable organizational reasons, but it showed that Plessner regarded his work as the vanguard of an open-minded, what might be called post-secular, European humanism.[15] "Man," Plessner said in a lecture in 1937, "faced with the dissolution of a world determined by Christianity and the ancients, now fully abandoned by God and in danger of sinking into animal nature, poses himself anew the question of the essence and aim of being human."

The new humanist must not turn back reflexively to the security of Christian faith to create a new society, he said, but neither could he close off dialogue with religious people and reject the possibility of God's existence.[16] The world after Nazism would still be post-Christian, but it must not be anti-Christian. The task Plessner set for a future Europe distinguished him from other prominent German anti-Nazi humanists, such as the philosopher Edmund Husserl, who held on to a purely secular definition of "European man."[17]

After the outbreak of the Second World War in 1939, but before Dutch authorities under Nazi occupation forced him out of his university position for the second time in his career, Plessner issued one last major statement on Germany before Hitler's fall. The book he published in 1941, titled *Laughing and Crying*, was on its surface a purely objective analysis, claiming to explain the "function" of two bodily phenomena that separate human nature from animal nature. Plessner's fairly questionable conclusion was that human beings laugh or cry when they become conscious of a loss of control over their bodies. Reviewing the book when it came out, one eminent Swiss psychologist expressed confusion as to why the author chose to focus narrowly on the breakdown of "bodily control" as the source of these phenomena. Plessner's scientific analysis seemed strange because at heart the book was really a humanistic argument about the future of Germany. Plessner was telling Germans, famously reputed for humorlessness and stoicism, to stop trying to rule an inherently unruly body politic. He was calling upon them to mitigate the "masculine" practice of self-control with the presumably feminine practice of self-surrender.[18]

For Plessner, this meant that Germans would literally surrender the idea of a sovereign state and instead embrace a mission to build a peaceful European union. In 1946, in a lecture he gave to an organization led by the Dutch socialist politician Gerrit Jan van Heuven Goedhart, Plessner proposed that Germans make a "positive out of the negative" of unconditional defeat: instead of trying to reconstruct a centralized German state that had proved itself "unfeasible" in the Weimar years, they should form an extremely loose federation in which the different German regions could cooperate more easily with their non-German neighbors in a larger European community. With no centralized pressure from Berlin, Germans in the Rhineland, Hessen, and Württemberg-Baden could work together more easily with the French, in Westfalia-Oldenburg more easily with the Dutch and Belgians, in Bavaria more easily with the Austrians, and in the eastern regions more easily with the Poles. "German youth is ready to take this path if it can be made clear to them that they must give up on the anachronism of the idea of the Reich for the sake of realizing European cooperation," he said.[19]

Furthermore, like the socialists who led the SPD in the Western zones of occupied Germany, Plessner felt that Germans should play an important role in keeping a future European community non-aligned in the emerging "cold war" between the United States and the Soviet Union. He argued against Wilhelm Röpke and others close to the Christian Democratic Union who advocated for an irrevocable marriage with the West. An active member of the Union of European Federalists, Plessner expressed concern that if Germans signed exclusive transatlantic partnerships with the Western countries, including the United States, they might alienate themselves from potential partners in communist countries and give up on what he called German youth's new "universal task" to "bring together East and West."[20] When it became clear in 1949 that West Germany would become a sovereign state and that Europe more generally was dividing into mutually hostile blocs, Plessner argued in Germany's main student newspaper that young people in the West should work culturally in whatever way they could to "strengthen the deliberations and feelings that fight against war" within the new reality.[21]

At the University of Göttingen, where he accepted a post as professor in 1950 and became involved in education policy, Plessner supported efforts to promote dialogue with the East. He worked with Lower Saxony's socialist cultural minister, Richard Voigt, who was attempting to design a regional unified school system in the spirit of non-aligned Europe. Unlike the regions led exclusively by Christian parties, Lower Saxony—where socialists were the dominant party in coalition with Christians and liberals—did not require its schools to teach Christianity, a policy that would have alienated Marxists. In an effort to gather all anti-fascist forces, socialists even included a Communist Party member in the government until 1948. Furthermore, the cultural ministry recommended that teachers promote an ideal of federated Europe separate from the "political, societal, and ideological opposition" between the United States and the Soviet Union.[22] In his own work as a scholar, Plessner also promoted

East-West cooperation. As newly elected president of the German Philosophical Society, he planned the group's annual conference for 1950 with the theme "Symphilosophein" (Greek for "philosophizing together") and invited communist thinkers from East Germany who argued for dialectical materialism.[23]

Neutral educational and scholarly principles such as the ones advocated in Lower Saxony became difficult to sustain as the Cold War intensified and fear of Soviet aggression increased among the West German population. Unless they took a militant stance against communism, politicians and teachers faced the danger of being branded as irresponsible, even traitorous. At the opening of a meeting in 1950 planned by the Congress for Cultural Freedom, a new organization of the non-communist left to which Plessner belonged, the writer Arthur Koestler called those who wanted to cooperate but not align with the West "half-virgins of democracy," referring to women who are comfortable with foreplay but not penetration.[24] Meanwhile, Chancellor Adenauer mounted pressure on the regional states to adopt laws decisively promoting Western culture, which for his government meant Christian values. The CDU leadership was adamant that Germany's renewal in a Western democracy depended on teaching Christian religion in the primary school (*Volksschule*) and the "humanism that derived from it" in the elite secondary school (*Gymnasium*).[25] At a speech in June 1952 to students at the University of Frankfurt, where Plessner was set to take over temporary directorship of the left-leaning Institute for Social Research, Adenauer said that while Germans were rightly proud of their independence, it was important at this moment to show commitment to their Western allies.[26]

Meanwhile, nationalist extremism seemed to be growing among the right wing of German youth and anti-Christian extremism among the left wing. In 1952, sixteen seats in Lower Saxony's state assembly were filled by members of the neo-Nazi Socialist Reich Party, and a major study registered a rise in "pro-Nazi orientations" among West Germans aged eighteen to twenty.[27] Plessner, who was in the process of having a new house built in Göttingen, received several antisemitic threats. On the other side of the political spectrum, in July the leaders of the ruling party in East Germany announced at their party conference that Christian churches would henceforth be subject to expropriation and surveillance as opponents of socialism. West Germany's Communist Party released a similarly anti-Christian platform in early November, calling for a "revolutionary subversion of the Adenauer government" in the struggle for German reunification.[28]

In this environment of political pressure and fear, Plessner and other educators close to the SPD seem to have taken the step to exclusive partnership with the pro-Western advocates of Christian education. Strikingly, he welcomed Göttingen students and faculty to the new semester in November 1952 with a grave lecture in the main auditorium on the origins of hatred in society, which he identified as "modern faithlessness." "It is palpably evident what can come of the appraisal of human existence when the theological backing handed down to him is taken away," he said. "Individual philosophers and free spirits may come to terms with this situation; the mass of the half-educated will not." Arguing that Germans were still in a state of political tutelage [*Vormundschaft*] and therefore in danger of channeling their frustration into hatred against others, he seemed to suggest that the masses could not do without religion until they matured.[29] He had moved from proposing dialogue between secular and religious humanists to urging Christianity's indispensability in public education. This move would be sure to cut off communication with communist philosophers who rejected religion from the principles of dialectical materialism. At the age of sixty, the longtime bachelor also decided to take the final step into matrimony with a young scholar in Frankfurt, Monika Tintelnot.

Under the new helm of Erich Ollenhauer, the socialist leadership of the SPD began to pledge more cooperation with Christian Democrats in their efforts to create an educational system and a foreign policy dedicated to a peaceful and unified Europe in partnership with the United States. Kurt Schumacher, the militant anti-church and anti-alignment politician who had led the party since its refounding, died the year before. In Lower Saxony, where Plessner lived and taught, socialists would work with their Christian political counterparts to make that state the first socialist-controlled region in the Federal Republic to require Christianity as a mandatory subject of study in public schools. Although students could opt out if they wished, teachers would be asked "to cultivate and educate the young people entrusted to them as citizens of a democratic and social state . . . on the foundation of Christianity, the assets of Western culture, and the inheritance of German self-cultivation [*Bildung*]."[30] This was the language of Adenauer's government, which campaigned on a platform to build a "European community in the spirit of Western Christianity." After the difficult electoral defeat of 1953, Ollenhauer even declared the SPD's willingness to cooperate, tentatively, with Adenauer's Christian government on a foreign relations endeavor that Schumacher had most opposed: military alliance with Western Europe against the Soviet Union.

A pamphlet released in 1953 by the European Youth Union, the new youth group associated with the Union of European Federalists in Germany to which Plessner belonged, explained some of the reasoning behind this commitment. The pamphlet was written by a young socialist associated with the SPD in Munich, Heinz Hahn. Titled *How Do I Hold a Discussion with Communists?* and featuring a cover illustration of an open hand confronting a closed fist, the pamphlet announced that the aim of the group was to develop a new idea for Europe that "substitutes partner-ship for class hatred, party hatred, national hatred" in a way that would "excite the youth of a whole continent." The problem with the communist was that he rejected that very idea of "partnership." The pamphlet quoted a recent report to the United States Senate, likely in one of the hearings led by Senator Joseph McCarthy, about how hate-filled communists were not interested even in cooperating with Christians who say they want to create a more just social order. Their minds were made up: they did not communicate ideas, only propagated them. For that reason, it was impos-sible for them to contribute to the "building up of a new societal order of partnership in Europe." Nevertheless, with its how-to guide for breaking their defenses and coaxing them into discussion, the group still held out hope for a more cooperative future.[31]

WESTERNISM AND THE "MANLY" PEACE

The socialist opposition's pledge to cooperate, even tentatively, with Adenauer was crucial because the chancellor needed its support in controversial policy proposals he had planned in late 1953 to convince the United States government of West Germans' readiness to begin regaining complete sovereign control over their country. First, Adenauer's new inte-rior minister, the Nazi-turned-Christian politician Gerhard Schröder, introduced legislation in the parliament for the creation of a new Federal Committee for the Education System (*Ausschuss für das Unterrichtswesen*), an institution designed to foster a Western-oriented European ideal in the various regionally controlled education systems. While not a ministry of education with powers of coercion, the plan ran the risk of appearing to regional leaders dangerously close to Weimar- and Nazi-era attempts to synchronize a federalist system. Second, Adenauer aimed to convince a wary population devastated by Nazi militarism of the necessity to rearm Germany and possibly even reintroduce mandatory military service.

With socialist support, the educational bill passed easily in late 1953, and the Committee for the Education System began its work in early 1954. The committee consisted of members appointed directly by the federal interior ministry and the president of the Permanent Conference of State Cultural Ministers. Both appointing bodies were headed by CDU politicians. Felix Messerschmid, one of the leading appointees, was a former youth leader in the Weimar Republic and the founder of a postwar study group in southwestern Germany dedicated to rewriting school text-books in the spirit of Christianity and European community. In his mani-festo, Messerschmid described the committee's task to reintroduce the educational insights of the old patriotic youth movement that had been lost in the Nazi period. In a country with a shattered and shameful image of itself, he wrote, students needed to relearn how to be proud of their fatherland and how to identify with it again. The teacher must serve as a political role model for students, as the youth movement had once shown. But instead of leading them into myths about German racial purity like the Nazis, the new German teacher would show the true history of the German nation and "of the greater unities"—Europe and the Western idea of liberal democracy—"into which it flows." Messerschmid failed to mention that the old patriotic youth leaders, including his own mentor in the Weimar years, had been skeptical of Germany's compatibility with Western liberal democracy and had been willing to partner with the Nazis twenty years earlier.[32]

No one in the Federal Republic represented the patriotic youth move-ment's shift away from nationalism and toward Westernism more than the educator and foreign policy scholar Arnold Bergsträsser, who had recently returned from a long emigration in the United States to reside again permanently in the land of his birth and lead a new program in political science at the University of Freiburg in southwestern Germany. That university had, in 1933, famously fallen under the leadership of the professor Martin Heidegger, the anti-Western philosopher whose works were popular among nationalist youth. Now, the region of Baden, which fell under French occupation after the war, had banned Nazi Party member Heidegger from teaching there. Bergsträsser, on the other hand, returned as a committed liberal democrat with influential American connections who could claim never having joined the Nazi Party. Once back in post-Nazi Germany, Bergstrasser was unparalleled in the number of young West German political leaders he helped train and in how many influential programs he helped shape.[33] Revered for his teaching, he came to be held in such esteem that Adenauer even floated his name for the republic's presidency, now a mostly symbolic role reserved for the country's most illustrious personalities.[34]

Bergsträsser's prominence had much to do with the image he created for himself as a patriot who had preserved unchanged the nation's precious cultural heritage in emigration while it was destroyed by the Nazis on German territory. As he made sure it was known, he spent the fifteen years from 1937 to 1952 as a grateful resident of the United States but renounced his recently gained American citizenship and his professorship at the University of Chicago to return out of a feeling of deep patriotism and Christian forgiveness. "Who has seen more of his homeland," Bergstrasser wrote in a musing on emigration reminiscent of the poet Heinrich Heine, "the one who exiles, or the exile who, out of love, refuses to be exiled?"[35] Upon his return, he claimed that he had confirmed things about the German tradition perhaps not as readily apparent to those who had been bombarded by the anti-American propaganda of the Nazis and had never witnessed the United States themselves: the profound ideas that linked Germans in an unbreakable "Western" chain not only to other Europeans but all the way to the Americans of the United States.[36]

In truth, Bergsträsser's presentation of his (and Germany's) past masked a shift in his earlier thinking before leaving Germany for the United States. Like so many German nationalists whose foremost ideal was cultural unity and maintenance of the state, he supported the revolt of German youth against "the West" and in 1933 officially endorsed the Hitler-Papen government as a protection against the communist threat in Germany. He did that despite his partial Jewish heritage, which along with his conservatism sabotaged his career after 1935 when Nazi students began disrupting and boycotting his lectures at the University of Heidelberg. Comparing the situation to Lorenzo Medici's role in bringing the crazed Savonarola to power in Renaissance Italy, Bergsträsser apparently recognized that conservative nationalists in Germany had called forth a leader, Hitler, who now existentially threatened them and the cultural assets of Christianity they hoped he would protect against the communists, the secularists, and the pacificists.[37]

In 1937, Bergsträsser used his high-level contacts from the youth movement and the university, including early opponents of Hitler at the highest echelons of the German army and in the American academic establishment, to arrange for his escape to the United States. There, he would attempt to convince American leaders that the Nazis represented a threat to all humanity and that they did not represent the culture of the "true Germany," which in its essence belonged to the West. In the later words of future chancellor Kurt Georg Kiesinger, Bergsträsser "confessed himself with decisiveness to the West."[38] He obtained a teaching appointment at the far western corner of the United States, near Los Angeles, at Scripps College, an elite private women's school where he taught courses in Western Civilization and on the spirit of German culture in the work of Johann Wolfgang von Goethe. The work of Goethe, he would argue in the English-language scholarship that came out of his years teaching in America, balanced what he called the typically feminine virtues of peace and love with the masculine virtues of discipline, force, and order.

When fellow German exiles who remembered the true facts of Bergsträsser's pre-Nazi past threatened to derail his new trajectory, Bergsträsser and his friends were forced into the position of having to justify his potential usefulness to the American government in helping create a pro-Western Germany after the fall of Hitler. Emil Gumbel, the socialist supporter of the League of Nations whose career had been ruined by nationalist students with the blessing of Bergsträsser, informed the Federal Bureau of Investigation that this man now masquerading as a committed liberal democrat once mentored student leaders who were now top officials in the Nazi regime. (Bergsträsser himself privately expressed regret for this, especially when he learned of their role in the Holocaust.) Sacked from his post at Scripps and in and out of alien internment camps for much of the war, Bergsträsser was able to regain a teaching post only through the character witness of other prominent

German émigrés of more credible anti-Nazi and pro-Western pedigree, such as Thomas Mann and Carl Joachim Friedrich (who had made their conversions to pro-Westernism in the 1920s).[39] The U.S. Congress began funding university programs to help familiarize American soldiers with Germany in preparation for the postwar occupation, and Bergsträsser was hired to chair the Committee on the History of Culture at the University of Chicago, whose president, a Goethe enthusiast, was hiring German émigré scholars to help shape a curriculum dedicated to the definition of "Western values."[40]

The pro-Western, anticommunist émigrés at elite American institutions such as the University of Chicago were able to use their new influence as experts on German culture to pressure the American military occupation to support conservative policies that they argued would help win over the defeated nation as a dependable partner of the West. In 1947 and 1948, together with a coterie of other scholars at the University of Chicago and with the support of the university's president Robert Maynard Hutchins, Bergsträsser advised the military government to abandon its attempts to impose an American-style unified high school system on Germans, a move that prominent local leaders, including the Bavarian cultural minister, were vigorously resisting. Some occupation officials argued that Germany's education system, which mixed church and state and used testing at age ten to separate out gifted students for studies leading to university, was undemocratic and perpetuated divisions of religion and class. The officials did not understand, Bergsträsser and his colleagues argued, the Pandora's box of the unified school system question in Germany. It would be better to return to the status quo ante and allow the continuation of the higher-tracked schools (Gymnasiums), where teachers trained future leaders in Greek and Latin and the ideals of self-formation (*Bildung*) in authors such as Goethe, thus preserving the "consciousness of the common ground of Western civilization." The military government's ambitious plans were famously dropped in 1949.[41]

"Do you remember Bergsträsser from Heidelberg?" asked the émigré political philosopher Hannah Arendt in a letter to her friend Karl Jaspers in 1949. "After he had successfully accommodated himself to the [Nazi] regime, it was shown that he had a whole string of Jewish ancestors." Arendt suggested it was deeply dishonest to profess that authentic German culture had always been rooted in the West, when only years before the same person had advocated German exceptionalism against those very same normative Western values.[42] To be fair, Bergsträsser expressed some recognition that a German commitment to a Western alliance could easily appear opportunistic.[43] It was also true that he never again spoke of his conservative-revolutionary days, when he urged German students to "resist" the paradigms imposed on them by the West through the League of Nations. Instead, he promoted the creation of a Western security community and helped found key transatlantic institutions, such as the sister think tanks American Council on Germany and Atlantic Bridge, organizations that still exist today. Before returning permanently to Germany in 1954, Bergsträsser lectured on American culture as a visiting professor at the universities in Erlangen and Frankfurt and worked for the U.S. State Department's High Commission on Germany as a foreign expert.

One explanation for the fact that few of Bergsträsser's collaborators back in Germany, including Helmuth Plessner, mentioned his past publicly is that they were so committed to combating radicalization among the youth and so single-mindedly committed to substituting partnership for old conflicts. After all, the values Bergsträsser expressed in lectures, such as the one he gave at the University of Freiburg in 1954, would have been compelling to a post-secular supporter of European community such as Plessner. To be part of "Europe, our Europe," he said, was not just to be born in a specific place, but to have certain ideals: to strive toward cultural freedom and social responsibility, to overcome divisions, and to understand norms and recognize their binding force." Bergsträsser had abandoned his earlier nationalist language and now called on Germans to "sacrifice an element of sovereignty" to a European entity in the "struggle for the art of peace."[44] In his work advising the CDU-led government in the state of Baden-Württemberg on how to foster political responsibility, liberal democracy, and European unity in high schools, Bergsträsser's goals also seemed laudable. Plessner did privately note Bergsträsser's "fractious and erratic" personality and inquired into his "prior political standing," but he generally recommended him as "a gentleman through and through and an unusually cultivated spirit of world experience."[45]

Just beneath the surface of Bergsträsser's public pronouncements on global unity and common European values boiled a hateful anticommunism that was potentially more of a problem for a partnership with open-minded humanists such as Plessner. One of Bergsträsser's doctoral students in Chicago, Wilma Eggers, remembered him throwing a briefcase across the room when she suggested the Communist Party co-founder Rosa Luxembourg as a possible dissertation topic.[46] Bergsträsser typically blamed these outbursts on his injury from the First World War, but his private letters on the "red threat" proved that there was real hatred of communists behind them.[47] In public, he preferred to let those affiliated with the new Evangelical and Catholic academies and adult education centers in the European movement hold countless talks and seminars on the threat of communism to the Christian way of life. The sociologist René König, who remembered this strategy from his student days in Berlin when anticommunism provided a common goal for Christian conservatives and Nazis, remembered the return of Bergsträsser's star and his "mushy" rhetoric as evidence that "nothing had changed in this country."[48]

But something had changed. Bergsträsser's prominence revealed a new discourse in German patriotism: a stated commitment to the value of peace, and a justification of military strength only in the "Western" posture of defense. Bergsträsser's old colleague Carl Schmitt, who unlike Bergsträsser had committed himself to the Nazis and now paid the consequences of a university teaching ban, argued that Germans were adopting the typical American ideology of "the West." In his book *Nomos of the Earth* (1950), Schmitt noted that the early leaders of the United States, men such as President Thomas Jefferson, held two simultaneous opinions of Europe: on one hand they hated it and wanted to separate from it, and on the other they imagined their people as derived from it and in fact a better version of it. For these early American nationalists, what made the "West" superior was the rejection of Europe's constant conflict and warfare. Schmitt quoted Jefferson in a Christian-inspired statement that would provide the prelude to America's hegemony over the Western hemisphere: "it should be that the meridian of the mid-Atlantic should be the line of demarcation between war and peace, on this side of which no act of hostility should be committed, and the lion and the lamb lie down in peace together." The only Western justification for war, therefore, was to defend against violations of the peace.[49]

Indeed, the promise to adopt a purely defensive military posture was crucial to the Federal Republic's entry into the North Atlantic Treaty

Organization (NATO), the military coalition that the United States formed in 1949 to forge military partnerships with Western European countries in defense against potential Soviet expansion. In August 1954, Adenauer's negotiations with the French for a specifically Western European security alliance against the Soviet Union (a proposed European Defense Community) fell through, scaring the Americans and prompting them to invite the Federal Republic to join NATO. Adenauer, leveraging parliamentary opposition as evidence that the Federal Republic's entry would cost him political capital at home, negotiated a deal that would give his government sovereignty over its foreign policy by May 1955. Naturally, leaders in the U.S. State Department expressed anxiety over the prospect of military alliance, even the possibility of sharing nuclear weapons, with a people whose leaders had recently embraced the value of conflict and struggle.

NATO members required the West German government to demonstrate proof that its new military would legitimize force only in a defensive posture. Likewise, the United Nations, founded after the war to replace the defunct League of Nations, granted observer status to the Federal Republic in 1955 but required evidence that it was a "peace-loving state" before granting full admission (Article 4 of the U.N. Charter). In light of these demands on Germans to "prove themselves politically," the German Committee for the Education System advised the government to promote harmonization among the divergent social studies curricula in the regional states.[50] That year, the new socialist-led government of Bavaria, headed by Wilhelm Hoegner, appointed Bergsträsser and Messerschmid as primary advisers for the creation of a new institution to be called the Academy of Political Self-Formation (*Akademie für Politische Bildung*), a project to provide teachers all over the country with common educational materials.

The academy proposal was not an easy sell among those in West Germany skeptical of educational centralization, especially those Catholic politicians who had staunchly opposed the creation of unified schools in both the Weimar Republic and the Third Reich, and again under the American military occupation. In February 1956, Bergsträsser gave a speech in the Bavarian state assembly to ensure Christian leaders that partnership with socialists in creating common materials would not undermine their efforts to promote Christian values. "We have nothing more necessary than security at this decisive moment in world history," Bergsträsser told the representatives. As a result, all parties dedicated to the maintenance of German existence must cooperate in creating a curriculum that fostered what he called "calm, manly, and healthy political thought."[51]

Bergsträsser's case for the new Academy for Political Self-Formation as an incubator for "calm, manly, and healthy political thought" was part of his larger vision for a new type of military service in a sovereign, post-Nazi Germany. In 1956, parliamentarians began discussing the possibility of conscription for men above eighteen, a previously unpopular idea now gaining traction even among socialists. Around this time, West German parents began listening to arguments that military service could inculcate values of peace-loving discipline instead of militarism. If public opinion polls can be trusted, many of them (especially mothers) supported the idea of male conscription because they worried that their teenage children (especially boys) were being influenced by a new American popular culture of rock 'n' roll and sexual promiscuity, rebelling against hard work and commitment.[52] The public face of the reconstituted West German military, General Hans Speidel—Erwin Rommel's chief deputy during the war, and the same man who helped spirit Bergsträsser out of Nazi Germany to America in 1937—promoted the armed services as a place to train young men with "clean" and "manly attributes."[53]

As a foreign policy adviser, Bergsträsser advocated militant force not in the use of arms, but in the "peaceful" leveraging of economic power. Elected as the first president and director of the new German Society for Foreign Policy (*Deutsche Gesellschaft für Auswärtige Politik*), an equivalent of the Council on Foreign Relations in the United States, he endorsed a manly posture against East Germany and the Soviet Union now that the West German government could finally determine its own policy.[54] Bergsträsser supported the adoption of the Hallstein Doctrine—named after Foreign Office strategist Walter Hallstein, who recommended Bergsträsser for the society's presidency—according to which the Federal Republic would use its powerful export economy to impose trade sanctions on any foreign state that opened diplomatic relations with East Germany. Helped along by his mediation in 1956, socialist opposition leaders such as the SPD chairman Ollenhauer and chairman of the SPD parliamentary faction Carlo Schmid came to support the Hallstein

Doctrine.[55] It was tough and manly, but the threat behind it was no longer military. They were convinced by the policy, akin to America's Marshall Plan, that the robust West German government would offer development aid to new postcolonial nations on the condition that they did not align with the Soviet bloc.[56]

Bergsträsser's ideas on education and foreign relations were reflected in the recommendations the German Committee for the Education System made to Adenauer's government in 1956 for coordinating the way West German schoolteachers would deal with communism and Eastern Europe in their classrooms. In March, the committee advised that teachers should emphasize that the Slavic peoples of the East were shaped by the religious culture of the Eastern Orthodox Church and thus did not belong to the historical cultures of Western (Catholic and Protestant) Christianity. However, they were still part of a larger community of European Christian descent. It was crucial, the committee wrote, for West German youth to appreciate the "seriousness and force of the intellectual, moral, and religious life" on which Slavic cultures had been built before communism and on which they would depend for reconstruction once they were "liberated" from it. Furthermore, the committee argued that West German students must still "process" the destruction Germans themselves had caused in Eastern Europe, for only when German youth properly grasped the collapse of European Christian culture that had enabled Nazism would they be able "to effectively represent" the Western ideals of freedom and peace in their arguments against communists.[57]

STRANGE BEDFELLOWS

The discomfort that German socialists sometimes felt when they found themselves "in bed"—or at least on the same planning committees—with militant anticommunists such as Bergsträsser became evident when it began to seem that the icy cold relations between the world's superpowers might be thawing. In the spring of 1956, news that Joseph Stalin's successor as leader of the Communist Party of the Soviet Union, Nikita Khrushchev, had given the green light for communist parties in Western Europe to participate in coalition politics in parliament and planned to grant more autonomy to Eastern European nations gave many West German socialists hope that the Federal Republic would no longer have to posture so aggressively. For a moment, it even seemed that the partnership the opposition and the regime had apparently struck to promote an exclusively Atlantic-oriented foreign policy might no longer be necessary. (Indeed, one of Khrushchev's main objectives in his policy of "de-Stalinization" was to separate Social Democrats in the Federal Republic from the Adenauer government.)[58]

Helmuth Plessner, certainly, was hopeful for a thaw. As the main German representative to the International Institute of Philosophy, whose members consisted almost exclusively of scholars from the non-communist world, Plessner supported what he called the "brave and wise resolution" in September 1956 to hold the following year's meeting in the Polish People's Republic, so that in the new era of de-Stalinization philosophers living in the West and the East could meet for the first time in a communist-led country.[59] The following month, Plessner also tried to convince the University of Göttingen to bring the Marxist philosopher Ernst Bloch, who taught in East Germany, for a lecture series that would aid in the mutual understanding of non-communists and communists.[60]

Journalistic exposés on the Nazi pasts of top figures in West German society also threatened to weaken the marriage of convenience between socialists and conservatives. Plessner, who had been working with the socialist-led cultural ministry in Lower Saxony to expose former Nazi personnel in the region's bureaucracy, expressed concern that some of the people Bergsträsser supported for membership in the German Society for Sociology—for example the staunch conservatives Helmut Schelsky and Arnold Gehlen—had been active members of the Nazi Party just years earlier. It also turned out that the author of one of West Germany's most popular books for teachers on democratic education, *Partnership: The Task of Political Education* (1953), was written by the Nazi educator Theodor Wilhelm under the pseudonym Friedrich Oetinger.[61] The historian Heinrich August Winkler aptly noted that such occurrences were not coincidental: the new ideal of a European community, understood as a committed and militant defender of Western liberal democratic values, appealed to so many former supporters of Nazism because it "provided a new context for their anti-communism."[62] The erupting scandal around Hans Globke, the author of a legal commentary on the Nuremberg Laws before becoming Adenauer's closest political adviser, seemed to be only the tip of an iceberg. A list of thousands of former Nazis in high administrative, political, and military posts, fully exploited by the East German government, threatened to hinder fragile partnerships that had been formed.[63]

Despite these signs, however, the Soviet government's repressive crackdown against new declarations of freedom in Poland and Hungary in late 1956 dashed the hopes for dialogue and drove the socialist opposition back into the arms of the Adenauer government. A top official in the German Democratic Republic was reported having said at a writers' conference that year that the goal of the ruling Socialist Unity Party was no longer to reunite East and West Germany. By the time votes came before the West German parliament in spring 1957 to approve the creation of a European Atomic Community and a European Economic Community of exclusively Western European nations, the socialist faction had little choice but to support it, in a complete turnaround from its opposition to such policies in the earlier part of the decade.

Although the socialist opposition and Adenauer's government remained strange bedfellows, their broad agreement on basic ideals to foster among youth demonstrated the political stabilization of the Federal Republic. As the political scientist Otto Kirchheimer noted in 1957, Germans' cooperation was "impressive" compared with the "violent dissension" that had marked the Weimar Republic. In part but not only because of a shrinking field of future options under the pressures of the Cold War, German educators ceased to clash over basic questions of democracy, the political usefulness of Christianity, and Germany's relationship to international law. They now shared a vision of partnership in a federated Europe, born of a common sense of existential threat and the product of a long process of partnership building with previously opposing groups. They had, as Kirchheimer wrote, "for better or for worse . . . effectively joined the Western community."[64] Debates persisted about how best to achieve their vision of a unified Europe in partnership with the United States—debates about tactics, timing, and posturing toward communists—but there was a distinct lack of ideological conflict or opposition of principle to the new regime.

CHAPTER NINE

The Culture of Christian Partnership

THE LATE 1950S IN THE FEDERAL REPUBLIC of Germany was not a time of social volatility or high political drama, as the 1920s, 1930s, and 1940s had been. Boosted by American Marshall Plan money and their will to reconstruct the country, Germans were producing unprecedented amounts of goods and jobs, so that even though workers' wages were not increasing proportionally to business owners' profits, the overall standard of living for the population was higher than in most, if not all, other European countries. In the parliamentary elections of September 1957, Adenauer's Christian bloc won an absolute majority of votes with the slogan "No Experiments," an affirmation of the political status quo. Some contemporary commentators argued that the socialist opposition, which received thirty percent, could not compete because it offered no truly alternative vision or ideology to that of the pro-Western ruling government. The platforms of the two major parties, the CDU and the SPD, varied more in technical strategies than ultimate aims. It was with one eye trained toward Germany at the end of the decade that the American sociologist Daniel Bell published an essay collection subtitled "On the Exhaustion of Political Ideas in the Fifties."[1]

But careful observers of the Federal Republic did notice a different kind of social drama unfolding. German society was becoming more ethnically diverse and self-consciously pluralistic. Germans were starting to critically examine their people's history of persecution of ethnic minorities and other peoples, especially those in Eastern Europe. Adenauer's government was beginning to negotiate agreements with southern European nations racked with high unemployment to import guest workers into Germany's booming economy. Regional governments were beginning to open their universities to thousands of foreign students.[2] The dominant culture was also changing. In 1957, in the months before the federal elections, West Germans celebrated a huge international building exposition called "Interbau," funded in large part by American tax dollars to symbolize German-American friendship and cultural diversity, in the divided former capital city of Berlin. Attended by over a million visitors, the exposition's opening showcased a soaring modernist building designed by an American architect and debuted a new work by the professor and composer of Christian sacred music, Max Baumann, entitled "Perspectives."[3]

Scholars of German history have often argued that the country's transformation from a society that valued cultural uniformity in the beginning of the twentieth century to one that valued cultural plurality by the end of the century resulted from the rise of a new post-Nazi generation. They argue that this generational cohort, whose formative experience was the fall of Hitler in 1945 (hence their generation's nickname "the '45ers"), was able to face Germany's genocidal past in a way the older generation could not, and in the process opened up society to cultural diversity. It was under this generation's leadership that German politicians began using the term "multiculturalism" and built a Holocaust memorial in the heart of the nation's capital. As a result, many have seen the '45ers as the people who truly "democratized" post-Nazi Germany.[4]

While there is some truth in such a Promised Land narrative, according to which Germans who came of age in the enslaved land of ethnic nationalism were unable to cross over into the multiculturalist land of milk and honey, it often leaves out an important aspect of the story. It was the generation born between 1890 and 1910 that first critically examined Germany's antisemitic past and expanded its cultural horizons in the late 1950s, not the generation born between 1920 and 1940. Significantly, they celebrated their cultural plurality in a strongly Christian key, driven in large part by competition with communists in East Germany. In response to the anti-Western smear campaigns of the

East German government and the crisis over the city of Berlin, cultural leaders in the Federal Republic attempted to show that an open society based on religious values was a superior foundation on which to reunify a future Germany. Interbau itself was largely a response to the new monumental apartment buildings constructed in the 1950s by the East German government to symbolize Soviet-German friendship and a future Germany that would use its resources not to liberate the international marketplace but to ensure the welfare of its workers.[5]

This chapter tells the story of two important but often forgotten men, Hans-Joachim Schoeps and Ernst Benz, who represent the midcentury shift away from a Weimar-era ideal of a uniform national culture (*Kulturstaat*) to a post-Nazi-era ideal of a diverse but still fundamentally Christian culture. These two best-selling authors made a striking pair. Schoeps was one of a very small number of German Jews who survived the war in emigration and returned to Germany despite having lost his family in the Holocaust. Benz was a conservative Protestant who advised the Nazi government on church questions before 1937 and, like so many conservatives, remained silent in the face of persecution against Jews— he even contributed to antisemitic prejudice as a university professor and then as an army chaplain on the eastern front in the worst areas of genocidal violence, occupied Poland and Ukraine. Yet in a gesture of reconciliation, these two men nurtured a close personal relationship and professional partnership after the war. Together they founded a journal dedicated to retelling the history of the European religious tradition, and both wrote for newspapers owned by the publishing magnate Axel Springer, who made it one of his missions in post-Nazi Germany to foster reconciliation between Germans and Jews. Like the other figures studied in this book, these men began laying the foundations for their future collaboration already before the war, in the midst of the German church struggle under Nazi rule.

The work of Schoeps and Benz in post-Nazi Germany resonated not only with large parts of the reading public but also with many in the generation of West Germany's rising elites. They spoke to a question that troubled many young West Germans who grew up in the 1950s under a strong Christian government: namely, the proper role of churches and faith in a liberal democracy. Were there values rooted in religion that a republic needs to promote in order for the people to be responsible citizens? If so, which religion(s)? "Precisely because the democratic order constitutes itself entirely from below," wrote one member of the young West German generation who would go on to become an influential political thinker and justice on the Constitutional Court, "it is dependent like no other form of state on what is brought into it by [the] individual."[6]

The cultural leaders of the Federal Republic, including Adenauer's interior minister responsible for youth affairs, Gerhard Schröder, and teachers such as Schoeps and Benz, made the case that the inculcation of faith in monotheistic religion was indeed necessary for the maintenance of a Western liberal democracy. They sought to convince young Germans that a confession to the value of monotheism necessitated a decisive rejection of antisemitism, which they cast as the epitome of hatred and the very opposite of Christian partnership. Partnership, of course, requires two parties, which meant it was also crucial for Christian leaders to find Jews who would endorse their conservative ideology and testify to their turn away from evil. Older West Germans thus began embracing Jews and Judaism, not only to show that they had changed as a people, but also to celebrate the teaching of a monotheistic view of humankind over the materialist conception advocated by schools in the communist bloc. As we will see, much of the younger '45er generation welcomed this transition, while others began to resist it.

ANTICOMMUNISM AND THE NEW PARTNERSHIP WITH THE JEWISH COMMUNITIES

One cannot understand why the late 1950s saw a spike in the level of West German public discussion about antisemitism and the Jews without contextualizing it in the international political dynamics of those years. West Germans felt increasingly squeezed. From one side, American-led NATO forces ramped up pressure on Adenauer's government to equip its new military with nuclear warheads, a move that many understood would provoke the Soviet Union and further hinder hopes for reunification. From the other side, the East German government was launching a massive propaganda campaign to discredit the Federal Republic by revealing the names of suspected antisemitic war criminals who escaped prosecution and now staffed the highest leadership positions in all realms of West German society, from judges to large business owners and from government advisers to university professors.[7] In its propaganda pamphlets of 1956, the Committee for German Unity in East Berlin pointed to West German opinion polls showing that more than twenty percent of the population still believed they were better off without Jews in their midst. The campaign highlighted the periodic desecration of Jewish cemeteries in the Federal Republic as well as a recently publicized case in which a high school teacher at an elite West German school told a half-Jewish student that he was surprised the Nazis had forgotten to gas him.[8]

In this tense political atmosphere, the middle-aged publishing magnate Axel Springer—as the owner of the only mass-circulation media outlets in West Germany, the individual probably most responsible for opinion making—changed the editorial policy of his publications in two key ways. First, he decided to prioritize the importance of German reunification under the sign of Christian partnership. Springer, who made a high-profile trip to East Germany to promote his proposal, claimed to have been inspired after reading about the historical figure Nikolaus von Flüe, a fifteenth-century Christian mystic known as a symbol of unity for the once-divided land now known as Switzerland. Second, he demanded of his journalists more attention to Judaism and the fate of the Jews. He said he had been struck by his friend Erich Lüth's statement at an Evangelical Academy meeting that an "emasculated majority of Christians, humanists, and democrats" in Germany had not yet "answered for the Jewish brother" who had been persecuted and murdered under their watch during the Nazi years.[9] For Springer, the German reunification question and the Jewish question were not unrelated.

Springer's favored author on the Jewish question over the subsequent years was his close friend Hans-Joachim Schoeps, in 1957 probably the best-known spokesperson for the decimated Jewish minority in Germany. He was one of the very few German Jews—estimated to be less than five percent of the pre-1933 population—who survived the war in exile and made the difficult choice to return to post-Nazi Germany.[10] Six million Jews in Europe had been hunted down and murdered during the war under Hitler's rule, and most German Jews who had been lucky enough to flee understandably preferred to remain far away. In West Germany, what was already a tiny minority of one percent before Hitler was now demographically microscopic—roughly thirty thousand, not even a tenth of a percentage point—many of them not even German-born but rather displaced older Jews from countries farther east.[11] Schoeps, therefore, was one of the few capable of writing and speaking on Jewish topics. Although he sometimes expressed controversial views and held little direct connection with the actual Jewish communities of post-Nazi Germany, he held the ear of Springer and other influential figures in West Germany interested in German-Jewish reconciliation, including the Protestant president of the Federal Republic, Theodor Heuss, and the Christian Democratic president of the federal parliament, Eugen Gerstenmaier. His lectures at the Bavarian university where he taught packed lecture halls, and his many books sold thousands and thousands of copies.

Schoeps's popularity as a speaker and author in Christian circles during the 1950s was due mainly to the function he served in West German society as a symbolic Jew. Many of his students at the University of Erlangen, one of the mainsprings of Protestantism in Germany, later attested that it was an inspiring gesture for the younger generation of Germans to see a Jewish intellectual returning to his homeland despite everything that had happened. Many knew him for the open letter he wrote to President Heuss in 1951 calling for Germans to reckon with anti-semitism and announcing himself as a Jew who had returned "even though my parents and almost all my relatives were killed or gassed in the camps." Schoeps's choice to give Germans a second chance was particu-larly poignant in light of the resolution passed in 1948 by the Jewish World Congress, a Zionist organization that claimed to speak for all Jews, insisting that Jews should "never again live on the blood-stained ground of Germany."[12] Upon his return, not a few Germans used Schoeps for exculpatory purposes, asking him to serve as a character witness in their denazification hearings or citing his love for Germany as proof that Nazi antisemitism had been an aberration of the nation's true Christian spirit. One historian called this public use of Jews in Germany "the white-washing of the yellow badge."[13]

The function Schoeps served as a Jewish alibi for Christian Germany, however, cannot alone explain the currency he enjoyed among West German audiences. To fully understand it, one must examine the political value he attached to an embrace of Judaism and the Jews. In his lectures and books, Schoeps argued that an appreciation of Judaism would promise both a revitalization of the healthiest conservative elements of the original unified German Empire of 1871, as well as an eradication of the antisemitic (and anti-Catholic) cancers that later became aggressive and eventually overtook Germany. This message resonated with many Protestant Germans who had once supported attempts in the Third Reich to mold a uniform German national culture, but after the church struggle of the mid-1930s began to regret their choice and look back more fondly to the cultural federalism of the old German Empire.

Like his friend Arnold Bergsträsser, Schoeps neglected to mention that he himself had been willing in 1933 to support the Nazi-led national revolution and had only turned against it in the subsequent years, when he transformed himself from a young conservative revolutionary into a self-described conservative liberal democrat. When the Nazi regime consolidated its power and radicalized its racial policies, Schoeps began to regret his earlier condemnation of Zionists and his earlier insistence that Jews should not emigrate from Germany despite persecution.[14] In the midst of the Nazi persecution of several conservative Protestants in the Confessing Church, Schoeps argued in a book titled *Jewish-Christian Religious Dialogue Through Nineteen Centuries* (1937) that common suffering under the Nazis should open up the possibility, for the first time in almost two thousand years of European history, of Christian and Jewish partnership against the current secular order.[15] Supported by the Jewish community of Berlin led by chief rabbi Leo Baeck, the book sold for a brief time in Jewish-only bookshops in Germany. By the time he fled the country after the Kristallnacht pogroms of 1938 and received a job teaching at a Protestant theology department in Sweden, Schoeps had already rethought the political categories of his youth, which had included anti-Americanism and anti-democratism.[16]

From neutral Sweden, a generally tolerant liberal democratic monarchy where the history of Christianity was taught in all public schools, Schoeps helped envision a post-Nazi Germany built on biblical principles. He used his access to the impressive theological library at the University of Uppsala to assemble massive amounts of educational materials to promote future Christian-Jewish partnership. The upsetting word he received from contacts inside Germany, that his parents had been deported along with most other German Jews to camps, no doubt only enhanced his sense of mission.[17] As it became clear that Hitler would thankfully be defeated, Schoeps helped build an organization of fellow émigrés (from what he called "diverse ideological camps," including some former SPD members) to lobby the Western Allies against the prospect of a prolonged military occupation. They argued that the German underground resistance was now ready, after the experience of Nazism, to avoid the problems of Weimar and lead Germans into a new functioning liberal democracy.[18] In a Swedish-language publication titled *What Shall Be Done with Germany?* (1944), Schoeps wrote that the oppositions that prevented Germans from cooperating in Weimar—mainly between Protestantism and Catholicism—had been "canceled out by a second distinction between Christianity and National Socialism." He rejected the idea, popular in American military circles, that Germany's youth had been brainwashed and needed foreign reeducation. On the contrary, he wrote, they were already ready to accept the vision that "the old and eternally new belief in the Ten Commandments will become Germany's spiritual salvation."[19]

Schoeps was not only one of the few German Jews to return after the war to the Western occupied zones from emigration, but also one of the first. Before much of the rubble had even been cleared, Schoeps wrote to his old friends now scattered across the globe that he had decided to help build the Christian political foundations of post-Nazi Germany "precisely as a Jew." According to what he told his older friend and fellow German Jewish author Margarete Susman, who remained in Swiss emigration, the first job he took upon arriving in the American-occupied zone in 1946 was with a Protestant relief organization in Stuttgart whose members wanted to come to terms with their guilt.[20] Older German-born Jewish intellectuals who had known Schoeps since the Weimar years, such as Leo Baeck and Martin Buber, expressed surprise but also deep respect for his commitment to the reconciliation of Germans and Jews despite the Holocaust. He received less support from Gershom Scholem, a Zionist who believed that theological reconciliation was impossible, and who had himself returned to Germany only to spirit the remaining vestiges of Jewish material culture to Palestine.[21]

An impression soon developed among Germany's tiny Jewish population that Schoeps was more interested in promoting Christian politics than he was in reconstituting Jewish life.[22] Over the first Cold War years, he spent most of his energies collaborating with Christian leaders who wanted Germans to recognize the church's complicity in Jewish persecution. In 1948, he engaged in lengthy correspondence with theologians such as Wilhelm Röpke's friend Karl Thieme, who also aimed to provide a moral foundation for post-Nazi Germany through Christian-Jewish partnership and a reckoning with antisemitic elements in the church. "As a Jewish German, I stand in solidarity with other decent Germans," Schoeps told listeners in 1949 at the first conference for Christian-Jewish Cooperation, "whereby their decency is not dependent on the decision of the denazification court."[23] This promise to forgive past antisemites harmonized with the policies of the Christian politician Adenauer, who promised to make material reparations to Jews and the State of Israel for Nazi crimes but also to amnesty Nazi Party members who had "atoned" for their past political sins.[24]

Schoeps made the case in his best-selling books that Nazism emerged because the modern German unified state had been built on insufficiently Christian, and ultimately Jewish, political foundations. In *The Honor of Prussia* (1951) and *The Other Prussia* (1952), both of which were published with a press led by a former antisemite, Schoeps told the history of a path not taken. Otto von Bismarck, the founder of modern Germany and its first chancellor, wrote its constitution in 1871 simply as a treaty between the leaders of the various German states to promote the welfare of the German people, with no reference to God. His conservative opponent Ernst Ludwig von Gerlach, Schoeps wrote, unsuccessfully opposed this constitution from his Calvinist standpoint, arguing that the laws of all states, whether monarchies or republics, must have sanction from a power higher than humanity to be legitimate.[25] The paradox of the whole story, Schoeps argued in the climax of *The Other Prussia,* was that Gerlach's conservative tradition, infamous for its anti-Jewish prejudices, was actually profoundly Jewish in its insistence that all law must have divine sanction. The leaders of the Weimar Republic and Nazi Germany, like Bismarck before them, ultimately rejected that conservatism with disastrous consequences.[26]

The ideas at the heart of Schoeps's Prussian story connected him to a transatlantic network of conservative political theorists who would help shape both German and American foreign policy in the years to come. Not only was Schoeps's work privately praised by former Nazis who had turned back to Christianity after Hitler's failed experiment, such as Carl Schmitt, but it was also embraced by younger conservative intellectuals on both sides of the Atlantic who worried about the cultural preconditions for protecting liberal democracy. The young conservative Irving Kristol, who greatly admired Schoeps's writings, recruited him to write articles on the common Jewish and Christian foundations of an ethical politics in the American Jewish Committee's magazine *Commentary*. The Harvard University graduate student Henry Kissinger asked him to contribute an article to the journal he edited, *Confluence*.[27] Schoeps's contemporary Erik Kuehnelt-Leddihn, the European correspondent for the conservative journal *National Review* and a formative influence on its founder William F. Buckley, told Schoeps in 1953 that what united conservatives on both sides of the ocean was "theism, the faith in a personal God that pulls us into responsibility," and that in this belief "synagogue and church form a primary factor."[28]

Schoeps, who like his historical lodestar Gerlach preferred liberal monarchies to republics, made himself the butt of some jokes when he led a short-lived campaign in 1954 to revive the German constitutional monarchy under the leadership of the Calvinist Hohenzollern family, but his ideas still resonated among younger conservatives.[29] The young Ernst-Wolfgang Böckenförde, on his way to becoming a Constitutional Court justice and perhaps Germany's premier legal theorist, pointed out to Schoeps after the two met at the Alpbach European Forum that, while much of the nation was sympathetic to the theocratic ideas represented by the old Prussian monarchy, conservative politics depended on the unbroken continuity of tradition. Liberal democratic monarchies such as the Netherlands, Denmark, Sweden, Belgium, and Norway enjoyed that continuity, but the new Germany did not. Schoeps agreed that the timing was inauspicious. But Böckenförde would go on to write in 1957, in language similar to that of Schoeps, that the liberal democratic state could not afford to be entirely neutral toward the belief systems of its citizenry.[30]

In 1957, the history of Germany's persecution of the Jews was thrust into mainstream West German political discourse by the East German government's delegitimization campaign. That year, the city council of West Berlin decided to invest in the rebuilding of the ruined Fasanenstrasse synagogue as a Jewish community center. The government of North Rhine–Westphalia decided to assist financially with the reconstruction of the beautiful Roonstrasse synagogue in Cologne.

In-depth reports of the trials of war criminals and the meetings and events of the Societies for Christian-Jewish Cooperation, which had been taking place for almost ten years, suddenly began to appear in the national press, in no small part thanks to the new editorial policy of Axel Springer and his press empire.[31] Schoeps, who spent much of his time in West Berlin and had recently published a volume of memoirs, was tapped to speak at the Day of German Unity in June 1958 in the giant square on the western side of the Brandenburg Gate, where he declared that "we are *one* nation, despite all the violence."[32]

Schoeps found widespread resonance with a pair of books he finished in 1958: one an extended essay extolling conservative virtues, the other a historical interpretation of Paul the Apostle from a Jewish standpoint. In typical conservative fashion, Schoeps worried in *Conservative Renewal* that although the political parties of West Germany were thankfully now "unified in all essential questions," German cultural leaders were not doing enough to raise a new generation of political elites who would carry on the values of social partnership and social cooperation that he claimed had achieved that consensus. They must recognize that republics, no matter how prosperous, are "structurally weak"—moneyed interest groups can easily buy elections and create cynicism—and therefore need "the building in of counterweights to stabilize the democracy." For Schoeps, this meant the strengthening of educational institutions that could translate traditional values into a modern idiom, beginning with attention to the core values of the Bible: "not everything," he wrote, but "some lines." In particular, he argued that the idea of the revealed Ten Commandments shared by Jews and Christians was indispensable. It is a testament to the popularity of these ideas that the Evangelical Academy in Lower Saxony recruited Schoeps in late 1958 to train one of the first crops of Bundeswehr officers in the spirit of biblical morality.[33]

Meanwhile, a crisis was developing over the status of West Berlin in the battle between the Federal Republic and the German Democratic Republic. In October 1958, East German government officials issued a secular "Ten Commandments of Socialist Morality" as part of a campaign to subordinate church influence and also delegitimize the West in general. One of the key spokespeople they put on their anti-Western campaign was a German of Jewish background named Albert Norden, who noted that the West German political leadership was full of unprosecuted war criminals and that the only solution to antisemitism there was the razing of religion and the building up of socialism.[34] With support from the Soviet Union, they made it clear that they would no longer tolerate the presence of Western forces in West Berlin as they consolidated their country. By the end of the month, Nikita Khrushchev sent his famous letter to the Western powers urging them to vacate West Berlin, sparking an international crisis for the next six months.

This geopolitical dynamic, more than any generational change, explains why the late 1950s saw a rise in the Jewish minority's profile and the official memorialization of its fate. It helps illuminate the paradox of why Germans in the Federal Republic would continue to consider Jews racially distinct and yet begin to associate their presence with a sign of Germany's commitment to an open democratic society. Chancellor Adenauer closed his speech at the rededication of the famous Cologne synagogue in September 1959 with the words, "we all want to be, with one another, a protection of order and a refuge and shield of justice."[35] It also sheds light on why the leaders of the socialist opposition in West Germany might have chosen the occasion of their annual conference in November to ensure voters that "socialism is no replacement for religion." Using the master language of post-Nazi Germany, the SPD leadership at Bad Godesberg declared the party was "always ready for a free partnership with the churches and religious communities," unlike socialism in the East.[36]

FROM THE THIRD REICH TO CULTURAL PLURALISM

At the very end of 1959, during the Christmas of that year, a wave of antisemitic events threatened to derail the West German government's attempt to present itself as a society that had atoned and matured. Foreign press outlets ran stories about a right-wing party whose members sprayed antisemitic graffiti on the synagogue in Cologne that Adenauer had rededicated just months before. In the weeks that followed, police counted five hundred separate antisemitic incidents throughout the country. Commentators raised the specter of renewed racism in Germany, and some leaders of Jewish organizations in the United States, such as the American Jewish Congress and the World Jewish Congress, wondered whether Germans had simply remained antisemitic behind a facade of official celebration of Judaism and Jews. The correspondent for the *New*

York Times in Germany wrote on January 2, 1960, "Like the symptoms of some long-dormant disease, a rash of anti-Semitic incidents burst out in West Germany this week, scarring the image of post-war Germany and foreigners alike."[37]

The West German government's response to old symptoms of hatred in the new Germany was mostly dismissive. In interviews with the foreign press, Adenauer's Christian interior minister Gerhard Schröder, a former Nazi Party member who embraced cultural diversity, downplayed the significance of the events, calling the perpetrators "hoodlums" and chalking up the graffiti as the result of "prejudices still living in a few young heads." He said that the government would reexamine what students were learning in schools and in churches about foreigners and minorities, but mostly he blamed the East German government for playing up the events as more important than they were.[38] Significantly, Schröder did not focus his remarks on antisemitism in particular, but on hatred in general. He and leaders in the regional governments suggested that as the West German population diversified culturally, with hundreds of thousands of refugees from the Eastern bloc countries, guest workers from Italy, Spain, Greece, and possibly Turkey, and exchange students from around the globe, schools simply needed to continue teaching youth about foreign cultures in a Christian European spirit of openness and partnership.[39]

Few West Germans were more valuable in educational efforts to combat communism and overcome "prejudice" than Ernst Benz, a university professor who wrote best-selling texts on foreign cultures from a Christian perspective. Franklin Littell, a long-standing American official in the Cultural Affairs Section of the High Commission on Germany and one of the founders of Holocaust studies in the United States, described Benz in 1959 as the "one great scholar of world reputation" who maintained Germany's tradition of studying religious culture in the footsteps of Max Weber.[40] He advised multiple institutions dedicated to European cultural integration, such as the German Commission for UNESCO. As dean of the theological faculty at the University of Marburg and director of its program in ecumenism, Benz wrote books on Christian engagement with Judaism, Hinduism, and Buddhism. In 1959 and 1960, Benz was arguing that Europeans would do especially well to engage with the ideas behind Buddhist and Hindu culture, which could act as bulwarks against the spread of communism in post-colonial Asian countries such as India or Vietnam.[41]

The students who took classes with Benz in West Germany would likely not have known much about their teacher's past and the transformation in his thinking since the Weimar and Nazi years. Like many who had lived through the war, he preferred not to speak about that time. However, reconstructing the story with the help of his recently discovered personal papers and his file from an American-funded denazification court helps us understand some of the logic of the turn away from a vision of cultural uniformity to one of cultural plurality in the Federal Republic. For in many ways, Benz, though an educated elite, expressed the outlook of mainstream conservative Protestants in Germany.

Benz's change in outlook seems to have taken place after 1937. Until then, he helped conceptualize the conservative revolutionary idea of a Third Reich, a Christian state with a uniform national culture. Despite his private opposition to racialism, he publicly supported the Nazi government and attempted to pull it toward pro-Christian policy through his conciliatory work between the pro-racialist German Christians and the anti-racialist Confessing Church. He joined the Nazi Party when the government required all civil servants to do so. By 1937, however, even the most hopeful conservatives in Germany had to admit the impossibility of church unification, and with it the failure of German cultural unification through a unified school system. Benz's mentor, Erich Seeberg, declared in 1938 that the best conservative Christians could hope for was a pluralistic spirit of mutual recognition and partnership among the conflicting sects.[42] Benz, according to a letter he wrote to a friend, began collecting library and archival materials in 1937 for a massive new book on Emanuel Swedenborg, the famous Scandinavian visionary who preached the diversity of divinity on earth. He would pursue this project on Christian pluralism with single-minded devotion, even lugging his books with him toward Poland when he enlisted as a German army chaplain in 1939, and then all the way into Russia in 1941 as part of Operation Barbarossa. He claimed to do much of the writing in a blockhouse near Bryansk, less than three hundred miles from Moscow.[43]

The Swedenborg project, which Benz began publishing in installments back in the Reich even while serving at the front, unsubtly implicated his own government in the modern process of de-Christianization typically associated with liberal or Marxist ideology. In articles for cultural journals in 1941 and 1942, Benz described how Swedenborg—an accomplished naturalist in early-eighteenth-century Europe who developed a theory of electricity decades before Benjamin Franklin conducted his famous experiment—was ridiculed by the German Enlightenment thinker Kant and the rationalist tradition that followed. For in addition to writing works on natural science, Swedenborg also published theological works in which he recorded mystical visions of ghosts and celestial beings. Benz showed that Kant, in his mean-spirited *Dreams of a Spirit Seer* (1766), disingenuously took Swedenborg's mystical visions out of context and tarred him as a fool worthy of "laughing at," ruining Swedenborg's reputation as well as that of his popularizer in Germany, Friedrich Oetinger. Kant even admitted in private to committing this unethical act in the service of "reason." But by ridiculing visionaries, Benz suggested, he destroyed the very essence of Christianity, beginning with the vision that Saul of Tarsus saw before he became Paul the Apostle.[44]

These implications ultimately put Benz on a collision course with the Nazi government, even when he publicly supported its policy to colonize Eastern Europe and cleanse it of Jews. In early 1942, the rising Nazi leadership, including especially Hitler's new chief deputy, Martin Bormann, was cutting all ties with the still divided churches in an attempt to shore up German unity and remake the racial landscape of Europe. Benz probably learned quickly of the memorandum Bormann circulated among party leaders declaring the "incompatibility" of Nazism and Christianity. As he served as chaplain in what Timothy Snyder has aptly called the "bloodlands" of Poland and Ukraine, Benz took a chance when he decided to self-publish a short pro-Christian report that his regular Protestant press dared not release. Titling it *The Religious Situation in the Ukraine,* Benz called for German assistance in the reconstruction of the Ukrainian Orthodox churches after decades of Soviet rule, led by cultural commissars who he claimed were typically Jewish. Though passionate in its conservative linkage of anticommunism and antisemitism, Benz's vision was entirely at odds with the party's plans for the destruction of Slavic culture in its new eastern empire.[45] Upon his return to the Reich in between tours in 1942, Benz found his mother's home in Meersburg, where he kept much of his library, "fully plundered," according to a letter. There are no records of his further contact with the party. Like most army chaplains, he seems to have carried out his duty to boost troop morale without promoting any active resistance against the regime. Benz redeployed to the western front, accompanied German soldiers during the American invasion of Normandy in the summer of 1944, and reported to the army's chief spiritual counselor, Franz Dohrmann, extraordinary stories about leading troops of different confessions in ecumenical Christian service as they faced death or capture.[46]

Benz emphasized his advocacy for the churches when he became friendly with military government officials in Marburg, which fell in the American occupation zone after the war. His successful denazification hearing of 1946, which as a party member he was required to undergo in order to regain a teaching post at the university, categorized his work to conserve Christianity as "resistance" and made no reference to his support for German imperial expansion or his antisemitic linkage of Jews and Bolshevism in his work on the Ukrainian churches.[47] Many in the top American occupation posts, including the military governors from 1946 to 1949, Joseph McNarney and Lucius Clay, were confessed Christians who expressed horror at the Nazi treatment of the churches and made it a top military priority to help rebuild them. Charles Hartshorne, the philosopher of religion from the University of Chicago who worked in the occupation to vet professors in the American zone, reported positively back to his colleague Arnold Bergsträsser in 1946 that he had met a man working on "mysticism, Swedenborg, and such topics" who "struck a chord" with him. Hartshorne was a member of the Unitarian Church, which in its origins in America drew heavily on the ideas of Emanuel Swedenborg.[48]

Benz's massive biography, *Swedenborg: Naturalist and Visionary*, which was cleared to be published in the American zone in 1948, emphasized the Christian pluralistic aspect of his thought. A famous partisan of the Dutch Republic, Swedenborg preached God's love for variety and a neo-Platonic conception of beauty as the influx of divine light. It was for that reason, Benz argued, that despite Kant's best efforts to destroy his reputation, Swedenborg's ideas survived and found fertile ground, not only in the pluralistic United States (among such people as Thomas Jefferson, Ralph Waldo Emerson, and William James) but also in the German-speaking world, among romantic writers such as Schelling and Hegel, who saw God's spirit represented diversely in the world. Christian pluralism—the recognition of multiple paths to the good not only in the various forms of Christianity, which Swedenborg held to be the true religion, but also in other religious expressions that recognized the universal in the plural—was for Benz a way out of the homogenizing tendencies of the transcendental idealism he saw manifested in Nazism.[49] He did not advocate the wholesale abandonment of the European Enlightenment. On the contrary, he suggested that Enlightenment-style reason must be rehabilitated in partnership with religion; without that partnership, it risked falling into animalistic barbarism.

Benz's emphasis on the importance of religious pluralism for the future of humanity resonated with many intellectual and political leaders in the United States who wanted to see religious faith flourish in the public life of Europe as a way to bring together a divided continent in partnership and contain the spread of communism. Secretary of state George Marshall, who announced his idea for helping reconstruct Europe at a Harvard University commencement in 1947, expressed a belief that America was a Christian nation and that faith was necessary for ethical political leadership. The Harvard-trained political scientist Karl Deutsch, who became one of the most prominent voices in American policy efforts to help rebuild Europe after the war, also shared a Swedenborgian commitment to Christian pluralism. In a pamphlet he wrote for a Unitarian youth group during the war, titled *Faith for Our Generation*, Deutsch declared that faith was necessary for postwar partnerships between previously conflicting parties. Christianity was particularly valuable, he argued, because of its simple emphasis on the idea that "man was created in the image of God."[50]

After the American military occupation cleared him to teach again at Marburg, where he was immediately elected dean of the theological faculty, Benz helped found several institutions that he believed would help promote Christian pluralism as the integrating aspect of European culture. In the 1950s, he established Germany's first academic program in ecumenical studies, where students could study comparative Christian religion with invited lecturers from all confessions and from all over the continent, including Eastern Orthodox scholars from the Eastern bloc. (One of his closest friends was Dmitrij Tschizewskij, a Ukrainian scholar of Eastern Christianity whose Jewish heritage forced him into hiding during the war before he could teach with Benz at Marburg and later at Harvard University.) The program intended to show how Europeans, also

those behind the Iron Curtain, were united by a shared history of a fundamentally Christian image of humanity. In their correspondence, he and
another close friend, the theologian Walter Nigg—incidentally, the same
author who inspired the newspaper magnate Axel Springer to launch his
Christian campaign for German reunification—agreed that it was the
"task of our generation" to emphasize the importance of the metaphysical
views of great European figures of the past.[51] Benz also volunteered to lead
the cultural section of a new "European Academy" in the town of
Schlüchtern dedicated to understanding the religious and cultural
"preconditions of a union of the European states," and took part in the
Cultural Conference of the European Movement in Lausanne, Switzerland,
in 1949.[52]

Together with the Jewish pro-Christian scholar Hans-Joachim
Schoeps, who briefly taught at the University of Marburg during the
American occupation before moving to the University of Erlangen in
Bavaria, Benz also built West Germany's premier journal of cultural
history over the course of the 1950s. The purpose of the *Zeitschrift für
Religions- und Geistesgeschichte,* as Benz described it in a letter to Schoeps
in 1953, was "to propagate a rehabilitation of idealist philosophy and
philosophy of religion." That rehabilitation was not simply an academic
exercise, but one that had important political implications as the West
German government entered into fierce rivalry with East Germany over
which side could claim moral authority to lead Germans back to reunifi-
cation.[53] From the beginning of the Cold War, leaders in the German
Democratic Republic attacked the idealist tradition of European
Christianity that Adenauer claimed as the cultural foundation of post-
Nazi Germany. Pointing to the support of Christian conservatives for
Hitler's policies in the east, German cultural leaders in the Socialist Unity
Party followed Karl Marx in arguing that Christianity was unsalvageably
implicated in the politics of prejudice, exploitation, and imperialism.
They claimed sole heirship of the true European ethical tradition and thus
sole inheritance of the European future.[54] A journal such as the one
co-edited by Benz, which featured a persecuted Jew at the top of its mast-
head, could contribute to a defense of the tradition.

Benz faced the materialist attacks against the European Christian
tradition head on. Christians in Germany had much to answer for in their
representations of cultural "others," he admitted, beginning with the

Slavic peoples. In numerous books and articles and radio addresses, Benz attempted to slay what he called the "rat king of prejudices and pejoratives" that surrounded the historical depiction of traditional Eastern European culture, which was rooted in Eastern Orthodoxy. Protestants, he noted, too often conflated Slavic culture with the repressive political leadership that frequently dominated the Russian Empire, assuming that the Eastern Church did not sufficiently value the dignity of the individual human soul.[55] Likewise, Europeans needed to abandon prejudices against other groups whose values they falsely imagined were incompatible with their own. In a speech he gave in India in 1957 and published in the journal *Islamic Culture,* Benz emphasized the influence of Muslim philosophers on European life through the transmission of Plato and Aristotle and neo-Platonic philosophy. Benz urged non-Muslims to "enter into a further discussion of common sources as a fruitful method to abolish, gradually, the mass of misunderstandings, traditional polemics and prejudices of the former centuries which have hindered today that better mutual understanding, which alone can be the basis of a new spiritual, ethical and cultural cooperation in our modern world in all freedom of mutual criticism and mutual respect."[56]

Benz also addressed the most damning stain of European Christianity: the prejudice against Jews that many critics claimed led to Christian inaction in the face of Nazi-led genocide. As late as 1942, as we have seen, Benz himself had contributed to that prejudice: in his chaplain's report on the religious situation in Ukraine, he depicted Jews as Soviet agents of Christian persecution and propagators of an atheistic Darwinism, even though he must have seen dozens of pious Jewish communities on his way through Poland with the army.[57] In 1958, Benz published a book explicitly intended to counteract those prejudices and instead establish "the starting points of a new encounter" between Christians and Jews. Learning from the work of a Jewish scholar he knew from an annual international conference on the European religious heritage, Gershom Scholem, Benz traced the largely unknown history of Jewish influence on Christian humanist culture all over Europe, especially in the German regions. Christian scholars during the Renaissance, he showed, recognized in Jewish mysticism a neo-Platonic conception of humanity so resonant with theirs that one had even "defended the esteem of the intellectual heritage of Judaism to the point of risking his life against the offices of the Inquisition in Cologne." Those Christians had not hermetically sealed themselves off from other cultures in "dogmatic correctness," but rather opened themselves up to "genuine community" with others "in an experience of transcendence which can only be called mystical." It was only with the Kantian Enlightenment, Benz argued, that this kind of mystical partnership was driven to the margins of Christianity as a "stepchild of theology."[58]

Historians have shown that while West Germans often looked to America as a model for a culturally pluralistic liberal democracy, they created institutions specific to their own historical patterns of culture and thought.[59] Benz's story confirms this picture. When he was invited to teach for a semester at Harvard University's Divinity School in early 1960, he told students there that European Christians who depended too much on the authority of clergy could learn from America's tradition of active congregations. But in post-Nazi Germany, Benz said, Germans created two types of Christian institutions that did not exist in America. First, there were the Evangelical Academies, adult education centers in almost all cities catering to educated laypeople with lectures on social issues from a Christian perspective. They served an estimated fifty thousand participants per year by the end of the 1950s. Second, there was the German Evangelical Church Assembly, a biennial congress that brought together members of Protestant churches from both sides of divided Germany to discuss common social and cultural problems.[60] Frank Littell, the State Department official responsible for overseeing church life in Germany and one of the people who organized Benz's appointment at Harvard, called the academies and the assembly "the real 'German miracle.' "[61]

The annual German Evangelical Church Assembly events were widely followed in West Germany's press, despite rapidly declining church attendance, because they were one of the few institutions of cultural partnership, if not the only one, between Germans in the two divided countries. The leaders of the German Democratic Republic, despite their hostility toward religion, reluctantly allowed church-goers to participate in the all-German events. The Church Day planned for the summer of 1961, scheduled to be held on both sides of divided Berlin, was to be especially significant because it would feature the first inclusion of a Jewish speaker and a special working group dedicated to Christian-Jewish reconciliation.[62] Benz's close friend Littell, who himself was a pioneer in Christian-Jewish interfaith dialogue and Christian self-reckoning after the Holocaust, explained the political symbolism of the assembly to an American audience in his book *The German Phoenix* (1960): "True and responsible political decision today requires the commitment to live with the opponent, to rule with the opposition," he wrote.[63]

Benz, who still resented the refusal of the Catholic Church to participate in ecumenical Christian events with Protestants, argued that the Protestant assemblies were vastly superior to the Catholic competitor institution: the Ecumenical Council (Vatican II), which Pope John XXIII announced at the end of the 1950s and hoped would provide a cultural foundation for a future unified Europe and ultimately unified world. Benz argued that although the convening of Catholic bishops to consult on the modernization of Catholic doctrine might be regarded as a "democratic gesture," it could not serve as an appropriate model of politics. Its hierarchical structure and its refusal to admit other confessions made it analogous to a "one-party state with an authoritarian head."[64] By contrast, the organizers of the German Evangelical Church Assembly saw their event as a precursor to the World Council of Churches in 1961, when Christians of all denominations would convene in a display of democratic unity in cultural diversity in New Delhi, India.

West Germany's educational policy of the late 1950s and early 1960s, which sought to counteract prejudice against minorities and yet "integrate" them into a Christian culture, was not unlike what Benz described as the ecumenical task of the Christian mission in the age of post-colonialism. This should not be surprising, as educational policy was set in no small part by leading members of the Protestant ecumenical movement; both the interior minister, Gerhard Schröder, and the longtime president of the West German parliament, Eugen Gerstenmaier, were active members of the Protestant ecumenical movement. "The most important point in the transformation of the world situation," Benz wrote in his *History of the Church in Ecumenical Perspective* in early 1961, "is the fact that a common, militant, and decisive opponent has confronted all religions in the form of dialectical materialism, which seeks to slowly but surely dispossess religions of their hitherto leading position and hijack their influence on cultural, spiritual, social and educational life." Communists were using the same tactics that Christianity had used on non-Christian religions in the past: staking an exclusive claim to truth and an exclusive inheritance of the future. In order not to weaken other religions' position against this more dangerous opponent, he argued, Christianity must sacrifice the claim that it possessed the sole path to the good.[65] This did not mean that Christians should renounce their claim to superiority. On the contrary. "All religions are 'good' insofar as all of them have the one end goal in view," he said in a public talk in 1960. "But the various religions reach only certain higher or lower experiences and understandings of the transcendental reality. Only Christianity leads up to the summit of the experience and understanding of God." As one of his beloved teachers, Rudolf Otto, once wrote, Christianity would remain the "first-born of his brothers."[66]

SMOLDERING SUSPICIONS

Although West German society as a whole was indisputably more inclusive than the Weimar Republic, let alone the Third Reich, cultural minorities in the Federal Republic could not help but suspect that the gospel of pluralist integration had its limits. West German laws made it clear that certain types of Christian values, which in many areas were Catholic values in particular, were still privileged. Those who entered into traditional partnerships of wedlock and had large families received many benefits from the state. Prohibition of business on Sundays remained the norm in most regions, and in early summer 1961 there was talk of extending it even to the large iron and coal factories in the industrial part of the country. Catholics in the CDU/CSU used their influence to push through a law in parliament making divorce more difficult. Women could not legally enlist a doctor to perform an abortion. Christian churches and Jewish synagogues, but not Muslim mosques, received the status of "corporations of public law," which gave them the right to collect taxes through the state. Muslim guest workers from Turkey who began arriving after 1961 soon would attest to hostility toward their cultural difference.

Gays and lesbians, who could be prosecuted for homosexuality, felt the force of these laws aimed at societal integration. Schoeps, who was gay and secretly involved with the International Committee for Sexual Equality's efforts to reform the Federal Republic's criminal code, chastised fellow Germans, comparing their refusal to speak out to defend Jews during the Nazi regime to their silence in the face of homosexual persecution in West Germany. "Ever since the persecution of Jews during the Third Reich," he reminded them in a widely discussed article, "the German people is suspected, in the eyes of the world, for harboring the tendency to torture, persecute, and terrorize its minorities."[67]

Suspicions also remained within the Jewish community itself, despite public displays of philosemitism. The daughter of the rabbi set to speak at the German Evangelical Church Assembly in Berlin in July 1961—chief rabbi of Baden-Württemberg Robert Raphael Geis, an émigré who had returned to Germany from Palestine in a particularly poignant expression of love for his fatherland—later remembered how clergy members who came to her father's house for interfaith dialogue would sometimes try to bless her secretly when her father left the room.[68] The suspicion that the Christians in Germany most involved in reconciliation with the Jews ultimately still hoped for their conversion to Christianity remained a constant thorn in the side of dialogue.

Nevertheless, things were different than they had been before. A week before the church assembly was set to open in Berlin in July 1961, the East German government announced that it would not allow events to take place on its side of the city. With support from the Soviet Union, a wall was going to be built separating East from West, to prevent infiltration of the border and flight from the German Democratic Republic. The events proceeded to take place on the Western side, where nearly forty thousand participants were present to see how, as one observer described it, "a Jewish speaker was able, for the first time since Christianity's break with Judaism, to address a large, official gathering of Christians on an equal footing and in an atmosphere of freedom and respect." A German Jewish visitor from Israel, a good friend of Schoeps, reported that a Star of David "of monumental size" glittered next to five crosses behind the speaker's lectern, "so that the symbol of the Church and that of the Synagogue stood vis-à-vis."[69]

CHAPTER TEN

Living with Liberal Democracy

"Our slogan might well be: Who wins the youth, wins the peace."

Institute for Social Research

The West German parliamentary elections of September 1961 seemed to augur a potential shift away from the Christian-dominated politics of the previous decade. The Social Democratic Party gained almost five percentage points from the previous election (thirty-six, from thirty-one in 1957), making it the largest vote-getting party in Germany for the first time since the Weimar Republic. Although the result was still insufficient to defeat the Christian bloc, which combined for forty-five percent, many argued that it was only a matter of time before the left came to power, in either a majority or coalition government. The Hamburg-based left-wing magazine *Der Spiegel* also noted the emergence of a group of independent, non-party-affiliated left-wing activists who, unsatisfied with the socialists' renunciation of Marxism and embrace of the American-led military alliance, were organizing around universities in the large cities.[1] These two developments provided good reason to believe that the era of longtime chancellor Konrad Adenauer, now eighty-five years old, was quickly coming to an end.

More critically, as one contemporary left-wing historian, Lutz Niethammer, pointed out, the younger West German intelligentsia increasingly faced a decision about the role their country would play in Europe in the coming post-Adenauer era. The geopolitical situation was changing in several important ways, Niethammer noted in a text

commissioned by the German Society for Foreign Policy. First, the establishment of such institutions as NATO and the European Economic
Community tied the hands of individual member nations in crucial
matters of policy, such as foreign relations with the Eastern bloc. Second,
in part due to the sealing of East-West borders culminating in the
construction of the Berlin Wall in 1961, the Soviet-led bloc was showing
impressive economic growth and innovation in a non-market-based
system, thwarting one of the key arguments in Adenauer's rhetorical
repertoire. The effectiveness of Christian anticommunism to integrate
the population of West Germany ideologically, therefore, was becoming
less effective, but no alternative ideology existed.[2]

It is in the context of this political situation that one must examine
the remarkable rise in prominence of the Institute for Social Research, a
small academic center whose work became a lodestar for left-wing politics
among secular West Germans in the 1960s. Affiliated with the University
of Frankfurt, the institute was directed by the sociologist Theodor W.
Adorno, though it was still more associated with the recently retired but
still active scholar Max Horkheimer. Both men, one in his late fifties and
the other in his mid-sixties, had returned from emigration in the United
States around the time of the division of Germany to reestablish what in
the Weimar years had been a privately funded incubator of Marxist sociology. In the 1950s and 1960s, it used private and public funds to research
social problems and make policy recommendations to the cultural and
education ministries, and sometimes even to large corporations.

That an institution which had previously been forced into exile
because of its Marxist politics had returned in the form of a quasi-state
agency in an age of extreme anticommunism was remarkable in itself.
Still more impressive, perhaps, is the fact that the Institute for Social
Research has come to represent West Germany's shift from the Christian
conservatism of the Adenauer era into the multicultural era of present-
day Germany. At the turn of the twenty-first century, a group of historians
characterized Horkheimer and Adorno as "the intellectual founders" of
the current Federal Republic, in light of the influence they exerted on the
generational cohort of educators and policy makers who came to power
in the late 1960s and 1970s.[3] The legacy of this tiny group of men—
otherwise known as the "Frankfurt school" of social thought—has,
against all odds considering their plight in the Weimar Republic, become

a central point of debate for commentators who trace the intellectual history of today's German culture and society.[4]

This chapter puts debates about the foundations of the Federal Republic into perspective by examining the function of the Institute for Social Research and its ideas within the larger political stabilization of postwar democracy. In particular, it examines the institute's role as a left-wing entity whose members were deeply disappointed with how the constitutional, economic, educational, and cultural reconstruction had played out in West Germany, and yet accepted the new liberal democracy's legitimacy, actively endorsing it against the alternative of the communist German Democratic Republic. In the early 1960s, Horkheimer and Adorno, the institute's main representatives, offered left-wing youth a method of challenging the status quo from within the confines of that status quo. But instead of subverting—overturning foundations from below, as radical groups including members of the institute itself had attempted during the Weimar years—they offered lessons to students in a new art of "immanent critique," a method of using the logic of an institution against the institution itself.

This chapter gives special attention to the institute's work on combating prejudice against cultural minorities, a part of its practice that has received less attention than others in the massive amounts of scholarship on the Frankfurt School. Horkheimer and Adorno presented an alternative to a specifically Christian ideology of partnership. Just as Nazi thinkers competed with Christian conservatives in the 1930s over how best to integrate a divided nation, critical theorists such as Horkheimer and Adorno competed with Christian conservatives in the 1960s over how best to integrate a divided Europe. The main difference lay in the fact that Horkheimer and Adorno never entirely subverted the ideology of Christian partnership. Rather, they lived and worked within it, attempting to reveal the contradictions they felt were inherent in its logic. In this way, they consciously contributed to the stabilization of the postwar democratic system, while trying to ensure through their influence that it did not remain a closed system incapable of becoming something new.

FROM SUBVERSIVE TO INSIDER

The University of Frankfurt in 1961 was, second to the Free University in walled-in West Berlin, the place that young left-wing students chose to study in the Federal Republic. Formerly the headquarters of the American military occupation, Frankfurt became the beating heart of the country's intellectual culture, known for its annual book fair. Its region, Hessen, was controlled by socialist governments, essentially since 1949, which meant that the professors appointed to the university and other schools of higher education were largely progressive. Frankfurt had a reputation as home of the secular left-wing intelligentsia at least since the Weimar Republic, and directly after the war, Hessen was one of the few regions to call for émigré scholars to return for immediate reinstatement.[5] It was the only region in the Federal Republic whose state constitution did not contain the phrase "responsibility before God," or something similar, in its preamble. The Hessian cultural ministry was also known to be at the vanguard of political education and teacher training for a critical reflection on Germany's genocidal and antisemitic past. After the antisemitic graffiti outbreak of 1959–1960, other West German regions scrambling to construct curricula to combat prejudice looked to Hessen as their model.[6]

No one in Hessen spent more time writing and speaking about prejudice than the recently retired social philosopher at the University of Frankfurt, Max Horkheimer. In fact, one of the main reasons the cultural ministry had recruited him back to Frankfurt so aggressively after the war was that the center he led in American exile, the Institute for Social Research, was in the process of completing a major empirical study on prejudice titled *The Authoritarian Personality.* Since then, Horkheimer had been twice elected rector of the university by the faculty (making him only the second unconverted Jew in German history to receive that honor and the first who was not even a German citizen), overseen an elaborate study on prejudice in Germany, and worked with the UNESCO International Institute for Education while splitting his teaching between Frankfurt and the University of Chicago. Already before the antisemitic outbreaks of 1959–1960, Horkheimer had been planning a permanent move to either the United States or Switzerland. Instead, in light of the events, he stopped all plans and applied to the U.S. Congress for special dispensation to continue residing in Germany without relinquishing American citizenship.[7] After he spoke on racial prejudice at the West German Foreign Office and organized a major conference on prejudice at the institute, the Christian interior minister Gerhard Schröder appointed him in August 1960 to a new twelve-person Commission to Advise the Federal Government in Questions of Political Education.[8]

Horkheimer's appointment to such a post was remarkable, almost shocking, for two reasons. First, Schröder was a staunch anticommunist locked in a battle with socialist politicians over what proved to be the most contested legislation of the 1960s: the ministry's proposals for so-called emergency laws. Even though the West German government regained almost all of its prewar sovereignty when it joined NATO, the Western Allies still retained one final legal power, perhaps the most essential, to declare states of emergency and override constitutional rights to defend the country against enemy attack. According to the treaty for entry into NATO, West Germans could not attain absolute sovereignty until their parliament adopted laws specifying the scope of acceptable executive power in case of such an emergency. Leaders in the SPD, concerned about protections for the rights of unions, were blocking all drafts coming out of the ministry, while Schröder accused his opponents of insufficient loyalty to the West and a creeping sympathy for Marxist and materialist ideology.[9] His choice of Horkheimer, a well-known Marxist and materialist himself, to sit on a commission of government insiders therefore demands an explanation.

Second, the fact that Horkheimer accepted the call was a puzzle in itself. Not only did Schröder have a Nazi past that he, like many officials in Adenauer's government, now renounced in favor of political Christianity, but he also represented all the aspects of liberal democratic politics that Horkheimer considered dangerous. Responsible for youth programs since 1953, Schröder described his task using the language of liberal nationalism: "integration" of the people, cultivation of "healthy" feelings for the national "organism," creation of a "harmonious order," and promotion of traditional Christian family units.[10] For secularist left-wing students, the question arose as to why Horkheimer would work with such a regime. One commentator in an East German newspaper offered a simple answer in August 1960: capitalists paid the institute's bills, so Horkheimer was beholden to them.[11] Some on the West German left would come to see it that way as well, but an examination of the development of Horkheimer's thought since the Weimar years suggests a more complex puzzle.

Horkheimer expressed suspicion of national integration policies since he first began his academic career in the early 1920s. Horrified by the way national attachments had turned Europeans against Europeans in the Great War—he was in love with a French woman at the time—Horkheimer rejected his parents' patriotism. The king of Bavaria had personally decorated his father, a textile business owner, for service to the fatherland during the war. Horkheimer later explained that he committed himself to intellectual labor, turning to the history of philosophy and psychology for insight into the roots of such conflict.[12] His first two serious pieces of writing were extended reflections on Kant's *Critique of Judgment*, which some regarded as the German Enlightenment's greatest expression of political philosophy.

In criticisms that presented an interesting comparison to the nationalist Alfred Baeumler, who was writing on the same text at the same time, Horkheimer argued that the structure of modern thinking inaugurated by the German Enlightenment was unable to forge genuine human cooperation. First, he argued, Kant's logic of community organization was trapped in a contradiction. On one hand, community was supposed to develop "organically," with all parts of a society naturally working without conflict toward a common purpose, and on the other, humans were supposed to build community individualistically, or "mechanically," first forming themselves through education and then "welding" themselves together. (Perhaps these metaphors had something to do with Kant's efforts to transcend the conflicts between Catholicism and Protestantism.) Second, Horkheimer pointed out, recent research in psychology showed that eighteenth- and nineteenth-century enlighteners were wrong to assume that individuals could make decisions based on logic and education alone. Material conditions mattered for how people behaved.[13]

As Martin Jay has pointed out, Horkheimer criticized Kant's separation of the private from the public sphere, and was more attracted (though of course with caveats) to a Hegelian vision of society that would synthesize the individual and public interest. Unlike Baeumler, who also engaged with Hegel, Horkheimer drew Marxist, not racist, conclusions from his materialist critique of Enlightenment thinking.[14] During the years leading up to his appointment at the Marxist-oriented Institute for Social Research in Frankfurt in 1931, Horkheimer saw no future for the categories of the nation or organized religion in political practice. He rejected all metaphysics and expressed confidence that the psychological impulses behind national and religious belonging could be translated into a different kind of completely secular politics. "The idea of the nation," he wrote, "contains a productive core": since the Enlightenment, it was the vehicle through which individuals overcame selfishness and became conscious of commonality. Likewise, one of religion's most important functions historically had been to "provide people in agony" with a symbolic device to express hope for change. A materialist critique of those institutions was therefore productive only so long as those impulses became "operative in other forms." "Today," he concluded in the years leading up to Hitler, "the form in which that core is alive is primarily the international solidarity of the exploited."[15] While uncomfortable with the particular manifestation of communism in the Soviet Union, the institute's members aimed to conceptualize a revolutionary socialist alternative to the liberal democratic Weimar Republic.

In 1932, Horkheimer and his colleagues saw that right-wing politicians in Germany, both Nazis and Christian conservatives, were aiming to consolidate the institutions of the nation and religion, and that therefore the work of the institute would naturally be targeted as subversive. They made moves to transfer its private funds out of the country to their sister office in Geneva, Switzerland, well before Hitler's appointment as chancellor. Because of this foresight, Horkheimer was able to continue organizing the institute's work after his emigration. By the time the Nazi government eliminated its political opposition and concluded its left-wing and antisemitic purges of the universities, the institute had successfully landed in the United States and used its academic contacts to establish a new branch in New York City.

The story of the institute and the talented leftist émigré authors who gathered around its temporary New York office in the subsequent years has been told many times over (and in ever finer-grain detail) by American and European scholars.[16] However, one tactical move crucial for the institute's eventual return to Germany is often neglected in those narratives and therefore will be emphasized here. Forced into exile as Marxists only to arrive in a country where Marxism was also considered subversive to the "American way of life," Horkheimer and his colleagues faced an existential choice. They could either slowly become irrelevant, losing funding sources and eventually dissolving as an organization, or they could continue to exist with new financial partners whose support would necessarily alter the face of their collective work. There was no substantial socialist movement in America to support them. Horkheimer received a depressing letter in 1935 from Henryk Grossman, one of the older original founders of the institute now living in French emigration: "We all fight for the great proletarian cause in the end. But with the breakdown of the labor movement, the satisfaction that every fighter used to get from recognition within the movement, earlier, before the war, is no longer possible."[17] Grossman referred to the schism in the German left between Social Democratic and Communist camps during the Great War, a division that marginalized such nonaligned socialists as the institute members during the Weimar Republic. Now, this already small circle of independent Marxists had been further splintered and displaced.

But the isolation of exile could also be productive. During the following years, a shift toward a new strategy of partnership became apparent in the institute based in New York. It is perhaps best highlighted in an exchange between Horkheimer and one of the institute's collaborators still residing in Europe, the independent author Walter Benjamin, as the institute was preparing to put together a primer for "materialism in Western philosophy" for future use by post-Nazi German university students. After reading Horkheimer's intended contribution, which consisted of a philosophical rejection of Christian theology—strikingly parallel again to Alfred Baeumler's nearly simultaneous criticism of Christianity's relationship to politics—Benjamin wrote to him on Christmas Eve 1936 with a gentle suggestion. Instead of creating an entirely new vocabulary for materialist philosophy—a strategy that seemed unconducive to education, because most people would be unfamiliar with the terms—they might profit more, at least "for a certain amount of time," he said, from the tactic of using people's "everyday language" in which materialist concepts are actually already "deeply embedded."[18] Sensing what Benjamin was getting at, Horkheimer "fully agreed" with "the stylistic demand to be unequivocal with regard to the decisive questions of today," among which "religion now figures again." Citing André Gide's recent note about the Soviet attack on religion, Horkheimer used the German phrase "one should not throw out the baby with the bathwater."[19]

The metaphors of education and babies in bathwater used in Horkheimer and Benjamin's exchange suggested a new tactic that would inform the manifesto Horkheimer wrote later that year as a guide for all the institute's future work in what he called "critical theory." No doubt, Gide wrote, the bathwater remained "dirty and smelly," but it must not be thrown out "with too much haste." Until the baby—that is, society—was mature enough to climb out of the bathwater on its own, Horkheimer suggested in the institute's programmatic essay of 1937, it was the engaged scholar's task to resist overly hasty abandonment of traditional categories and institutions. Left-wing scholars should avoid advocating immediate application of closed theories meant to supersede the past, such as Marx's theory of society in *Capital*. They should resist the temptation to "constantly call every particular theoretical content radically into question and always start again from scratch," as some existentialists were currently doing. Instead, their proper calling was to reflect actively on the role the intelligentsia *itself* might be playing in the perpetuation of societal injustices, through the very institutions that supported the critic.[20] In this turn away from frontal attack toward subversive immanent critique, Horkheimer self-consciously swapped the role of the revolutionary for that of the educator—the critical schoolteacher. In a letter to his closest colleague, he compared the role to the Hebrew prophets, who criticized the group from within the group.[21]

The institute's tactical shift manifested in subsequent years in temporary affiliations with groups that Horkheimer and his collaborators privately criticized as part of humankind's continuing immaturity, but regarded as necessary to preserve at least temporarily.[22] With news in America about the German pogroms of 1938 and then especially with the terrifying reports of mass killings during the world war, this tactic took on special urgency in light of the physical threat posed to the Jewish population in Europe, including Horkheimer's and many of the other institute affiliates' own Jewish families. With the independent funds that initially supported their studies in emigration running out, Horkheimer took on the institute's first major outside contract with an organization called the American Jewish Committee (AJC). The AJC's leadership had long been interested in enlightening public opinion and combating prejudice against Jews and other minority populations in the United States. In the eyes of the institute, the AJC was a typical "liberal" organization—that is, despite its relatively progressive politics, it was willing to conform to America's foundational values of capitalist political economy, national exceptionalism, and spiritual politics of social harmony based on Christian (or now perhaps "Judeo-Christian") outlook.[23] Institute leaders had decided to live temporarily within the confines of this new benefactor even if it opened them up to charges of betrayal.

Just as he became the "scientific adviser" to the AJC's series *Studies on Prejudice,* Horkheimer was also co-writing a book with Adorno for an exclusively European audience, a challenging critique of groups like the AJC and other American liberal organizations fighting against prejudice through the promotion of liberal democratic institutions. The final product, *Dialectic of Enlightenment,* published in German by a press in the Netherlands, included an appended section where Horkheimer and Adorno argued that liberals were fooling themselves if they believed that prejudice could be overcome simply by asserting that human beings are created equal. They wrote sarcastically that such liberal organizations seemed to believe that the only task remaining to create harmony in society was to iron out the kinks through "policy for minorities and democratic strategy."[24]

At root, Horkheimer and Adorno argued, antisemitism was not the result of age-old stereotypes or conspiracy theories regarding communism and finance capitalism, but rather, like all prejudices, a possible side effect of the structure of Enlightenment-style thinking itself. Kant, who for Horkheimer and Adorno epitomized that style of thinking, was the case in point. The eighteenth-century philosopher looked down on the mystical visions of Emanuel Swedenborg and other Christian myths, envisioning a world founded on logic instead of faith, they noted. However, he preserved an ideal of society as biological organism, in which every part has its "use" or "purpose" for the whole. "Where the humanly wants to become like nature," Horkheimer and Adorno wrote in an extension of the metaphor, it often despairs of the individual "organs" that do not conform to the desired purpose: not because they "hate" those groups, but on the contrary, because their loving desire to integrate them is thwarted and then turns to disgust. Like Ernst Benz, then, Horkheimer recognized a tragedy in Kant's turn against Swedenborg and his visions. But unlike Benz's story, the tragedy in *Dialectic of Enlightenment* was not the dying out of Christianity, but rather the potential of self-cannibalization in secular philosophy.[25]

Horkheimer and Adorno's *Dialectic of Enlightenment* was by no means a call for Europeans to give up on the German Enlightenment's continual striving toward an ideal of rational society capable of lifting humanity from the warm bath of national and religious belonging. The main purpose of their message was rather to demonstrate that a key step in reaching such a goal—what they called "the emancipation of society from antisemitism," where antisemitism was a stand-in for prejudice in general—depended on ending the way people think about human institutions such as the family, religious groups, and the nation. Until people stopped regarding those institutions as harmonious organic communities of common purpose, they would not be capable of practicing "enlightenment empowered over itself."[26]

When Horkheimer and his core colleagues decided to return to Germany with the institute after the war, and regained their teaching posts at the University of Frankfurt, they came with the intention of transmitting those basic insights of critical theory to the next generation: as they put it, to influence in whatever small way "the mentality and philosophy of university students, the leaders-to-be in all branches of national life."[27] The Hessian politicians who recruited them were liberal socialists who were familiar primarily with the institute's work on the AJC's *Studies on Prejudice*. At the official reopening ceremony of the institute in 1952, attended by officials of the Federal Republic such as the country's liberal president Theodor Heuss, Horkheimer used Germany's liberal language of the Enlightenment in a kind of immanent critique. Speaking of the institute's goals for the education of youth in post-Nazi Germany, Horkheimer used the Kantian educational term *Bildung*, which was often used to refer to both self-formation of the individual and self-formation of the people (*Volksbildung*). When he used it, however, he said that the "most important and ultimate goal of self-formation" was to gain the theoretical tools "to endure standing alone" against an existing order that demands conformity.[28]

In terms of their own research, the institute's directors continued their practice forged in emigration of living with, contracting with, and defending liberal West German and American institutions against criticism from "totalitarian" regimes—now the Eastern bloc countries—even as they critiqued and in very indirect ways subverted those institutions from within. Left-wing émigrés who returned instead to the eastern, communist side of Germany, such as Bertolt Brecht and Hanns Eisler, chided them for making their immanent critiques too timid, compared with their outright dismissals of communist policy. One of the institute's former collaborators who stayed behind in the United States, Herbert Marcuse, even wondered in early 1960 if his former colleagues had not begun "fostering Cold War ideology."[29]

Had Horkheimer spent his energies undermining the central institutions of the West German state, he likely would not have been able to reestablish the Institute for Social Research in Frankfurt and successfully gather around it a small but talented group of younger West German left-wing intelligentsia. Neither would he have been appointed to Gerhard Schröder's commission to advise the federal government on political education and gained the prestige that allowed him, in the years after 1960, to promote his outlook on Jews and Germany and the roots of anti-semitism and other prejudices. He likely would not have gained the necessary platform from which to advertise his group's critical theory, which actually challenged the Christian conservatism advocated by Schröder's ministry.

Horkheimer used his platform as government adviser to critique the dominant post-Nazi ideology of Christian humanism from within itself. In a book edited by the country's most prominent journalist, he argued that the Enlightenment tradition of Christian humanism contained within it a deep appreciation for one particular aspect of Judaism, the tradition out of which Christianity grew. Pointing to Kant's comment in *The Critique of Judgment* that the Jewish ban on images of God was "sublime," Horkheimer argued that a "reverence for the absolute as negation" lay deep inside the cultural DNA of Germany. Just as in Jewish religion one was always wary of "naming and defining the absolute" and more concerned with "breaking idols," so the great German philosophers maintained a strict dualism between what exists now and what ought to exist in the future.[30] Remarkably, Horkheimer was roughly paraphrasing Alfred Baeumler's Nazi characterization of the Jewish spirit as a hindrance to conformity, but now in a positive light. In emphasizing this aspect of humanism, Horkheimer challenged the assumption that the only thing Christians and Jews held in common was a desire to conserve the traditional faith in God. Christians and Jews in Germany could also partner, he suggested, in their common tradition of *challenging* tradition.

One can explain Horkheimer's insistence on affinities in part through the institute's research findings that people have a psychological need to feel positive about their own heritage (national, religious, or familial) when they confront its dark past. In his short pamphlet on the German Enlightenment in 1962, which he dedicated to the institute's benefactors at the Dresdner Bank for supporting its efforts in educating a generation that would "no longer be susceptible" to totalitarian politics, Horkheimer emphasized the potentially positive political aspects of a religious attitude that took the negative aspects of Kant's philosophy seriously. He took special note of the fact that unlike the main representatives of their counterparts in Western Europe, the German-speaking Enlighteners took the idea of religion seriously and did not attack it frontally or leave it to wither as an antiquated but perhaps pleasant institution. It was Kant's serious engagement with the negative, or Jewish, aspect of religion, he claimed, that made him the greatest philosopher of the Enlightenment, for in refusing to deny the existence of God, and yet also refusing to "make him into a safeguard of commandments," he pointed a way forward toward emancipation. Horkheimer passionately insisted that, although there could be no simple adoption of Enlightenment values as expressed by Kant, his ideas were "infinitely timely." The insistence on reconciling individual freedom and common interests "still contains the truth of socialism in it," he concluded. "While the East against which Europe wants to compete has driven out the Kantian heritage, the West possesses in itself the idea of social justice in its most sublime form." And it was not simply "the West" in general, but Germans in particular, he insisted, who had best access to this idea.[31]

These ideas explain why Horkheimer was so upset when he read that Eugen Gerstenmaier, the Christian politician presiding over parliament for the previous ten years, declared in 1963 that the Federal Republic was no longer affected by the disease of antisemitism.[32] Gerstenmaier made the declaration shortly after the announcement that the popular new American president, John F. Kennedy, was set to make a visit to West Germany. Horkheimer was livid. In a letter he penned to Gerstenmaier in June 1963 but never sent—probably for fear of subverting the delicate German-American partnership—Horkheimer accused Gerstenmaier of saying such things to reassure the former Allies that West Germans were politically mature. He worried about the psychological effects of such statements on young Germans who would be forced to think of their parents and their past as having been infected with disease. The true source of hate, which was rooted in economic structures, had not been overcome. And it was the responsibility of politicians to ensure, no matter "what the cost," he wrote—and despite the fact that educational policy was handled by the individual states—that life in Germany be made "brighter, more humane, and more civilized than anywhere else in the Western world." He pointed in particular to the importance of better teacher education.[33]

Horkheimer began attending synagogue and celebrating Jewish holidays such as Passover in these later years. But his turn to the religion of his parents was more than the typical "return to roots" that often occurs in one's older age. It was also a silent but studied resistance against the Christian political culture of the Federal Republic: against what he privately considered its drive to conformity, its premature reconciliation of oppositions, and its pretense of social partnership when the balance of power between the social partners was not yet equal.

A NON-RELIGIOUS ALTERNATIVE FOR EUROPEAN CULTURE

By the time of President Kennedy's visit to the Federal Republic in late June 1963, most mainstream commentators in the West had long declared the postwar reconstruction there a success story. Norbert Muhlen, a seasoned reporter on German affairs, wrote a hopeful report in 1962 on the country's Jewish population and in 1963 noted the "remarkably stable" edifice of the new German democracy, even if it still retained something of an "aura of wait-and-see among most observers."[34] The biggest story, perhaps, was the cooperation of the two largest parties, the SPD and the CDU, on foreign policy. The image of Kennedy's visit that American newspaper editors used most frequently was not coincidentally a shot of him in front of the Brandenburg Gate in West Berlin, flanked on one side by Adenauer, the aged Christian politician, and on the other by Willy Brandt, the up-and-coming socialist politician who represented his party's new course of unequivocal Western orientation.

But within Germany, the wait-and-see approach seemed justified. The Harvard University political scientist Carl J. Friedrich, who lauded the stabilization of the new Federal Republic and characterized Adenauer's efforts to integrate Germany into the European Community as part of a great task of nation-building analogous to the leaders of post-colonial states in Asia and Africa, was right to note that deep uncertainties still existed about the "viability"—the ability to live on as a self-sustaining system—as Adenauer's tenure came to a close.[35] A new generation was coming into power, and to them the CDU's approach seemed increasingly stale and subservient. When Adenauer finally retired midway through his term in October 1963, many regarded his replacement, the free-market economist Ludwig Erhard, as bereft of new ideas and overly reliant on West German economic success and American patronage.

It was true that the economy was still booming: the postwar cycle that had spurred talk of miracles had just peaked, and average unemployment rates were near zero. The message of Erhard's book *Prosperity for Everyone* (1957) still resonated among many. However, young left-wing students, now attending university with a cohort from all over the world as Germany became more culturally diverse, was increasingly knowledgeable about, and resentful of, American global interventionism and their own government's perceived subservience to it.[36] Many protested the idea of NATO-controlled nuclear weapons on Germany's soil. Ulrike Meinhof, a young journalist writing after Kennedy's assassination later that year in one of the main publications of the Socialist German Students League (*Sozialistischer Deutscher Studentenbund,* or SDS), advocated a move away from financial and military dependency on the United States. Although she advocated respect for the treaties already on the books, she argued that it was time Germans asserted their sovereignty and created policy better suited to their geographical position—which was, after all, "not on the Atlantic but in Central Europe." In particular, she insisted that they "end the latent civil war between the Federal Republic and the GDR."[37] This call for peace and engagement, increasingly resonant among West German youth, required a plan for European integration not provided by the dominant Christian ideology underpinning the West German state.

Among the university teachers to whom SDS students and other young left-wing political activists looked for guidance on such matters, the sociologist Theodor W. Adorno was by far the most highly regarded. Adorno, sixty years old and now the official face of the Institute for Social Research in Frankfurt, was less cautious and more engaged with students than his older colleague Horkheimer, despite their broad agreement on political developments in Germany. After returning from emigration in the United States, renouncing his American citizenship and reacquiring the German citizenship that had been revoked by the Nazis, Adorno became a regular speaker for SDS chapters opening up at different universities around the country. While Horkheimer concentrated on academics and personnel, Adorno was the voice responsible for the popularization of the institute's work. He received the most prestigious writing award in the country, the Goethe Medal, and according to one journalist immersed in left-wing politics, his writings "belonged to the hand luggage of every intellectual" in the early 1960s.[38]

Adorno's popularity in the leftist milieu was a function not only of his politics or his provocative (if dense) cultural commentary, but of what he represented for the possible future of European integration independent of American sponsorship. Adorno was a European and a German, and presented himself as such. The reason he gave for returning from exile, aside from "the ancient tradition that those who were driven from their homeland by a tyrant return after his downfall," was that he "simply belongs to Europe and to Germany," a statement corroborated by his exhortation to fellow émigrés in the United States not to conform to American norms but to develop the "critical ideas which are native to our thought and which were exterminated in Europe."[39] In a postwar society many young Germans considered conformist and restorative in its dominant ideals for the Christian family, Adorno represented resistance: his very name, Theodor W. Adorno, suggested with his middle initial—short for Wiesengrund—a dissonant heritage of a German Jewish father and an Italian Catholic mother. He became known for a line from his first popular book in post-Nazi Germany, *Minima Moralia* (1950): "the whole is the untrue."[40] At the same time, like Horkheimer, Adorno was no outsider. In 1963, his colleagues elected him to the prestigious chair of the German Society for Sociology, an organization where specialists exchanged research on European and national integration, youth, and family issues often used by policy makers and educators.

Adorno's focus on the process of "integration" upon his return to Europe requires some explanation, given that, during the Weimar years as a clever and ambitious young student of philosophy and musical composition, he was more interested in promoting the active process of *dis*integration. Like many cultural critics in the 1920s and 1930s, his opinions about art and philosophy self-consciously paralleled his political outlook. The composer he nearly idolized, Arnold Schoenberg, pushed the German classical tradition of composition to what seemed like its limit, deriving atonality, where works lacked a central key, from contrapuntal polyphony. The philosopher he wrote his thesis on, Edmund Husserl, embedded the German idealist conception of the autonomous self as far as it could go without becoming completely identical with the social. The Protestant theologian on whom he wrote his dissertation, Søren Kierkegaard, protested so much against Christian dogma that all that remained of Christianity was an existential leap of faith.[41] This might explain Adorno's relatively sanguine reaction to the rise of Hitler, which may have seemed to him like the ultimate conclusion in the immanent logic of nationalism before it collapsed from the weight of its own absurdities and laid the ground for a radical new international socialism. He soon came to see that as a pipe dream, though he still expressed a belief that Hitler's regime would not last long.[42]

During his exile in the United States after 1938, working full-time for Horkheimer's institute, Adorno critiqued the psychological theories of integration dominant in American social scientific circles. In the course of his research on personality types and prejudice, Adorno found a literature that presented racial and other types of prejudice as a disease, an aberration from so-called healthy norms. Social scientists spoke of the "un-churching" of Americans and the loss of religious and community-oriented values, as did the leaders of the National Conference of Christians and Jews.[43] Psychiatrists portrayed prejudice as a disease of the mind, evidence of an unintegrated or maladjusted personality typical in neurotic patients. Near the end of the war, as social scientists and psychologists were mobilized to advise on the occupation of Germany, many argued that Germans needed to be "re-educated"—a term from psychiatry normally used in reference to schizophrenics.[44]

Adorno and his co-authors of The Authoritarian Personality, the institute's study of college-aged students and the correlation between prejudicial (or ethnocentric) attitudes on one hand and susceptibility to anti-democratic propaganda ("proto-fascist" leanings) on the other, radically challenged mainstream religionists and psychiatrists on the nature of integration. Adorno interpreted the data collected by the institute's subcontractors to suggest that prejudice—far from being the product of an unintegrated personality, as the communitarians claimed—actually served an *integrative* function for the rational individual in society. Those who registered high levels of prejudice were found to be often "better 'adjusted' " in their familial and communal life than those scoring low levels.[45] The paradox, and the reason Adorno put the word in quotation marks, was that those people who appeared well-adjusted on the surface often showed signs of psychological immaturity—a weak sense of self, insecurity, and anxiety about one's own lack of power in the world, a need to depend on parental and especially paternal figures—and thus "over-adjusted" to groups and the historical suspicion or hostility those groups held toward outsiders. Thus the adoption of group prejudices served a functional role for this "normal" type of person, who, for the same reasons, might be suited to following strong leaders in politics instead of engaging in democratic dialogue.[46] The authors located the problem of authoritarian behavior in the emotionally cold home and the public pressure to integrate.

Furthermore, religious identification did not seem to prevent hostility against out-groups. For though the "Christian doctrine of universal love" was certainly opposed to prejudice and indeed historically linked to the roots of equal rights for minorities, Adorno wrote, people's attachment to religion in the twentieth century had less to do with doctrinal content than with community building, which could easily lend itself "to subservience, over-adjustment, and in-group loyalty which covers up hatred against the disbeliever, the dissenter, the Jew."[47] The general implication Adorno and his co-authors drew, therefore, without making specific recommendations, was that simply confronting myths about individual minority groups or physically desegregating (facilitating contact between) majorities and minorities would not be an effective means of combating prejudice, unless more focus was placed on preventing deeper trends in the way people were socialized into groups from birth onward.[48]

When socialist politicians in Hessen recruited Adorno and Horkheimer to return to Germany to continue their research, many Germans did not value their mode of inquiry or the types of recommendations they made. Their large empirical study on prejudice and guilt in the Federal Republic (*Group Experiment*), published in 1955, received little public attention. Part of the reason might have been the timing: the study cast a poor light on the society just as the East German government began its campaign to reveal antisemites in the Federal Republic. Perhaps more important, Adorno concluded that West Germans' continuing prejudice against the Jews resulted from the guilt they felt for the genocide.[49] Most social-psychological literature in West Germany, like in America, located the roots of prejudice in moral failings, social isolation, or inferiority complexes stemming from a shattered sense of self and national identity. The Coordinating Council of the Federal Republic's Societies for Christian-Jewish Cooperation, a lay organization that focused much of its efforts on combating prejudice, promoted religion and exposure to other cultures as a cure for hatred. The interior ministry recommended historical literature that presented Germany's past in a positive, or at least tolerable, way so as to avoid shame and aggression.[50] *Group Experiment* did none of that.

Adorno used the opportunity of an educators' conference sponsored by the Societies for Christian-Jewish Cooperation (SCJC) in 1958 to pose questions about how prejudice and the past were discussed in West Germany. First, he asked whether the phrase "working through the past" (*Aufarbeitung der Vergangenheit*), so modish among educators in the late 1950s, suggested that the eradication of prejudice depended entirely on the moral choices of individuals, when in reality material factors also played a role. Faced with the real threat of being devoured by the Soviet Union, Germans were being kept in a state of prolonged dependence on the United States and thus given an excuse to claim democratic immaturity. By submitting to a powerful foreign authority to protect them against communism, they were retroactively justifying their old support of Hitler.[51]

To the dismay of some of the members of the SCJC in attendance, Adorno did not count discussion of the Christian or Jewish image of humanity among the methods to responsibly combat prejudice.[52] Instead, in the discussion after his speech, Adorno suggested that the main origin of the problem was "alienation," which begins in basic processes of socialization on the first day of school: "For the first time, the child is torn away from the protection of the family, from this prolonged mother love so to speak, and comes to feel the coldness of a world with which it is not identical." The child who "experiences coldness, fear, the pressure of the collective" often "saves himself" by shifting negative attention on to others. Adorno wondered aloud to the pedagogues in the room if it would be possible "to develop forms in the first school years through which this suppression of the individual, and indeed every individual, through the collective is no longer admissible." When an audience member asked about religion, Adorno responded that the Christian churches did belong to the forces that currently "dam up" prejudice, but religion alone could not neutralize its ultimate sources, which lay deeper in the very process of group formation to which church organizations were also subject.[53]

It was not a coincidence that Adorno's reputation began to rise as the war of words between East and West entered a new stage of bombast during the Berlin crisis. Reunification seemed further away than ever, and the integration of continental Europe into a tighter economic form or common market under the American sphere of influence seemed more and more an inevitability. "Frontiers will go, technocracy will come into its own at last, and national animosities will dwindle away into mere parochial dislikes," wrote the German-born political commentator George Lichtheim, an admirer of the institute's critical theory, as part of his analysis of the "new Europe" in 1962 and 1963. "Life will become duller, though more prosperous, and—for the great majority—more pleasant. The elite will have supra-national [European] schools and colleges for its children—it is already beginning to set them up in Strasbourg and Florence—and in due course the citizenry will catch on and learn to talk the new European language," even if they would oppose American hegemony in the Western world.[54]

To be sure, Adorno must have been pleased with some of these developments in Western Europe and West Germany in particular. The continent no longer felt like it was on the brink of chaos and dictatorship and war. Most West Germans supported the efforts of the Jewish state attorney of Hessen, Fritz Bauer, to bring some of the many war criminals remaining free in the country to justice, in what became known as the Frankfurt-Auschwitz trials beginning in December 1963. The unemployment rate was near zero. Furthermore, the younger generation seemed to be more anti-authoritarian than their parents, which thrilled Adorno. As even socialist observers such as the émigré writer Lichtheim noted, there was much to celebrate in the Federal Republic and the "new Europe" when compared with what had come before.[55]

Adorno cautioned against resting on these laurels. He critiqued West Germany's elites, who, in the face of the new prosperity, seemed to be giving up on public ideals and instead withdrawing into the private sphere. In a short book published in 1964, *The Jargon of Authenticity: On*

the German Ideology, Adorno argued that the words West German educators used to talk about new educational practice revealed a deep pessi-
mism about the possibilities of creating a just collective world. Their
words, which he argued derived from existentialism but "resembled the
Christian," revolved around all kinds of allegedly "authentic" activities:
"encounters" between "partners," "genuine dialogue," "statements," et
cetera. The idea was to give individuals tools to create brief meaning for
their own lives within an atomized market society, not to improve that
society as a whole. It celebrated fair play in the "authentic" private sphere,
what Adorno called "disorganization as principle of organization," while
denying the possibility of consensus in the public sphere.[56]

Indeed, the educators and economic elites that Adorno challenged
for promoting such principles admitted as much. Otto-Friedrich Bollnow,
Germany's leading philosopher of education and co-founder of the
journal Benz and Schoeps published, promoted in his *Existential
Philosophy and Pedagogy* (1959) reverence for what he called the "most
holy and fragile thing": individual human "encounters" and "partnerships." Bollnow, who came from a background of anti-authoritarian and
anti-conformist school projects, admitted to having lost his Weimar-era
"faith in the creative powers of men."[57] Likewise, Arnold Bergsträsser,
who was a friend of Bollnow, Benz, and Schoeps, and now led the Institute
for Research in Cultural Studies in Freiburg, also used the existentialist-
religious terms of authenticity in describing the importance of political
and economic links with the peoples of Asia, Africa, Latin America, and
the Middle East, bringing students from those regions into Germany and
sending German students to those regions. In a programmatic statement
on the humanitarian tasks of cultural studies, he wrote that nothing
promoted world understanding (and economic development) better than
"the immediate encounter with people of other nations."[58]

Adorno urged students to envision a new Enlightenment project of
constructing a secular polity, free of quasi-Christian underpinnings. In
his lectures on "History and Freedom" at the University of Frankfurt
beginning in winter 1964 (which would form the basis for his master-
work *Negative Dialectics*), Adorno offered what became his most lasting
immanent critique of Kant's critical philosophy. Kant's noble, idealistic,
and never-to-be-abandoned dream in *Critique of Judgment* was to join
theoretical and practical reason together, Adorno said: to combine the

truth of the whole with the interests of the thinking individual by establishing laws maximizing freedom. But Kant, famously a cold fish, proceeded from the assumption that the ideal thinking individual was someone who responsibly judged beauty and truth by suppressing his own desires, as a cool observer contemplates the merits of a portrait of a nude. "In the shape of objectivity, of so-called logical reason, reason has its origin in the suppression of impulse and of impulses of the will," he said in his penultimate lecture of February 1965.[59] Form, discipline, content, and political education were still necessary to democracy. But the will and desire that initiates the noble pursuit of universal values in the first place—the libidinal warmth that draws people together—would have to be acknowledged and affirmed if future political projects were not to be purely instrumental.

THE PRICE OF STABILITY?

As parliamentary elections approached later in 1965, political commentators observed some indications that the momentum of political Christianity and the social market economy was beginning to lag. The economic growth rate, so robust for the past decade, helping the Christian bloc to its landslide victories, was slowly flattening out, and East German growth threatened to surpass it.[60] Ludwig Erhard, running as the incumbent chancellor, campaigned not on grand visions for the future, but on the consolidation of what had already been achieved. In March, he and his adviser Rüdiger Altmann rolled out their campaign slogan "The Formed Society," essentially a call for more order within the structures that had already been built. Erhard argued in his speeches that the market economy would run smoothly and continue to grow only if Germans remained connected as "social partners." Otherwise, society would devolve into a chaos of competing interests. The slogan, which used the past participle "formed," contrasted strikingly with the dominant political rhetoric of the Weimar-era governments, which almost always spoke in the present or future tense about the "coming society" or the "nascent people" (das werdende Volk). "We are somebody again," Erhard said of Germany in a speech of March 1965.[61]

Many younger intellectuals on the left expressed frustration that the leaders of the SPD in Germany, their only potential representation in parliament, did not offer what they considered a true alternative to the

CDU in the election cycle. The SPD campaign slogans they put on posters—with the phrases "Yes," "SPD-1965," "Sure is Sure," and "Forward with Willy Brandt"—all consciously eschewed any sense of real conflict with the status quo, or even with their political opponents. In light of this, Erhard delivered a speech ramping up for the campaign in which he compared Social Democrats to "slow-worms" of the social market economy: "they want to nest themselves warmly into what we have built."[62] Given the SPD leadership's official renunciation of Marxist ideologies and the banning of Marxist student groups such as the Socialist German Students League from membership, many on the activist student left were inclined to agree with Erhard on that point at least.

When the students looked to their teachers Horkheimer and Adorno for alternative visions for a future society, however, they were denied any positive image. The closest Adorno came to something concrete was a definition of good art in the text he was completing on aesthetic theory in 1965: it must "be able to integrate layers of material and details into their immanent law of form" while not "erasing the fractures left by the process of integration, preserving instead in the aesthetic whole the traces of those elements which resisted integration."[63] Horkheimer and Adorno never endorsed explicitly political art. To the dismay of many participants in the left-wing student movement, these critical teachers, to whom they owed so much for their own outlook on history and society, refused to make what they thought was the logical step toward attacking the foundations upon which Cold War Germany had been reconstructed. The two men assiduously avoided signing their names or affiliating their institute with any pacifist or anti-American movement they felt might endanger the new liberal democracy by playing into the hands of Soviet propaganda. Horkheimer persuaded Adorno, who for several years had been considering speaking out about the centrist tack of the Social Democratic Party and its decision to ban the SDS from its ranks, to hold his tongue. The accusation among some students that they had become "establishment" figures was therefore not entirely inaccurate.

These facts raise the question of the institute's role in the reconstruction of Germany. Did it rob left-wing politics of militancy and serve precisely the social function Horkheimer and Adorno so often critiqued— as a pressure valve that released steam from the system? Horkheimer's defense of traditional institutions and Adorno's failure to engage in the party political sphere could easily be regarded as ineffectual. At the same time, the institute and its leading theorists did provide an alternative approach, if not a concrete vision, to the Christian-dominated reconstruction. Students could take up their ideas as an intellectual spur for many different movements in constitutional theory, economics, education, and theology.[64] It was probably due to their decision to work with the establishment and remain acceptable to the main political parties of the Federal Republic that their ideas could be transmitted to West German students at all.

Besides, few predicted that the status quo could be radically altered through parliamentary means. The critic and activist Ulrike Meinhof, who still regarded the Social Democratic Party as the only possible vehicle for "getting rid of Erhard and his team," argued in her columns leading up to the elections in September 1965 that even with Erhard gone, no vision of a concrete alternative to the liberal market economy would likely emerge among the centrist socialists in parliament. And the chances of an actually anticapitalist party getting significant votes were slim. The reason, Meinhof argued, was that most people on the lower rungs of West German society were resigned to the inevitability of wealth inequality. Using a zoological metaphor, Meinhof said there were many "wounded dogs" in the Federal Republic, but they lacked the will to bite.[65]

Meinhof's predictions about the level of consensus among the main political parties were proved right on election day. The German Peace Union, the only party to call for socialization of big industry and neutrality in the Cold War, did not receive the necessary five percent to qualify for a delegation in parliament. The Christian bloc, which supported the continued rule of Erhard as chancellor, received forty-seven percent, and the socialists followed with almost forty percent. The SPD had tacked so far to the center that former chancellor Adenauer even suggested to Erhard the possibility of a "grand coalition." Erhard decided against the idea, but the similarity in the platforms of the two largest parties was striking. Christian politicians accused socialist politicians of aping them on pro-Western foreign policy; socialist politicians accused Christian politicians of stealing their ideas on public works and welfare.

The left-wing intelligentsia represented by the Institute for Social Research could easily have pounced on the parties' commitment to capitalist America and the socialists' betrayal of their roots as a workers' party.

They could have criticized all that had been built in the post-Nazi period, beginning with the founding ideology of partnership—as Friedrich Nietzsche had done to the ideologies of democratism and liberalism in the late nineteenth century. But they never did. Their most damning critiques always remained private and their public critiques always immanent. Therefore, while Horkheimer and Adorno were the least politically "significant" of all the figures studied in this book in the creation of post-Nazi Germany, their support of the new liberal democracy was perhaps the strongest endorsement of its legitimacy. The fact that they did not publicly advocate its overturning showed that the experience of loss over the course of the Nazi regime and the Second World War had been so great that even the most radical of post-Nazi Germany's critics were ready to partner with the new order to avoid something potentially worse.

Conclusion

STABILITY IS THE MOST COMMON REFRAIN ASSOCIATED with today's Germany. From high politics to economics and foreign relations to cultural policy, foreigners know the Federal Republic as the sturdy rock of Europe. Refugees from all over the world see it as a destination of safety. This has been true ever since the mid-1960s, when the memory of democratic collapse was still fresh and the pain caused by Nazi racial dictatorship still raw. "People do not love our blue eyes," said a leading West German politician, Rainer Barzel, in a visit with American Jewish groups, including Holocaust survivors, in 1965. "They value us, when at all, as dependable, stable, social partners."[1] I have argued in this book that the stability Germany became so well known for can only be understood in the context of shifting political dynamics inside the country from the pre-Nazi period to the post-Nazi period.

The story presented here challenges the way we often imagine modern German history as a process of political maturation initiated by defeat and occupation after the Second World War. According to the familiar narrative, the trauma of utter destruction under Hitler's military rule shocked Germans into reconsidering their relationship to Western-style liberal democracy. After the Western governments got them back on their feet, the story goes, successive generations of Germans confronted their dark past of nationalism, authoritarianism, antisemitism, and

268

imperialism. They continued to learn democracy and mature politically, and the future got brighter. This book, by contrast, suggests that there was never such a thing as a German body politic that could mature. The German nation-state founded in 1871 consisted of subsets of people with specific affiliations, interests, and ideals for the future—ideals many came to see as mutually exclusive. Faced with material destruction at the hands of the Nazi government in the years after 1937, Germans themselves imagined the framework for a more stable political structure before the arrival of American troops. Groups of people who before the rise of Hitler advanced opposing visions for the future of their country—like lions and lambs—allied with each other as new partners.

The reconstruction of post-Nazi Germany relied so much on the reconciliation of previously conflicting groups that "partnership" became its foundational ideology. The Germans who rebuilt the educational system in the Federal Republic, West Germany's intelligentsia, were the lions and lambs of the Weimar Republic in their youth. They lived through and participated in the social, economic, political, and cultural conflicts that tore apart German society before Hitler's rise. They also witnessed the Nazi attempt to overcome those conflicts, and some supported Hitler publicly before opposing him as he led Europe and the world into a catastrophic war. When this generation of Germans, who had seen so much, designed courses of education for the rising post-Nazi generations, they celebrated the ideal of partnership precisely to avoid the earlier conflicts. Before Germany was physically destroyed by bombs, it was already riven by opposing groups and ideologies.

We can verify the centrality of the partnership ideal in the post-Nazi reconstruction because the student protesters of the late 1960s attacked it with such vigor in their attempt to subvert the postwar societal order. In those years, a generation of students in their twenties and thirties, having grown up in relative prosperity, began questioning what had been lost in the successful search for political stability in Germany. These articulate socialist student leaders of the "new left," who wrote articles, distributed pamphlets, led rallies, held teach-ins, disrupted lectures, and occupied university classrooms, tried to recover precisely the radical values and visions for the future the older generation had pushed aside in the name of partnership. They protested the Social Democratic Party's abandonment of Marxist secularism and the goal of economic socialization. They looked askance at the number of former Nazis reintegrated into public service in a policy of reconciliation. Perhaps most dramatically, they rejected the Cold War alliance that both the Christian government and the socialist parliamentary opposition had signed with the United States, making them accessories to the repressive operations the American military was waging across the globe in the fight against communism. In short, they sought to undermine all the partnerships that the older generation studied in this book painstakingly nurtured over three decades.

The student rebellion arose in the midst of a government collapse—a situation some student leaders hoped was a sign of instability in West Germany but turned out to be the opposite. In 1966, the Christian-liberal coalition of Ludwig Erhard, who staked his political success on economic prosperity in close alliance with America, fell apart when a recession caused a huge spike in unemployment. It was the first collapse of a parliamentary coalition since the rise of the Nazis. Fearing a power vacuum, the leaders of the country's two main political rivals, the Christian bloc and the socialists, announced in November that they would partner together to form a replacement government. Together, this "grand coalition" would include nearly ninety percent of the total seats in parliament. Kurt Georg Kiesinger, a Nazi Party member turned Christian politician, would serve as chancellor, and Willy Brandt, who had fled the Nazis into Swedish exile before returning to become a leader of the reconstituted socialist party, would help him choose cabinet ministers as vice chancellor. West Germans called the new regime a "cabinet of national reconciliation." We might be tempted to call it a government of lions and lambs.

American foreign policy specialists and mainstream West German journalists celebrated the reconciliation of lions and lambs as a mark of political maturation. "The alliance between Christian and Social Democrats marks the end of ideology and the triumph of pragmatism," wrote the editor of the centrist newspaper *Die Zeit* in an American journal in the spring of 1967. In a confidential paper prepared for the State Department, American officials described the creation of the Kiesinger-Brandt government as a sign of West Germans' successful path from "tutelage" to "independence" without "rupturing cooperation and partnership with the U.S."[2] Socialist student leaders, meanwhile, regarded the grand coalition as the culmination of a long process of ideological compromise they must openly protest. Organizing in the Socialist German Students League (SDS), the youth branch of the SPD that had been expelled from party affiliation because of its refusal to break with Marxism, the protesters walked into the lecture halls of their universities in the summer semester of 1967 with the intention of undermining the very teachers who had orchestrated the post-Nazi partnerships.

The SDS targeted all the lions and lambs discussed in this book. They attacked Ernst Fraenkel, head of the country's most prestigious training institute for socialist party politicians in West Berlin, as representative of the SPD's betrayal of Marxism and direct democracy in partnership with the liberal judiciary.[3] The young political scientist Johannes Agnoli, who helped organize a new socialist "extra-parliamentary opposition" that could provide a real alternative to the West German capitalist economy, went after Fraenkel's partner in the reconstruction, Gerhard Leibholz, for arguing that true democracy consisted only of party politics and a strong constitutional court.[4] SDS protesters lambasted the idea of a "social market economy," which politicians in the Christian bloc, using the ideas of Wilhelm Röpke, celebrated as a balance between individual freedom and social welfare. In 1967, the sociology graduate student Rudi Dutschke, who was raised Christian in East Germany before coming to the Federal Republic, led rallies across the country to challenge the idea that a Christian economy based on Jesus's teachings could be anything but socialist.[5] They also criticized Oswald von Nell-Breuning, the Catholic Church hierarchy's main representative of social ethics, for what they considered his naive belief that the conflicts between capital and labor could be reconciled in a "social partnership," simply by encouraging profit sharing and including workers in oversight boards. Citing the writer Rolf Hochhuth's statement that "the class war is not yet over," they called for the more combative approach of the Weimar-era unions.[6]

Sick of a university system they believed perpetuated Cold War anticommunism and justified brutal interventions in places like Vietnam, student protesters allied with Asian and African foreign exchange students to demand more power over the curricula in their course of study and the hiring of new professors. Leaders of the Freiburg chapter of the SDS protested the Arnold-Bergstraesser-Institut, a university-affiliated think tank founded to advise the West German government on development aid to Third World countries that pledged to fight communism.[7] After May 1967, protesters ramped up their demands for university control when a police officer in West Berlin shot and killed a young student protesting the visit of an Iranian leader whom many considered an anticommunist American puppet. The recently retired Helmuth Plessner, who had himself been a mentor to student leaders in the SDS just after the war, warned a gathering at West Germany's main teacher's college in June that some members of the organization were taking on what he called a dangerous anti-establishmentarianism.[8]

The angriest confrontations of SDS leaders were reserved for the cultural guardians of West Germany's partnership ideal: those who used the moral authority of Christian penitence and the nation's history of antisemitism to stave off challenges to the post-Nazi order. SDS spokespeople called for a boycott of the newspapers owned by Axel Springer, the wealthy publisher who in 1967 prohibited the editors in his press empire from printing any article that criticized the West German constitution, partnership with America, the social market economy, or support of the Jews and the State of Israel. During Christmas of that year, Springer personally commissioned his good friend, the German Jew and Holocaust survivor Hans-Joachim Schoeps, to write an op-ed comparing the SDS to neo-Nazi groups and calling on the grand coalition government to crack down with police force.[9] The students recognized that a deep grammar of Christianity underlay the ideology of partnership in West Germany, and that Christian partnership with Jews and Judaism held a special place in that moral ideal. This is one of the reasons the SDS leadership was attracted to the young professor of philosophy Jacob Taubes, a critic of Schoeps who rejected the cooperation between Christians and Jews in the service of liberal politics.[10]

The arguments of the SDS leaders were severely damaged by the violence that broke out at some of their demonstrations in 1968. During the Christian Holy Week of that year, a twenty-four-year-old right-wing student—rumored to be an avid reader of the Springer press—shot and nearly killed Dutschke, the public face of the protest movement. That Easter Sunday, instead of partaking in the annual peace marches against nuclear weapons, roughly fifty thousand protesters converged on twenty different West German cities, forcibly blocking the delivery of Springer-owned publications. For the first time, some threw stones and Molotov cocktails at police officers. Ulrike Meinhof, a journalist widely read in SDS circles, called for students to stop acting "like sheep" and move from

protest to outright "resistance."[11] The West German public turned against
these developments. Three days after Easter, the Christian theologian
Ernst Benz circulated a document among all the country's institutions of
higher education, garnering more than a thousand signatories to guard
against the demands of the violent students.[12] In May, with support from
the majority of the West German population, the grand coalition government passed a law that allowed police to take tougher action against any
group that challenged the liberal democratic order.[13]

As numerous historians of the postwar period have pointed out, the
protests culminating in 1968 led to some concrete changes as these
students turned into the leaders of today's Germany. Critical of the explicitly Christian culture of the reconstruction years, the protest generation
led a transition from mere openness to active celebration of difference in
the multiculturalism of today. Critical of conservative gender roles and
male dominance in political life—a public opinion poll from the late
1960s found that more than forty percent of respondents in West
Germany agreed with the statement "Politics is an affair for men"—the
protest generation helped guide a shift in attitudes about sexual equality
and social mores.[14] The fact that all the figures featured in this book were
men reflected the reality of Germany's public sphere in the pre-1968 era.
By contrast, the public face of the Federal Republic at the turn of the
twenty-first century has been a woman, the Christian politician Angela
Merkel.

However, the protesters were unsuccessful in undoing the partnerships that underpinned the creation of post-Nazi Germany's basic institutions and structures. The majority of the West German population in
1968 roundly rejected their challenge to the partnership ideal. Seventy
percent polled supported the grand coalition government of lions and
lambs.[15] Even Max Horkheimer and Theodor W. Adorno, the left-wing
professors at the Institute for Social Research in Frankfurt whose call to
resist the status quo had inspired many of the protest leaders to begin
with, defended the partnership of the critical intellectual with the liberal
democratic state. In May 1968, Horkheimer wrote in an introduction to
the institute's Weimar-era Marxist writings: "It seems to me necessary to
say openly that a questionable democracy, with all its deficiencies, is still
better than dictatorship, to which a revolution today would necessarily
lead." Adorno, even as he released a statement in support of the students'

protests, called in the police to remove the SDS leaders occupying their building.[16]

The leaders of today's Germany, therefore, might look different than they did before 1968, but the institutions they work in are the same ones the Weimar generation of lions and lambs built. Their attempts to build up a regime of human rights, to balance the free market with social welfare, to hold the European Union together, and to integrate refugees all reveal a profound continuity with the consensus formed in those first post-Nazi years.

NOTES

INTRODUCTION

1. *The Architectural Forum* 107 (1957), 189.
2. Terence Prittie, *Germany* (New York: Time-Life, 1968), 15.
3. Hans Speier and Walter Davidson, *West German Leadership and Foreign Policy* (New York: Row, Peterson, 1957), 122; Wilhelm Grotkopp et al., eds., *Germany, 1945–1954* (Cologne: Boas International, 1954), 127.
4. Bertram Gross, introduction to Hans-Joachim Arndt, *West Germany* (Syracuse, N.Y.: Syracuse University Press, 1966), ix.
5. Mike Mason, *Development and Disorder: A History of the Third World Since 1945* (Hanover, N.H.: University of New England Press, 1997), 80.
6. Noah Feldman, *What We Owe Iraq* (Princeton: Princeton University Press, 2006), 1. See also Ray Salvatore Jennings, *The Road Ahead: Lessons in Nation Building from Japan, Germany, and Afghanistan* (Washington, D.C.: U.S. Institute of Peace, 2003), and James Dobbins et al., *America's Role in Nation-Building: From Germany to Iraq* (Santa Monica, Calif.: RAND, 2003).
7. These tales seem to have originated with the stories told by American occupation soldiers themselves. See Susan Carruthers, *The Good Occupation: American Soldiers and the Hazards of Peace* (Cambridge: Harvard University Press, 2016).
8. Nils Gilman, *Mandarins of the Future: Modernization Theory in Cold War America* (Baltimore: Johns Hopkins University Press, 2003), 5–15; for representative theoretical works see Karl Deutsch, *The Nerves of Government* (New York: Free Press of Glencoe, 1963), Walter Rostow, *The Stages of Economic Growth: A Non-Communist Manifesto* (Cambridge: Cambridge University Press, 1960), and

Daniel Lerner, *The Passing of Traditional Society: Modernizing the Middle East* (Glencoe, Ill.: Free Press, 1958).

9. Karl Deutsch, "Some Problems in the Study of Nation-Building," in *Nation-Building*, ed. Karl Deutsch and William Foltz (New York: Atherton, 1963); Karl Deutsch and Lewis J. Edinger, *Germany Rejoins the Powers* (Stanford: Stanford University Press, 1959), esp. 37–38, 111–132, 247.

10. For a review of the literature in connection with modernization, see Axel Schildt, *Die Sozialgeschichte der Bundesrepublik Deutschland bis 1989/1990* (Munich: Oldenbourg, 2007), 67–110. For studies on "re-education" and "re-orientation" through exchange programs and curriculum, see Richard Bessel, *Germany 1945: From War to Peace* (New York: HarperCollins, 2009), Brian Puaca, *Learning Democracy* (New York: Berghahn, 2009), and James Tent, *Mission on the Rhine* (Chicago: University of Chicago Press, 1982); on "Americanization" and "Westernization" in the late 1950s and early 1960s, see Anselm Doering-Manteuffel, *Wie westlich sind die Deutschen?* (Göttingen: Vandenhoeck & Ruprecht, 1999), and Volker Berghahn, *The Americanisation of West German Industry, 1945–1973* (New York: Berg, 1986); on liberalization and generation, see Christina von Hodenberg, *Konsens und Krise: eine Geschichte der westdeutschen Medienöffentlichkeit* (Göttingen: Wallstein, 2006), and Ulrich Herbert, ed., *Wandlungsprozesse in Westdeutschland* (Göttingen: Wallstein, 2002).

11. Konrad Jarausch, *After Hitler: Recivilizing Germans, 1945–1995* (New York: Oxford University Press, 2006), quoted here 12–16, 98–102. Jarausch further argues that in contrast to the Federal Republic, the institutions of the German Democratic Republic promoted unhealthy learning, encouraging regression toward ideology, lack of empathy, and extractive economy.

12. Compare for example Edmund Spevack, *Allied Control and German Freedom* (Münster: Lit, 2001) with Richard L. Merritt, *Democracy Imposed: U.S. Occupation Policy and the German Public, 1945–1949* (New Haven: Yale University Press, 1995).

13. Jarausch, *After Hitler*, 11. On the death of the older historiography on modern Germany, see Helmut Walser Smith, "When the *Sonderweg* Debate Left Us," *German Studies Review* 31, no. 2 (2008), 225–240.

14. Daron Acemoğlu and James Robinson, *Why Nations Fail: The Origins of Power, Prosperity, and Poverty* (New York: Crown, 2012).

15. Mario Rainer Lepsius, *Demokratie in Deutschland* (Göttingen: Vandenhoeck & Ruprecht, 1993), 25–50.

16. See for example Otto Hintze, "Rede, gehalten zur Feier der fünfundzwanzigjährigen Regierung Seiner Majestät des Kaisers u. Königs Wilhelm II.," in *Hohenzollern-Jahrbuch* 17 (1913), 91–95.

17. Friedrich Meinecke, "Um Freiheit und Vaterland" (November 1917), in *Werke*, vol. 2, ed. Georg Kotowski (Darmstadt: Toeche-Mittler, 1958), 213.

18. See Geoff Eley et al., eds., *German Modernities from Wilhelm to Weimar: A Contest of Futures* (New York: Bloomsbury, 2016), and Rüdiger Graf, *Die Zukunft der*

Weimarer Republik: Krisen und Zukunftsaneignungen in Deutschland, 1918–1933 (Munich: Oldenbourg, 2008).

19. Hans Zehrer, "Absage an den Jahrgang 1902," *Die Tat* 20, no. 10 (1929/1930), 740–748.

20. Rüdiger Graf, "Either-Or: The Narrative of 'Crisis' in Weimar Germany and in Historiography," *Central European History* 43, no. 4 (2010), 592–615, quoted here at 600.

21. On this generation's involvement with Nazism see Michael Wildt, *Generation of the Unbound* (Jerusalem: Yad Vashem, 2002), and Ulrich Herbert, *Arbeit, Volkstum, Weltanschauung* (Frankfurt: Fischer, 1995), 31–58. On the more recent research on their involvement with reconstruction, see Udi Greenberg, *The Weimar Century: German Émigrés and the Ideological Foundations of the Cold War* (Princeton: Princeton University Press, 2014); Sean Forner, *German Intellectuals and the Challenge of Democratic Renewal* (New York: Cambridge University Press, 2014); and Marcus Payk, *Der Geist der Demokratie* (Munich: Oldenbourg, 2008).

22. Alexander Gallus and Axel Schildt, eds., *Rückblickend in die Zukunft: Politische Öffentlichkeit und intellektuelle Positionen in Deutschland um 1950 und um 1930* (Göttingen: Wallstein, 2011), foreword.

23. Samuel Moyn, *Christian Human Rights* (Philadelphia: University of Pennsylvania Press, 2015), 99. For the new scholarship on Catholic thought in particular see Piotr Kosicki, *Catholics on the Barricades: Poland, France, and "Revolution," 1939–1956* (New Haven: Yale University Press, 2017); James Chappel, *The Pope's Divisions: Catholicism and the Salvation of European Democracy, 1920–1960* (Cambridge: Harvard University Press, forthcoming 2018); and Giuliana Chamedes, "Reinventing Christian Europe: Vatican Diplomacy, Transnational Anticommunism, and the Erosion of the Church-State Divide (1917–1958)" (Ph.D. dissertation, Columbia University, 2012).

24. For an emphasis on this function of Christian ideology see Maria D. Mitchell, *The Origins of Christian Democracy: Politics and Confession in Modern Germany* (Ann Arbor: University of Michigan Press, 2012).

25. Theodor Heuss, "Um Deutschlands Zukunft," in *Aufzeichnungen 1945–1947*, ed. Eberhard Pikart (Tübingen: Wunderlich, 1966), 207.

26. Max Warren, *Partnership: The Study of an Idea* (London: SCM, 1956), 11–13.

27. Deborah Kalb et al., eds., *State of the Union: Presidential Rhetoric from Woodrow Wilson to George W. Bush* (Washington, D.C.: CQ, 2006), 627–640.

28. Pierre Viénot, *Is Germany Finished?* (New York: Macmillan, 1932), 17.

PART ONE: CONFLICT

1. Ralph Haswell Lutz, *The German Revolution, 1918–1919* (Palo Alto: Stanford University Press, 1922), 57.

2. Cyril Brown, "New Popular Idol Rises in Bavaria," *New York Times* (November 21, 1922), 18.

3. Friedrich Curtius, *Hindernisse und Möglichkeit einer ethischen Politik* (Leipzig: Verlag Naturwissenschaften, 1918), 1.

4. Max Weber, *Politik als Beruf* (Munich: Duncker & Humblot, 1919), 66–67.
5. Leonard Nelson, *Führer-Erziehung als Weg zur Vernunft-Politik* (Leipzig: Der Neue Geist, 1922), 5–6.
6. Friedrich Ebert, "Brief an den Ausschuss der Deutschen Jugend-Verbänden" (December 31, 1923), in *Schriften, Aufzeichnungen, Reden*, vol. 2, ed. Friedrich Ebert, Jr. (Dresden: Reissner, 1926), 315–316.

1: THE CONSTITUTIONAL CRISIS

1. See Thomas Lamont, "The Dawes Plan and European Peace," *Proceedings of the Academy of Political Science in the City of New York* 11, no. 2 (1925), 177–184. On the specifics of the plan see Adam Tooze, *The Deluge: The Great War, America, and the Remaking of the Global Order, 1916–1931* (New York: Penguin, 2014), and Stephen Schuker, *The End of French Predominance in Europe: The Financial Crisis of 1924 and the Adoption of the Dawes Plan* (Chapel Hill: University of North Carolina Press, 1974).
2. Simeon Strunsky, "German Democracy's New Test: In the Pending Struggle for Power, the Workers Are the Principal Champions of Popular Rule, with the Middle Classes Striving Now to Assert Themselves in the Affairs of the Nation," *New York Times* (August 21, 1932), 11. For a historian's argument to that effect see Jeffrey Herf, *Reactionary Modernism: Technology, Culture, and Politics in Weimar and the Third Reich* (New York: Cambridge University Press, 1984).
3. See Margaret Anderson, *Practicing Democracy: Elections and Political Culture in Imperial Germany* (Princeton: Princeton University Press, 2000).
4. For two of the first extended discussions of this issue see Ronald Dworkin, *Taking Rights Seriously* (Cambridge: Harvard University Press, 1977), and Josef Esser, *Vorverständnis und Methodenwahl in der Rechtsfindung* (Frankfurt am Main: Athenäum, 1970).
5. Carl Schmitt, *Die geistesgeschichtliche Lage des heutigen Parlamentarismus* (Berlin: Duncker & Humblot, 1923).
6. *Juristische Wochenschrift* (January 8, 1924), 90. Specifically, the judges referred to the regime's consideration to forbid the revaluation of loan agreements to approximate the value of the old contracts under new market conditions. See Gerald Feldman, *The Great Disorder: Politics, Economics, and Society in the Great Inflation, 1914–1924* (Princeton: Princeton University Press, 1993), 810–821.
7. James Bryce, *Modern Democracies*, vol. 2 (New York: Macmillan, 1921), 84.
8. Carl J. Friedrich, "The Issue of Judicial Review in Germany," *Political Science Quarterly* 43, no. 2 (1928), 189–191.
9. See Wolfgang Wehler, *Der Staatsgerichtshof für das Deutsche Reich* (Ph.D. dissertation, Bonn, 1979), 26–39, 64–67. On the impossibility of deriving authority for judicial review from the constitutional document itself, see Richard Thoma, "Das richterliche Prüfungsrecht," *Archiv des öffentlichen Rechts* 4 (1922), 267–286.
10. I use the term "liberal" for *bürgerlich* instead of "bourgeois" to avoid confusion, since "bourgeois" in English typically refers to the middle or upper-middle-class.

11. Recent historians of the Weimar Republic have begun to leave this debate out of the narrative, for example Eric Weitz, *Weimar Germany* (Princeton: Princeton University Press, 2007). For excellent specialized treatments of the debates, see Peter C. Caldwell, *Popular Sovereignty and the Crisis of German Constitutional Law* (Durham: Duke University Press, 1997), and Helge Wendenburg, *Die Debatte um die Verfassungsgerichtsbarkeit und der Methodenstreit der Staatsrechtslehre in der Weimarer Republik* (Göttingen: Schwartz, 1984).

12. See Carl-Ludwig Holtfrerich, *Die deutsche Inflation, 1914–1923* (Berlin: de Gruyter, 1980), 317.

13. Heinrich Triepel, "Der Weg der Gesetzgebung nach der neuen Reichsverfassung," *Archiv für öffentliches Recht* 39 (1920), 534–537; Heinrich Triepel, "Staatsgewalt und bürgerliche Freiheit," *Internationale Monatsschrift für Wissenschaft, Kunst, und Technik* 10 (1916), 1033–1034.

14. Heinrich Triepel, *Goldbilanzen-Verordnung und Vorzugsaktien* (Berlin: De Gruyter, 1924), 4–24.

15. His father seems to have remained supportive of the Jewish community in Germany. His name was among the list of benefactors for the main rabbinical academy in Berlin. See *Bericht der Hochschule für die Wissenschaft des Judentums* 30 (1912), 44.

16. See Rudolf Smend, "Gerhard Leibholz zum 70. Geburtstag," *Archiv des öffentlichen Rechts* 96 (1971), 568.

17. Gerhard Leibholz, *Fichte und der demokratische Gedanke* (Freiburg: Boltze, 1921). For Leibholz's intellectual biography, see Manfred Wiegandt's excellent *Norm und Wirklichkeit* (Baden-Baden: Nomos, 1995); Anikó Szabó, *Vertreibung, Rückkehr, Wiedergutmachung* (Göttingen: Wallstein, 2000), 378. On Fichte's vision see A. C. Armstrong, "Fichte's Conception of a League of Nations," *The Journal of Philosophy* 29, no. 6 (1932), 153–158.

18. See Kenneth Barnes, "Dietrich Bonhoeffer and Hitler's Persecution of the Jews," in *Betrayal*, ed. Robert Ericksen and Susanna Heschel (Minneapolis: Fortress, 1999), 111.

19. Hans Nawiasky noted approvingly that Leibholz's study "further expanded and underpinned" Triepel's ideas. *Die Gleichheit vor dem Gesetz im Sinne des Art. 109* (Berlin: De Gruyter, 1927), 40–41.

20. Gerhard Leibholz, introduction to *Gleichheit vor dem Gesetz* (Berlin: Liebmann, 1925), 13. On the influence of Leibholz's theory see Christoph Link, *Der Gleichheitssatz im modernen Verfassungsstaat* (Baden-Baden: Nomos, 1982), 25.

21. Leibholz, *Gleichheit vor dem Gesetz*, 17–25. Leibholz suggested that these values spread with Christianity but were no longer dependent on Christian faith, citing the French Protestant theologian Henri Bois, "La démocratie et l'Évangile," in *Les démocraties modernes*, ed. Paul Doumergue (Paris: Ernest Flammarion, 1921), 88–89.

22. Leibholz, *Gleichheit vor dem Gesetz*, 19–21.

23. Ibid., 79–85, 114–115.

24. Ibid., 22–28, 129–131. Leibholz praised Hans Kelsen for having conceived Austria's new constitutional court, but criticized him for not making "equality before the law" the central standard. This was part of his larger critique of the legacy of Jean-Jacques Rousseau's idea of the democratic general will, which Kelsen adopted in his *Vom Wesen und Wert der Demokratie* (Tübingen: Mohr, 1920).

25. Leibholz, *Gleichheit vor dem Gesetz*, 142.

26. For Hindenburg's statement in 1919 about the Social Democrats, see *Stenographische Berichte über die öffentlichen Verhandlungen des 15. Untersuchungsausschusses der verfassungsgebenden Nationalversammlung*, vol. 2 (Berlin: Verlag der norddeutschen Buchdruckerei und Verlagsanstalt, 1920), 700–701.

27. *Entscheidungen des Reichsgerichts in Zivilsachen*, vol. 111, 320–335; Feldman, *The Great Disorder*, 813; see also Caldwell, *Popular Sovereignty and the Crisis of German Constitutional Law*, 153–154.

28. Hindenburg's letter to his former campaign manager Friedrich von Loebell (May 22, 1926) was published in the *Frankfurter Zeitung* (June 8, 1926) and reproduced in Walter Hubatsch, *Hindenburg und der Staat* (Göttingen, 1966), 237–239. For context see Franklin C. West, *A Crisis in Weimar* (Philadelphia: American Philosophical Society, 1985).

29. For the amendment proposal, see Gerhard Anschütz, *Empfiehlt es sich, die Zuständigkeit des Staatsgerichtshofs auf andere als die im Art. 19 Abs. 1 RVerf. bezeichneten Verfassungsstreitigkeiten auszudehnen* (Berlin: De Gruyter, 1926); Leibholz, *Gleichheit vor dem Gesetz*, 100.

30. The published version, appearing as Walter Simons, "Die Vertrauenskrise der deutschen Justiz," *Deutsche Juristen-Zeitung* 31 (1926), 1665ff., was heavily redacted. See also his "Richtertum und Sozialismus," *Evangelisch-Sozial* 32, no. 1 (January/March 1927), 33–35, where he "took nothing back" from what he said in Munich. See Daniel Siemens, "Die 'Vertrauenskrise der Justiz' in der Weimarer Republik," in *Die "Krise" der Weimarer Republik*, ed. Moritz Föllmer and Rüdiger Graf (Frankfurt am Main: Campus, 2005), 139–164.

31. *Gesetz gegen die gemeingefährlichen Bestrebungen der Sozialdemokratie vom 21. Oktober 1878, Reichsgesetzblatt*, Nr. 34 (1878), 351.

32. On the negotiations see Ludwig Richter, "SPD, DVP und die Problematik der Grossen Koalition," in *Demokratie in Deutschland und Frankreich, 1918–1933/40*, ed. Horst Müller (Munich: Oldenbourg, 2002), 153–182.

33. Quoted in Heinrich August Winkler, *Weimar, 1918–1933* (Munich: Beck, 1998), 263, emphasis added.

34. *Das Heidelberger Programm* (Berlin: Vorstand der Sozialdemokratischen Partei Deutschlands, 1925).

35. See Hugo Sinzheimer, "The Development of Labor Legislation in Germany," trans. Daniel B. Shumway, *Annals of the American Academy of Political and Social Science* 92 (November 1920), 39–40.

36. See for example Karl Korsch, "Der tote Sinzheimer und der lebende Marx," *Internationale Presse-Konferenz* (1923), 1843–1844.
37. Hugo Sinzheimer, "Chronik," *Die Gesellschaft* 4, no. 6 (August 1929), 642–643. For his use of Kant see Hugo Sinzheimer, introduction to *Grundzüge des Arbeitsrechts* (Jena: Fischer, 1921). Emmanuel Lévy, *La vision socialiste du droit* (Paris: M. Giard, 1926); Édouard Lambert, *Le gouvernement des juges et la lutte contre la legislation sociale aux États-Unis* (Paris: M. Giard, 1921).
38. Simone Ladwig-Winters, *Ernst Fraenkel* (Frankfurt: Campus, 2009), 45–60.
39. Ernst Fraenkel, "Die Wirtschaftsschule des Deutschen Metallarbeiterverbandes in Bad Dürrenberg," *Die Tat* (July 1926), 333–334; Ernst Fraenkel, "Der Film als sozialistische Kunstform," *Jungsozialistische Blätter* 5, no. 3 (March 1926), 77. On Fraenkel and Austro-Marxism see Hubertus Buchstein, "Von Max Adler zu Ernst Fraenkel: Demokratie und pluralistische Gesellschaft in der sozialistischen Demokratietheorie der Weimarer Republik," in *Demokratisches Denken in der Weimarer Republik*, ed. Christoph Gusy (Baden-Baden: Nomos, 2000), 543–606.
40. Ernst Fraenkel, *Zur Soziologie der Klassenjustiz* (Berlin: Laub, 1927), 8–11. For Simons's argument on Christianity and the law see Walter Simons, *Christentum und Verbrechen* (Leipzig: Strauch, 1925).
41. See Todd Weir, *Secularism and Religion in Nineteenth-Century Germany: The Rise of the Fourth Confession* (New York: Cambridge University Press, 2014), epilogue.
42. Fraenkel, *Zur Soziologie der Klassenjustiz*, 15–29.
43. Ibid., 30–35. The reference was to the judgment of the Reichsgericht of February 11, 1926.
44. See Claudia Schöningh, *"Kontrolliert die Justiz"* (Munich: Fink, 2000), 119–254.
45. Ernst Feder, "Die Bedeutung der Presse für die Entwicklung des Rechtsgefühls," *Deutsche Presse* 22–23 (1927), 304; Martin Löwenthal, "Zur Prüfung der Verfassungsmässigkeit von Vorschriften des Reichsrechts," *Deutsche Juristen-Zeitung* 32, no. 18 (1927), 1234–1238.
46. Fritz Naphtali, ed., *Wirtschaftsdemokratie* (Berlin: Verlagsgesellschaft des Allgemeinen Deutschen Gewerkschaftsbundes, 1928), 175–181, quotation from 179–180. Many of these ideas were developed from Otto Bauer's foundational theory of nation-states, *Die Nationalitätenfrage und die Sozialdemokratie* (Vienna: Volksbuchhandlung, 1924; original printing, 1907).
47. See Hermann Müller, *Die November-Revolution* (Berlin: Bücherkreis, 1928), 279–286.
48. William Patch, "Class Prejudice and the Failure of the Weimar Republic," *German Studies Review* 12, no. 1 (1989), 35–54. Patch was right to highlight intensification in the rhetoric of class conflict in these years, but his explanation—that the "absence of economic or diplomatic crisis encouraged regression to the mentality of class conflict deeply engrained in most Germans during the Wilhelminian era"—did not take into account the all-important crisis of the judiciary in the years directly preceding 1927.
49. Carl Schmitt, *Verfassungslehre* (Munich: Duncker & Humblot, 1928), 142.

50. Rudolf Smend, *Verfassung und Verfassungsrecht* (Munich: Duncker & Humblot, 1928).
51. On Simons's resignation, see Horst Gründer, *Walter Simons als Staatsmann, Jurist und Kirchenpolitiker* (Neustadt an der Aisch: Schmidt, 1975), 251–258.
52. Gerhard Leibholz, *Das Wesen der Repräsentation unter besonderer Berücksichtigung des Repräsenativsysem* (Berlin: De Gruyter, 1929).
53. Gerhard Leibholz, *Zu den Problemen des faschistischen Verfassungsrechts* (Berlin: Walter de Gruyter, 1928), 39.
54. Gerhard Leibholz, review of Max von Rümelin's *Die Gleichheit vor dem Gesetz* (Tübingen: Mohr, 1928), in *Archiv für Rechts- und Wirtschaftsphilosophie* 22, no. 3 (April 1929), 489–491.
55. Clemens Nörpel, "Die Prüfung der Verfassungsmässigkeit von Vorschriften des Reichsrechts," *Die Arbeit* 6, no. 6 (June 1929), 373; Franz L. Neumann, "Gegen ein Gesetz über Nachprüfung der Verfassungsmässigkeit von Reichsgesetzen," *Die Gesellschaft* 6, no. 6 (June 1929), 517–536; Gustav Radbruch, "Parteienstaat und Volksgemeinschaft," *Die Gesellschaft* 6, no. 8 (August 1929), 101.
56. Ernst Fraenkel, "Kollektive Demokratie," *Die Gesellschaft* 6, no. 8 (August 1929), 103–118. Such Social Democratic proposals should not be seen as attempts to create permanent alliances with bourgeois groups. They were tactical maneuvers, much like the decisions of Social Democratic party leaders in Germany and Austria to join coalition governments with liberal parties if, and only if, as Otto Bauer argued in the late 1920s, "circumstances were favorable." Bauer quoted in Charles Gulick, *Austria from Habsburg to Hitler*, vol. 2 (Berkeley: University of California Press, 1948), 1396. For a different view see Udi Greenberg, *The Weimar Century: German Émigrés and the Ideological Foundations of the Cold War* (Princeton: Princeton University Press, 2014), chapter 2.
57. Charles Maier noted that such a model of interest-group mediation (what he called "corporatism") was perhaps one of the few national policy options left available for Social Democrats in an era of parliamentary deadlock. Charles Maier, *Recasting Bourgeois Europe: Stabilization in France, Germany, and Italy in the Decade After World War I* (Princeton: Princeton University Press, 1975).
58. On the historiographical debate about welfare programs as a factor of Weimar democracy's collapse, see Jürgen Baron von Kruedener, ed., *Economic Crisis and Political Collapse: The Weimar Republic, 1924–1933* (New York: Berg, 1990).
59. Franz L. Neumann, *The Rule of Law: Political Theory and the Legal System in Modern Society* (Dover, N.H.: Berg, 1986), 277, from a reprint of his dissertation of 1936.

2: SECTARIAN VISIONS OF THE ECONOMY

Epigraph: Quoted in Wilhelm Solzbacher, *Pius XI: Als Verteidiger der menschlichen Persönlichkeit* (Luzern: Vita Nova, 1939), 249.

1. On the appointment see William L. Patch, Jr., *Heinrich Brüning and the Dissolution of the Weimar Republic* (Cambridge: Cambridge University Press, 1998), 72ff.

2. See Andreas Dorpalen, *Hindenburg and the Weimar Republic* (Princeton: Princeton University Press, 1964), 138–139.

3. See Wolfram Kaiser et al., eds., *Political Catholicism in Europe, 1918–1945* (New York: Routledge, 2005), and Martin Conway, *Catholic Politics in Europe, 1918–1945* (New York: Routledge, 1997).

4. For a description of the Kulturkampf, see Margaret Lavinia Anderson, *Windthorst: A Political Biography* (New York: Oxford University Press, 1981).

5. One of the assassins was himself Catholic but appeared to despise political Catholicism. See Cord Gebhardt, *Der Fall des Erzberger-Mörders Heinrich Tillessen* (Tübingen: Mohr, 1995), 22–23.

6. On Brüning's unsuccessful efforts to form an interconfessional party during the Weimar Republic see Maria D. Mitchell, *The Origins of Christian Democracy* (Ann Arbor: University of Michigan Press, 2012), 16–22. For background see Noel Cary, *The Path to Christian Democracy: German Catholics and the Party System from Windhorst to Adenauer* (Cambridge: Harvard University Press, 1996).

7. Heinrich Hermelink, *Katholizismus und Protestantismus in der Gegenwart, vornehmlich in Deutschland* (Stuttgart: Perthes, 1923), 49, 63–68.

8. Karl Ludwig Schmidt, "Die Notwendigkeit der Einheit der Christen für die Darstellung der christlichen Wahrheit," in *Dokumente zur Lausanner Konferenz über Glauben und Verfassung* (Bern: Stämpfli, 1927), 557–562; Karl Veidt, *Der Kulturkampf unserer Zeit* (Berlin: Deutsche Nationale Schriftenvertriebsstelle, 1929).

9. Pius XI, *Rundschreiben über die Förderung der wahren Einheit der Religion* (Freiburg: Herder, 1928); Franz Xaver Münch, "Der katholische Gedanke. Sinn und Ziel," *Katholische Gedanke* 1, no. 1 (1928), 1–2, 10.

10. See Jonathan Wright, *Gustav Stresemann: Weimar's Greatest Statesman* (New York: Oxford University Press, 2002), 133–135, and Dietrich Orlow, *Weimar Prussia, 1925–1933: The Illusion of Strength* (Pittsburgh: University of Pittsburgh Press, 1991), 56–57.

11. For a detailed narrative, see Patch, *Heinrich Brüning and the Dissolution of the Weimar Republic,* chapter 2, especially 83–94.

12. The other original members were Bernhard Dernburg, Hermann Dersch, Wilhelm Engler, Hans Frick, Wilhelm Polligkeit, Adolf Tortilowicz von Batocki-Friebe, and Friedrich Zahn.

13. Gangolf Hübinger, *Kulturprotestantismus und Politik: Zum Verhältnis von Liberalismus und Protestantismus im Wilhelminischen Deutschland* (Tübingen: Mohr, 1994), 31–37.

14. See Marie-Louise Plessen, *Die Wirksamkeit des Vereins für Socialpolitik von 1872–1890* (Berlin: Duncker & Humblot, 1975).

15. Wilhelm Röpke, *Der Cicero auf dem Dorfe,* ed. Werner Pries (Horb: Geiger, 2002), 29; Hans Jörg Hennecke, *Wilhelm Röpke: Ein Leben in der Brandung* (Zurich: Neue Zürcher Zeitung, 2005), 16–18.

16. There was of course no one "Protestant voice" to represent in Germany. Röpke did, however, exemplify the mainstream view among educated Protestants who

had become self-described secular liberals. The fact that he was not a member of any self-declared Protestant organizations was also typical.

17. Wilhelm Röpke, "Weg und Ziel staatsbürgerlicher Erziehung," in *Staatsbürgerliche Erziehung an den deutschen Universitäten* (Marburg: Bauer, 1920), esp. 3–5. Most analyses of Röpke's work do not deal with his early years in Weimar, starting only with the post-1933 years. See, for example, John Zmirak, *Wilhelm Röpke* (Wilmington, Del.: ISI, 2001), and Samuel Gregg, *Wilhelm Röpke's Political Economy* (Northampton, Mass.: Elgar, 2010). One recent exception is Jean Solchany, *Wilhelm Röpke, l'autre Hayek* (Paris: Sorbonne, 2015).

18. Wilhelm Röpke to Gustav Heinemann, November 19, 1923, quoted in Hennecke, *Wilhelm Röpke*, 45.

19. Wilhelm Röpke, *Geld und Aussenhandel* (Jena: Fischer, 1925), 30.

20. See Wilhelm Röpke, "Der kapitalistische Geist," *Jahrbücher für Nationalökonomie und Statistik* (1924), 347. On the influence of Weber more generally, see Joshua Derman, *Max Weber in Politics and Social Thought* (New York: Cambridge University Press, 2012), 24–25.

21. Wilhelm Röpke to Edward Alsworth Ross, March 22, 1927, Edward Alsworth Ross Papers, Box 15, Wisconsin Historical Society Archives.

22. Röpke, "Das problematische Amerika," *Mitteilungen des Jenaer Instituts für Wirtschaftsrecht* (May 1927), 1–4; Röpke, "Die Gewerkschaftsbewegung in den Vereinigten Staaten von Amerika," *Jahrbücher für Nationalökonomie und Statistik* 127, no. 3 (1927), 493–495.

23. Hennecke, *Wilhelm Röpke*, 60. Röpke's wife translated Ross's book *Standing Room Only?* (1927) into German. Ross, *Raum für alle?*, trans. Eva Röpke (Stuttgart: Deutsche Verlagsanstalt, 1929).

24. Röpke, "Sozialökonomische Betrachtungen üben den abnehmenden Bevölkerungszuwachs," *De Economist* (1930), 647–652; Wilhelm Röpke, *Nationalsozialisten als Feinde der Bauern* (Hanover: Meister, 1930). Röpke urged opposition to the Nazi Party not because of its racism but because of its "hostility to property," the same phrase that farmers often used to describe the platforms of the Catholic Center since Matthias Erzberger's tax reforms.

25. Hennecke, *Wilhelm Röpke*, 76.

26. See for example Wilhelm Röpke, "Die Ursachen der gegenwärtigen Wirtschaftskrise," *Leipziger Neueste Nachrichten* (February 3, 1931).

27. *The Unemployment Problem in Germany* (London: H.M. Stationery Office, 1931), 41–42.

28. Ibid., 44–63, especially 48–49.

29. Otto Veit, "Ein Weg zur Arbeitschaffung," *Magazin der Wirtschaft* (May 8, 1931), 787.

30. Patch, *Heinrich Brüning*, 157; Hak-Ie Kim, *Industrie, Staat und Wirtschaftspolitik: Die konjunkturpolitische Diskussion in der Endphase der Weimarer Republik 1930–1932/33* (Berlin: Duncker & Humblot, 1997), 65–66.

31. See further Heinrich August Winkler, *Der Weg in die Katastrophe: Arbeiter und Arbeiterbewegung in der Weimarer Republik 1930 bis 1933* (Berlin: Dietz, 1987), 314–315.

32. Wilhelm Röpke, "Ein Weg aus der Krise," *Frankfurter Zeitung* (May 7, 1931), and Röpke, "Das Brauns-Kommission und seine Kritiker," *Soziale Praxis* 40, no. 21 (May 21, 1931), 665–671.

33. Wilhelm Röpke, "Deutschland und die Weltwirtschaftskrise (Schluss)" *Sparkasse* 51, no. 10 (May 15, 1931), 197–200; see also Eduard Heimann, "Kreditpolitik auf Grund öffentlicher Aufträge," *Magazin der Wirtschaft* 7 (May 15, 1931), 831–834. Röpke's choice of metaphor to describe the government's interventions, "work of healing" (*Sanierungswerk*), was significant. In his mind, Brüning's regime failed to understand the German economy properly as part of a larger world-economic machine whose engine needed to be reignited. Instead, the cabinet apparently regarded the national economy as an organism that could be "healed" by redistributing energies within the body.

34. Reichsministerium des Innern, ed., *Reichsgesetzblatt Teil 1, 1931* (Berlin: Reichsverlagsamt, 1931), 279–314.

35. Wilhelm Röpke, "Praktische Konjunkturpolitik: Die Arbeit der Brauns-Kommission," *Weltwirtschaftliches Archiv* 34 (1931), 450; Antonie Hopmann, "Bekämpfung der Arbeitslosigkeit," *Soziale Berufsarbeit* 11, no. 8 (August 1931), 135–136.

36. Wilhelm Röpke, *Der Weg des Unheils* (Berlin: Fischer, 1931), 14.

37. See Patch, *Heinrich Brüning*, chapters 4 and 5.

38. On the anti-Protestantism of his older brother Tilmann Pesch, from whom Heinrich Pesch took many ideas, see Hermann-Josef Grosse Kracht, "Biographie Heinrich Pesch (1854–1926)," in *Das System des Solidarismus*, ed. Hermann-Josef Grosse Kracht, Tobias Karcher, and Christian Spiess (Berlin: Lit, 2007), 14–15.

39. Heinrich Pesch, *Lehrbuch der Nationalökonomie*, vol. 1 (Freiburg: Herder, 1905), esp. 138–139, 381–382.

40. See the publications of the Kommission für christliches Völkerrecht founded in 1917, especially those written by the chairman of the commission Joseph Mausbach, *Naturrecht und Völkerrecht* (Freiburg: Herder, 1918), and Heinrich Pesch, *Ethik und Volkswirtschaft* (Freiburg: Herder, 1918).

41. Siegfried Kracauer, "Deutsche Geist und deutsche Wirklichkeit" (1922), in *Siegfried Kraceur Schriften*, ed. Inka Mulder-Bach, vol. 5, part 1 (Frankfurt: Suhrkamp, 1990), 1958.

42. See Eberhard Grein, *Für die soziale Marktwirtschaft: Oswald von Nell-Breuning, Reformer und Jesuit* (Sankt Ottillien: EOS, 2011), 20. Unfortunately, like Brüning, Nell-Breuning burned all his personal papers, so we must reconstruct his ideas solely from his published work.

43. Willy Hellpach, "Die katholische Kulturoffensive," *Der neue Merkur* 8 (February 1925), republished in *Die Rückkehr aus dem Exil*, ed. Karl Hoeber (Düsseldorf: Schwann, 1926), 139–152.

44. Karl Bachem, *Vorgeschichte, Geschichte, und Politik der Deutschen Zentrumspartei*, vol. 8 (Cologne: Bachem, 1931), 362. For example, Nell-Breuning's pamphlet *Proletarier oder Kapitalisten-Religion?* (Kevalaer: Bercker, 1926) went through its 25,000th copy printed in 1928.

45. Oswald von Nell-Breuning, *Grundzüge der Börsenmoral* (Freiburg: Herder, 1928), esp. 18–20, 120–155.

46. *Lehren und Weisungen der österreichischen Bischöfen über soziale Fragen der Gegenwart* (Wien: Typographische Anstalt, 1926).

47. Oswald von Nell-Breuning, *Kirche und Kapitalismus* (Mönchengladbach: Volksverein, 1929), 7–8. For his arguments against Austrian Catholic critics ("universalists" or theorists of *Ganzheit* such as the editors of the Austrian Catholic periodical *Schönere Zukunft*, Ottmar Spann and Eugen Kogon), see Nell-Breuning, "Kapitalismus und Börse," *Allgemeine Rundschau* 25, no. 30 (1928), 468–469, and Nell-Breuning, "Wirtschaft und Moral der Wirtschaftslehre und Dogmatik," *Allgemeine Rundschau* 25, no. 39 (1928), 614–615. For more on Spann and his attack against the solidarists, see Janek Wassermann, *Black Vienna* (Ithaca: Cornell University Press, 2014), and on the broader conflict between German and Austrian Catholics on these issues, see Anton Rauscher, *Der soziale und politische Katholizismus* (Munich: G. Olzog, 1981), 354–355. On the importance of "accidentalism" in Catholic doctrine see James Chappel, *The Pope's Divisions: Catholicism and the Salvation of European Democracy* (Cambridge: Harvard University Press, forthcoming 2018).

48. Nell-Breuning, *Kirche und Kapitalismus*, 8.

49. Oswald von Nell-Breuning, *Jakobinischer, bolshewistischer und christlicher Eigentumsbegriff* (Mönchengladbach: Volksverein, 1929), 10–12; Nell-Breuning, *Sinnvoll geleitete Wirtschaft* (Mönchengladbach: Volksverein, 1929), 1–3; Nell-Breuning, *Die Eigentum in der Auffassung des Freiherrn vom Stein* (Mönchengladbach: Volksverein, 1929), 2–3; and Nell-Breuning, *Rationalisierung der Verteilung* (Mönchengladbach: Volksverein, 1929). Nell-Breuning associated the "Jacobin" concept of property with one of Wilhelm Röpke's other mentors, Johann Victor Bredt, the leader of the Economics Party of the Middle Class. See *Erinnerungen und Dokumente von Joh. Victor Bredt, 1914–1933*, ed. Martin Schumacher (Düsseldorf: Droste, 1970), 35–36.

50. Pius XI's choice of Nell-Breuning and Gustav Gundlach suggests the Vatican's preference for a more flexible approach (arbitrating between the German and Austrian bishops), given that most Catholics in the world currently lived in societies with a capitalist type of economy. See Johannes Schasching, *Zeitgerecht, zeitbedingt: Nell-Breuning und die Sozialenzyklika Quadragesimo anno nach dem Vatikanischen Geheimarchiv* (Bornheim: Ketteler, 1994), 19–23.

51. Oswald von Nell-Breuning, "Wirtschaftsfreiheit und wirtschaftliche Machtstellungen," *Deutsche Arbeit* 15, no. 8 (1930), 393–406.

52. Oswald von Nell-Breuning, "Katholische Siedlungsdienst," *Stimmen der Zeit* 121, no. 1 (April 1931), 40–45.

53. Gustav Gundlach, "Zur Eigentumsfrage," *Stimmen der Zeit* 121 (July 1931), 296–298, 302.

54. Heinrich Brüning, *Memoiren, 1918–1934* (Stuttgart: Deutsche Verlagsanstalt, 1970), 270.

55. The syntax " 'ordines' nimirum, quibis inserantur homines non pro munere" was purposefully vague to account for different political forms.

56. See William Patch, Jr., "Fascism, Catholic Corporatism, and the Catholic Trade Unions of Germany, Austria, and France," in *Between Cross and Class,* ed. Lex Heerma van Voss et al. (New York: Peter Lang, 2005), 185.

57. For statistics on the growth of the Nazi Party see Detlef Mühlberger, *Hitler's Followers: Studies in the Sociology of the Nazi Movement* (New York: Routledge, 1991), 132. For the popularity of the idea see Walter Schüle, *Der berufsständische Gedanke in der wirtschaftspolitischen Diskussion seit 1919* (Ph.D. dissertation, University of Mannheim, 1933); Erich List, *Der Berufsständegedanke in der deutschen Verfassungsdiskussion seit 1919* (Leipzig: Brandstetter, 1930).

58. [Theodor Heuss], "Quadragesimo anno," *Der Staat seid Ihr* 1, no. 15 (June 8, 1931). Derek Hastings, *Catholicism and the Roots of Nazism: Religious Identity and National Socialism* (New York: Oxford University Press, 2010).

59. Oswald von Nell-Breuning, "Um den berufsständischen Gedanken. Zur Enzyklika 'Quadragesimo anno' vom 15. Mai 1931," *Stimmen der Zeit* 122 (October 1931), 36–50. Although he argued that a free incorporation was to be preferred, Nell-Breuning noted that according to the Vatican's teaching an obligatory membership in a vocational estate would theoretically be "justified." In his official line-by-line commentary of *Quadragesimo anno,* Nell-Breuning further distanced the church from the top-down "corporative state" in Italy. Nell-Breuning, *Die soziale Enzyklika* (Cologne: Katholische Tat, 1932), 173–176.

60. See Patch, *Heinrich Brüning,* 179–193, and on the *Wirtschaftsbeirat* in particular see Gerhard Schulz, *Zwischen Demokratie und Diktatur* (Berlin: De Gruyter, 1992), 613–626. On the Catholic proposals see Oswald von Nell-Breuning, "Soziale Nutzung des Bodens. Entwurf eines Gesetzes zur Ausführung von Art. 155 RV," in *Der Deutsche Weg* Nr. 49 (September 3, 1931), and Karl Muth, "Grossstadt und Siedlung," *Hochland* 29 (November 1931), 132.

61. See "Vierte Verordnung des Reichspräsidenten zur Sicherung von Wirtschaft und Finanzen und zum Schutz des inneren Friedens," *Reichsgesetzblatt,* Teil 1 (December 9, 1931), 700–745.

62. Friedrich Dessauer, preface to first edition (November 1931), *Im Kampf mit der Wirtschaftskrise* (Frankfurt: Carolus, 1932), vi–vii, 138–159.

63. Oswald von Nell-Breuning, "Die gegenwärtige Krise und Wege zu ihrer Überwindung," in *Rhein-Mainische Volkszeitung* (December 8, 1931); Nell-Breuning, "Wirtschaftsfragen vor dem Völkerbund," *Katholik* (October 4, 1931), 1–3, text of a speech he gave in Geneva. Nell-Breuning later argued at a conference of the People's Association in Mönchengladbach in October 1932

that Brüning had "open[ed] the door as much as possible in the direction" of creating a "true *berufsständische Ordnung*" with his December 1931 decrees. See his contribution "Wirtschaft und Recht," in *Wettbewerbsfreiheit und berufsständische Ordnung*, 58.

64. See Hermann Graml, *Zwischen Stresemann und Hitler: Die Aussenpolitik der Präsidialkabinette Brüning, Papen und Schleicher* (Munich: Oldenbourg, 2001), 205.

65. Patch, *Heinrich Brüning*, 198.

66. Quoted in Harry Louis Nathan, *Free Trade To-day* (London: Victor Gollancz, 1929), 235.

67. See Claudia Lepp, "Konservativ-christlicher Widerstand: Das Beispiel Gerhard Ritter," in *Jahrbuch für badische Kirchen- und Religionsgeschichte*, vol. 2, ed. Albrecht Ernst et al. (Stuttgart: Kohlhammer, 2008), 69–90.

68. For a general introduction see Theo Balderston, *Economics and Politics in the Weimar Republic* (Cambridge: Cambridge University Press, 2002), and more specifically on the Lautenbach Plan see Hansjorg Klausinger, "German Anticipations of the Keynesian Revolution?: The Case of Lautenbach, Neisser, and Röpke," *European Journal of the History of Economic Thought* 6, no. 3 (1999), 378–403.

69. Wilhelm Röpke, *Krise und Konjunktur* (Leipzig: Quelle & Meyer, 1932), 115–121 and 131–138. The quotation is from the translation by Vera C. Smith, *Crisis and Cycles* (London: William Hodge, 1938), 180, 217.

70. Gustav Gundlach, "Staat, Gesellschaft, und Wirtschaft in der individualistischen Ära unter katholischer Sicht," in *Die berufsständische Ordnung*, ed. Joseph van der Velden (Cologne: J.P. Bachem, 1932), 39.

71. See in particular Johannes Gickler, "Die Arbeitnehmer in der berufsständischen Ordnung," in *Die berufsständische Ordnung*, ed. Joseph van der Velden (Cologne: J.P. Bachem, 1932), 103–121; Oswald von Nell-Breuning, "Der gesellschaftspolitische Vorstoss des deutschen Katholizismus," *Das Neue Reich* 14, no. 35 (May 28, 1932), 683–685.

72. Josef Dobretsberger, *Freie oder gebundene Wirtschaft?* (Munich: Duncker & Humblot, 1932), 10–11.

73. Franz von Papen, in *Der Ring* (April 16, 1932). See also Christoph Hübner, *Die Rechtskatholiken, die Zentrumspartei und die katholische Kirche in Deutschland bis zum Reichskonkordat von 1933* (Berlin: Lit, 2014), 686–689.

3: THE BATTLE OVER NATIONAL EDUCATION

Epigraph: Siegfried Kracauer, "Über Arbeitslager," *Frankfurter Zeitung* (October 1, 1932), in *Siegfried Kracauer Schriften*, ed. Inka Mülder-Bach, vol. 5, part 3 (Frankfurt: Suhrkamp, 1990), 110.

1. Jonathan Israel, *Revolutionary Ideas: An Intellectual History of the French Revolution from The Rights of Man to Robespierre* (Princeton: Princeton University Press, 2014), chapter 14; *Journal of the Proceedings of the National Teachers' Association at the First Anniversary* (Albany, N.Y.: Cruikshank, 1858).

2. *Rapport sur l'instruction publique* (1793), quoted in Lynn Hunt, *Politics, Culture, and Class in the French Revolution* (Berkeley: University of California Press, 1984), 68.

3. Walther Schotte, *Das Kabinett Papen-Schleicher-Gayl* (Leipzig: Kittler, 1932).

4. See further F. L. Carsten, *The Reichswehr and Politics, 1918 to 1933* (London: Oxford University Press, 1966), chapter 8.

5. See Berthold Petzinna, *Erziehung zum deutschen Lebensstil: Ursprung und Entwicklung des jungkonservativen "Ring"-Kreises, 1918–1933* (Berlin: Akademie, 2000), 257–274.

6. "To the Nazi Colors Flock German Students," *New York Times Magazine* (January 17, 1932).

7. Friedrich von der Leyen, "Gedanken zur Hochschulreform," *Deutsche Rundschau* 184 (1920), 247ff.

8. Heinrich Brüning, *Memoiren* (Stuttgart: Deutsche Verlagsanstalt, 1970), 617.

9. See Heinrich August Winkler, *Weimar, 1918–1933*, 3rd edition (Munich: Beck, 1998), 486–487.

10. See Roger Chickering, *Imperial Germany and a World Without War: The Peace Movement and German Society, 1892–1914* (Princeton: Princeton University Press, 1975), chapter 4.

11. See the posthumously published Max Scheler, *Die Idee des Friedens und des Pazifismus* (Leipzig: Neue Geist, 1931).

12. Walter Benjamin to Gershom Scholem, December 1, 1920, in Benjamin, *Gesammelte Briefe*, vol. 2, ed. Christoph Gödde and Henri Loditz (Frankfurt: Suhrkamp, 1996), 108–109.

13. Carola Dietze, *Nachgeholtes Leben: Helmuth Plessner, 1892–1985* (Göttingen: Wallstein, 2006), 26–30, 45. Driesch's comments regarded Plessner's Habilitationsschrift, *Die Einheit der Sinne* (Bonn: Cohen, 1923). The directors of the Richard Avenerius Foundation awarded the Prize of the Academy of Sciences to Plessner in 1932.

14. For the early critics of the empire's lack of political education, see Paul Rühlmann, *Wege zur Staatsgesinnung: Beiträge zur politischen Pädagogik* (Berlin: Deutsche Verlagsgesellschaft für Politik und Geschichte, 1919), and Max Weber, *Politik als Beruf* (Munich: Duncker & Humblot, 1919). See also Hugo Preuss, *Das deutsche Volk und die Politik* (Jena: Diederichs, 1915).

15. Helmut [*sic*] Plessner, "Staatskunst und Menschlichkeit," *Volkswacht für Schlesien und Posen* (November 9, 1920); Hellmut [*sic*] Plessner, "Politische Erziehung in Deutschland," *Die Zukunft* 30, no. 6 (November 5, 1921), esp. 152–163. Plessner did not intend "race" in the *völkisch* meaning but in the sense of a class of statesmen.

16. Helmuth Plessner, *Die Grenzen der Gemeinschaft: Eine Kritik der sozialen Radikalismus* (Bonn: Cohen, 1924), especially 9–13, 87–102.

17. See Siegfried Kracauer's review in "Philosophie der Gemeinschaft," *Frankfurter Zeitung* (October 30, 1924), and Robert Drill to Plessner, November 18, 1924, Helmuth Plessner Papers, 130.248, Bibliotheek der Rijksuniversiteit Groningen.

18. F. J. J. Buytendijk and Helmuth Plessner, "Die Deutung des mimischen Ausdrucks," *Philosophische Anzeiger* 1 (1925), 72–126. For context see Helmut Lethen's *Cool Conduct: The Culture of Distance in Weimar Germany* (Berkeley: University of California Press, 2002).

19. Helmuth Plessner, *Die Stufen des Organischen und der Mensch* (Berlin: De Gruyter, 1928), 341–346. It is clear from his private papers that Plessner explicitly intended the system outlined in *Die Stufen des Organischen* to establish a philosophical foundation of his critique of social radicalism in *Die Grenzen der Gemeinschaft* (for which some of his mentors, including Max Scheler, had criticized him for being insufficiently systematic).

20. Zentralinstitut für Erziehung und Unterricht, "Richtlinien für die Gestaltung des staatsbürgerlichen Unterrichts," in *Staatsbürgerliche Erziehung*, ed. F. Lampe and G. H. Francke (Breslau: Hirt, 1926).

21. Theodor Litt, "Die philosophische Grundlagen der staatsbürgerlichen Erziehung," in *Staatsbürgerliche Erziehung*, 19–38. On his fascination with Plessner's work see the private correspondence between Theodor Litt and Helmuth Plessner, September 19, 1925, Plessner Papers, 33.37, and Litt to Plessner, February 9, 1928, Plessner Papers, 34.23, where he wrote of his "great veneration" for the younger scholar. For an excellent analysis of Litt's use of Plessner's ideas, see Peter Dudek, *Grenzen der Erziehung im 20. Jahrhundert* (Bad Heilbrunn: Klinkhardt, 1999), 81–136.

22. Theodor Litt, *Geschichte und Leben*, 2nd edition (Leipzig: Teubner, 1928), 32–34, 144–145. The first edition was published in 1925. For Litt's commitment to international understanding see Theodor Litt, *Nationale Erziehung und Internationalismus* (Berlin: E.S. Mittler und Sohn, 1920).

23. Hans Hellmuth Preuss, "La fédération universitaire pour la S.d.N.," *L'Europe Nouvelle* 9 (1926), 1512.

24. Jonathan French Scott, *The Menace of Nationalism in Education* (New York: Macmillan, 1926), 209.

25. Hugo Lehbert, "Einige Probleme aus der Methodik des Unterrichts in der Geschichte und Bürgerkunde," *Vergangenheit und Gegenwart* 16, no. 7 (1926), 397. For context see Larry Jones, "German Liberalism and the Alienation of the Younger Generation in the Weimar Republic," in *In Search of a Liberal Germany*, ed. Konrad Jarausch and Larry Jones (Oxford: Berg, 1990), 287–321.

26. On the debate see Peter E. Gordon, *Continental Divide: Heidegger, Cassirer, Davos* (Cambridge: Harvard University Press, 2010). On Cassirer's ideas and their resonance with Stresemann's diplomacy, see Emily Levine, *Dreamland of Humanists* (Chicago: University of Chicago Press, 2014), 199.

27. Gerhard Noack, " 'Staatsbürgerkunde.' Vorträge (mit Aussprache) zu Breslau," *Vergangenheit und Gegenwart* 21, no. 1 (1931), 67.

28. For the proposal see "Vorschläge des Studienrats Dr. Hugo Lötschert zu der durch den Völkerbund geforderten Reform der geschichtlichen Lehrbücher," *Vergangenheit und Gegenwart* 21, no. 3 (1931), 208–215.

29. Cited by Ernst Wilmanns in his report of the conference, "Lehrgang, 'Völkerbund und Schule,' Köln 1.-3. Juni 1931," *Vergangenheit und Gegenwart* 21, no. 9 (1931), 560. For context see Sven Pflifka, *Zwischen nationaler Gewissheit und transnationalen Hoffnungen* (Idstein: Schulz-Kirchner, 2011), 292–303.

30. Wilhelm Mommsen, "Äusserung zu Dr. H. Lötscherts Vorschlägen," *Vergangenheit und Gegenwart* 21, no. 4 (1931), 222–225.

31. Ernst von Hippel approached Plessner in 1929 to contribute to a "Politics and Civic Education" series for the publisher Junker & Hauptmann, but Plessner did not take up the offer until the summer of 1931, when he furiously wrote the piece in two weeks. Ernst von Hippel to Helmuth Plessner, November 9, 1929, Plessner Papers, 131.86. This is also noted by Helmut Lethen, "Sich in Form bringen," in *Die kulturelle Moderne zwischen Demokratie und Diktatur*, ed. Bernd Wirkus (Konstanz: UVK, 2007), 185.

32. Helmuth Plessner, *Macht und menschliche Natur* (Berlin: Junker & Hauptmann, 1931), 40–78. I have translated *Bodenlosigkeit* as "groundlessness" instead of "unfathomability," as one sometimes sees it. For the object of Plessner's critique see Heidegger, *Sein und Zeit*, erste Hälfte (Halle: Niemeyer, 1927), especially 117–125, and for useful context see Hans-Peter Krüger, "Die Leere zwischen Sein und Sinn. Helmuth Plessners Heidegger-Kritik in 'Macht und menschliche Natur' (1931)," in *Die Weimarer Republik zwischen Metropole und Provinz*, ed. Wolfgang Bialas and Burkhard Stenzel (Cologne: Böhlau, 1996), 177–199. Some scholars have argued, I think misleadingly, that Plessner was attempting to "ground" Carl Schmitt's idea of politics (as struggle between enemies) in philosophical anthropology. See Rüdiger Kramme, *Helmuth Plessner und Carl Schmitt* (Berlin: Duncker & Humblot, 1989). While Plessner did adopt Schmitt's definition of politics as the struggle between enemies, the ultimate value he intended to communicate was suprastate authority and international law, while Schmitt rejected that value.

33. Plessner, *Macht und menschliche Natur*, 89–92. For another explication of this point see Hans-Peter Krüger, "Das Öffentliche: John Dewey im Vergleich mit Helmuth Plessner," in *Handlung und Erfahrung*, ed. Bettina Hollstein et al. (Frankfurt: Campus, 2011), 160–165. There was some concern over what Plessner's theory—the idea that a person could "belong" only to one "people"— meant for Germany's Jewish population. See Ludwig Feuchtwanger in his review of *Macht und menschliche Natur* in the *Bayerische Israelitische Gemeindezeitung* (October 15, 1931), 309–311. Indeed, Plessner's relationship to his own Jewish heritage on his father's side seems to have been fraught. See Dietze, *Nachgeholtes Leben*, epilogue.

34. Lieselotte Steveling, *Juristen in Münster: Ein Beitrag zur Geschichte der Rechts- und Staatswissenschaftlichen Fakultät der Westfälischen Wilhelms-Universität Münster/Westf.* (Berlin: Lit, 1999), 185.

35. Franz von Papen, speech to the Lausanne Conference, republished in *Weimar Republic Sourcebook*, ed. Anton Kaes et al. (Berkeley: University of

California Press, 1994), 81–82; William Patch, Jr., *Heinrich Brüning and the Dissolution of the Weimar Republic* (New York: Cambridge University Press, 1998), 277.

36. Giselher Wirsing, "Papens Notverordnung. Der Weg in den Hunger," *Die Tat* 24, no. 4 (July 1932), 305–308.

37. See Peter Gay, *The Dilemma of Democratic Socialism: Eduard Bernstein's Challenge to Marx* (New York: Columbia University Press, 1952).

38. Dietrich Orlow, *Weimar Prussia, 1918–1925: The Unlikely Rock of Democracy* (Pittsburgh: University of Pittsburgh Press, 1986).

39. For a good synopsis of these developments see Dietrich Orlow, *Weimar Prussia, 1925–1933* (Pittsburgh: University of Pittsburgh Press, 1991), especially chapter 8.

40. Frederick Birchall, "Reich Cabinet Firm on Threat to Arm," *New York Times* (July 30, 1932), 1.

41. Rundschreiben des Reichsministers des Innern Wilhelm Freiherr von Gayl an die Unterrichtsminister der deutschen Länder und den Minister für Wissenschaft, Kunst und Volksbildung in Preussen, July 28, 1932, reprinted in *Acta Borussica*, 2. Reihe: Preussen als Kulturstaat, vol. 3.2, Dokumente: Die Kontroverse um staatsbürgerliche Bildung und Erziehung in Preussen (1901–1933), ed. Hartwin Spenkuch (Berlin: Akademie, 2012), 377–380.

42. "Papen Denies Aims for a Dictatorship," *New York Times* (July 30, 1932), 2.

43. See further Eberhard Kolb and Wolfram Pyta, "Die Staatsnotstandsplanung unter den Regierungen Papen und Schleicher," in *Die deutsche Staatskrise, 1930–1933*, ed. Heinrich August Winkler (Munich: Oldenbourg, 1992), 166.

44. George Soloveytchik, "Germany—Chaos or Dictatorship?" *The Nineteenth Century and After* (September 1932), 314–317.

45. Walther Schotte, *Der neue Staat* (Berlin: Neufeld & Henius, 1932). For context see Heinrich August Winkler, *Der Weg in die Katastrophe* (Berlin: Dietz, 1987), 726, and Axel Schildt, *Militärdiktatur mit Massenbasis? Die Querfrontkonzeption der Reichswehrführung um General von Schleicher am Ende der Weimrarer Republik* (Frankfurt: Campus, 1981), 73.

46. Günther C. Behrmann, "Arnold Bergsträsser," in *Jugendbewegt geprägt*, ed. Barbara Stambolis (Göttingen: V&R, 2013), 107–108. Unfortunately, no correspondence from before Bergsträsser's emigration from Germany in 1937 is available in his personal papers at the Bundesarchiv Koblenz.

47. For a description of the case from 1924 to 1932, see Arthur D. Brenner, *Emil J. Gumbel* (Boston: Brill, 2001), 96–143.

48. Arnold Bergsträsser, "Ko-referat zur Ausländer Frage," presentation delivered July 27, 1920, at the 2nd German Student Conference in Göttingen, Bergsträsser Papers, N1260/102, 1–2, Bundesarchiv Koblenz; Bergsträsser, *Die wirtschaftlichen Mächte und die Bildung des Staatswillens nach der deutschen Revolution* (Dissertation, Heidelberg, July 1923), especially foreword and 112–120. For a good biographical background see Horst Schmitt, "Ein 'typischer

Heidelberger im Guten wie im Gefährlichen.' Arnold Bergsträsser und die
Ruperto Carola, 1923–1936," in *Heidelberger Sozial- und Staatswissenschaften*, ed.
Reinhart Blomert et al. (Marburg: Metropolis, 1997), 168–169.

49. Bergsträsser's slightly younger colleague Carl Friedrich traveled to the United
States to coordinate exchanges with U.S. colleges, while Bergsträsser remained
in Germany to coordinate intra-European exchanges. On Friedrich's efforts, see
Udi Greenberg, *The Weimar Century: German Émigrés and the Ideological
Foundations of the Cold War* (Princeton: Princeton University Press, 2015),
chapter 1.

50. Martin Spahn, *Die Bedeutung des Geschichtsunterrichts für die Einordnung des
Einzelnen in das Gemeinschaftsleben* (Berlin: Mittler, 1918), 3; Elisabeth
Blochmann, *Die Flugschrift "Gedencke, daß du ein Teutscher bist": Ein Beitrag
zur Kritik der Publistik und der diplomatischen Aktenstücke* (Berlin: De Gruyter,
1923).

51. Arnold Bergsträsser, "Die Jugendbewegung und die Universitäten," in
Jugendbewegung und Universität (Karlsruhe: Braun, 1927), 16–17, 23–27. This
was an explicit attack on Plessner's friend Theodor Litt, who was arguing at the
time that instructors should limit themselves to serving as critical facilitators.
See Theodor Litt, *Möglichkeiten und Grenzen der Pädagogik* (Leipzig: Teubner,
1926), 9–10.

52. Eugen Rosenstock, "Dienstpflicht," *Deutsche Rundschau* 219, no. 7 (April 1929),
13. For background on the labor camps see Felix Raabe, *Die Bündische Jugend:
ein Beitrag zur Geschichte der Weimarer Republik* (Stuttgart: Brentano, 1961),
96–101. On the individuals behind the project see Günter Brakelmann,
Helmuth James von Moltke (Munich: Beck, 2007), 54. Moltke's two advisers,
Rosenstock and Adolf Reichwein, were both members of the *Wandervögel* and
shared a vision of the teacher as inspirational leader.

53. See Ger van Roon, ed., *Helmuth James Graf von Moltke: Völkerrecht im Dienste der
Menschen* (Berlin: Siedler, 1986), 14–15.

54. See Friedrich Fiederlein, *Der deutsche Osten und die Regierungen Brüning, Papen,
Schleicher* (Dissertation, Würzburg, 1966), 262–265. For more context see T.
Hunt Tooley, *National Identity and Weimar Germany: Upper Silesia and the
Eastern Border, 1918–1922* (Lincoln: University of Nebraska Press, 1997), and
Henryk Zielinski, "The Social and Political Background of the Silesian
Uprisings," *Acta poloniae Historica* 26 (1972), 73–108.

55. *Appeal of the "Deutscher Volksbund" of Polish Silesia concerning the admission
of children to the primary German minority schools in the Voïvodie of Silesia*
(Geneva: League of Nations, 1927); Peter Dudek, *Erziehung durch Arbeit:
Arbeitslagerbewegung und freiwilliger Arbeitsdienst, 1920–1935* (Opladen:
Westdeutsche Verlagsanstalt, 1988), especially 150–163. For Piłsudski's
connection to Silesia, see Wacław Jedrzejewicz, *Piłsudski, a Life for Poland*
(New York: Hippocrene, 1982), 142–157.

56. "Germany Protests on Poland to League," *New York Times* (November 29,
1930), 8.

57. On Bergsträsser's role in the Deutsch-Französische Studienkomitee with Pierre
    Viénot, see Guido Müller, *Europäische Gesellschaftsbeziehungen nach dem Ersten
    Weltkrieg* (Munich: Oldenbourg, 2005).

58. Arnold Bergsträsser, "Frankreich und die deutschen Wahlen," *Deutsch-
    französische Rundschau* 4, no. 1 (January 1931), 30–54.

59. Andrée Viénot to her mother, December 1, 1930, and Andrée Viénot to
    Wladimir d'Ormesson, January 16, 1931, d'Ormesson, quoted in Gaby
    Sonnabend, *Pierre Viénot* (Munich: Oldenbourg, 2005), 201.

60. Arnold Bergsträsser, *Sinn und Grenzen der Verständigung zwischen Nationen*
    (Munich: Duncker & Humblot, 1930), especially 20–28; Bergsträsser, *Staat und
    Wirtschaft Frankreichs* (Stuttgart: Deutsche Verlags-Anstalt, 1930), especially
    212–312. Carl Schmitt, *Der Völkerbund und das politische Problem der
    Friedenssicherung* (Leipzig: Teubner, 1930), 31.

61. Max Clauss to Arnold Bergsträsser, August 5, 1932, quoted in Müller,
    Europäische Gesellschaftsbeziehungen, 285–286.

62. Giselher Wirsing, *Zwischeneuropa und die deutsche Zukunft* (Jena: Diederichs,
    1932), 7. For context see György Ranki, *Economy and Foreign Policy: The Struggle
    of the Great Powers for Hegemony in the Danube Valley, 1919–1939* (New York:
    Columbia University Press, 1983).

63. Adam Tooze, *Statistics and the German State, 1900–1945* (New York: Cambridge
    University Press, 2001), 176.

64. Arnold Bergsträsser to Paul Ravoux (French chief of Deutsch-französische
    Studienkomitee in Berlin), August 1, 1932, quoted in Müller, *Europäische
    Gesellschaftsbeziehungen*, 283–284.

65. The proper definition of "fascism" in the interwar period is naturally contested
    by historians. For scholarship that emphasizes the principles of political
    leadership outlined here, see Reto Hoffman, *The Fascist Effect: Japan and Italy,
    1915–1952* (Ithaca: Cornell University Press, 2015), and Stanley Payne, *A History
    of Fascism, 1914–1945* (Madison: University of Wisconsin Press, 1995).

66. Arnold Bergsträsser, *Geistige Grundlagen des deutschen Nationalbewußtseins in der
    gegenwärtigen Krise* (Stuttgart: Deutsche Verlags-Anstalt, 1933), 3–18.

67. Cited by Hans Peter Bleuel and Ernst Klinnert, *Deutsche Studenten auf dem Weg
    ins Dritte Reich* (Gütersloh: Sigbert Mohn, 1967), 202.

68. Arnold Bergsträsser, "Politische Bildung und Erziehung der Jugend."
    Bergsträsser Papers, Band 106.

69. Hans E. Friedrich, "Über die Einigung zwischen Deutschland und Frankreich,"
    Die Christliche Welt (September 17, 1932), 849–853.

70. Helmuth Plessner, "Das Wiedergeburt der Form im technischen Zeitalter. Rede
    zum 25. Jubiläum des Deutschen Werkbundes 1932," republished in Plessner,
    Politik–Anthropologie–Philosophie, ed. Salvatore Giammusso and Hans-Ulrich
    Lessing (Munich: Fink, 2001), 85–86; see Joan Campbell, *The German
    Werkbund* (Princeton: Princeton University Press, 1978), 224.

71. Arnold Bergsträsser, lecture on "Humanismus" (undated, late 1932), Arnold
    Bergsträsser Papers, Band 118.

72. Carl Bausteadt, "Siebenter Lehrgang zur Politischen Propädeutik am Staatsbürgerkundlichen Seminar der Deutschen Hochschule für Politik in Berlin, 19. bis 24. September 1932," *Vergangenheit und Gegenwart* 22, no. 11 (1932), 636.

73. Otto Meissner to Adolf Hitler, November 24, 1932, quoted in Joachim Fest, *Hitler*, trans. Richard and Clara Winston (New York: Harcourt, 1974), 350.

74. Quoted in Carl Landauer, *European Socialism: A History of Ideas and Movements from the Industrial Revolution to Hitler's Seizure of Power*, vol. 2 (Berkeley: University of California Press, 1960), 1477.

4: THE PROBLEM OF CULTURE

1. See Carole Fink, *Defending the Rights of Others: The Great Powers, the Jews, and International Minority Protection, 1878–1938* (New York: Cambridge University Press, 2004), chapter 10.

2. Hugo Preuss, "Die heutige politische Lage des Reiches und das deutsche Judentum," *Jüdisch-liberale Zeitung* (June 26, 1925), 6.

3. For different approaches that focus on class and economics, see Götz Aly, *Hitler's Beneficiaries: Plunder, Racial War, and the Nazi Welfare State*, trans. Jefferson Chase (New York: Holt, 2006), and Peter Pulzer, *The Rise of Political Anti-Semitism in Germany and Austria* (Cambridge: Harvard University Press, 1964); for explanations focusing on cultural prejudice, see Kevin Spicer, *Antisemitism, Christian Ambivalence, and the Holocaust* (Bloomington: Indiana University Press, 2007).

4. See Sharon Gillerman, *Germans into Jews* (Palo Alto: Stanford University Press, 2009), and Michael Brenner, *The Renaissance of Jewish Culture in Weimar Germany* (New Haven: Yale University Press, 1996).

5. See Marjorie Lamberti, *The Politics of Education: Teachers and School Reform in Weimar Germany* (New York: Berghahn, 2002), 151–170.

6. Franz A. Lütz, "Die Frage der Simultanschule nach der Weimarer Verfassung vom 11. August 1919" (Dissertation, Giessen, 1928), vi; Detlev Peukert, *The Weimar Republic: The Crisis of Classical Modernity*, trans. Richard Deveson (New York: Hill & Wang, 1992), 141.

7. According to statistics given in "Um die Gemeinschaftsschule," *Internationale Zeitschrift für Erziehung* 6 (1937), 228.

8. For details of what his duties would be, see Carl Heinrich Becker's memorandum for Schleicher, "Vorschläge für eine Vereinfachung der kulturpolitischen Doppelarbeit im Reich und Preussen" (undated, December 1932), in Carl Heinrich Becker Papers, Geheime Staatsarchiv preussischer Kulturbesitz Berlin, Nr. 1380; for context see Erich Wende, *C. H. Becker, Mensch und Politiker* (Stuttgart: Deutsche Verlags-Anstalt, 1959), 97.

9. Axel Schildt, *Militärdiktatur mit Massenbasis? Die Querfrontkonzeption der Reichswehrführung um General von Schleicher am Ende der Weimarer Republik* (Frankfurt: Campus, 1981), 56–58; F. L. Carsten, *The Reichswehr and Politics, 1918 to 1933* (London: Oxford University Press, 1966), 317.

10. Heinrich Muth, "Schleicher und die Gewerkschaften 1932. Ein Quellenproblem," *Vierteljahrsheft für Zeitgeschichte* 29 (1981), 189–215, as well as Dieter Emig and Rüdiger Zimmermann, "Das Ende einer Legende: Gewerkschaften, Papen und Schleicher, Gefälschte und echte Protokolle," *Internationale wissenschaftliche Korrespondenz zur Geschichte der deutschen Arbeiterbewegung* 12, no. 1 (March 1976), 19–43. For further context see Heinrich August Winkler, *Der Weg in die Katastrophe* (Berlin: Dietz, 1987), 746–753.

11. Kurt von Schleicher, radio address of December 15, 1932, published in *Akten der Reichskanzlei, Weimarer Republik: Das Kabinett von Schleicher* (Boppard am Rhein: Boldt, 1986), quoted here 101–115.

12. Andreas Dorpalen, *Hindenburg and the Weimar Republic* (Princeton: Princeton University Press, 1964), 404.

13. See Carl Heinrich Becker, *Secondary Education and Teacher Training in Germany* (New York: Teachers College, 1931), 14.

14. Shlomo Shafir, "American Jewish Leaders and the Emerging Nazi Threat (1928–1933)," *American Jewish Archives* 31 (1979), 179.

15. "Ein Denkmal für die gefallenen deutschen Juden," *C.V.-Zeitung* (November 25, 1932), 3–4; for more in-depth coverage "Feierstunden des RjF," *Der Schild* (November 24, 1932), 1–3. For more on the Reichsbund jüdischer Frontsoldaten at this time, see Arnold Paucker, "Der jüdische Abwehrkampf," in Werner Mosse and Arnold Paucker, *Entscheidungsjahr 1932* (Tübingen: Mohr, 1966), 405–499.

16. Hans-Joachim Schoeps, *Die letzten dreissig Jahre* (Stuttgart: Klett, 1956), 72–73.

17. For an in-depth analysis of the programs see Günther Grünthal, *Reichsschulgesetz und Zentrumspartei in der Weimarer Republik* (Düsseldorf: Droste, 1968).

18. See Moritz Werner, "Staat und Erziehung," *Der Morgen* (December 1925), 588; Ludwig Basnizki, "Jüdische Erziehung?" *Jüdisch-liberale Zeitung* (February 4, 1927), 3; Hans-Joachim Schoeps, "Um den Sinn der konfessionellen Schule" (undated, most likely 1929), Schoeps Papers, Kasten 30, Mappe 1, 1–5.

19. On German Jewish voting patterns, see Ernest Hamburger and Peter Pulzer, "Jews as Voters in the Weimar Republic," *Leo Baeck Institute Year Book* (1985), 8–49.

20. On Hellpach's proposal, see Claudia-Anja Kaune, *Willy Hellpach (1877–1955)* (Frankfurt: Peter Lang, 2005), 247. For his comments on Freud and the Jewish psyche see Willy Hellpach, *Politische Prognose für Deutschland* (Berlin: Fischer, 1928), especially 77–78, 364–377. Schoeps reported on his seminar with Hellpach in a letter to Martin Rade, June 6, 1928, in Friedrich Wilhelm Kantzenbach, "Die wissenschaftliche Werden von Hans-Joachim Schoeps und seine Vertreibung aus Deutschland 1938. Eine Dokumentation aus den Briefen von Hans-Joachim Schoeps an Martin Rade im Nachlass M. Rade, Marburg," *Zeitschrift für Religions- und Geistesgeschichte* 32 (1980), 331.

21. For Rade's argument on state neutrality toward religion, see Johanna Jantsch, ed., *Der Briefwechsel zwischen Adolf von Harnack und Martin Rade* (Berlin: de

Gruyter, 1996), 121–130. Some of Schoeps's articles included "Max Brod," *Die Christliche Welt* (February 16, 1929), 181–186, and "Die geistige Gestalt Franz Kafkas," *Die Christliche Welt* (August 17, 1929), 761–771. Schoeps finished his dissertation under the supervision of the historian of religion (and Jewish-born convert to Christianity) Joachim Wach but because of the Nazi rise to power could not publish it until 1935. Hans-Joachim Schoeps, *Geschichte der jüdischen Religionsphilosophie* (Berlin: Vortrupp, 1935).

22. Claudia Bruns, *Politik des Eros: Der Männerbund in Wissenschaft, Politik und Jugendkultur (1880–1934)* (Cologne: Böhlau, 2008), 438, and Fritz Stern, *The Politics of Cultural Despair: A Study in the Rise of the Germanic Ideology* (Berkeley: University of California, 1961), 226–229.

23. Hans Blüher, *Deutsches Reich, Judentum und Sozialismus* (Munich: Steinicke, 1919), esp. 10–21.

24. Hans Blüher, *Die Erhebung Israels gegen die christlichen Güter* (Hamburg: Hanseatische Verlagsanstalt, 1932), 189–193.

25. On Kafka and Blüher, see Iris Bruce, *Kafka and Cultural Zionism* (Madison: University of Wisconsin Press, 2007), 148. Schoeps helped Kafka's longtime editor Max Brod co-edit an edition of the deceased author's unpublished stories: *Beim Bau der Chinesischen Mauer: ungedruckte Erzählungen und Prosa aus dem Nachlass,* ed. Brod and Schoeps (Berlin: Kiepenheuer, 1931).

26. Hans-Joachim Schoeps, "Zu Hans Blühers: Die Erhebung Israels gegen die christlichen Güter," *C.V.-Zeitung* (January 15, 1932), 5–6; Schoeps, *Rückblicke,* 77. Their subsequent correspondence was published in a separate volume by a Christian press: Hans Blüher and Hans-Joachim Schoeps, *Streit um Israel* (Hamburg: Hanseatische Verlagsanstalt, 1933).

27. See Gershom Scholem, "Offener Brief an den Verfasser der Schrift 'Jüdischer Glaube in dieser Zeit,' " *Bayerische Israelitische Gemeindezeitung* (August 15, 1932).

28. Hans-Joachim Schoeps, *Jüdischer Glaube in dieser Zeit* (Berlin: Philo, 1932), esp. 1–3, 36–62, 85–87.

29. Eduard Strauss, one of the leading educators at Franz Rosenzweig's Jüdische Lehrhaus in Frankfurt, praised Schoeps for attempting to overcome "the extreme rationalistic mode of thought" that had characterized much of Jewish thought since the Enlightenment. Eduard Strauss, "Eine jüdische Theologie?" *Der Morgen* 8, no. 4 (October 1932), 313.

30. Schoeps, *Jüdischer Glaube in dieser Zeit,* 45–50; Salomon Ludwig Steinheim, *Die Politik nach dem Begriffe der Offenbarung, als Theokratie* (Leipzig: Teubner, 1845), esp. 58–59, 107–110. For more on Schoeps's interpretation of Steinheim, see Gary Lease, *"Odd Fellows" in the Politics of Religion* (Berlin: De Gruyter, 1994), 191–210. For an excellent analysis of Schoeps's work in relation to Karl Barth's notion of "return" (*Umkehr*), see Marc Krell, *Intersecting Pathways* (New York: Oxford University Press, 2003), 47ff. On other attempts in the Weimar Republic to emulate Barth in a Jewish key, see Benjamin Lazier, *God Interrupted: Heresy and the European Imagination Between the World Wars* (Princeton: Princeton

University Press, 2008), and Samuel Moyn, *Origins of the Other: Emmanuel Levinas Between Revelation and Ethics* (Ithaca: Cornell University Press, 2005).

31. "Ein Deutsche Hochschullehrer" [Oskar Stillich], *Deutschvölkischer Katechismus*, Heft 2: *Völkische Organisationen* (Leipzig: Oldenburg, 1931), 224.

32. Ernst Robert Curtius, *Deutscher Geist in Gefahr* (Stuttgart: Deutsche Verlags-Anstalt, 1932), 24, 84–96.

33. *Wir deutschen Juden, 321–1932* (Berlin: Centralverein der deutschen Staatsbürger jüdischen Glaubens, 1932), 26.

34. L.H., "Burgfrieden?" *C.V.-Zeitung* (Dec. 2, 1932), 489.

35. The NSDAP received more than forty-two percent of the vote in Thuringian state parliament elections on July 31, 1932, compared with under thirty-five percent in the local (communal) elections of December 3, 1932.

36. [Hans-Joachim Schoeps,] "Der Sieg der preussischen Konservatismus über die Hitlerbewegung," *Der Ring* 6, no. 1 (January 6, 1933), 11–12.

37. For the current state of research on Schröder, see Ulrich Soénius, "Bankier und 'Geburtshelfer'—Kurt Freiherr von Schröder," in *Bewegen, verbinden, gestalten: Unternehmer vom 17. bis zum 20. Jahrhundert*, ed. Ulrich Soénius (Cologne: Stiftung Rheinisch-Westfälisches Wirtschaftsarchiv, 2003), 335–350.

38. Karl Dietrich Bracher, *Die Auflösung der Weimarer Republik* (Stuttgart: Ring, 1955), 691.

39. See a Marxist interpretation in David Abraham, *The Collapse of the Weimar Republic* (Princeton: Princeton University Press, 1981), 172, and the contrasting psychological interpretation in Henry Ashby Turner, Jr., *Hitler's Thirty Days to Power* (Reading, Mass.: Addison-Wesley, 1996), 42. Neither corresponds to Papen's own comments in his memoirs, where he claimed that he "felt no personal animosity towards Schleicher" but did differ with him on matters of "policy," and that Hitler "backed up with enthusiasm my efforts to support the rights of the Churches by special treaties, though knowing full well that these privileges would meet with violent opposition from many of his supporters. . . . To begin with, I believed, mistakenly, that in Church questions it would be possible to wean him away from the radical wing of his party and make him support our own point of view." Franz von Papen, *Memoirs*, trans. Brian Connell (London: Andre Deutsch, 1952), 225–261. Memoirs are inherently suspect as historical sources, but in this case I see no reason not to take his claims seriously.

40. During his governorship of Prussia from July to November 1932, Papen appointed two ministers of culture, the Catholic Aloys Lammers and the Protestant Wilhelm Kähler, who had been intimately involved in the contractual efforts to secure the rights and finances of the Catholic and Protestant churches in Prussia in 1929 and 1931, respectively. On the importance of Papen's Catholicism for the alliance with Hitler, see Larry Eugene Jones, "Franz von Papen, Catholic Conservatives, and the Establishment of the Third Reich, 1933–1934," *Journal of Modern History* 83, no. 2 (2011), 272–318.

41. Wilhelm Kähler, *Noch hundert Tage bis Hitler*, ed. Eckhard Oberdörfer (Schernfeld: SH-Verlag, 1993), esp. 64–70, 89–90. For context see Eckhard Oberdörfer, "Wilhelm Kähler—Ein vergessener Preussischer Kultusminister," *Geschichte und Gegenwart* 12 (1993), 114.

42. Erich Seeberg, *Staat und Religion* (Tübingen: Mohr, 1932), esp. 15–31; Seeberg, *Gottfried Arnold* (Meerane: Herzog, 1923), 142–160, 199–202.

43. For the history of the project, see Stefan Rebinich, "Die Altertumswissenschaften und die Kirchenväterkommission an der Akademie," in *Die königlich Preussische Akademie der Wissenschaften zu Berlin im Kaiserreich*, ed. Jürgen Kocka et al. (Berlin: Akademie, 1999), 199–233.

44. On his studies in Italy see Friedrich Wilhelm Kantzenbach, "Ernst Benz—wie ich ihn sehe und verstehe," *Zeitschrift für Religions- und Geistesgeschichte* 29 (January 1977), 289–290.

45. Giorgio Agamben, *Opus Dei: An Archaeology of Duty*, trans. Adam Kotsko (Stanford: Stanford University Press, 2013), 126; Herbert Grundmann, review of *Ecclesia spiritualis*, in *Historische Zeitschrift* 154, no. 1 (1936), 129.

46. For context on Marius Victorinus's significance in early Christianity, see Marcia Colish, *The Stoic Tradition from Antiquity to the Early Middle Ages*, vol. 2 (Boston: Brill, 1985), 131–142.

47. Ernst Benz, *Marius Victorinus und die Entwicklung der abendländischen Willensmetaphysik* (Stuttgart: Kohlhammer, 1932), 173–179.

48. Ibid., 417–426. Benz referred to Marius Victorinus's treatise *Against Arius* (A.D. 361).

49. Lamberti, *The Politics of Education*, 209; Rainer Bölling, *Sozialgeschichte der deutschen Lehrer* (Göttingen: Vandenhoeck & Ruprecht, 1983), 113.

50. See Else Gräfin von Rittberg, *Der Preussische Kirchenvertrag von 1931: seine Entstehung und seine Bedeutung für das Verhältnis von Staat und Kirche in der Weimarer Republik* (Ph.D. dissertation, University of Bonn, 1960).

51. Karl Barth, "Warum führt man den Kampf nicht auf der ganzen Linie? Der Fall Dehn und die 'dialektische' Theologie," *Frankfurter Zeitung* (February 15, 1932), 6. Barth's protest regarded the Protestant theologian Günther Dehn, whose lectures were being interrupted by Nazi student groups in Halle.

52. Ernst Benz to Erich Seeberg, February 5, 1932, Erich Seeberg Papers, Bundesarchiv Koblenz, N 1248, 3a.

53. Ernst Benz to Erich Seeberg, April 27, 1932, Erich Seeberg Papers, 3a.

54. Ernst Benz to Erich Seeberg, November 27, 1932, Erich Seeberg Papers, 3a.

55. The manifesto of the Nationalsozialistische Frauenbund (1932), which formed in 1931, is quoted in Richard Steigmann-Gall, *The Holy Reich: Nazi Conceptions of Christianity, 1919–1945* (Cambridge: Cambridge University Press, 2003), 147, emphasis in the original; Heinrich Hoffmann, *Das braune Heer: Leben, Kampf und Sieg der SA und SS* (Berlin: Zeitgeschichte, 1932). On the acquiescence of conservative Christian women's groups to alliances with National Socialism, see Michael Phayer, *Protestant and Catholic Women in Nazi Germany* (Detroit: Wayne State University Press, 1990), and Claudia Koonz,

Mothers in the Fatherland: Women, the Family, and Nazi Politics (New York: Routledge, 1986).

56. On the complex negotiations, see William Patch, Jr., *Heinrich Brüning and the Dissolution of the Weimar Republic* (New York: Cambridge University Press, 1998), 272–290, and Carl Landauer, *European Socialism: A History of Ideas and Movements,* vol. 2 (Berkeley: University of California Press, 1960), 1477–1488.

57. Otto Meissner, *Staatssekretär unter Ebert–Hindenburg–Hitler* (Hamburg: Hoffmann & Campe, 1950), 265.

58. Quoted in Christoph Strohm, *Die Kirchen im Dritten Reich* (Munich: Beck, 2011), 17.

59. The headline in the *Völkischer Beobachter* (February 9, 1933) upon Rust's appointment was "Our Confession of Christianity." Cited in Steigmann-Gall, *The Holy Reich,* 122.

60. Quoted in Bernd Sösemann, " 'Auf Bajonetten lasst sich schlecht sitzen.' Propaganda und Gesellschaft in der Anfangsphase der nationalsozialistischen Diktatur," in *Geschichtsbilder,* ed. Thomas Stamm-Kuhlmann et al. (Stuttgart: Franz Steiner, 2003), 389.

61. Hans-Joachim Schoeps, "Die talmudische Königslehre," *Die Christliche Welt* (February 4, 1933), 129–131.

62. George Goetz, "Treue halten," *Jüdisch-liberale Zeitung* (February 15, 1933), 1–2. The editors of the *J-lZ* also agreed with the manifesto that Schoeps published later in the month which reiterated the Germanness of Jews (though they noted that it was now "too late to vault on the warhorse"). "Deutscher Vortrupp— Gefolgschaft deutscher Juden," *Jüdisch-liberale Zeitung* (March 15, 1933), 4. For details on Schoeps's manifesto, see Carl J. Rheins, "Deutscher Vortrupp, Gefolgschaft deutscher Juden 1933–1935," *Leo Baeck Institute Year Book* (1981), 207–229.

63. See Léon Poliakov and Josef Wulf, eds., *Das Dritte Reich und seine Denker* (Berlin: Arani, 1957), 90. For Papen's assurances in a speech on February 24, 1933, see *Appell an das deutsche Gewissen* (Oldenburg: Stalling, 1933), 39.

64. Ernst Benz to Erich Seeberg, March 5, 1933, Erich Seeberg Papers, 3a.

65. Adolf Hitler, "Regierungserklärung vom 23.03.1933," quoted in Georg Denzler, ed., *Die Kirchen im Dritten Reich: Christen und Nazis Hand in Hand?,* vol. 2 (Frankfurt: Fischer, 1984), 41–42.

66. See Josef Becker, "Zentrum und Ermächtigungsgesetz 1933," *Vierteljahrshefte für Zeitgeschichte* 9 (1961), 195–210.

67. Leo Baeck, "Das deutsche Judentum und die Erneuerung Deutschlands," *Israelitisches Familienblatt* 35, no. 14 (April 6, 1933), 2.

68. Erich Seeberg to Rudolf Smend, April 18, 1933, cited in Thomas Kaufmann, " 'Anpassung' als historiographisches Konzept und als theologisches Programm," in *Evangelische Kirchenhistoriker im "Dritten Reich,"* ed. Thomas Kaufmann and Harry Oelke (Gütersloh, 2002), 229.

69. Erich Seeberg to Adolf Deissmann (former dean of the Berlin theological faculty), April 23, 1933, cited in Hartmut Ludwig, "Die Berliner Theologische

Fakultät 1933 bis 1945," in *Die Berliner Universität in der NS-Zeit*, vol. 2, ed. Rüdiger vom Bruch (Wiesbaden: Franz Steiner, 2005), 96–97. One of Seeberg's students, Dietrich Bonhöffer, had written to Seeberg on April 21 with a request for an official statement from the Berlin faculty on the case of Paul Tillich in Frankfurt.

5: TWO COMPETING IDEALS FOR A THIRD REICH

Epigraphs: "Rundfunkansprache des Ministers Göring," in *Die nationalsozialistische Revolution*, ed. Walther Gehl (Breslau: Hirst, 1933), 69–70; Edgar Jung, *Sinndeutung der deutschen Revolution* (Oldenburg: Stalling, 1933), 24.

1. Mark Mazower, *Hitler's Empire: How the Nazis Ruled Europe* (New York: Penguin, 2009), 223.
2. Michael André Bernstein, *Foregone Conclusions: Against Apocalyptic History* (Berkeley: University of California Press, 1994).
3. Hermann Rauschning, *Die Revolution des Nihilismus* (Zürich: Europa-Verlag, 1938), and Rauschning, *Gespräche mit Hitler* (Zürich: Europa-Verlag, 1939).
4. On the false impression of Hitler's anti-Christianity and a discussion of Rauschning, see Richard Steigmann-Gall, *The Holy Reich: Nazi Conceptions of Christianity, 1919–1945* (New York: Cambridge University Press, 2003), 28–29.
5. Franz von Papen, "Die christlichen Grundsätze des Dritten Reich," *Germania* 64, no. 14 (January 15, 1934), 1; Papen, introduction to Heinrich Rogge, *Nationale Friedenspolitik* (Berlin: Junker & Dünnhaupt, 1934), xi. Compare these to Papen's memoirs, *Der Wahrheit eine Gasse* (Munich: List, 1952), 321.
6. For context see David Kaiser, *Economic Diplomacy and the Origins of the Second World War: Germany, Britain, France, and Eastern Europe, 1930–1939* (Princeton: Princeton University Press, 2015), chapters 2 and 3.
7. Arthur Moeller van den Bruck, *Das Dritte Reich* (Berlin: Der Ring, 1923).
8. See Larry Eugene Jones, "Conservative Antisemitism in the Weimar Republic: A Case Study of the German National People's Party," in *The German Right in the Weimar Republic*, ed. Larry Eugene Jones (New York: Berghahn, 2014), 79–107.
9. See further Noah Strote, "The Birth of the 'Psychological Jew' in an Age of Ethnic Pride," *New German Critique* 39, no. 1 (2012), 199–224, and Steven Aschheim, *Culture and Catastrophe: German and Jewish Confrontations with National Socialism and Other Crises* (New York: New York University Press, 1996), chapter 3.
10. Erich Vögelin, *Rasse und Staat* (Tübingen: Mohr, 1933), especially 182–208.
11. Adolf Hitler, *Hitlers zweites Buch: Ein Dokument aus dem Jahre 1928*, ed. Gerhard Weinberg (Stuttgart: Deutsche Verlagsanstalt, 1961), chapter 9, quoted here 120. Hitler simultaneously expressed the belief that America's downfall would come from the disintegrating racial solidarity of the American idea's core cultural carriers, the Anglo-Saxons, demonstrated by the Civil War between them over black emancipation. See Klaus Fischer, *Hitler and America* (Philadelphia: University of Pennsylvania Press, 2011), chapter 1.

12. Edgar Jung, *Die Herrschaft der Minderwertigen: Ihr Zerfall und ihre Ablösung durch ein neues Reich* (Berlin: Verlag Deutsche Rundschau, 1927), 24. I use here the translation in *The Rule of the Inferiour*, vol. 1, ed. and trans. Alexander Jacob (Lewiston, U.K.: Mellen, 1995), 29–30.

13. "Regierungserklärung des Reichskanzlers im Reichstag," published in *Freiburger Zeitung* (March 23, 1933), 1.

14. Jung, *Sinndeutung der deutschen Revolution*, 35–36, 97–103.

15. See Götz Aly, *Hitler's Beneficiaries: Plunder, Racial War, and the Nazi Welfare State*, trans. Jefferson Chase (New York: Holt, 2008); Claudia Koonz, *The Nazi Conscience* (Cambridge: Harvard University Press, 2003).

16. For a good analysis of the boycott see Frank Bajohr, *"Aryanisation" in Hamburg: The Economic Exclusion of Jews and the Confiscation of Their Property in Nazi Germany* (New York: Berghahn, 2002), 28–34.

17. See the reproductions of the flyer of April 12, 1933, in Werner Tress, ed., *"Wider den undeutschen Geist": Bücherverbrennung 1933* (Berlin: Parthas, 2003).

18. For a timeline of the events see Anna-Maria Gräfin von Lösch, *Der nackte Geist: Die Juristische Fakultät der Berliner Universität im Umbruch von 1933* (Tübingen: Mohr Siebeck, 1999), 134–135.

19. Unfortunately little has been written on his and Monroe's involvement in the *Review of International Education (Internationale Zeitschrift für Erziehung)*. Monroe, who along with Ellwood Cubberley is known in the literature on American education as a consensus historian, advised the governments of China, the Philippines, Turkey, and Iraq.

20. For a biographical introduction see Christian Tilitzki, *Die deutsche Universitätsphilosophie in der Weimarer Republik und im Dritten Reich*, Teil 1 (Berlin: Akademie, 2002), 545–592.

21. Alfred Baeumler, *Kants Kritik der Urteilskraft* (Halle: M. Niemeyer, 1923), vii–viii, 62–66. On the pride German educators took in this idealism, see Fritz Ringer, *The Decline of the German Mandarins: The German Academic Community, 1890–1933* (Cambridge: Harvard University Press, 1969).

22. Baeumler, *Kants Kritik*, 25–39, 95. See also Alfred Baeumler, "Politischer Intellektualismus," *Das neue Deutschland* 9 (1920), 222–225.

23. For the affinities between Steiner's schools and National Socialist visions for education, see Peter Staudenmaier, *Between Occultism and Nazism: Anthroposophy and the Politics of Race in the Fascist Era* (Boston: Brill, 2014).

24. Alfred Baeumler, introduction to Johann Jakob Bachofen, *Der Mythus von Orient und Occident*, ed. Manfred Schröter (Munich: Beck, 1926). For a good analysis see David Pan, *Sacrifice in the Modern World: On the Particularity and Generality of Nazi Myth* (Evanston, Ill.: Northwestern University Press, 2012), chapter 2.

25. Alfred Rosenberg, *Der Mythus des 20. Jahrhunderts* (Munich: Hoheneichen, 1930), especially 667–670.

26. Friedrich Nietzsche, *Unpublished Writings from the Period of Unfashionable Observations*, trans. Richard Gray (Stanford: Stanford University Press, 1995), 163; Nietzsche, "On Truths and Lies in an Extramoral Sense" (1873), in *Nietzsche*

and the Death of God: Selected Writings, trans. Peter Fritzsche (Long Grove, Ill.: Waveland, 2007), 47–50. Baeumler argued that Nietzsche, despite his antipathy to thuggish antisemitism, was "in the most profound sense antipathetic to the Jews, in whom he saw the authentic priest natures." Alfred Baeumler, foreword to *Nietzsche der Philosoph und Politiker* (Leipzig: P. Reclam, 1931), 158.

27. Alfred Baeumler, "Antrittsvorlesung" (May 10, 1933), published in Baeumler, *Männerbund und Wissenschaft* (Berlin: Junker & Dünnhaupt, 1934), 123–134.

28. See Léon Poliakov and Josef Wulf, eds., *Das Dritte Reich und seine Denker* (Berlin: Arani, 1957), 90.

29. "Die Universität im neuen Reich. Ein Vortrag von Prof. Martin Heidegger," *Heidelberger Neueste Nachrichten* (July 1, 1933), republished in *Nachlese zu Heidegger*, ed. Guido Schneeberger (Bern: 1962), 73–75. On the context of the speech see Steven Remy, *The Heidelberg Myth: The Nazification and Denazification of a German University* (Cambridge: Harvard University Press, 2002), chapter 1.

30. See Anton Ritthaler, "Eine Etappe auf Hitlers Weg zur ungeteilten Macht. Hugenbergs Rücktritt als Reichsminister," *Vierteljahrshefte für Zeitgeschichte* 8, no. 2 (1960), 193–219.

31. Oswald von Nell-Breuning in *Rhein-Mainische Volkszeitung* (July 23, 1933), cited in Johannes Messner, "Der deutsche Katholizismus nach dem Reichskonkordat," *Schönere Zukunft* (August 13, 1933), 1100. For the historiographical debates about Center complicity, see Rudolf Morsey, *Der Untergang des politischen Katholizismus* (Stuttgart: Belser, 1977), 9; for the concept of "self-synchronization," see Karl Dietrich Bracher et al., *Die nationalsozialistische Machtergreifung* (Cologne: Westdeutscher Verlag, 1960), passim.

32. *Gesetz über den Neuaufbau des Reiches* (January 30, 1934), and *Gesetz über die Aufhebung des Reichsrats* (February 14, 1934).

33. In an article in the Nazi Party's main academic journal, Baeumler lauded the argument made by the nineteenth-century Danish theologian Søren Kierkegaard, that a separation of church and state would benefit both parties involved. Alfred Baeumler, "Gedanken über Kierkegaard," *Nationalsozialistische Monatshefte* 5 (February 1934), 167–180, reprinted in Baeumler, *Studien zur deutschen Geistesgeschichte* (Berlin: Junker & Dunnhaupt, 1937), 96.

34. See NSLB Gau Sachsen, *Erziehungs- und Unterrichtsplan für die achtklassige Volksschule* (Dresden: Meinhold, 1934). Another proposal from Gau Westphalia-South was more favorable to Christian education. See NSLB Westfalen-Süd, *Nationalsozialistischer Erziehungs- und Unterrichtsplan* (Dortmund: Crüwell, 1934). For further context see Friedhelm Kraft, *Religionsdidaktik zwischen Kreuz und Hakenkreuz* (Berlin: De Gruyter, 1996), chapter 3.

35. See for example Edgar Jung, "Deutschland ohne Europa," *Deutsche Rundschau* (February 1934), 73–78; Franz von Papen, *Rede des Vizekanzlers von Papen vor dem Universitätsbund, Marburg 17. Juni 1934* (Berlin: Germania, 1934).

36. Adolf Hitler, *Rede des Reichskanzlers Adolf Hitler vor dem Reichstag am 13. Juli 1934* (Berlin: Müller, 1934).

37. Carl Schmitt, "Der Führer schützt das Recht. Zur Reichstagsrede Adolf Hitlers vom 13. Juli 1934," *Deutsche Juristenzeitung* 15 (August 1, 1934), 945–950; Carl Schmitt, *Staat, Bewegung, Volk* (Hamburg: Hanseatische Verlagsanstalt, 1933), 14–30. For good context see Raphael Gross, *Carl Schmitt and the Jews*, trans. Joel Golb (Madison: University of Wisconsin Press, 2007), and Joseph Bendersky, *Carl Schmitt, Theorist for the Reich* (Princeton: Princeton University Press, 1983).

38. See Hitler's speech at the Juristentag in Leipzig in October 1933, cited in *Hitler: Reden und Proklamationen, 1932–1945*, ed. Max Domarus (Munich: Süddeutscher Verlag, 1965), 305; Carl Schmitt, "Die Wendung zum totalen Staat," *Europäische Revue* 7, no. 4 (1931), 242–250.

39. See Klaus-Jürgen Müller, *Das Heer und Hitler: Armee und nationalsozialistisches Regime, 1933–1940* (Berlin: De Gruyter, 1969), chapter 4.

40. Published in *Reichstagung in Nürnberg* (Berlin: Weller, 1934), 91.

41. Horace Kallen, *Individualism: An American Way of Life* (New York: Liveright, 1933).

42. Hermann Beck, *The Fateful Alliance: German Conservatives and Nazis in 1933* (New York: Berghahn, 2008), 148; see also Robert Gellately, *Backing Hitler: Consent and Coercion in Nazi Germany* (New York: Oxford University Press, 2001), 16–17.

43. Quoted in "Die Feier des Luthertages," *Sonntagsblatt für innere Mission* 84, no. 49 (1933), republished in Günther van Norden, *Der deutsche Protestantismus im Jahr der nationalsozialistischen Machtergreifung* (Gütersloh: Mohn, 1979), 131–134.

44. Shelley Baranowski, "The 1933 German Protestant Church Elections: Machtpolitik or Accommodation?" *Church History* 49, no. 3 (1980), 298–315. On Pro-Deo in Germany, see Stéphanie Roulin, *Un credo anticommuniste: La commission Pro Deo de l'Entente internationale anticommuniste, ou la dimension religieuse d'un combat politique, 1924–1945* (Lausanne: Antipodes, 2010), 303–333. See also Lorna Waddington, "The Anti-Komintern and Nazi Anti-Bolshevik Propaganda in the 1930s," *Journal of Contemporary History* 42, no. 4 (2007), 573–594.

45. Steigmann-Gall, *The Holy Reich*, 45.

46. See Hans-Werner Prahl, *Uni-formierung des Geistes: Universität Kiel im Nationalsozialismus*, vol. 2 (Kiel: Schmidt & Klaunig, 2007), 107.

47. *Das Wort der bekennenden Kirche: die Erklärung der Barmer Bekenntnissynode aus dem Jahre 1934* (Gladbeck: Schriftenmissions-Verlag, 1934).

48. Müller cited in Georg May, *Interkonfessionalismus in der deutschen Militärseelsorge vom 1933 bis 1945* (Amsterdam: Grüner, 1978), 20; bishop Johann Jakob von Hauck cited in Doris Bergen, "Catholics, Protestants, and Christian Antisemitism in Nazi Germany," *Central European History* 27, no. 3 (1994), 339.

49. See Klaus Scholder, *The Year of Disillusionment: 1934, Barmen and Rome* (Philadelphia: Fortress, 1988); Horst Kater, *Die Deutsche Evangelische Kirche in den Jahren 1933 und 1934* (Göttingen: Vandenhoeck & Ruprecht, 1970).

50. *Evangelium im Dritten Reich* 3 (1934), quoted in Kurt Meier, *Die theologische Fakultäten im Dritten Reich* (Berlin: De Gruyter, 1996), 326.

51. Lothar Mertens, *"Nur politisch Würdige": Die DFG-Forschungsförderungen im Dritten Reich, 1933–1937* (Berlin: Akademie, 2004), 317; Andreas Lippmann, *Marburger Theologie im Nationalsozialismus* (Munich: Saur, 2003), 229–231. Benz replaced Hermann Hermelink.

52. Ernst Benz, *Ecclesia Spiritualis* (Stuttgart: Kohlhammer, 1934), 3–174.

53. The analogy between Islam and Bolshevism was standard practice among the Christian propagandists (both Protestant and Catholic) in the Anti-Komintern and the Pro-Deo Commission. For example, Konrad Algermissen, *Die gottlosenbewegung der Gegenwart und ihre Überwindung* (Hanover: Giesel, 1933), 107.

54. Benz, *Ecclesia Spiritualis*, 387–404.

55. Untitled, *New York Times* (March 3, 1935), 9.

56. On Kerrl see Folker Schmerbach, *Das "Gemeinschaftslager Hanns Kerrl" für Referendare in Jüterbog, 1933–1939* (Tübingen: Mohr Siebeck, 2008), 153–170, as well as Steigmann-Gall, *The Holy Reich*, chapter 5.

57. Dietrich Bonhöffer, "Die Bekennende Kirche und die Ökumene," *Evangelische Theologie* 7 (August 1935), 245–262. For context see Shelly Baranowski, "Consent and Dissent: The Confessing Church and Conservative Opposition to National Socialism," *Journal of Modern History* 59, no. 1 (1987), 53–78.

58. Kerrl's speech is published in *Reichstagung in Nürnberg, 1935: Der Parteitag der Freiheit*, ed. Hanns Kerrl (Berlin: Weller, 1935), 407–418.

59. *Bishop George Bell: House of Lords Speeches and Correspondence with Rudolf Hess* (New York: Peter Lang, 2009), 187–189.

60. "Rebel Churchmen Face Nazi Threat of Treason Trials," *New York Times* (December 6, 1935), 15.

61. Adolf Schlatter, *Wird der Jude über uns siegen?* (Essen: Freizeiten, 1936), 3–4.

62. Letter to the editor signed by Emil Balla, Ernst Benz, Heinrich Frick, Georg Wünsch, Adolf Jülicher, and Rudolf Otto, published in *The Times* (January 11, 1936). For context see Andreas Lippmann et al., eds., *Marburger Theologie im Nationalsozialismus* (Neukirchener Verlag, 1998), 83–85.

63. See the declaration in *Junge Kirche* 4 (March 1936), 289–290, and *Die Christliche Welt* 50 (1936), 369–370. The proposal, signed by Ernst Benz, Ernst Ludwig Dietrich, Erich Seeberg, Robert Winkler, Georg Wobbermin, and Konrad Weiss, was published along with an undated letter they had sent in mid-December 1935 to Education Minister Bernard Rust. For context see Matthias Wolfes, *Protestantische Theologie und moderne Welt* (Berlin: Walter de Gruyter, 1999), especially 341–366.

64. See Gesine Gerhard, *Nazi Hunger Politics: A History of Food in the Third Reich* (New York: Rowman & Littlefield, 2015), 52–53; Gerhard Weinberg, *Hitler's Foreign Policy, 1933–1939* (New York: Enigma, 2005), 272.

65. "Finance of German Rearmament. Rumours of New Taxes," *The Times* (April 24, 1936), 16.

66. See Adam Tooze, *The Wages of Destruction: The Making and Breaking of the Nazi Economy* (New York: Penguin, 2008), chapter 7; Timothy Mason, "Internal Crisis and War of Aggression, 1938–1939," in Mason, *Nazism, Fascism, and the Working Class*, ed. Jane Caplan (Cambridge: Cambridge University Press, 1995), 108–109.

67. "Denkschrift Hitlers über die Aufgaben eines Vierjahresplans" (August 1936), published in *Vierteljahrshefte für Zeitgeschichte* 3, no. 2 (1955), 204.

68. Otto Koellreutter, *Deutsches Verfassungsrecht*, 2nd ed. (Berlin: Junker & Dünnhaupt, 1936), 192–195; Koellreutter, *Deutsches Verwaltungsrecht* (Berlin: Junker & Dünnhaupt, 1936), 136–137; Koellreutter, *Grundriß der Allgemeinen Staatslehre* (Tübingen: Mohr, 1933), especially 106–110, 250–255. On his three-year campaign against Carl Schmitt, see Peter Caldwell, "National Socialism and Constitutional Law: Carl Schmitt, Otto Koellreutter, and the Debate over the Nature of the Nazi State, 1933–1937," *Cardozo Law Review* 16 (1994), 399–427. Koellreutter waged his campaign against Schmitt in coordination with Hans Gerber, the dean of the law school at Leipzig, who was involved in reconciliation efforts among the Protestant churches.

69. Franz Böhm, *Die Ordnung der Wirtschaft als geschichtliche Aufgabe und rechtsschöpferische Leistung* (Stuttgart: Kohlhammer, 1937).

70. See Stephen Gross, *Export Empire: German Soft Power in Southeastern Europe, 1890–1945* (New York: Cambridge University Press, 2016), 194. For context on Gördeler and Schacht, see Peter Hoffmann, *Carl Goerdeler and the Jewish Question, 1933–1942* (Cambridge: Cambridge University Press, 2011), 13–15.

71. On Fritsch's views on the chaplaincy see Klaus-Jürgen Müller, *Das Heer und Hitler: Armee und nationalsozialistisches Regime, 1933–1940* (Stuttgart: Deutsche Verlags-Anstalt, 1969), 195–204. Dohrmann was officially neutral in the church struggle between German Christians and the Confessing Church, but actually closer to the latter. Rarkowski was appointed against the wishes of the Catholic bishops of Germany. See Lauren Rossi, *Wehrmacht Priests* (Cambridge: Harvard University Press, 2015).

72. May, *Interkonfessionalismus in der deutschen Militärseelsorge*, 127–128.

73. See Jeremy Noakes, "The Oldenburg Crucifix Struggle of November 1936: A Case Study of Opposition in the Third Reich," in *The Shaping of the Nazi State*, ed. Peter Stachura (New York: Barnes & Noble, 1978), 210–233.

74. Quoted in Meier, *Die theologische Fakultäten im Dritten Reich*, 337, and Michael Garleff, ed., *Deutschbalten, Weimarer Republik, und Drittes Reich*, vol. 1 (Cologne: Böhlau, 2008), 294. Seeberg's conversation with Rosenberg in August 1936 reported by Paul Tillich, in *Ein Lebensbild in Dokumenten*, ed. Renate Abrecht and Margot Hahl (Stuttgart: Evangelisches Verlagswerk, 1980), 263–264.

75. See Joseph Goebbels et al., eds., *Gebt mir vier Jahre Zeit!: Dokumente zum ersten Vierjahresplan des Führers* (Munich: Eher, 1937).

76. See the reports by the German delegation to the annual international conference on public education held in Geneva, Switzerland, in July 1935 and July 1936. "The Development of German Education 1934/35," *Internationale Zeitschrift für*

Erziehung 4 (1935), 297; "The Development of German Education 1935/36," *Internationale Zeitschrift für Erziehung* 6 (1937), 211.

77. Alfred Rosenberg, diary entry for November 22, 1936, *Die Tagebücher von 1934 bis 1944*, ed. Jürgen Matthäus and Frank Bajohr (Frankfurt: Fischer, 2015), 222; Joseph Goebbels, diary entry for January 5, 1937, *Tagebücher*, Teil 1, vol. 3, ed. Elke Fröhlich (Munich: Saur, 1987), 5.

78. Diary entry for January 18, 1937, Alfred Rosenberg, *Die Tagebücher von 1934 bis 1944*, 234.

79. On Sauckel see Gerhard Besier, *Die Kirchen und das Dritte Reich: Spaltungen und Abwehrkämpfe, 1934–1937* (Berlin: Propyläen, 2001), 565; on Himmler and Bormann, see Steigmann-Gall, *The Holy Reich*, especially chapter 7.

80. *Brethren in Adversity: Bishop George Bell, the Church of England, and the Crisis of German Protestantism, 1933–1939*, ed. Andrew Chandler (Rochester, N.Y.: Boydell, 1997), 129. Like with Voltaire, whom Bell quoted, the goal of those who wanted to "crush the infamy" was not physically to destroy the churches, but rather to separate them from, and subordinate them to, the state.

81. "Um die Gemeinschaftsschule," *Internationale Zeitschrift für Erziehung* 6 (1937), 228.

82. Alfred Baeumler, "Die deutsche Schule im Zeitalter der Totalmobilmachung," *Weltanschauung und Schule* (April 1937); Uwe Werner, *Anthroposophen in der Zeit des Nationalsozialismus* (Munich: Oldenbourg, 1999), 218.

83. Goebbels reported that the transportation minister Paul von Eltz-Rübenach accused Hitler at the meeting of ministers on January 31, 1937, of "suppressing the churches" as he refused to join the party. Goebbels, entry for January 31, 1937, *Tagebücher*, Teil 1, vol. 3, 29.

84. Ernst Benz, "Nietzsches Ideen zur Geschichte des Christentums," *Zeitschrift für Kirchengeschichte* 56 (1937), 169–313, quoted here on 313.

85. Heinz Lonicer, quoted in May, *Interkonfessionalismus in der deutschen Militärseelsorge*, 115–116.

PART TWO: PARTNERSHIP

1. For an excellent essay on conflicting versions of Niemöller's "poem," see Harold Marcuse, "The Origin and Reception of Martin Niemöller's Quotation 'First they came for the communists . . .' " in *Remembering for the Future: Armenia, Auschwitz, and Beyond*, ed. Michael Berenbaum et al. (St. Paul, Minn.: Paragon House, 2016).

2. Gregory Bateson, "Culture Contact and Schismogenesis," *Man* 35 (December 1935), 183.

3. For a different argument that accords more agency and influence to particular individuals and their ideas on post-Nazi Germany, see Udi Greenberg, *The Weimar Century: German Émigrés and the Ideological Foundations of the Cold War* (Princeton: Princeton University Press, 2015).

4. See Stefan Scheil, *Transatlantische Wechselwirkungen* (Berlin: Duncker & Humblot, 2012), Arnd Bauernkämpfer, Konrad Jarausch, and Marcus Payk,

eds., *Demokratiewunder: Transatlantische Mittler und die kulturelle Öffnung Westdeutschlands, 1945–1970* (Göttingen: Vandenhoeck & Ruprecht, 2005), 11–37.

5. See Sebastian Ullrich, *Der Weimar-Komplex: das Scheitern der ersten deutschen Demokratie und die politische Kultur der frühen Bundesrepublik, 1945–1959* (Göttingen: Wallstein, 2009), 329–335.

6. Raymond Aron, "Fin de l'âge idéologique?" in *Sociologica*, ed. Theodor Adorno and Walter Dirks (Frankfurt: Europäische Verlagsanstalt, 1955), 219–233; Edward Shils, "The End of Ideology?" *Encounter* 5 (November 1955), 52–58; Daniel Bell, *The End of Ideology: On the Exhaustion of Political Ideas in the Fifties* (Glencoe, Ill.: Free Press, 1960).

6: THE CREATION OF CONSTITUTIONAL CONSENSUS

Epigraph: Gerhard Leibholz, *Re-educating Germans?* (London: National Peace Council, 1944), 14.

1. On his importance on the court, see Justin Collings, *Democracy's Guardians: A History of the German Federal Constitutional Court, 1951–2000* (New York: Oxford University Press, 2015), 6.

2. Gerhard Leibholz to Ernst Fraenkel, August 23, 1953, Ernst Fraenkel Papers, NL 274/10, Bundesarchiv, Koblenz.

3. On the broader process throughout Western Europe see René Marcic, *Vom Gesetzesstaat zum Richterstaat* (Vienna: Springer, 1957).

4. Jan-Werner Müller, *Contesting Democracy* (New Haven: Yale University Press, 2011), 146–147. For a comparative analysis of constitutional courts implemented in other Western European countries, see Hideo Wada, *Continental Systems of Judicial Review* (Tübingen: J.C.B. Mohr, 1982).

5. For example, Tony Smith, *America's Mission*, expanded edition (Princeton: Princeton University Press, 2012), 158; Lawrence Meir Friedman, *American Law in the Twentieth Century* (New Haven: Yale University Press, 2004), 577.

6. See Gerhard Göhler, "Vom Sozialismus zum Pluralismus. Politiktheorie und Emigrationserfahrung bei Ernst Fraenkel," *Politische Vierteljahresschrift* 27 (1986), 6–27; Joachim Perels, "Überwindung des NS-Systems durch Pluralismus—Ernst Fraenkel," *Kritische Justiz* 40, no. 3 (2007), 286–296; Uwe Backes, "Vom Marxismus zum Antitotalitarismus: Ernst Fraenkel und Richard Löwenthal," in *Totalitarismuskritik von links*, ed. Mike Schmeitzner (Göttingen: Vandenhoeck & Ruprecht, 2007), 327–354. Udi Greenberg has claimed, I think mistakenly, that Fraenkel's efforts in the Weimar and Bonn republics represent an unbroken continuity of vision. See Greenberg, *The Weimar Century: German Émigrés and the Ideological Foundations of the Cold War* (Princeton: Princeton University Press, 2015), chapter 2.

7. Geoff Eley, *Forging Democracy: The History of the Left in Europe, 1850–2000* (New York: Oxford University Press, 2002), 317.

8. Erich Matthias, *Sozialdemokratie und Nation* (Stuttgart: Deutsche Verlags-Anstalt, 1952).

9. Report of August–September 1934, republished in *Deutschland-Berichte der Sozialdemokratische Partei Deutschlands*, ed. Klaus Behnken (Frankfurt: Zweitausendeins, 1980), 459. For more context, see Gerd-Rainer Horn, *Socialists Respond to Fascism: Ideology, Activism, and Contingency in the 1930s* (New York: Oxford University Press, 1996), 64–66. On Ulbricht's frustration, see Carola Stern, *Ulbricht: A Political Biography* (New York: Praeger, 1965), 67.

10. See Douglas G. Morris, "The Dual State Reframed: Ernst Fraenkel's Political Clients and His Theory of the Nazi Legal System," *Leo Baeck Institute Yearbook* (2013), 5–21.

11. See Ernst Fraenkel [pseud. Fritz Dreher], "Der Sinn illegaler Arbeit," *Sozialistische Warte* (November 1935), 241–247.

12. Ernst Fraenkel [pseud. Conrad Jürges], "Das Dritte Reich als Doppelstaat," *Sozialistische Warte* 12 (January 15, 1937), 41; Fraenkel, "Das Dritte Reich als Doppelstaat," 1, Fortsetzung, *Sozialistische Warte* 12 (February 1, 1937), 53–55; Fraenkel, "Das Dritte Reich als Doppelstaat," 2, Fortsetzung, *Sozialistische Warte* 12 (February 15, 1937), 88–90.

13. See Boris Böhm, *"Die Entscheidung konnte mir niemand abnehmen—": Dokumente zu Widerstand und Verfolgung des evangelischen Kirchenjuristen Martin Gauger (1905–1941)* (Dresden: Stiftung Sächsische Gedenkstätten zur Erinnerung an die Opfer politischer Gewaltherrschaft, 1997).

14. The Lutheran wing of the Confessing Church (Rat der Evangelisch-Lutherischen Kirche Deutschlands, or Lutherrat for short) was at the time considering whether to participate in the pacification efforts of the ministry of church affairs. For Fraenkel's recollection see Ernst Fraenkel, "Vorwort zur deutschen Ausgabe," *Der Doppelstaat* (Frankfurt: Fischer, 1974), 17.

15. Martin Gauger, *Bekenntnis und Kirchenregiment in ihrer Beziehung zueinander* (Elberfeld: Evangelische Gesellschaft für Deutschland, 1936). I quote from his dissertation, "Beziehungen zwischen Bekenntnis und Kirchenregiment" (Ph.D. dissertation, University of Münster, 1935), esp. 9–26.

16. Fraenkel, *Der Urdoppelstaat*, in *Gesammelte Schriften*, vol. 2 (Baden-Baden: Nomos, 1999), 383–384, 394–395. I quote from the original German version, before it was edited and translated into English.

17. Ibid., 380–381. Fraenkel relied on the studies of the liberal Protestant theorist Ernst Troeltsch for these historical arguments, distilled in Troeltsch, *Die Soziallehren der christlichen Kirchen und Gruppen* (Tübingen: Mohr, 1912).

18. Fraenkel, *Der Urdoppelstaat*, 376–384. Fraenkel quoted a liberal Protestant who had recently emigrated from Nazi Germany to the United States: "our ethics descend from the Christian religion, our politics from the ancient state." The citation was to Werner Jäger, *Paideia: Die Formung des griechischen Menschen*, vol. 1 (Berlin: De Gruyter, 1936), 411.

19. Fraenkel, *Der Urdoppelstaat*, 394–397. Fraenkel found this point important enough to italicize: *"The explicit clarification of the relationship of Marxist socialism and rational natural right is of decisive importance."*

20. Hugo Marx, *The Case of the German Jews vs. Germany* (New York: Egmont, 1944), 46–47.

21. Heinrich Rommen, *Die ewige Wiederkehr des Naturrechts* (Leipzig: Hegner, 1936).

22. Fraenkel, *Der Urdoppelstaat*, 397. On Burke see Peter Stanlis, *Edmund Burke and the Natural Law* (Ann Arbor: University of Michigan Press, 1958).

23. Simon Ladwig-Winters, *Ernst Fraenkel: Ein politisches Leben* (Frankfurt: Campus, 2009), 127. For context see Konrad Jarausch, *The Unfree Professions: German Lawyers, Teachers, and Engineers, 1900–1950* (New York: Oxford University Press, 1990), 146.

24. See Max Lerner, "The Supreme Court Revolution," *The Nation* (June 11, 1938), 660–661. For context see William Leuchtenberg, *The Supreme Court Reborn: The Constitutional Revolution in the Age of Roosevelt* (New York: Oxford University Press, 1995); William Ross, *A Muted Fury: Populists, Progressives, and Labor Unions Confront the Courts, 1890–1937* (Princeton: Princeton University Press, 1994).

25. Hugo Preuss remembered that Social Democrats made explicit reference to the "notorious practices of the American Supreme Court" when they scuttled the proposal for judicial review at the convention in 1919. Preuss quoted in Fritz Morstein Marx, *Variationen über richterliche Zuständigkeit zur Prüfung der Rechtsmässigkeit des Gesetzes* (Berlin: Rothschild, 1927), 32–33.

26. Ernst Fraenkel [pseud. Emil Kleinfrank], "Es ist später, als Ihr denkt," *Freie sozialistische Tribüne* (1939), 749–753, 773–776, review of Max Lerner, *It Is Later Than You Think: The Need for a Militant Democracy*, 2nd edition (New York: Viking, 1943), xvi–xviii.

27. Michael Stolleis, *Darker Legacies of Law in Europe* (Oxford: Hart, 2003), 8.

28. On the attraction see Eric Kurlander, *Living with Hitler: Liberal Democrats in the Third Reich* (New Haven: Yale University Press, 2009), in particular his treatment of Hermann Höpker-Aschoff, the future president of the Federal Republic's Constitutional Court. On Bumke see Dieter Kolbe, *Reichsgerichtspräsident Dr. Erwin Bumke: Studien zum Niedergang des Reichsgerichts und der deutschen Rechtspflege* (Karlsruhe: Müller, 1975), 143–145.

29. Manfred Wiegandt, *Norm und Wirklichkeit: Gerhard Leibholz (1901–1982)* (Baden-Baden: Nomos, 1995), 39–41.

30. See Susanne Benöhr, *Das faschistische Verfassungsrecht Italiens aus der Sicht von Gerhard Leibholz* (Baden-Baden: Nomos, 1999).

31. Gerhard Leibholz, "Il Secolo XIX e lo Stato totalitario del presente," *Rivista Internazionale di Filosofia del Diritto* 18 (January–February 1938), 13–39.

32. Ibid.

33. See George Bell's comments in M. S. Leigh, ed., *Christianity in the Modern State* (London, 1936), 151, and William Temple, *Christian Democracy* (London: Student Christian Movement Press, 1937).

34. See Eberhard Bethge, *Dietrich Bonhoeffer: Theologian, Christian, Contemporary*, trans. Eric Mosbacher, revised edition (Minneapolis: Fortress, 2000), 560, and

Tom Lawson, *The Church of England and the Holocaust: Christianity, Memory, and Nazism* (Woodbridge: Boydell, 2006), 41–53.

35. See Matthew Grimley, *Citizenship, Community, and the Church of England* (New York: Oxford University Press, 2004), 83.

36. See Spectator [pseud. Gerhard Leibholz], "National-Socialism and the Church," *The Contemporary Review* (October 1939), 473–484.

37. Dietrich Bonhoeffer to Leibholz Family, March 7, 1940, in *Dietrich Bonhoeffer Works*, vol. 15, trans. Dirk Schulz, ed. Victoria J. Barnett (Minneapolis: Fortress, 1996), 300–301.

38. Leibholz wrote frequently for the newsletter of the principal organizer of the Oxford Conference, J. H. Oldham; "For a New Society," *Time* (January 21, 1941), 61–62. For the proceedings, see George Brereton Code, *Archbishop of York's Conference, Malvern* (London: Industrial Christian Fellowship, 1941).

39. See for example *The Moot Papers: Faith, Freedom, and Society, 1938–1944*, ed. Keith Clements (London: Bloomsbury, 2015). For context see Stefan Collini, *Absent Minds: Intellectuals in Britain* (Oxford: Oxford University Press, 2006).

40. Gerhard Leibholz, *Christianity Politics and Power* (London: Sheldon, 1942).

41. See Gerhard Ringshausen, "Gerhard Leibholz: Bonhoeffers Schwager als Vertreter des Widerstands in England," in *Exile and Patronage: Cross-Cultural Negotiations Beyond the Third Reich*, ed. Andrew Chandler et al. (Berlin: Lit, 2006), 91–108.

42. "Bormann-Rundschreiben vom 9.6.1941 über das Verhältnis Nationalsozialismus–Christentum," reprinted in *Kirchenkampf in Deutschland, 1933–1945*, ed. Friedrich Zipfel (Berlin: De Gruyter, 1965), 511–516.

43. Walther Bierkamp, "Document D-75: Secret Decree of The Reichsleiter Bormann Regarding the Relationship of National Socialism to Christendom [translation]" (December 12, 1941), in *Nazi Conspiracy and Aggression*, vol. 6 (Washington, D.C.: Government Printing Office, 1946), 1035–1036; "Revealing Memorandum by Martin Bormann," *The Spiritual Issues of the War*, no. 121 (February 26, 1942); J. O. Reicheinheim, "The Nazi Destruction of Christian Marriage," *The Tablet* (February 28, 1942), 4.

44. Gerhard Leibholz, "Germany Between West and East," *Fortnightly* (October 1942), republished in *Politics and Law* (Leyden: Sythoff, 1965).

45. See Ernst-Albert Scharffenorth, "Die Aufgabe der Kirche in Kriegszeiten. Der Einsatz von George Bell und Gerhard Leibholz für eine konstruktive Deutschlandpolitik Großbritanniens, 1941–1943," *Kirchliche Zeitgeschichte* 1, no. 1 (1988), 94–115. Robert Vansittart's best-selling book was *Black Record: Germans Past and Present* (London: Hamilton, 1941).

46. Gerhard Leibholz, "The Foundations of Justice and Law in the Light of the Present European Crisis," *Dublin Review* (January 1943), 35–36; originally published in J. H. Oldham's *Christian News-Letter* (December 2, 1942).

47. Leibholz, "The Foundations of Justice and Law," 48–49. See the original in *Holmes–Pollock Letters*, vol. 2 (Cambridge: Cambridge University Press, 1942), 217. Leibholz's concept of constitutional consensus around the principles of

Western Christianity did not require one to *identify* as a Christian. It was, however, necessary that non-Christians recognized Western Christianity as the "origin" of the European culture of legality and therefore the churches as its spiritual center. Gerhard Leibholz, *Re-educating Germans?*, 11. On the importance of restraint in the court Leibholz later helped build, see Donald Kommers and Russell Miller, *The Constitutional Jurisprudence of the Federal Republic of Germany*, revised edition (Durham: Duke University Press, 2012), 33–34; Edward McWhinney, "Judicial Restraint and the West German Constitutional Court," *Harvard Law Review* 75 (1961), 5–38.

48. See Daniel Pick, *The Pursuit of the Nazi Mind: Hitler, Hess, and the Analysts* (New York: Oxford University Press, 2012).

49. Gerhard Leibholz to George Bell, May 4, 1944, in *An der Schwelle zum gespaltenen Europa: Der Briefwechsel zwischen George Bell und Gerhard Leibholz*, ed. Eberhard Bethge and Ronald C. D. Jasper (Stuttgart: Kreuz, 1974), 147. On the foundation of the group, see the article "Gegner der Nazis bilden hier einen Ausschuss für ein demokratisches Deutschland. Vom Zentrum bis zur Linken alles darin vertreten," *New Yorker Staats-Zeitung und Herold* (May 3, 1944), 1.

50. Gerhard Leibholz, "The Opposition Movement in Germany," *New English Weekly* (October 19, 1944), republished in *Politics and Law*, 213.

51. Fraenkel and Leibholz returned despite counsel from friends and their own initial misgivings. See Ernst Fraenkel to the Suhr family, March 23, 1946, in *Gesammelte Schriften*, vol. 3, ed. Gerhard Göhler (Baden-Baden: Nomos, 1999), 389–395; and the letters between Bell and Leibholz from 1945 to 1947 in *An der Schwelle zum gespaltenen Europa*, esp. 238–239, 266.

52. See Jeffrey Herf, "Multiple Restorations: German Political Traditions and the Interpretation of Nazism, 1945–1946," *Central European History* 26, no. 1 (1993), 21–55.

53. Theodor Heuss, "Um Deutschlands Zukunft," in *Aufzeichnungen 1945–1947*, ed. Eberhard Pikart (Tübingen: Wunderlich, 1966), 207.

54. Walter Menzel, *Der Aufbau der Deutschen Republik* (Bielefeld: SPD Vorstand, 1947), 7, 35, 40. Significantly, he cited the German Christian idealist philosopher Christian Wolff for his definition of natural law. See also the socialist Gustav Radbruch's definition of natural law in "Gesetzliches Unrecht und übergesetzliches Recht," *Süddeutsche Juristen-Zeitung* 1 (1946), 105–108.

55. For details of the meeting see Wolfgang Benz, "Föderalistische Politik in der CDU/CSU. Die Verfassungsdiskussion im 'Ellwanger Kreis' 1947/48," *Vierteljahrshefte für Zeitgeschichte* 25, no. 4 (1977), 776–820.

56. See Walter Strauss, *Das Problem der Verfassungsänderung nach der Weimarer Reichsverfassung* (Dissertation, Heidelberg, 1924); see also Friedemann Utz, *Preusse, Protestant, Pragmatiker: Der Staatssekretär Walter Strauss und sein Staat* (Tübingen: Mohr Siebeck, 2003), 18–19.

57. Josef Beyerle, "Das Christentum als Voraussetzung und Grundlage der gesamten Politik in der CDU und CSU!" (May 1, 1947), in Walter Strauss Papers, 001/1, Archiv für Christlich-Demokratische Politik,

Konrad-Adenauer-Stiftung, Sankt Augustin. For the theory behind this, see Adolf Süsterhenn, "Das Naturrecht," *Die Kirche in der Welt* 1 (1947), 55–62. The political practice of consulting with theologians was normal for the Catholic Center Party in the Weimar years, but contrary to the position of the old Lutheran churches and liberal parliamentarians who insisted that religion and party politics remain separate.

58. Hans Ehard, *Freiheit und Föderalismus* (Munich: Pflaum, 1947), 38; Paul Binder, "Zur Wirtschaftspolitik der CDU" (September 20, 1947), Ellwangen, in Walter Strauss Papers, 001/1.

59. Karl Polak, *Marxismus und Staatslehre* (Berlin: Einheit, 1947); Polak, *Die Weimarer Verfassung* (Berlin: Kongress, 1948), esp. 48. See also Marcus Howe, *Karl Polak: Parteijurist unter Ulbricht* (Frankfurt: Klostermann, 2002), 85–86.

60. See Heike Amos, *Die Entstehung der Verfassung in der Sowjetischen Besatzungszone/DDR, 1946–1949* (Münster: LIT, 2006), esp. 153–163.

61. Not including five nonvoting members from West Berlin.

62. Mangoldt and Leibholz later co-edited the most prestigious journal of constitutional law, and Leibholz would also complete the commentary on the Grundgesetz that Mangoldt was working on at the time of his premature death in 1953. See Leibholz's obituary, "Hermann von Mangoldt," *Jahrbuch des öffentlichen Rechts der Gegenwart* 2 (1953), iii–iv.

63. Hermann von Mangoldt, *Rechtsstaatsgedanke und Regierungsformen in den Vereinigten Staaten von Amerika* (Essen: Essener Verlagsanstalt, 1938), especially 278–312.

64. Nineteenth meeting of the Ausschuss für Grundsatzfragen, November 9, 1948, *Der Parlamentarische Rat, 1948–1949: Akten und Protokolle*, vol. 5/1: Ausschuss für Grundsatzfragen, ed. Deutschen Bundestag und Bundesarchiv (Boppard am Rhein: Harald Boldt, 1993), 519.

65. See especially the case made by the SPD's Carlo Schmid at the third and fourth meetings of the Ausschuss für Grundsatzfragen, September 21 and 23, 1948, in *Der Parlamentarische Rat, 1948–1949: Akten und Protokolle*, vol. 5/1, 40–43, 63–67. While there is no evidence that Schmid borrowed directly from Fraenkel's *Dual State*, the logical arguments were strikingly similar (and similarly forced, based on Edmund Burke). He said, "It is not about saying, from out of a philosophical natural law thinking: man is essentially determined by this and that, so this and that natural law result. Instead we must proceed from a *historical* natural law concept, which is only apparently a contradiction in itself, and say: In this sphere of historical development, we Germans are not ready to live below a standard of freedom that guarantees to man this and that, and those freedoms cannot be affected by the state."

66. In the constitutions ratified in 1946 and 1947, "Out of trust in God" (Württemberg-Baden), "In the consciousness of responsibility before God" (Bavaria and Rheinland-Pfalz) and "In obedience to God" (Württemberg-Hohenzollern). The constitution of Hesse, where the SPD was strongest, contained no such invocation.

67. Nineteenth meeting of the Ausschuss für Grundsatzfragen, November 9, 1948, in *Der Parlamentarische Rat, 1948–1949*, vol. 5/1, 509, 518–519.

68. Leibholz, "Die Struktur der neuen Verfassung," *Deutsche Verwaltung* (November 15, 1948), 73–75. He cited former Marxist and now Christian social rights advocate Stafford Cripps, *Toward Christian Democracy* (New York: Philosophical Library, 1946).

69. Thirty-first meeting of the Ausschuss für Grundsatzfragen, November 16, 1948, *Das Parlamentarische Rat*, vol. 5/2, ed. Deutschen Bundestag und Bundesarchiv (Boppard am Rhein: Harald Boldt, 1993), 554. The SPD members present were Ludwig Bergsträsser, Fritz Eberhard, Friederike Nadig, Albert Rosshaupter, and Elisabeth Selbert.

70. *Der Parlamentarische Rat, 1948–1949: Akten und Protokolle*, vol. 5/2, Ausschuss für Grundsatzfragen, ed. Deutschen Bundestag und Bundesarchiv (Boppard am Rhein: Harald Boldt, 1993), 578. In the plenary meetings of the Parliamentary Council the word "holy" was removed from Art. 1 para. 1.

71. The lower courts would be barred only from reviewing new legislation; they could to some extent review the compatibility of Nazi-era legislation with the new Basic Law. On the specificities of the Constitutional Court in this respect and its difference from the U.S. system, see Kommers and Miller, *The Constitutional Jurisprudence of the Federal Republic of Germany*, 3–78.

72. Rudolf Katz, "Bundesverfassungsgericht und U.S.A. Supreme Court," *Die öffentliche Verwaltung* 7, no. 4 (February 1954), 98–100.

73. Donald Kommers, "Building Democracy: Judicial Review and the German *Rechtsstaat*," in *The Postwar Transformation of Germany: Democracy, Prosperity, and Nationhood*, ed. John Brady et al. (Ann Arbor: University of Michigan Press, 1999), 94–121; Donald Kommers, "Procedures for the Protection of Human Rights in Diffuse Systems of Judicial Review," in *The Protection of Fundamental Rights by the Constitutional Court*, ed. European Commission for Democracy Through Law (Strasbourg: Council of Europe, 1996), 96–124.

7: CHRISTIAN ECONOMICS?

1. Walter Eucken and Fritz W. Meyer, "The Economic Situation in Germany," *Annals of the American Academy of Political and Social Science* 260 (November 1948), 56–58; survey from August 1948, cited in A. J. and R. L. Merritt, eds., *Public Opinion in Occupied Germany* (Urbana: University of Illinois Press, 1970), 258–259.

2. For the reaction to the reforms in East Germany see Jonathan Zatlin, *The Currency of Socialism: Money and Political Culture in East Germany* (Cambridge: Cambridge University Press, 2007), chapter 1. On the aftermath of the reforms in West Germany, see Karl Hardach, *The Political Economy of Germany in the Twentieth Century* (Berkeley: University of California Press, 1980), 145.

3. Hans Habe, *Our Love Affair with Germany* (New York: Putnam & Sons, 1953), 81.

4. See Uwe Furhmann, "Stuttgart 1948 und die soziale Marktwirtschaft," in *Zwischen Ignoranz und Inszenierung*, ed. Henning Fischer et al. (Münster: Westfälisches Dampfboot, 2012), 95–128, and Jörg Roesler, *Die Wiederaufbaulüge der Bundesrepublik* (Berlin: Dietz, 2008), 47–56. For general context see Gerhard Beier, *Der Demonstrations- und Generalstreik vom 12. November 1948* (Frankfurt: Europäische Verlagsanstalt, 1975).

5. Jeffrey Sachs, "Building a Market Economy in Poland," *Scientific American* (March 1992), 40; Naomi Klein, *The Shock Doctrine* (New York: Macmillan, 2007), 101.

6. Ludwig Erhard, "Social Order Creates Prosperity and Security" (April 26, 1961), in *The Economics of Success*, trans. J. A. Arengo-Jones and D. J. S. Thomson (London: Billing and Sons, 1963), 354.

7. See Christoph Buchheim, "Die Währungsreform 1948 in Westdeutschland," *Vierteljahrsheft für Zeitgeschichte* 36, no. 2 (April 1988), 221; Manfred Görtemaker, *Geschichte der Bundesrepublik Deutschland* (Munich: Beck, 1999), 159. In June the SPD fraction in the council also attempted to create a supervisory board that would have required Erhard's agency to receive prior approval before eliminating controls on individual goods, but the CDU/CSU representatives helped overrule that as well. See James C. Van Hook, *Rebuilding Germany: The Creation of the Social Market Economy, 1945–1957* (New York: Cambridge University Press, 2004), 166.

8. Alfred Mierzejewski, *Ludwig Erhard: A Biography* (Chapel Hill: University of North Carolina Press, 2004), 73.

9. Oswald von Nell-Breuning to Wilhelm Röpke, October 31, 1948, Wilhelm Röpke Papers, Ordner 12, Institut für Weltwirschaft, Cologne.

10. The exact numbers are difficult to ascertain. One historian put Catholics at forty-five percent of the population of West Germany in 1948, with the rest Protestant or unaffiliated. See Bernard Cook, ed., *Europe Since 1945: An Encyclopedia*, vol. 1 (New York: Routledge, 2001), 503. Tony Judt reported that the number was over fifty percent in the 1950s. Judt, *Postwar: A History of Europe Since 1945* (New York: Penguin, 2005), 267. On the influence of refugees from Eastern Europe on the confessional demographics of West Germany, see Paul F. Myers and W. Parker Mauldin, *Population of the Federal Republic of Germany and West Berlin* (Washington, D.C.: Bureau of the Census, 1952), 45–46.

11. See Maria D. Mitchell, *The Origins of Christian Democracy: Politics and Confession in Modern Germany* (Ann Arbor: University of Michigan Press, 2012), 99.

12. D., "Anti-Kollektivismus," *Neue Zürcher Zeitung* (November 20, 1948).

13. Wilhelm Röpke to Marcel van Zeeland, June 16, 1941, published in Röpke, *Der innere Kompass: Briefe* (Zürich: Rentsch, 1976), 40–41.

14. Wilhelm Röpke, "Fascist Economics," *Economica* 2, no. 5 (February 1935), 98–99; Röpke, review of Johannes Messner's *Die berufständische Ordnung*, in *Monatsschrift für Kultur und Politik* 2 (April 1937), 327–328. Röpke urgently pleaded with his friend and fellow free-market theorist Alexander Rüstow to tone down his "attacks on Christianity, theology, immortality, etc.," as they

would levy a "heavy cost" on the influence of their arguments. Letter from late 1941 quoted in Kathrin Meier-Rust, *Alexander Rüstow: Geschichtsdeutung und liberales Engagement* (Stuttgart: Klett, 1993), 79.

15. Wilhelm Röpke, *Die Gesellschaftskrisis der Gegenwart* (Zürich: Rentsch, 1942), 288–289. Compare these with the proceedings of the Society for Social Policy, in Franz Boese, ed., *Verhandlungen des Vereins für Sozialpolitik in Dresden, 1932* (Munich: Duncker & Humblot, 1932). Dieter Haselbach has dated the development of what became known as "neo-liberalism" to that earlier period. See Dieter Haselbach, *Autoritärer Liberalismus und Soziale Marktwirtschaft* (Baden-Baden: Nomos, 1991).

16. Röpke, *Die Gesellschaftskrisis der Gegenwart*, 13–14. He appears to have begun writing about a "third way" in a book he wrote largely for a Catholic audience in Austria and in which he explicitly cited Catholic theorists; Röpke, *Die Lehre von der Wirtschaft* (Vienna: Springer, 1937), 187–193.

17. Friedrich Hayek to Wilhelm Röpke, June 6, 1942, Wilhelm Röpke Papers, Ordner 7.

18. "Oekonomie des Humanismus?" *Solothurner Anzeiger* (June 30, 1942), Röpke Papers, Ordner 97b. See further Jean Solchany, *Wilhelm Röpke, l'autre Hayek* (Paris: Sorbonne, 2015), 41–43.

19. Wilhelm Röpke, "Der Beveridgeplan," *Schweizer Monatshefte* 23, nos. 3/4 (1943), 169.

20. Karl Thieme to Hans Urs von Balthasar, April 15, 1943, Karl Thieme Papers, ED 163/4, Institut für Zeitgeschichte, Munich. Karl Thieme to Wilhelm Röpke, February 8, 1943; Röpke to Thieme, July 29, 1943; and Thieme to Röpke, August 4, 1943; Röpke to Thieme, May 20, 1944. Karl Thieme Papers, ED 163/67. For the articles that came out of their correspondence, see Röpke, "Die Enzyklika 'Quadragesimo anno' in der heutigen Diskussion," *Schweizer Rundschau* 44, no. 2 (1944–1945), 88–97, and Thieme, "Korporativismus als entarteter Föderalismus!" *Schweizer Rundschau* 44, no. 3 (1944–1945), 172–181.

21. See Wilhelm Röpke, *Gegen die Brandung* (Zürich: Rentsch, 1959), 371–373. On the proposed committee, see "Entwurf einer Resolution des Ausschusses der Christl. Bekenntniss D'lands zur Mitarbeit am Wiederaufbau," September 1944, Karl Thieme Papers, ED 163/3. On Welles see Christopher O'Sullivan, *Sumner Welles: Postwar Planning and the Quest for a New World Order, 1937–1943* (New York: Columbia University Press, 2008).

22. Wilhelm Röpke, *Civitas Humana* (Zürich: Rentsch, 1944), section on economy, 297–401. For a complete list of the other planned educational materials, see Ausschuss der christlichen Bekenntnisse Deutschlands zur Mitarbeit am Wiederaufbau, "Lehrmittel für die deutsche Jugend-Erziehung nach Hitler," undated, probably early 1945, in Karl Thieme Papers, ED 163/3.

23. Wilhelm Röpke, *The German Question*, trans. E. W. Dickes (London: Allen & Unwin, 1946), 97.

24. Christlich-Demokratische Union Deutschlands, *Das Ahlener Programm* (Düsseldorf: DGB, 1947).

25. Albert Lotz, "Liberalismus und Liberalität," *Rheinischer Merkur* (September 6, 1947), 3–4.

26. Wilhelm Röpke, "Die Heilung der deutschen Wirtschaft," published in Informationsdienst B des CDU-Zonenausschusses, March 3, 1948, courtesy of Stiftung Bundeskanzler-Adenauer-Haus, I/08.10, Bl. 133, 13–14, originally in *Rheinischer Merkur* (February 28, 1948).

27. On the importance of the Catholic Church in the Wirtschaftsrat, see Christian Glossner, *The Making of the German Post-War Economy: Political Communication and Public Reception of the Social Market Economy After World War Two* (New York: I.B. Tauris, 2010), 80–106.

28. Oswald von Nell-Breuning, "Aus der Aussprache auf der 1. Sitzung des Wissenschaftlichen Beirats bei der Verwaltung für Wirtschaft am 23./24. Januar 1948 in Königstein im Taunus," in Nell-Breuning, *Wirtschaft und Gesellschaft*, vol. 1 (Freiburg: Herder, 1956), 158.

29. On the Vatican's commitment to the Marshall Plan, see Giuliana Chamedes, "Reinventing Christian Europe: Vatican Diplomacy, Transnational Anticommunism, and the Erosion of the Church-State Divide (1917–1958)" (Ph.D. dissertation, Columbia University, 2012), 290–304.

30. Hermann Pünder, "Die Entstehung der Sozialen Marktwirtschaft," in *Ludwig Erhard: Beiträge zu seiner politischen Biographie*, ed. Gerhard Schröder et al. (Frankfurt: Propyläen, 1972), 190; on the Catholic factor in the CDU Sozial-Ausschuss, see Mitchell, *Origins of Christian Democracy*, 159.

31. On the question of the "influence" of Röpke's ideas on Erhard's policies, see two contrasting arguments in John Zmirak, *Swiss Localist, Global Economist* (Wilmington, Del.: ISI, 2001), and Alfred Mierzejewski, "Water in the Desert? The Influence of Wilhelm Röpke on Ludwig Erhard and the Social Market Economy," *Review of Austrian Economics* 19 (2006), 275–287.

32. Walter W. Heller, "Tax and Monetary Reform in Occupied Germany," *National Tax Journal* 2, no. 3 (September 1949), 218–225. On the East German currency reform see Zatlin, *The Currency of Socialism*, chapter 1.

33. Wilhelm Röpke to Erik Kuehnelt-Leddihn, September 28, 1948, Röpke Papers, Ordner 12.

34. Franz Walter, "Katholizismus in der Bundesrepublik," *Blätter für deutsche und internationale Politik* 41, no. 9 (1996), 1103.

35. "Gemeinsames Hirtenwort der am Grabe des hl. Bonifatius versammelten Erzbischöfe und Bischöfe Deutschlands vom 26. August 1948," in *Die katholische Kirche im demokratischen Staat*, ed. Alfons von Fitzek (Würzburg: Naumann, 1981), 69–70.

36. Walter Strauss to Egbert Munzer, August 31, 1947, cited in Friedemann Utz, *Preusse, Protestant, Pragmatiker* (Tübingen: Mohr Siebeck, 2003), 119. Munzer, a Catholic philosopher and advocate of interconfessional partnership who had emigrated to Canada during the National Socialist years, was probably responsible for recommending Nell-Breuning to Strauss. See Oswald von Nell-Breuning to Heinrich Rommen, January 16, 1950, in Heinrich A. Rommen

Papers, Box 1, Folder 29, Georgetown University Special Collections, Washington, D.C.

37. Sternberger, *The Social Sciences in Western Germany* (Washington, D.C.: Library of Congress, 1950), 14–15. For a good comparative overview of these parties in Western Europe, see Tom Buchanan and Martin Conway, eds., *Political Catholicism in Europe, 1918–1965* (New York: Oxford University Press, 1996).

38. See James Chappel, *The Pope's Divisions: Catholicism and the Salvation of European Democracy, 1920–1960* (Cambridge: Harvard University Press, forthcoming 2018).

39. See Chamedes, "Reinventing Christian Europe," chapter 7.

40. Oswald von Nell-Breuning, *Zur Programmatik politischer Parteien* (Cologne: Bachem, 1946), 14.

41. Oswald von Nell-Breuning, "Um die 'berufsständische Ordnung,' " *Stimmen der Zeit* 142 (April 1948), 6–19. See also "Gutachten vom 1. April 1948," in *Der Wissenschaftliche Beirat beim Bundesministerium für Wirtschaft*, ed. Bundesministerium für Wirtschaft (Göttingen: Otto Schwartz, 1973), 1–6. See Nell-Breuning's letters to Röpke from October 31, 1948, as well as from May 31, 1949, Röpke Papers, Ordner 12.

42. Elisabeth Noelle and Eric Peter Neumann, eds., *Jahrbuch der öffentlichen Meinung, 1947–1955* (Allensbach: Verlag für Demoskopie, 1956), 154–155. Erik Nölting, *Es weht ein neuer Wind von Frankfurt?* (Düsseldorf: Westdeutsche Verlagsanstalt, 1949), 5, 10, 16.

43. Oswald von Nell-Breuning, "Wirtschaftliche Menschenführung," *Rheinischer Merkur* (February 12, 1949), 3–4; "Hirtenwort der deutschen Bischöfe zur Bundestagswahl am 14.8.1949," in *Die katholische Kirche im demokratischen Staat*, 86. For more context see Wolfgang Schroeder, *Katholizismus und Einheitsgewerkschaft* (Bonn: Dietz, 1992), 97–111.

44. Henry Ashby Turner, *The Two Germanies Since 1945* (New Haven: Yale University Press, 1987), 54–55. See further Klaus Gotto, "Die deutschen Katholiken und die Wahlen in der Adenauer-Ära," in *Katholizismus im politischen System der Bundesrepublik*, ed. Albrecht Langner (Paderborn: Schöningh, 1978), 7–33.

45. Oswald von Nell-Breuning, foreword to *Zur Wirtschaftsordnung*, ed. Oswald von Nell-Breuning and Hermann Sacher (Freiburg: Herder, 1950).

46. See Josef Frings, ed., *Verantwortung und Mitverantwortung in der Wirtschaft* (Cologne: Bachem, 1949), and Gustav Gundlach (adviser to Pope Pius XII), *Die Kirche zur heutigen Wirtschafts- und Gesellschaftsnot* (Berlin: Morus, 1949), 32; see further Mitchell, *The Origins of Christian Democracy*, 196–197.

47. Oswald von Nell-Breuning, "Joint Management and Profit Sharing in Western Germany," *Christus Rex* (Ireland) 4, no. 3 (1950), 228; Nell-Breuning, "Der Beitrag des Katholizismus zur Sozialpolitik der Nachkriegszeit," in *Katholizismus, Wirtschaftsordnung, und Sozialpolitik, 1945–1963*, ed. Albrecht Langner (Paderborn: Schöningh, 1980), 113.

48. Nell-Breuning, *Zur Programmatik politischer Parteien*, 14.

49. Nell-Breuning to Heinrich Rommen, January 16, 1950, Heinrich A. Rommen Papers, Box 1, Folder 29, Georgetown University Special Collections. In February 1950, Erhard was pressured to reluctantly introduce government job-creation measures, although they were minimal compared with Weimar-era standards. See Werner Abelshauser, "The Economic Policy of Ludwig Erhard," EUI Working Paper no. 80 (January 1984), 22.

50. Pope Pius XII, "The Problem of Unemployment," trans. Robert J. McEwen and Eugene Burns, *Review of Social Economy* 8, no. 2 (1950), 136.

51. Oswald von Nell-Breuning, "Vollbeschäftigung," *Michael* (June 11, 1950), republished in *Wirtschaft und Gesellschaft heute*, vol. 1 (Freiburg: Herder, 1956), 168.

52. Oswald von Nell-Breuning, "Zur Neuordnung der Wirtschaft," *Rheinischer Merkur* (August 19, 1950). See further Alan Milward, *The Reconstruction of Western Europe, 1945–1951* (Berkeley: University of California Press, 1984), 362–420.

53. Ludwig Erhard to Wilhelm Röpke, May 22, 1950, Ludwig Erhard Papers, 4/59, Ludwig-Erhard-Stiftung, Bonn.

54. Wilhelm Röpke, *Ist die deutsche Wirtschaftspolitik richtig?* (Stuttgart: Kohlhammer, 1950), 9.

55. The proposal called to promote forced savings for employees by increasing profit-sharing in the form of company shares (as opposed to simply higher wages), a so-called *Investivlohn*, and to convene an organization of unions and employers to facilitate this. On the context of the ministry's rejection of his proposal, see Yorck Dietrich, *Eigentum für jeden: Die vermögenspolitischen Initiativen der CDU und die Gesetzgebung, 1950–1961* (Düsseldorf: Droste, 1996), 146. For the original presentation to the Beirat, see Nell-Breuning, "Einkommensgestaltung in der sozialen Marktwirtschaft," in *Wirtschaft und Gesellschaft*, vol. 1, 403–410.

56. Ernst Molis to Konrad Adenauer, September 17, 1950, in *Die Kabinettsprotokolle der Bundesregierung*, vol. 3, ed. Ulrich Enders and Konrad Reiser (Boppard am Rhein: Boldt, 1986), 117–118. Adenauer also asked Heinemann to resign after long suspecting him of taking his role as president of the Protestant Church Synod more seriously than his party. For more context see Anselm Doering-Manteuffel, *Katholizismus und Wiederbewaffnung: Die Haltung der deutschen Katholiken gegenüber der Wehrfrage, 1948–1955* (Mainz: Grünewald, 1981), 105–108. Later, it was revealed that it was regime policy to ask applicants about their confession before hiring them for federal government jobs. See Jürgen Bevers, *Der Mann hinter Adenauer: Hans Globkes Aufstieg vom NS-Juristen zur Grauen Eminenz der Bonner Republik* (Berlin: Christoph Links, 2009), 113–115.

57. Bruno Six, during a discussion on the second day of the conference, October 21, 1950, in *Erster Parteitag der Christlich-Demokratischen Union Deutschlands* (Bonn: CDU, 1950), 48. For more context on the interconfessional tensions, see Martin

Greschat, "Konfessionelle Spannungen in der Ära Adenauer," in *Katholiken und Protestanten in den Aufbaujahren der Bundesrepublik,* ed. Thomas Sauer (Stuttgart: Kohlhammer, 2000), 19–34.

58. On the confrontation of the Church and the union leadership in January and February 1951, see Schröder, *Katholizismus und Einheitsgewerkschaft,* 119–122.

59. Wilhelm Röpke to Gertrud Fricke, January 25, 1951, in *Der innere Kompass,* 115; for his complaints about union strategy, see his letters of January 16 and February 26, in ibid., 111–114, 115–116. Röpke was not anti-union but rather anti-regulation. He had long praised the unions in the United States for helping raise the wages of workers. In fact, his belief in the beneficial nature of unions in general led to a chill between him and Hayek within the free-market-oriented Mont Pelerin Society. See Yves Steiner, "The Neoliberals Confront the Trade Unions," in *The Road from Mont Pelerin: The Making of the Neoliberal Thought Collective,* ed. Philip Mirowski and Dieter Plehwe (Cambridge: Harvard University Press, 2009), 188.

60. Alfred Müller-Armack, "Stil und Ordnung der Sozialen Marktwirtschaft" (originally delivered August 28, 1951), published in Nils Goldschmidt and Michael Wohlgemuth, *Grundtexte zur Freiburger Tradition der Ordnungsökonomik* (Tübingen: Mohr Siebeck, 2008), 457–464. For his wartime work see Alfred Müller-Armack, *Die Genealogie der Wirtschaftsstile* (Stuttgart: Kohlhammer, 1941), and Alexander Rüstow's long criticism of the book's emphasis on Protestantism in Rüstow, "Die Konfession in der Wirtschaftsgeschichte," *Revue de la Faculté des Sciences Economiques de l'Université d'Istanbul* 3 (1941/1942), 362–389.

61. Oswald von Nell-Breuning, "Thesen zu einer Grundsatzdebatte," *Finanz-Archiv* 13, no. 3 (1952), 401, published from the presentation at the working conference of the Wissenschaftlicher Beirat from January 19 to 20, 1952. After reading Müller-Armack's article "Die heutige Gesellschaft nach evangelischem Verständnis," Nell-Breuning was concerned by Müller-Armack's reference to "different starting points" among Protestants and Catholics. Nell-Breuning to Müller-Armack, March 19, 1952, in Müller-Armack Papers, CDU-Archiv, Konrad-Adenauer-Stiftung, ACDP 01-236-060/1.

62. Hermann-Josef Grosse Kracht, " 'Nichts gegen die Soziale Marktwirtschaft, den das ist verboten' (Konrad Adenauer). Sondierungen zur religiösen Tiefengrammatik des deutschen Wirtschafts- und Sozialmodells im Anschluss an Alfred Müller-Armack und Oswald von Nell-Breuning," *Ethik und Gesellschaft,* no. 1 (2010), 1–55.

63. See Herbert Giersch et al., *The Fading Miracle: Four Decades of Market Economy in Germany* (New York: Cambridge University Press, 1992), 52–58; Martin Greschat, "Konfessionelle Spannungen in der Ära Adenauer," 19–34; Mitchell, *The Origins of Christian Democracy,* 197.

64. A. R. L. Gurland, *Ursprünge und Entwicklung bis 1953,* ed. Dieter Emig (Frankfurt am Main: Europäische Verlagsanstalt, 1980), 11–12.

8: THE EDUCATION OF WESTERN EUROPEANS

1. Erich Ollenhauer, *Nach der Entscheidung,* speech in front of leading functionaries of the SPD, September 17, 1953 (Bonn: SPD, 1953), 29.

2. Otto Kirchheimer, "Notes on the Political Scene in West Germany," *World Politics* 6, no. 3 (April 1954), 321.

3. See, for example, the session and discussion on Germany led by Fritz Stern in 1954, published in *Proceedings of the Academy of Political Science* 26, no. 2 (January 1955), 46–100, and the first systematic analysis of the postwar German stabilization, Henry C. Wallich, *Mainsprings of the German Revival* (New Haven: Yale University Press, 1955).

4. Konrad Adenauer, Regierungserklärung, October 20, 1953, in Hans Ulrich Behn, ed., *Die Regierungserklärungen der Bundesrepublik Deutschland* (Munich: Olzog, 1971), 35–60.

5. On the origins of the forum see the memoirs of one of its founders, Otto Molden, *Odyssee meines Lebens und die Gründung Europas in Alpbach* (Munich: Amalthea, 2001).

6. "Motor des Fortschritts," *Die Zeit* (October 1, 1953). For other reports see Herbert Zdarzil, "Europäisches Forum Alpbach," *Wissenschaft und Weltbild* 6 (1953), 309–310; Robert Hofmann, "Alpbach," *Österreichiesche Monatshefte* 9 (1953), 571–572.

7. Arnold Bergsträsser to Helmuth Plessner, May 2, 1954, Helmuth Plessner Papers, Bibliotheek der Rijksuniversiteit Groningen, 153.185.

8. Ollenhauer, *Nach der Entscheidung,* 18–20. For context see Talbot Imlay, " 'The Policy of Social Democracy Is Self-Consciously Internationalist': The German Social Democratic Party's Internationalism After 1945," *Journal of Modern History* 86, no. 1 (March 2014), 81–123, and Udo Löwke, *Die SPD und die Wehrfrage, 1949–1955* (Bad Godesberg: Neue Gesellschaft, 1976).

9. See Nikolaus Jackob, ed., *Wahlkämpfe in Deutschland* (Wiesbaden: Verlag für Sozialwissenschaften, 2007), esp. 97–136.

10. Ollenhauer, *Nach der Entscheidung,* 15.

11. See Carola Dietze, *Nachgeholtes Leben: Helmuth Plessner, 1892–1985* (Göttingen: Wallstein, 2006), 359–360.

12. Ibid., 86–88.

13. Helmuth Plessner, *Das Schicksal deutschen Geistes im Ausgang seiner bürgerlichen Epoche* (Zürich: Niehan, 1935), especially 22–24, 135–156. On Plessner's own contributions to the suspicion of ideology through his embrace of Lebensphilosophie in the 1920s, see Jan-Werner Müller, "The Soul in the Age of Society and Technology: Helmuth Plessner's Defensive Liberalism," in *Confronting Mass Democracy and Industrial Technology: Political and Social Theory from Nietzsche to Habermas,* ed. John McCormick (Durham: Duke University Press, 2002), 139–162.

14. See Todd Weir's excellent *Secularism and Religion in Nineteenth-Century Germany: The Rise of the Fourth Confession* (New York: Cambridge University Press, 2014).

15. For more context see Dietze, *Nachgeholtes Leben*, 123–129. Plessner made contacts at this time with the Nederlandsche Christen Studenten Vereeniging, a Dutch student group that would be active in the European resistance against Nazism, and published in their journal *Eltheto*.

16. Helmuth Plessner, "Die Aufgabe der philosophischen Anthropologie" (1937) in *Gesammelte Schriften*, vol. 8 (Frankfurt: Suhrkamp, 1983), 33–51, quoted at 34–35. This was his inaugural lecture as a promoted full professor at the University of Groningen. The article focused on the origins of philosophical anthropology in the thought of the left-wing Hegelians Ludwig Feuerbach and Karl Marx, who were crucial to the development of socialist ideology.

17. Edmund Husserl, "Philosophy and the Crisis of European Man" (1935), in *Phenomenology and the Crisis of Philosophy*, trans. Quentin Lauer (New York: Harper, 1965), 149–162.

18. Helmuth Plessner, *Lachen und Weinen: Eine Untersuchung der Grenzen menschlichen Verhaltens*, 3rd edition (Bern: Francke, 1961), esp. 153–156. The quotation is from p. 156. See the review by Ludwig Binswanger in *Schweizer Archiv für Neurologie und Psychiatrie* 48 (1941), 158–163. To my knowledge, no one has studied *Lachen und Weinen* as a political text. The section on laughing is littered with jokes about European authoritarian-democratic leaders and the state of Germany in particular. One of his analyses centers on Hans Reimann's joke that "Germany is an egg of Columbus: one need only push on its end [in German, *auf die Spitze treiben* also means to drive it to extremes] and it will be able to ride by itself" [a reference to Bismarck's remark about universal suffrage, "I have helped the German people into the saddle; it will know how to ride by itself"]. The humor, Plessner suggested, resided in the image of a person trying to control uncontrollable things (an egg, a horse, democratic politics) only by destroying the bodily integrity of the thing itself and in the process making himself look foolish. Plessner, *Lachen und Weinen*, 132–133.

19. "Deutschlands Zukunft," *Hamburger Akademische Rundschau* 2 (1948), 324–334, quoted at 333. This was the German version of the speech he originally gave to the Committee for Active Democracy on November 3, 1946, published first as "Opmerking over de toekomst van Duitsland," in the brochure *Debat over Duitsland* (Amsterdam: Vrij Nederland, 1947).

20. Plessner was one of the earliest supporters of the Europa-Union founded in Switzerland in 1934, and in the Netherlands a member of the Europeesche Actie, one of the founding organizations of the Union of European Federalists. On these organizations and their efforts to create a nonaligned European bloc see Sergio Pistone, *The Union of European Federalists: From the Foundation to the Decision on Direct Election of the European Parliament (1946–1974)* (Milan: Giuffrè Editore, 2008), chapter 1. Plessner also began mentoring the young socialist student leader in Göttingen Dietrich Goldschmidt, who supported the message of non-alignment in his capacity as editor of Germany's main university newspaper. See Goldschmidt's exchange with Gerhard Leibholz in *Deutsche Universitäts-Zeitung* 4, no. 6 (March 25, 1949), 7–8.

21. Helmuth Plessner, "Die Friedens-Chance," *Deutsche Universitäts-Zeitung* 4, no. 18 (September 23, 1949), 5–6.

22. See the guidelines issued by the ministry on April 16, 1949, published in spring 1951, *Richtlinien für den Unterricht an den Schulen des Landes Niedersachsen: Geschichtsunterricht an höheren Schulen* (Braunschweig: Niedersächsische Kulturministerium, Westermann, 1951), esp. 28–30, 56. On the general "permissiveness" and flexibility known to be given to teachers in Lower Saxony, see Thomas Ellwein, *Pflegt die deutsche Schule Bürgerbewusstsein?* (Munich: Isar, 1955), 178–179.

23. Helmuth Plessner, ed., *Symphilosophein: Bericht über den Dritten Deutschen Kongress für Philosophie, Bremen, 1950* (München: Lehnen, 1952).

24. Arthur Koestler, speech from Eröffnungskundgebung reproduced in *Der Monat* 2, nos. 22/23 (July/August 1950), 355–356.

25. See Wolfgang Gudenschwager, *Zur Kulturpolitik der CDU 1945 bis 1952* (Berlin: Christlich-Demokratische Union, 1970), 18–21.

26. Konrad Adenauer, " 'Verständigung, Frieden und Freiheit': Ansprache in der Frankfurter Universität," in *Konrad Adenauer,* ed. Hans-Peter Schwarz (Stuttgart: Deutsche Verlagsanstalt, 1975), 255–256.

27. See Norbert Frei, *Adenauer's Germany and the Nazi Past: The Politics of Amnesty and Integration,* trans. Joel Golb (New York: Columbia University Press, 2002), 285.

28. *Rettet das Vaterland: Programm zur nationalen Wiedervereinigung Deutschlands* (Frankfurt: Parteivorstand der KPD, 1952). On the SED's 1952 convention see Gerhard Besier and Stephan Wolf, *"Pfarrer, Christen und Katholiken": das Ministerium für Staatsicherheit der ehemaligen DDR und die Kirchen* (Neukirchen-Vluyn: Neukirchener, 1991).

29. Helmuth Plessner, "Über Menschenverachtung" (delivered November 22, 1952), also published in the Festschrift for Karl Jaspers, *Offener Horizont* (Munich: Piper, 1953), 319–327. I quote from the republished text in Plessner, *Gesammelte Schriften,* vol. 8, ed. Günter Dix et al. (Frankfurt: Suhrkamp, 1983), 114–115.

30. "Gesetz über das öffentliche Schulwesen in Niedersachsen," *Niedersächsisches Gesetz- und Verordnungsblatt* 8, no. 19 (September 15, 1954), 89–92.

31. Bund Europäischer Jugend, *Wie diskutiere ich mit Kommunisten?* (Bonn: Seminar des Bundes Europäischer Jugend, 1954).

32. See Felix Messerschmid, "Der Ausschuss," *Geschichte in Wissenschaft und Unterricht* 5 (August 1954), 451–452. Arnold Bergsträsser's student Heinrich Schneider later noted that Messerschmid's postwar support for a federal plan of Western-oriented education was "unbelievable"; in the Weimar years, Messerschmid was the protégé of the Catholic youth leader Romano Guardini, who was famously skeptical of Western democracy. Heinrich Schneider, "Anfänge einer Akademie: Die Startjahre in Tutzing," in *Politische Bildung im Wandel der Zeit: 50 Jahre Akademie für Politische Bildung,* ed. Heinrich Oberreuter (Munich: Olzog, 2007), 29.

33. On Bergsträsser's influence in the development of political science, see Horst Schmitt, *Politikwissenschaft und freiheitliche Demokratie* (Baden-Baden: Nomos, 1995). For an argument that emphasizes the agency of returnees, see Alfons Söllner, "Normative Westernization? The Impact of Remigres on the Foundation of Political Thought in Post-War Germany," in *German Ideologies Since 1945*, ed. Jan-Werner Müller (New York: Macmillan, 2003), 40–60.

34. Wolfgang Wagner, *Die Bundespräsidentenwahl, 1959* (Mainz: Matthias-Grünewald Verlag, 1972), 7.

35. Arnold Bergsträsser, "Der Emigrant," undated ms., written during his Chicago period, probably early 1950s, Arnold Bergsträsser Papers, Band 134, NL260 Bundesarchiv Koblenz.

36. See Vanessa Conze, *Das Europa des Deutschen: Ideen von Europa in Deutschland zwischen Reichstradition und Westorientierung* (Munich: De Gruyter, 2005), 233–234.

37. Arnold Bergsträsser, *Lorenzo Medici* (Frankfurt: Vittorio Klostermann, 1936), 3–30.

38. Kurt Georg Kiesinger, "In Memoriam Arnold Bergsträsser," in *Weltpolitik als Wissenschaft: Geschichtliches Bewusstsein und politische Entscheidung* (Cologne: Westdeutscher Verlag, 1965), 18.

39. See Klaus-Dieter Krohn, "Der Fall Bergsträsser in Amerika," *Exilforschung* 4 (1986), 254–275.

40. See the contributions in Arnold Bergsträsser et al., eds., *Deutsche Beiträge zur geistigen Überlieferung* (Chicago: University of Chicago Press, 1947–1953). For the context of the émigré circles at Chicago around Hutchins, see Joachim Radkau, *Die deutsche Emigration in den USA: Ihr Einfluss auf die amerikanische Europapolitik, 1933–1945* (Düsseldorf: Bertelsmann, 1971), 214–218.

41. See Hal Foust, "AMG Educator Assails Critics of High Schools. Answers 13 Germans at University of Chicago," *Chicago Daily Tribune* (March 29, 1948), 28; Study Group for German Problems, University of Chicago, "Secondary Education in Germany" (1947), memo on the Report of the U.S. Education Mission to Germany, in Arnold Bergsträsser Papers, Band 125. On the failure of the American plan see James Tent, *Mission on the Rhine: "Reeducation" and Denazification in American-Occupied Germany* (Chicago: University of Chicago Press, 1982), esp. chapter 5.

42. Hannah Arendt to Karl Jaspers, June 3, 1949, in *Hannah Arendt–Karl Jaspers Correspondence, 1926–1969*, ed. Lotte Kohler and Hans Saner, trans. Robert and Rita Kimber (New York: Harcourt Brace, 1992), 136–137.

43. Arnold Bergsträsser, "Memorandum über die Frage, welche Erscheinungen in der deutschen geistigen Situation der Gegenwart zu Erwartungen für die Zukunft berechtigen" (1953), Arnold Bergsträsser Papers, Band 133.

44. Arnold Bergsträsser, "Europa als geistige und politische Wirklichkeit," *Freiburger dies universitatis* (1954), quoted at 69–70, 75, 79.

45. One of his first appointments after permanently returning was to serve on a committee created by the minister of culture in Baden-Württemberg to give

recommendations for political education and strengthening social sciences in the school system, especially at the elite Gymnasiums. See Arnold Bergsträsser, "Politische Bildung in Baden-Württemberg," in *Wirken solange es Tag ist* (Stuttgart: NWZ, 1957), 47–53; Helmuth Plessner to Alexander Rüstow, August 19, 1955, Plessner Papers, 146.75.1–2.

46. Wilma Eggers, personal email correspondence, December 18, 2009.

47. Arnold Bergsträsser to Arthur A. Cohen, April 19, 1948, Bergsträsser Papers, Mappe 90.

48. René König to Helmut Schelsky, February 26, 1980, in *René König Schriften*, vol. 1, ed. Mario and Oliver König (Opladen: Leske + Budrich, 2000), 209. König's exact phrase to describe Bergsträsser's rhetoric was the even less flattering "breiige Geschwafel." While the academies, which were generally open forums for discussion, did not endorse any particular policy, it is fair to say that they were generally anticommunist. For context on the Protestant academies, see Rulf Jürgen Treidel, *Evangelische Akademien im Nachkriegsdeutschland* (Stuttgart: Kohlhammer, 2001); on the Catholic academies, Oliver Schütz, *Begegnung von Kirche und Welt* (Paderborn: Schöningh, 2004); and on the more ecumenical Christian academies, Axel Schildt, *Zwischen Abendland und Amerika* (Munich: Oldenbourg, 1999).

49. Carl Schmitt, *The Nomos of the Earth in the International Law of the Jus Publicum Europaeum*, trans. G. L. Ulmen (New York: Telos, 2006), quoted at 287.

50. "Gutachten zur Politischen Bildung und Erziehung" (January 22, 1955), in *Empfehlungen und Gutachten des Deutschen Ausschusses für das Erziehungs- und Bildungswesen, 1953–1965* (Stuttgart: Klett, 1966), 827–838.

51. Arnold Bergsträsser, "Das Wesen der Politischen Bildung" (February 22, 1956), published in Messerschmid's new journal for political education, *Freiheit und Verantwortung* 1, no. 1 (June 1956), 4–5, 12. The debates in the Bavarian parliament are reproduced in *Kristallisationskern politischer Bildung*, ed. Heinrich Oberreuter (Munich: Olzog, 2009), 451–466. For context, see Thies Marsen, *Zwischen Reeducation und politischer Philosophie: Der Aufbau der politischen Wissenschaft in München nach 1945* (Munich: Fink, 2001), 93f.

52. See Uta Poiger, *Jazz, Rock, and Rebels* (Berkeley: University of California Press, 2000), esp. chapter 6, and Sebastian Kurme, *Halbstarke* (Berlin: Campus, 2006).

53. See Hans Speidel, *Invasion 1944: Ein Beitrag zu Rommels und des Reiches Schicksal* (Tübingen: Wunderlich, 1949), and his introduction to Ludwig Beck, *Studien* (Stuttgart: Koehler, 1955).

54. On the Deutsche Gesellschaft für Auswärtige Politik, see Christian Haase, *Pragmatic Peacemakers* (Augsburg: Wissner, 2007), 122–123.

55. On the "Hallstein Doctrine" see William Glenn Gray, *Germany's Cold War: The Global Campaign to Isolate East Germany, 1949–1969* (Chapel Hill: University of North Carolina Press, 2003). On Hallstein's endorsement of Bergsträsser, see Daniel Eisermann, *Aussenpolitik und Strategiediskussion* (Munich: Oldenbourg, 1999), 96–97.

56. See Arnold Bergsträsser, "Die weltpolitische Dynamik der Gegenwart," in *Die internationale Politik 1955*, ed. Arnold Bergsträsser and Wilhelm Cornides (Munich: Oldenbourg, 1958), esp. 36–43.

57. "Osteuropa in der deutschen Bildung" (March 16, 1956), in *Empfehlungen und Gutachten des Deutschen Ausschusses für das Erziehungs- und Bildungswesen, 1953–1965*, 839–846. For more context on the teaching of history and the goal of "processing" the events in eastern Europe in the 1950s, see Nicolas Berg, *Der Holocaust und die westdeutsche Historiker* (Göttingen: Wallstein, 2003).

58. Hope M. Harrison, *Driving the Soviets Up the Wall: Soviet–East German Relations, 1953–1961* (Princeton: Princeton University Press, 2011), 64–65.

59. Helmuth Plessner, "Säkularisierung des Marxismus. Der Philosophenkongress in Warschau," *Deutsche Universitätszeitung* 12, nos. 17/18 (September 27, 1957), 21.

60. Helmuth Plessner to Hermann Heimpel, October 19, 1956, Plessner Papers, 154.137.

61. See Helmuth Plessner to Richard Voigt, July 19, 1954, Plessner Papers, 156.316. For more context on this struggle, see Anikó Szabó, *Vertreibung, Rückkehr, Wiedergutmachung: Göttinger Hochschullehrer im Schatten des Nationalsozialismus* (Göttingen: Wallstein, 2000), esp. 265–289. Indeed, Bergsträsser even collaborated on a book edited by two former SS officers who had been camouflaging their identities since 1945: Hans Schwerte and Wilhelm Spengler, eds., *Denker und Deuter im heutigen Europa*, introduction by Arnold Bergsträsser (Oldenburg: Gerhard Stalling, 1954). Friedrich Oetinger, *Partnerschaft: die Aufgabe der politischen Erziehung* (Stuttgart: Metzler, 1953).

62. Heinrich August Winkler, *Der lange Weg nach Westen*, vol. 2 (Munich: C.H. Beck, 2000), 175; on the same theme see also Denis Goeldel, *Le tournant occidental de l'Allemagne après 1945* (Strasbourg: Presses Universitaires de Strasbourg, 2005).

63. For an introduction to the German Democratic Republic government's use of this past, see Jeffrey Herf, *Divided Memory: The Nazi Past in the Two Germanys* (Cambridge: Harvard University Press, 1997), chapter 6.

64. Otto Kirchheimer, "The Political Scene in West Germany," *World Politics* 9, no. 3 (April 1957), 433–445.

9: THE CULTURE OF CHRISTIAN PARTNERSHIP

1. Daniel Bell, *The End of Ideology: On the Exhaustion of Political Ideas in the Fifties* (Glencoe, Ill.: Free Press, 1960).

2. Axel Schildt and Detlef Siegfried, *Deutsche Kulturgeschichte: Die Bundesrepublik von 1945 bis zur Gegenwart* (Munich: Hauser, 2009), 204ff.

3. See Frank-Manuel Peter, *Das Berlin Hansaviertel und die Interbau 1957* (Erfurt: Sutton, 2007).

4. For general arguments to this effect, see Franz-Werner Kersting et al., eds., *Die zweite Gründung der Bundesrepublik* (Stuttgart: Franz Steiner, 2010); Jens Hacke, *Philosophie der Bürgerlichkeit: Die liberalkonservative Begründung der Bundesrepublik* (Göttingen: Vandenhoeck & Ruprecht, 2008); A. Dirk Moses,

German Intellectuals and the Nazi Past (New York: Cambridge University Press, 2007); Christina von Hodenberg, *Konsens und Krise: eine Geschichte der westdeutschen Medienöffentlichkeit* (Göttingen: Wallstein, 2006); and Jan-Werner Müller, *Another Country: German Intellectuals, Unification, and National Identity* (New Haven: Yale University Press, 2000), 37–45.

5. See Gregory Castillo, "Constructing the Cold War: Architecture, Urbanism, and the Cultural Division of Germany, 1945–1957" (Ph.D. dissertation, University of California, Berkeley, 2000), 383–395.

6. Ernst-Wolfgang Böckenförde, "Das Ethos der modernen Demokratie und die Kirche," *Hochland* 50, no. 1 (1957), 10. On the importance of the church-state problem to the younger generation of West German political thinkers, see also Wilhelm Hennis's recollections in his preface to the reissue of his 1951 dissertation, *Das Problem der Souveränität: Ein Beitrag zur neueren Literaturgeschichte und gegenwärtigen Problematik der politischen Wissenschaften* (Tübingen: J.C.B. Mohr, 2003), vi.

7. A small sample included *Bundesrepublik—Paradies für Kriegsverbrecher* (Berlin Ost: Ausschuss für Deutsche Einheit, 1956), *Antisemitismus in der Bundesrepublik* (Berlin Ost: Ausschuss für Deutsche Einheit, 1956), and *Judenmörder und Kriegsverbrecher an den Hebeln der Macht* (Berlin Ost: Ausschuss für Deutsche Einheit, 1956). For context see Manfred Wilke, *The Path to the Berlin Wall*, trans. Sophie Perl (New York: Berghahn, 2014), especially chapter 5.

8. See Werner Bergmann, *Antisemitismus in öffentlichen Konflikten: Kollektives Lernen in der politischen Kultur der Bundesrepublik, 1949–1989* (Berlin: Campus, 1997), 192–199.

9. The quotation is from Erich Lüth, *Deutschland und die Juden nach 1945* (Hamburg: Aktion Friede mit Israel, 1957), 4. On Springer's claim to have been inspired by Flüe, see Uwe Wolff, *Das Geheimnis ist mein: Walter Nigg, eine Biographie* (Zürich: Theologische Verlag, 2009), 263, 425–426, and Hans-Peter Schwarz, *Axel Springer: Die Biographie* (Berlin: Propyläen, 2008), 250–270. For context on Springer and the Jews more generally see *Bild dir Dein Volk!: Axel Springer und die Juden,* ed. Dmitrij Belkin and Raphael Gross (Göttingen: Wallstein, 2012).

10. The true number is uncertain because of the difficulty in defining who actually counted as Jewish. See Marita Krauss, *Heimkehr in ein fremdes Land: Geschichte der Remigration nach 1945* (Munich: Beck, 2001).

11. See Michael Brenner, *After the Holocaust,* trans. Barbara Harshav (Princeton: Princeton University Press, 1997).

12. Hans-Joachim Schoeps, "Ein neuer Antisemitismus im Werden?" published in several newspapers including *Die neue Zeitung* (June 14, 1951).

13. Frank Stern, *The Whitewashing of the Yellow Badge: Antisemitism and Philosemitism in Postwar Germany* (New York: Oxford University Press, 1992). Schoeps's personal papers are full of requests from conservatives who desired the attestation of a "full Jew" to clear their record in military occupation

denazification courts. Hans-Joachim Schoeps Papers, NL 148, Ordner 97, Staatsbibliothek zu Berlin.

14. On Schoeps's advocacy for accommodation with the regime in its early years, see the works from his publishing house, Hans-Joachim Schoeps, *Wir deutsche Juden* (Berlin: Vortrupp, 1934), and the collection he edited, *Wille und Weg des deutschen Judentums* (Berlin: Vortrupp, 1935). By 1937, however, he was publishing pamphlets endorsing America as a potential land of emigration. For more context, see Carl Rheins, "Deutscher Vortrupp, Gefolgschaft deutscher Juden, 1933–1935," *Leo Baeck Institute Year Book* 26 (1981), 207–229.

15. Hans-Joachim Schoeps, *Jüdisch-christliches Religionsgespräch in 19. Jahrhunderten: Geschichte einer Auseinandersetzung* (Berlin: Vortrupp, 1937).

16. Schoeps had originally wanted to emigrate to the United States but could not find a Jewish theological seminary that would take him, despite the support of Columbia University's Salo Baron and the New School's Alvin Johnson. See Schoeps Papers, Ordner 94, and the Karl O. Paetel Papers, Box 6, German and Jewish Intellectual Émigré Collection, State University of New York at Albany. In 1939 he was able to secure a position at the University of Uppsala through the help of the Protestant theologians Anton Fridrichsen and Gösta Lindeskog.

17. For the tragic story of Schoeps's parents, see Astrid Mehmel, "Ich richte nun an Sie die grosse Bitte, eine zweckdienliche Eingabe in dieser Sache zu machen . . .," *Zeitschrift für Religions- und Geistesgeschichte* 52, no. 1 (2000), 38–46.

18. Gründungsaufruf of the "Deutsche Vereinigung 1945," cited by Helmut Müssener, *Exil im Schweden* (Munich: Hanser, 1974), 220. On the Vereinigung, see also Hans-Joachim Schoeps, *Die letzten dreissig Jahre* (Stuttgart: Klett, 1956), 128–130, and Erwin Leiser, *Gott hat kein Kleingeld* (Cologne: Kiepenheuer & Witsch, 1993). The Vereinigung was founded in January 1945 and chaired by the socialist politician Kurt Heinig, but it also had many conservative members.

19. Hans-Joachim Schoeps (pseud. Joachim Frank), *Vad skall det bli av tyskarna?* (Stockholm: Rabén & Sjögren, 1944), 79–92, 111–114. I am very grateful to my late colleague Walter Jackson of North Carolina State University for his help translating the Swedish text.

20. Hans-Joachim Schoeps to Margarete Susman, August 6, 1946, Margarete Susman Papers, 88.11.920, Literaturarchiv Marbach. See also his letters to Karl Barth from September 25, 1945, and April 8, 1946, reprinted in *Menora* (1991), 128–129.

21. Leo Baeck to Hans-Joachim Schoeps, November 15, 1946, and Gershom Scholem to Schoeps, March 24, 1947, Schoeps Papers, Ordner 97.

22. Hans Lamm to Hans-Joachim Schoeps, December 9, 1948, Schoeps Papers, Ordner 109.

23. Quoted in the report on the meeting of May 30, 1949, "Gottlosigkeit. Feind der Christen und Juden," *Abendzeitung* (May 31, 1949). The conference papers were published as *Welt ohne Hass* (Berlin: Christian Verlag, 1950). Schoeps's correspondence with Thieme, who was the religious adviser for the Koordinierungsrat der Gesellschaften für Christlich-Jüdische Zusammenarbeit,

can be found in the Karl Thieme Papers, ED163/73, Institut für Zeitgeschichte, Munich. On the pioneering leadership of Thieme on Christian-Jewish relations, see John Connelly, *From Enemy to Brother* (Cambridge: Harvard University Press, 2012), esp. 190–238.

24. Konrad Adenauer, "Erste Regierungserklärung" from September 20, 1949, in *Reden, 1917–1967*, ed. Hans-Peter Schwarz (Stuttgart: Deutsche Verlagsanstalt, 1975), 163. On Adenauer's policy of amnesty, see Norbert Frei, *Adenauer's Germany and the Nazi Past*, trans. Joel Golb (New York: Columbia University Press, 2002), chapter 1. On his policy of reparations for the Jews, see Ronald Zweig, *German Reparations and the Jewish World: A History of the Claims Conference* (Boulder: Westview, 1987).

25. Hans-Joachim Schoeps, *Das andere Preussen* (Stuttgart: Vorwerk, 1952), esp. 1–50. Gerlach supported monarchy as the ideal form of state because a king could best represent God's authority, but Schoeps pointed out that in Gerlach's eyes "the republic, too, could be a legitimate authority" as long as its leaders were conscious of their divine responsibility as legislators. The quotation is from p. 15. Also see Schoeps, *Die Ehre Preussens* (Stuttgart: Vorwerk, 1951).

26. Schoeps, *Das andere Preussen*, 59.

27. Irving Kristol to Hans-Joachim Schoeps, April 7, 1949, Schoeps Papers, Ordner 110; Henry Kissinger to Hans-Joachim Schoeps, September 17, 1953, Schoeps Papers, Ordner 121. Schoeps wrote two articles for *Commentary* in 1950 and 1953, but his work never ended up appearing in *Confluence*. Among the younger generation in Germany, one of the foremost theorists of the "new right," Hellmut Diwald (b. 1924), considered himself a protégé of Schoeps.

28. Erik Kuehnelt-Leddihn to Hans-Joachim Schoeps, January 13, 1953, Schoeps Papers, Ordner 102.

29. On his campaign, see the long profile "Die Ehre Preussens," in *Der Spiegel* (March 3, 1954), which noted that roughly thirty percent of the West German population in polls favored a return of the monarchy but that idea enjoyed less support among the younger generation.

30. Ernst-Wolfgang Böckenförde to Hans-Joachim Schoeps, September 5, 1954, Schoeps Papers, Ordner 203. For more description see Frank-Lothar Kroll, *Geschichtswissenschaft in politischer Absicht* (Berlin: Duncker & Humblot, 2010), 70–80; Böckenförde, "Das Ethos der modernen Demokratie und die Kirche," 10–12.

31. Hans Gerd Sellenthin, *Geschichte der Juden in Berlin und des Gebäudes Fasanenstrasse 79/80* (1959), 125–128. Kauders, *Democratization and the Jews*, 201; on Springer's directive to the editors of *Bild* to broaden coverage of the Jews in late 1957, see Karl Christian Führer, "Schuld und 'Selbstbesinnung,' " in *Bild dir dein Volk!*, 18.

32. Manuscript of Schoeps's speech, "Ansprache zur 17. Juni-Feier, 1958," in Schoeps Papers, Kasten 26, Mappe 3.

33. Hans-Joachim Schoeps, *Konservative Erneuerung* (Berlin: Haude & Spener, 1958), 19–20, 77–82, 101–131; Hans-Joachim Schoeps, *Paulus* (Tübingen:

J.C.B. Mohr, 1959). Schoeps gave an address titled "Die Wandlung des Autoritätsgedankens von der Französischen Revolution bis zur Gegenwart," at the Evangelische Akadamie Loccum during a Tagung für Offiziere, October 21–25, 1958; Schoeps Papers, Ordner 104.

34. See Bernd Schaefer, *The East German State and the Catholic Church, 1945–1989*, trans. Jonathan Skolnik and Patricia Sutcliffe (New York: Berghahn, 2010), esp. 73–96; A. James McAdams, *Germany Divided: From the Wall to Reunification* (Princeton: Princeton University Press, 1993), 23–30; on Norden, see Herf, *Divided Memory: The Nazi Past in the Two Germanys* (Cambridge: Harvard University Press, 1997), 170–184.

35. Kauders, *Democratization and the Jews,* chapter 4; Adenauer's speech republished in Günther Ginzel and Sonja Güntner, *"Zuhause in Köln": Jüdisches Leben 1945 bis heute* (Cologne: Böhlau, 1998), 117.

36. *Grundsatzprogramm der Sozialdemokratischen Partei Deutchlands* (Bonn: Vorstand der SPD, 1959), 21. See also Willi Kreiterling, *Kirche, Katholizismus, Sozialdemokratie: von der Gegnerschaft zur Partnerschaft* (Bonn: Verlag Neue Gesellschaft, 1969).

37. Sydney Gruson, "Anti-Semitic Incidents Point Up Weaknesses in the New Germany," *New York Times,* January 2, 1960, E5; see also the letter to the editor from Kurt Grossman, "Anti-Semitism in Germany: Urgency Seen for Measures to Aid Democratic Forces," in the same issue.

38. Quoted in Torsten Oppelland, *Gerhard Schröder: Politik zwischen Staat, Partei und Konfession* (Düsseldorf: Droste, 2002), 324–325. See also Bergmann, *Antisemitismus in öffentlichen Konflikten,* 235–249.

39. For context on the guest worker programs see Herbert Ulrich, *A History of Foreign Labor in Germany, 1880–1980,* trans. William Templer (Ann Arbor: University of Michigan, 1990), 225–226.

40. Franklin Littell to Richard Leach, March 16, 1959, copy in Ernst Benz Papers. My heartfelt thanks are due to Benz's wife, Brigitte, and son, Balthasar, who allowed me access to Ernst Benz's personal papers. The papers were stored in the family's garage in Marburg and left unexamined for years until Balthasar and I discovered them in September 2014. Because the boxes have not been professionally archived and numbered, I will refer to source materials simply with the notation "Ernst Benz Papers."

41. Ernst Benz, "Asiatische Jugend zwischen Christentum, Buddhismus und Kommunismus," *Zeitschrift für Ganzheitsforschung* 3 (1959), 12–22. On the German Commission for UNESCO, see Manfred Regnery, "Die Diskussion über die deutsche auswärtige Kulturpolitik zwischen 1957 und 1963 unter besonderer Berücksichtigung der Deutschen Unesco-Kommission" (Ph.D. dissertation, Freiburg, 1973).

42. Erich Seeberg, "Gründe für das Scheitern der Reichskirche," in *Menschenwerdung und Geschichte: Aufsätze* (Stuttgart: Kohlhammer, 1938).

43. Ernst Benz, letter dated 1944, addressee name unfortunately made illegible by decay, Ernst Benz Papers.

44. Ernst Benz, "Immanuel Swedenborg als geistiger Wegbahner des deutschen Idealismus und der deutschen Romantik," *Deutsche Vierteljahrsschrift für Literaturwissenschaft und Geistesgeschichte* 19 (1941), 10–12; Benz, "Das mysteriöse Datum: Zu Kants Kritik an Swedenborg," *Zeitschrift für Kirchengeschichte* 61 (1942), 217–255. Benz's essay is dated June 29, 1942. The last pages are incorporated almost verbatim (although expanded) in the first book he was finally able to release after the war, *Swedenborg in Deutschland* (Frankfurt: Klostermann, 1947).

45. Ernst Benz, *Die religiöse Lage in der Ukraine* (Marburg: R. Friedrich's Universitäts-Buchdruckerei), 1942; Timothy Snyder, *Bloodlands: Europe Between Hitler and Stalin* (New York: Basic, 2010). The reconstruction of the Orthodox churches was often considered part of Ukrainians' national reconstruction in 1941 and 1942; thus Benz's advocacy for the Eastern church could be seen as subversive. For context on Reichskommissar Erich Koch's background and his actions against the Orthodox Church in Ukraine, see Wendy Lower, *Nazi Empire-Building and the Holocaust in Ukraine* (Chapel Hill: University of North Carolina Press, 2005), esp. 36–38, 119–122. Benz tried to publish a more polished version of the book with the Protestant press Kohlhammer, but it claimed a lack of paper. Kohlhammer Verlag to Ernst Benz, July 6, 1943, Ernst Benz papers.

46. Ernst Benz to Feldbischof [Franz Dorhmann], September 6, 1944, Ernst Benz Papers. Benz fit the general description outlined by Doris Bergen: military chaplains during the war were typically not ideological Nazis, but rather conservatives sent to the hottest areas of fighting during the war to maximize morale. In general, they did not actively resist the Hitler regime. Doris Bergen, "German Military Chaplains in World War II and the Dilemmas of Legitimacy," *Church History* 70, no. 2 (2001), 232–247.

47. Spruchkammer Aktz 3935/46, Ernst Benz, November 18, 1946, RG 260, Series 313 (A1), Box 201, National Archives, College Park, Maryland. The file includes Benz's claim that he rejected requests to work on both Alfred Rosenberg's anti-Catholic *Handbuch zur Romfrage* and at the Jena Institut zur Erforschung des jüdischen Einflusses in der deutschen evangelischen Kirche, a project described in Susannah Heschel, *The Aryan Jesus: Christian Theologians and the Bible in Nazi Germany* (Princeton: Princeton University Press, 2008). I could not verify those claims. According to Heschel's research, Benz was present at planning meetings where the removal of "Jewish influence" from theological faculties was discussed, but I found no evidence (in either his published materials or his personal papers) of his involvement with the actual institute.

48. Charles Hartshorne to Arnold Bergsträsser, undated [probably 1946], Arnold Bergsträsser Papers, Mappe 89.

49. Ernst Benz, *Emanuel Swedenborg: Naturforscher und Seher* (Munich: Hermann Rinn, 1948), esp. 252–264, 412–414.

50. Karl Deutsch, *Faith for Our Generation: A Study Unit on Youth and Religion* (Boston: American Unitarian Youth, 1943).

51. Walter Nigg to Ernst Benz, September 19, 1947; Ernst Benz to Walter Nigg, October 4, 1947, Ernst Benz Papers.

52. See the description of the Schlüchtern project in Robert Strobel, "Europäische Akademie," *Die Zeit* (November 4, 1948); on his involvement in Lausanne Graf von Trauttmannsdorff, Bericht des Generalsekretärs über die Kultur-Konferenz der europäischen Bewegung in Lausanne, December 1949, Ernst Benz Papers.

53. Ernst Benz to Hans-Joachim Schoeps, February 16, 1953, Ernst Benz Papers.

54. See for example A. Demal, "Wurzeln der nazistischen Ideologie in der Philosophie Hegels," *Einheit* 2, no. 2 (February 1947), 171–176; David Guest, "Über den dialektischen Materialismus," *Einheit* 2, no. 7 (July 1947), 665–675.

55. Benz argued that in fact the opposite was true: communism resonated in Russia precisely because the Eastern church held the mystical belief in "the deification of man as the goal of God's incarnation" so dear. Ernst Benz, "Menschenwürde und Menschenrecht in der Geistesgeschichte der Ostkirche," in *Die Ostkirche und die russische Christenheit*, ed. Ernst Benz (Tübingen: Furche, 1949), esp. 61–63; Ernst Benz, *Die Ostkirche im Lichte der protestantischen Geschichtsschreibung von der Reformation bis zur Gegenwart* (Freiburg: K. Alber, 1952).

56. Ernst Benz, "The Islamic Culture as Mediator of the Greek Philosophy to Europe," *Islamic Culture* 35, no. 3 (1961), 165. The essay was based on his lecture of July 25, 1957, for the Islamic Culture Board of Hyderabad, India.

57. See Benz, *Die religiöse Lage in der Ukraine,* esp. 25–33, 47ff.

58. Ernst Benz, *Christliche Kabbala: Ein Stiefkind der Theologie* (Zürich: Rhein, 1958), 7–8.

59. For two good introductions to the theme, see Michael Ermarth, "Counter-Americanism and Critical Currents in West German Reconstruction, 1945–1960," in *Americanization and Anti-Americanism,* ed. Alexander Stephan (New York: Berghahn, 2005), 25–50, and Anselm Doering-Manteuffel, "Dimensionen von Amerikanisierung in der deutschen Gesellschaft," *Archiv für Sozialgeschichte* 35 (1995), 1–34.

60. "Der Professor der Kirchengeschichte," *The Unauthorized Version* (journal of the Harvard Divinity School student association) 3, no. 1 (April 26, 1960), 3. On the academies see Axel Schildt, *Zwischen Abendland und Amerika: Studien zur westdeutschen Ideenlandschaft der 50er Jahre* (Munich: Oldenbourg, 1999), 121–122. On the Kirchentag see Benjamin Carl Pearson, "Faith and Democracy: Political Transformations at the German Protestant Kirchentag, 1949–1969" (Ph.D. dissertation, University of North Carolina at Chapel Hill, 2007).

61. Franklin Littell to Ernst Benz, February 27, 1956; Benz to Littell, March 8, 1956, Frank Littell Papers, Box 5.

62. See Dirk Palm, *"Wir sind doch Brüder!": Der evangelische Kirchentag und die deutsche Frage, 1949–1961* (Göttingen: Vandenhoeck & Ruprecht, 2002).

63. Franklin Littell, *The German Phoenix* (New York: Knopf, 1960), 89.

64. See Ernst Benz, "Die Konzilsankündigung des Papstes Johannes XXIII," *Evangelische Welt* 13, no. 5 (March 1, 1959), 113–116.

65. Ernst Benz, *Kirchengeschichte in ökumenischer Sicht* (Leiden: Brill, 1961), 9–11.

66. Ernst Benz, "Ideen zu einer Theologie der Religionsgeschichte," in *Abhandlungen der Geistes- und Sozialwissenschaftlichen Klasse,* Nr. 5 (Wiesbaden: Akademie der Wissenschaften und der Literatur in Mainz, 1960), 493.

67. Hans-Joachim Schoeps, "Soll Homosexualität strafbar bleiben," *Der Monat* (December 1962), 25; Schoeps, "Homosexualität und Bibel," *Zeitschrift für evangelische Ethik* 6 (1962), 369–374; see also his *Was ist der Mensch?* (Göttingen: Musterschmidt, 1960), esp. part 3, chapter 3. For context see Philipp Nielsen, " 'The Moral Sensibility of the People': Collective and Individual, Past and Future in the Decriminalization of Homosexuality in West Germany," *American Historical Review,* forthcoming.

68. Jael Geis in conversation with the author, February 18, 2008, Berlin.

69. Schalom Ben-Chorin, "The Youth Wants to Make Good the Sins of Their Fathers . . . But the Old Prejudices Against the Jews Are Still Smoldering," in *The Politics of Postwar Germany,* ed. Walter Stahl (New York: Praeger, 1962), 393; see also Dietrich Goldschmidt and Hans-Joachim Kraus, eds., *Der ungekündigte Bund* (Stuttgart: Kreuz, 1962), 10. Almost half of the attendees came in from the German Democratic Republic, as the event was forbidden by the East German regime. The Jewish speaker was Robert Raphael Geis (1906–1972), a returnee from Palestine and the chief rabbi of Baden.

10: LIVING WITH LIBERAL DEMOCRACY

Epigraph: Institute of Social Research, "Memorandum on the Elimination of German Chauvinism" (August 1942), Max Horkheimer Papers, Universitätsarchiv Frankfurt, XI/172/27.

1. "Geist und Macht," *Der Spiegel* (December 13, 1961).

2. Lutz Niethammer, "Traditionen und Perspektiven der Nationalstaatlichkeit," in *Aussenpolitische Perspektiven des westdeutschen Staates,* vol. 2 (Munich: Oldenbourg, 1971), 13–48.

3. Clemens Albrecht et al., *Die intellektuelle Gründung der Bundesrepublik* (Frankfurt: Campus, 1999). While it is provocative to claim that any one single institution or school of thought could lay "*the* intellectual foundation" for the stabilization of a country—especially when the authors clearly oppose the strategies of this school—neither can the stature of Horkheimer and Adorno from the mid-1960s onward be denied.

4. See the review article by Frank Biess on the new intellectual history of the Federal Republic in *History and Theory* 51 (May 2012), 221–245, and the roundtable discussion on "The Intellectual History of the Federal Republic," in *German History* 27, no. 2 (2009), 244–258.

5. See Wolfgang Schivelbusch, *Intellektuellendämmerung: zur Lage der Frankfurter Intelligenz in den zwanziger Jahren* (Frankfurt: Suhrkamp, 1985); Grosshessisches Staatsministerium, report April 27, 1946 (Doc. 50), Hessiches Hauptstadtarchiv, Wiesbaden, Abteilung 504, Sig. 313.

6. See Johann Zilien, *Politische Bildung in Hessen von 1945 zu 1965* (Frankfurt: Lang, 1994).

7. "Memorandum Friedrich Pollock–Max Horkheimer, Beschluß vom 11. Mai 1959," in Max Horkheimer, *Gesammelte Schriften*, vol. 18, ed. Gunzelin Schmid Noerr (Frankfurt: Fischer, 1996), 453–454.

8. Horkheimer's lecture at the Bundesaussenministerium (Auswärtiges Amt) was titled "Das rassische Vorurteil gegen farbige Studenten" on January 29, 1960; the Conference on Antisemitism and Other Prejudices was held at the Institute on August 9/10, 1960. Report to Ministry of Culture on Institute for Social Research activities in 1960, Hessiches Hauptstadtarchiv, Wiesbaden, IfS Series Band 4, Abt. 504, Nr. 12.270.

9. Gerhard Schröder, *Kompromiss mit der SPD?* (Bonn: Bundesgeschäftsstelle der CDU Deutschlands, 1961). Among other things, Schröder pointed to the communist past of the SPD's acting chairman, despite the latter's assurance that his party now took the Western and European treaties as their foundation for foreign policy with the East. See Torsten Oppelland, *Gerhard Schröder* (Düsseldorf: Droste, 2002), 298–316, 350–370; Herbert Wehner, *Bundestagsreden*, ed. Manfred Schulte (Bonn: AZ-Studio, 1971), 206.

10. For Schröder's language about national integration and Europe at this time, see Oppelland, *Gerhard Schröder*, 316–332.

11. Hawe, "Ein Gesinnungslineal," *Neues Deutschland* (August 20, 1960).

12. Max Horkheimer, "Nachwort zu *Porträts deutsch-jüdischer Geistesgeschichte*" (1961), in *Gesammelte Schriften*, vol. 8, ed. Gunzelin Schmid Noerr (Frankfurt: Fischer, 1985), 176.

13. Max Horkheimer, *Zur Antinomie der teleologischen Urteilskraft* (1922), in *Gesammelte Schriften*, vol. 2, ed. Gunzelin Schmid Noerr (Frankfurt: Fischer, 1987), esp. 40–60, quotation here at 60.

14. See Martin Jay, *The Dialectical Imagination: A History of the Frankfurt School and the Institute for Social Research, 1923–1950* (New York: Little, Brown, 1973), esp. 46–53. Horkheimer was familiar with Baeumler's work. Max Horkheimer, *Über Kants Kritik der Urteilskraft als Bindeglied zwischen theoretischer und praktischer Philosophie* (1925), in *Gesammelte Schriften*, vol. 2, 75. Alfred Baeumler, *Hegels Ästhetik* (Munich: Beck, 1922).

15. Max Horkheimer (pseud. Henrich Regius), *Dämmerung* (Zürich: Oprecht & Helbling, 1934), 116–119.

16. See the bibliographies in Thomas Wheatland, *The Frankfurt School in Exile* (Minneapolis: University of Minnesota Press, 2009), and Eva-Maria Ziege, *Antisemitismus und Gesellschaftstheorie* (Frankfurt: Suhrkamp, 2009).

17. Henryk Grossman to Max Horkheimer and Friedrich Pollock, February 7, 1935, in Horkheimer, *Gesammelte Schriften*, vol. 15, ed. Gunzelin Schmid Noerr (Frankfurt: Fischer, 1995), 316.

18. Walter Benjamin to Max Horkheimer, December 24, 1936, in Horkheimer, *Gesammelte Schriften*, vol. 15, 800. On the materialism reader planned in 1936

but subsequently scrapped, see Herbert Marcuse to Theodor Adorno and Max Horkheimer to Theodor Adorno, May 6, 1936, in Horkheimer, *Gesammelte Schriften*, vol. 15, 517–519. Horkheimer's contribution was a criticism of Theodor Haecker, a German Catholic who had remained in Germany and written *Der Christ und die Geschichte* (Leipzig: Hegner, 1935). See also Alfred Baeumler, "Theodor Haecker—ein Apologet der Kirche," *Wille und Macht: Führerorgan der nationalsozialistischen Jugend* 3, no. 20 (October 15, 1935), 2–7.

19. Max Horkheimer to Walter Benjamin, January 11, 1937, in Horkheimer, *Gesammelte Schriften*, vol. 16, 24–25. Horkheimer cited these "important" recent lines under the subtitle "The Struggle Against Religion" from André Gide, who had just returned from a trip to the Soviet Union, published in November 1936 with the double-entendre title of *Return from the USSR*, trans. Dorothy Bussy (New York: Knopf, 1937), 78–82.

20. Max Horkheimer, "Traditionelle und kritische Theorie," *Zeitschrift für Sozialforschung* 6, no. 2 (1937), 284–285.

21. Max Horkheimer to Friedrich Pollock, September 20, 1937, quoted in Helmut Dubiel, *Theory and Politics*, trans. Benjamin Gregg (Cambridge, Mass.: MIT Press, 1985), 52. See also Max Horkheimer, "Die Juden und Europa," *Zeitschrift für Sozialforschung* 8 (1939), 115–137.

22. Theodor W. Adorno and Max Horkheimer, *Briefwechsel, 1927–1969*, vol. 1, ed. Christoph Gödde and Henri Lonitz (Frankfurt: Suhrkamp, 2003), 143–145, 153–157.

23. On the role of liberal Jewish organizations such as the AJC before and during the war, see Wendy L. Wall, *Inventing the "American Way": The Politics of Consensus from the New Deal to the Civil Rights Movement* (New York: Oxford University Press, 2008), parts 1 and 2; Marc Dollinger, *Quest for Inclusion: Jews and Liberalism in Modern America* (Princeton: Princeton University Press, 2000), chapter 4.

24. Max Horkheimer and Theodor W. Adorno, *Dialektik der Aufklärung* (Amsterdam: Querido, 1947), 200. The main part of the text was published with this press in 1944, with the "Elements of Antisemitism" section appended in a second edition three years later. See also Institute for Social Research (Gurland), "Analysis of Central-Verein Policy in Germany," undated, probably 1945, 1–2, Arkadij Gurland Papers (unprocessed), in Max Horkheimer Archive, Universitätsarchiv Frankfurt.

25. Horkheimer and Adorno, *Dialektik der Aufklärung*, 39.

26. Ibid., 212, 244.

27. Institut für Sozialforschung, "Memo re: Anti-democratic Trends in West-German Universities," December 1949, Max Horkheimer Archive, IX/247/15c.

28. Institut für Sozialforschung, *Ein Bericht über die Feier seiner Wiedereröffnung* (1952), translated in Wiggershaus, *The Frankfurt School*, 445–446.

29. Herbert Marcuse to Theodor W. Adorno, January 24, 1960, quoted in Horkheimer, *Gesammelte Schriften*, vol. 18, 469.

30. Horkheimer, "Nachwort zu *Porträts deutsch-jüdischer Geistesgeschichte*" (1961), in *Gesammelte Schriften*, vol. 8, esp. 175–195. See also Max Horkheimer, "Über das Vorurteil" (1961), in *Gesammelte Schriften*, vol. 8, 200.

31. Max Horkheimer, "Kants Philosophie und die Aufklärung," in *Um die Freiheit* (Frankfurt: Europäische Verlagsanstalt, 1962); quotations are from 31, 36, and 40–41.

32. See the snippet of Gerstenmaier's article which Horkheimer read, "Es gibt keinen Antisemitismus mehr," *Frankfurter Allgemeine Zeitung* (March 16, 1963).

33. Max Horkheimer to Eugen Gerstenmaier (unsent), June 10, 1963, in Horkheimer, *Gesammelte Schriften*, vol. 18, 548–553.

34. Norbert Muhlen, *The Survivors* (New York: Crowell, 1962); Muhlen, introduction to *The Politics of Postwar Germany*, ed. Walter Stahl (New York: Praeger, 1963), xi.

35. Carl J. Friedrich, introduction to Peter Merkl, *The Origins of the West German Republic* (New York: Oxford University Press, 1963), xv–xvi; Carl J. Friedrich, "Nation-Building?" in *Nation-Building*, ed. Karl Deutsch and William Foltz (New York: Atherton, 1963), 31.

36. See Quinn Slobodian, *Foreign Fronts: Third-World Politics in Sixties West Germany* (Durham: Duke University Press, 2012), chapter 1.

37. Ulrike Meinhof, "Deutschland ohne Kennedy," *konkret* 12 (December 1963), 6.

38. Hans Magnus Enzensberger quoted in Stefan Müller-Doohm, *Adorno*, trans. Rodney Livingstone (Malden, Mass.: Polity, 2005), 410. For more on Adorno's early influence on SDS circles, see Martin Klimke, *The Other Alliance: Student Protest in West Germany and the United States in the Global Sixties* (Princeton: Princeton University Press, 2010), chapter 1.

39. Theodor W. Adorno, "Auf die Frage: Warum sind Sie zurückgekehrt," *Deutsche Post* 14 (December 12, 1962), republished in *Gesammelte Schriften*, vol. 19, part 1, ed. Rolf Tiedemann (Frankfurt: Suhrkamp, 1986), 394; Theodor W. Adorno, "Fragen an die intellektuelle Emigration" (May 27, 1945), in *Gesammelte Schriften*, vol. 20, ed. Rolf Tiedemann and Klaus Schultz (Frankfurt: Suhrkamp, 1986), 355.

40. Theodor W. Adorno, *Minima Moralia* (Frankfurt: Suhrkamp, 1951), 80. See Evelyn Wilcock, "Negative Identity: Mixed German Jewish Descent as a Factor in the Reception of Theodor Adorno," *New German Critique* (Autumn 2000), 169–187.

41. See John Abromeit, *Max Horkheimer and the Foundations of the Frankfurt School* (New York: Cambridge University Press, 2011), Excursus II. Horkheimer appreciated Adorno's critical mind but was originally wary of his interest in metaphysics until they jointly came to adopt immanent critique as the method of critical theory.

42. Adorno wrote to Walter Benjamin in 1934 that he was not optimistic that the replacement regime after Nazism would be socialist. Instead, it would probably be "right-wing anarchy." Theodor Wiesengrund Adorno to Walter Benjamin, April 21, 1934, in *The Complete Correspondence, 1928–1940*, ed. Henri Lonitz, trans. Nicholas Walker (Cambridge: Harvard University Press, 1999), 45–46.

When Adorno's students thirty years later asked him about his political miscalculations during the early Nazi years, he admitted he had naively misjudged the situation. Theodor W. Adorno, open letter to Schröder in *Diskus* (January 1963), reproduced in Theodor W. Adorno, *Gesammelte Schriften*, vol. 19, ed. Rolf Tiedemann and Klaus Schultz (Frankfurt: Suhrkamp, 1984), 637–638.

43. Wall, *Inventing the "American Way,"* 177–178.

44. The term "re-education" was popularized during the war through the psychiatrist Richard Brickner, M.D., *Is Germany Curable?* (New York: Lippincott, 1943). For context see Jeffrey Olick, *In the House of the Hangman: The Agonies of German Defeat, 1943–1949* (Chicago: University of Chicago Press, 2005), 58–64.

45. T. W. Adorno, "Types and Syndromes," in Adorno et al., *The Authoritarian Personality* (New York: Harper & Row, 1950), 748. Horkheimer summarized the integrative nature of prejudice well as he and Adorno were preparing their research: "One simply learns to speak disrespectfully of Jews as one would learn to curse, tell dirty jokes, drink heavily, or to rage about taxes and strikes." Max Horkheimer to Adorno, October 11, 1945, in *Gesammelte Schriften*, vol. 17, ed. Gunzelin Schmid Noerr (Frankfurt: Fischer, 1996), 657–659. See also Horkheimer's and Adorno's essays in Ernst Simmel, ed., *Anti-Semitism: A Social Disease* (New York: International Universities Press, 1946).

46. T. W. Adorno, "Prejudice in Interview Material," in *The Authoritarian Personality*, 609–612.

47. T. W. Adorno, "Some Aspects of Religious Ideology as Revealed in the Interview Material," in *The Authoritarian Personality*, 728–730.

48. "Conclusions," in *The Authoritarian Personality*, 973.

49. Their study of nearly two thousand subjects ("opinion-leading" members of communities from around the major cities of West Germany), the data for which was collected by graduate students hired by the institute mostly in 1950, took five years to process and finally publish and enjoyed little success. The main results and Adorno's interesting conclusions have been helpfully edited and translated by Jeffrey Olick in *Group Experiment and Other Writings* (Cambridge: Harvard University Press, 2011), and *Guilt and Defense* (Cambridge: Harvard University Press, 2010).

50. Walter Jacobsen, *"Lauter Vorurteile!"* (Bonn: Bundeszentrale für Heimatsdienst, 1956), esp. 15–18; Hermann Heimpel, *Der Mensch in seiner Gegenwart* (Göttingen: Vandenhoeck & Ruprecht, 1957), 165. For more context see Nicolas Berg, *Der Holocaust und die westdeutschen Historiker* (Göttingen: Wallstein, 2003).

51. Theodor W. Adorno, "Was bedeutet: Aufarbeitung der Vergangenheit," in *Gesammelte Schriften*, vol. 10/2 (Frankfurt: Suhrkamp, 177), 560–561.

52. Ibid., 563–570.

53. Clemens Albrecht was correct to suggest that this subjective side was the only "padagogisierbar" or applicable aspect of Adorno's theories on prejudice. See Albrecht et al., *Die intellektuelle Gründung*, 401. That is not to say, however, that *therapy* was Adorno's goal, as Albrecht suggested.

54. "Diskussion zum Referat Professor Adornos," in *Bericht über die Erzieherkonferenz am 6. u. 7. November 1959 in Wiesbaden* (Frankfurt: Deutscher Koordinierungsrat der Gesellschaften für Christlich-Jüdische Zusammenarbeit, 1959), 24–25, 29–30. See also Theodor W. Adorno, "Zur Bekämpfung des Antisemitismus heute," in *Erziehung vorurteilsfreier Menschen* (Frankfurt: Deutsche Koordinierungsrat der Gesellschaften für Christlich-Jüdische Zusammenarbeit, 1963), 15–31.

55. George Lichtheim, "The New Europe," *Commentary* (April 1, 1962), as part of his book *The New Europe* (New York: Praeger, 1963).

56. Theodor W. Adorno, *Jargon der Eigentlichkeit: Zur deutschen Ideologie* (1964), in *Gesammelte Schriften*, vol. 4, ed. Rolf Tiedemann (Frankfurt: Suhrkamp, 1973), 416–417.

57. Otto-Friedrich Bollnow, *Existenzphilosophie und Pädagogik* (Stuttgart: Kohlhammer, 1959), 11; Bollnow, *Die pädagogische Atmosphäre* (Heidelberg: Quelle & Meyer, 1964).

58. Arnold Bergsträsser, "Gedanken zu Verfahren und Aufgaben der kulturwissenschaftlichen Gegenwartsforschung," in *Kulturen im Umbruch*, ed. Gottfried-Karl Kindermann (Freiburg: Rombach, 1962), 401–422.

59. Theodor W. Adorno, "Will and Reason" (February 23, 1965), in *History and Freedom: Lectures, 1964–1965*, ed. Rolf Tiedemann, trans. Rodney Livingston (New York: Wiley, 2014), 256.

60. A. James McAdams, *East Germany and Detente* (New York: Cambridge University Press, 1985), 57.

61. Quoted in *Ich der Kanzler: Professor Erhards barockes Poesiealbum*, ed. Erhard Kortmann and Fritz Wolf (Bergisch Gladbach: Gustav Lübbe, 1966), 29.

62. Quoted in Ibid., 18.

63. Theodor W. Adorno, *Ästhetische Theorie*, in *Gesammelte Schriften*, vol. 7, ed. Gretel Adorno and Rolf Tiedemann (Frankfurt: Suhrkamp, 1970), 18.

64. See for example Dagmar Herzog, *Sex After Fascism: Memory and Morality in Twentieth-Century Germany* (Princeton: Princeton University Press, 2005), esp. chapters 3 and 4.

65. Ulrike Meinhof, "Hochhuth," *konkret* (August 1965), reprinted in Meinhof, *Dokumente einer Rebellion* (Hamburg: konkret, 1972), 55; Meinhof, "Wahlen," *konkret* (September 1965), in ibid., 56.

CONCLUSION

1. Rainer Barzel, *Auf dem Drahtseil* (Munich: Droemer-Knauer, 1978), 28.

2. Theo Sommer, "Bonn Changes Course," *Foreign Affairs* (April 1967), 478; "Paper Prepared in the Department of State" (May 5, 1968), in *Foreign Relations of the United States, 1964–1968*, vol. 15: Germany and Berlin (Washington, D.C.: Government Printing Office, 1999), 662–663.

3. In the spring of 1967, students at the Free University in West Berlin published a scathing review of the class Fraenkel taught that semester, accusing him of reducing the German workers' movement's once robust conception of

democracy—which in the Weimar Republic included liberation from oligarchy through parliamentary supremacy and direct democracy in the form of plebiscites—to a set of bureaucratic institutions that protected property rights and ensured periodic elections. See "Seminarrezension," and "Prof. Dr. Fraenkel nimmt Stellung," *FU-Spiegel* (May 1967), republished in *Hochschule im Umbruch*, Teil 4: Die Krise (1964–1967), ed. Siegward Lönnendonker and Tilman Fichter (Berlin: Pressestelle der FU Berlin, 1975), 420–422; also Joachim Bergmann, "Konsensus und Konflikt," *Das Argument* 9, no. 42 (1967), 41–59. They referred to his major work, Ernst Fraenkel, *Deutschland und die westlichen Demokratien* (Stuttgart: Kohlhammer, 1964).

4. Johannes Agnoli, "Thesen zur Transformation der Demokratie," *Konturen: Zeitschrift für Berliner Studenten*, no. 31 (1967), 3–17. He referred to Leibholz's arguments in such texts as Gerhard Leibholz, *Demokratie und Erziehung* (Hildesheim: Gerstenberg, 1967).

5. See Michael Karl, *Rudi Dutschke* (Frankfurt: Neue Kritik, 2003), 173–181.

6. See Frank Deppe et al., *Kritik der Mitbestimmung: Partnerschaft oder Klassenkampf?* (Frankfurt: Suhrkamp, 1969); Rolf Hochhuth, "Der Klassenkampf ist nicht zu Ende," *Der Spiegel* (May 26, 1965), 28–44.

7. See Quinn Slobodian, *Foreign Front: Third-World Politics in Sixties West Germany* (Durham: Duke University Press, 2012), and Dorothee Weitbrecht, *Aufbruch in die Dritte Welt: der Internationalismus der Studentenbewegung von 1968 in der Bundesrepublik* (Göttingen: Vandenhoeck & Ruprecht, 2012).

8. "Grenzen der Gemeinschaft: Vortrag Prof. Helmuth Plessner (Zürich) im Rahmen der Pädagogischen Hochschultage," *Nordwest-Zeitung* (June 24, 1967). He dusted off his old text *The Limits of Community: A Critique of Social Radicalism* for republication in 1967.

9. Hans-Joachim Schoeps, "Gefahren für den demokratischen Rechtsstaat: Der Radikalisierung entgegentreten," *Die Welt* (December 29, 1967). The SDS chapter at the university where he taught in Bavaria responded by interrupting Schoeps's lectures to remind students of their professor's past support of Kurt von Schleicher in the Weimar Republic. See Lothar Strogies, *Die Ausserparlamentarische Opposition in Nürnberg und Erlangen* (Erlangen: Palm & Enke, 1996).

10. See Jerry Z. Muller, *The Transgressive Rabbi: The Life and Times of Jacob Taubes* (Princeton: Princeton University Press, forthcoming 2017).

11. Ulrike Meinhof, "Vom Protest zum Widerstand," *konkret* (May 1968), 5. For documentation of the Easter Sunday action see Siegward Lönnendonke, ed., *Linksintellektueller Aufbruch zwischen "Kulturrevolution" und "kultureller Zerstörung"* (Opladen: Westdeutscher Verlag, 1998).

12. *Marburg Manifest von 17. April 1968*, Ernst Benz Papers.

13. The government was also motivated by fear of what was happening across the border in France. See Kristin Ross, *May '68 and Its Afterlives* (Chicago: University of Chicago Press, 2002), 60–63.

14. Elisabeth Noelle and Eric Peter Neumann, eds., *Jahrbuch der öffentlichen Meinung, 1965–1967* (Allensbach: Verlag für Demoskopie, 1967), 151. On multiculturalism see A. Dirk Moses, *German Intellectuals and the Nazi Past* (New York: Cambridge University Press, 2007), chapter 10; on the shift in sexual mores see in particular Dagmar Herzog, *Sex After Fascism: Memory and Morality in Twentieth-Century Germany* (Princeton: Princeton University Press, 2005).

15. Noelle and Neumann, eds., *Jahrbuch der öffentlichen Meinung, 1965–1967*, 201.

16. Max Horkheimer, "Vorwort zur Neupublikation seiner Aufsätze aus der 'Zeitschrift für Sozialforschung'" (1968), in *Frankfurter Schule und Studentenbewegung: Dokumente*, ed. Wolfgang Kraushaar (Hamburg: Rogner & Bernhard bei Zweitausendeins, 1998), 348ff.